OCEAN

CHUKCHI SEA

o. Vrangelya

VOSTOCHNO-SIBIRSKOYE MORE

Anadyrsky zaliv

Pevek

Anadyr

BERING SEA

1785

Severnaya Zemlya

Novosibirskiye ostrova

MORE LAPTEVYKH

mys Chelyuskin

Koryakskoye nagore

2562

o. Karaginsky

Komandorskiye ostrova

1146

poluostrov oz. Taymyr

Taymyr

Khatanga

Tiksi

Verkhoyansky khrebet

khrebet Cherskogo

g. Pobeda 3003

Verkhoyansk

2389

Sredinny khrebet

4688

zaliv Shelikhova

vlk. Klyuchevskaya Sopka

g. Kamen 1664

Lena

Yana

Indigirka

Kolyma

Kolymskoye nagore

Magadan

Sredno-

Vilyuy

Yakutsk

FAR EAST

poluostrov Kamchatka

Petropavlovsk-Kamchatsky

m. Lopatka

sibirskoye

Nizhnyaya Tunguska

Mirny

Aldan

o. Iony

SEA OF OKHOTSK

ploskogorye

Podkamennaya Tunguska

Lena

Amga

Shantarskiye ostrova

o. Sakhalin

1609

Kurilskiye ostrova

Angara

Vitim

3072

2255

Stanovoy khrebet

Tatarsky proliv

Stanovoye

Tynda

Komsomolsk-na-Amure

Yuzhno-Sakhalinsk

Krasnoyarsk

Bratsk

nagore

Zeya

Amur

2090

Khabarovsk

a y a n

oz. Baikal

Chita

Shilka

Blagoveshchensk

Sikhote-Alin

2290

g. Munku-Sardyk 3491

Irkutsk

Ulan-Ude

Selenga

Argun

Da Hinggan Ling

Hailar

Qiqihar

Yichun

Songhua jiang

oz. Khanka

Hokkaidō

Sapporo

Yenisey

Changajn Nuruu

2000

Ulaan Baatar

Kerulen

Harbin

Nakhodka

Vladivostok

Sendai

Hajn Nuruu

Changchun

2750 Paektu-san

SEA OF JAPAN

Honshū

MONGOLIA

2034

Shenyang

NORTH KOREA

JAPAN

Tōkyō

Fuji-san 3776

G O B I

P'yŏngyang

Nagoya

Baotou

Beijing

Sŏul

Ōsaka

CHINA

Huang He

Tianjin

Lüda

SOUTH KOREA

Pusan

Shikoku

Kitakyūshū

6385

Yinchuan

Shijiazhuang

Jinan

Qingdao

YELLOW SEA

INSIGHT ◉ GUIDES

RUSSIA

www.insightguides.com/Russia

⊙ Walking Eye App

Your Insight Guide now includes a free app and eBook, dedicated to your chosen destination, all included for the same great price as before. They are available to download from the free Walking Eye container app in the App Store and Google Play. Simply download the Walking Eye container app to access the eBook and app dedicated to your purchased book. The app features an up-to-date A to Z of travel tips, information on events, activities and destination highlights, as well as hotel, restaurant and bar listings. See below for more information and how to download.

MULTIPLE DESTINATIONS AVAILABLE

Now that you've bought this book you can download the accompanying destination app and eBook for free. Inside the Walking Eye container app, you'll also find a whole range of other Insight Guides destination apps and eBooks, all available for purchase.

DEDICATED SEARCH OPTIONS

Use the different sections to browse the places of interest by category or region, or simply use the 'Around me' function to find places of interest nearby. You can then save your selected restaurants, bars and activities to your Favourites or share them with friends using email, Twitter and Facebook.

FREQUENTLY UPDATED LISTINGS

Restaurants, bars and hotels change all the time. To ensure you get the most out of your guide, the app features all of our favourites, as well as the latest openings, and is updated regularly. Simply update your app when you receive a notification to access the most current listings available.

Shopping in Oman still revolves around the traditional souks that can be found in every town in the country – most famously at Mutrah in Muscat, Salalah and Nizwa, which serve as showcases of traditional Omani craftsmanship and produce ranging from antique khanjars and Bedu jewellery to halwa, rose-water and frankincense. Muscat also boasts a number of modern malls, although these are rare elsewhere in the country.

TRAVEL TIPS & DESTINATION OVERVIEWS

The app also includes a complete A to Z of handy travel tips on everything from visa regulations to local etiquette. Plus, you'll find destination overviews on shopping, sport, the arts, local events, health, activities and more.

HOW TO DOWNLOAD THE WALKING EYE

Available on purchase of this guide only.
1. Visit our website: www.insightguides.com/walkingeye
2. Download the Walking Eye container app to your smartphone (this will give you access to both the destination app and the eBook)
3. Select the scanning module in the Walking Eye container app
4. Scan the QR code on this page – you will be asked to enter a verification word from the book as proof of purchase
5. Download your free destination app* and eBook for travel information on the go

* Other destination apps and eBooks are available for purchase separately or are free with the purchase of the Insight Guide book

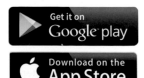

Contents

THE BEST OF RUSSIA: TOP ATTRACTIONS

From St Petersburg to Moscow, capitals past and present, to the vast and mysterious Siberia on board the mythical Trans-Siberian Railway, here, at a glance, are Russia's highlights.

△ **Red Square, Moscow**. This vast cobbled space is Russia's epicentre, a witness to medieval executions, May 1st parades of ballistic missile launchers and a million Russian wedding photographs. See page 150.

▽ **The Hermitage, St Petersburg**. The Hermitage's bamboozling collections of Old Masters, sculptures, antiquities and archaeology is a powerful symbol of Russia's imperial past. You'd need several weeks to see it all. See page 208.

△ **The Kremlin, Moscow**. Once the original Moscow, this fortress became the seat of religious power, tsarist rule and then Soviet might, and is still the centre of power of today's Russian Federation. See page 147.

△ **Lake Baikal**. The world's deepest lake is so remote and isolated it has evolved its own eco-system, with hundreds of species unique to its waters. It's also the most interesting stop on the Trans-Siberian railway. See page 276.

△ **Palace Square, St Petersburg**. Behind the Winter Palace is a key landmark in St Petersburg's turbulent history: Palace Square has witnessed murder, conspiracy and the coup that ousted the last tsar. See page 195.

△ **Golden Ring**. Long before Moscow became Russia's top dog, numerous principalities surrounded and rivalled the city. The kremlins of Vladimir and Suzdal have survived to this day and form the highlights of a Golden Ring tour. See page 172.

▷ **St Basil's, Moscow**. No one will believe you've been to Moscow without a picture with this psychedelic church on Moscow's Red Square in the background. See page 151.

◁ **Trans-Siberian Railway**. A ride on the Trans-Siberian Railway across the steppe from Moscow to the Pacific is one of the world's classic rail journeys. See page 128.

▽ **Kizhi's churches**. Situated in Russia's undervisited north, these elaborate wooden churches on Kizhi Island were assembled without nails or modern tools in the 17th century. See page 220.

△ **Siberia**. There are few places left on earth as untamed as Siberia, a huge adventure playground. However, it's not all blank spaces on the map – Siberia's cities have fascinating tales to tell. See page 260.

THE BEST OF RUSSIA: EDITOR'S CHOICE

From unique attractions such as a leader's mausoleum, Lake Baikal and the Hermitage to excursions through tsarist retreats and sacred resurrected churches, Russia is fascinatingly diverse. Here at a glance are our recommendations, plus some tips and tricks even the locals won't always know about.

BEST ADVENTURES

Trans-Siberian Railroad. A ride on the Trans-Siberian train, through Russia's heartland, is one of the world's epic journeys. See page 128.

Great Baikal Trail. Pack your hiking boots for a ramble around Lake Baikal or join an army of volunteers working on this ambitious project. See page 276.

The Altai. This remote area in Siberia's south is one huge outdoor playground with enough snow-capped mountains and fast flowing rivers to last a lifetime. See page 267.

BAM Railway. The 'other' Trans-Sib starts life in Tayshet, Eastern Siberia before crossing some mind-boggling remote backcountry on its way to the Pacific. See page 270.

Volga River. A trip along the Volga River, Europe's longest, offers the chance to explore some of Russia's ancient settlements. See page 233.

Adventures in Siberia. As industries carve tiny paths though this remote wilderness, tourists are able to explore some of the world's finest natural settings – from virgin forests to killer whales. See page 274.

Moscow Metro.

ONLY IN RUSSIA

Moscow's Metro. Underneath the capital's streets lies Moscow's metro system, a sprawling palace of marble and coloured stone lit by chandeliers and decorated with sculpture and mosaics. See page 170.

Tuvan throat singing. Little-visited Tuva is cut off from the rest of Russia by high mountains. Experience the Tuvan's mindboggling throat singing at the Centre for Tuvan Culture in Kyzyl. See page 125.

Petrodvorets. Russia's imitation of Versailles was once the primary country residence of the tsars. It's now open for all to see. See page 204.

Dachas. The dacha is a fixture of Russian life: families spend as much of the summer as possible in these rudimentary houses, enjoying simple countryside pleasures. See page 71.

130 Kvartal. Irkutsk has dedicated an entire neighbourhood to the preservation of timber architecture, filling traditional structures with cafés, restaurants, bars and shops. See page 272.

Sochi. The city that hosted the most expensive Olympics in history is a balmy, almost subtropical place popular with Russian holidaymakers. See page 254.

Annunciation Cathedral inside Kazan's Kremlin.

The Red Vineyards at Arles by Van Gogh, Pushkin Museum.

BEST MUSEUMS AND GALLERIES

Tretyakov Galleries. Moscow's Tretyakov and New Tretyakov galleries house a fine collection of icons and Russian artworks from the early 20th century. See page 165.

State Armoury Museum. The elaborate fittings of Russia's imperial state, from silk ball gowns to enormous jewels and Fabergé eggs, are preserved in the Kremlin's finest museums. See page 147.

Pushkin Museum of Fine Arts, Moscow. The collection of Impressionist art at this exquisite museum is second only to the Louvre's. See pages 167.

Tuvan National Museum. Kilos of Scythian gold fill a specially guarded room at Tuva's main museum. The exhibition is one of Siberia's cultural highlights. See page 269.

Krasnoyarsk Regional Museum. Possibly the world's only museum housed in an Art Nouveau mock-Egyptian temple, this museum of local history is a must-see on the Trans-Siberian Railway. See page 268.

BEST CHURCHES

Church of the Resurrection. St Petersburg's most fantastic church pays tribute to Russia's murdered tsar Alexander II with a gaudy assembly of folk styles. See page 200.

Sergiev Posad Monastery. A refuge for Peter the Great and a site of pilgrimage, this complex on the Golden Ring is a beautiful rival to the Kremlin. See page 175.

Kizhi's Churches. These amazing wooden churches were assembled without nails or modern tools. See page 220.

Cathedral of Christ the Saviour. The history of Russia's largest cathedral is complicated: built to commemorate the defeat of Napoleon in 1812, destroyed for the

Palace of the Soviets under Stalin, and recently rebuilt by Moscow's mayor-builder Luzhkov as a symbol of the resurgent city. See page 168.

Novodevichy Convent, Moscow. This monastery once housed unwanted brides of state, but is now the final resting place of some of Russia's most famous people, including Khrushchev, Chekhov and the circus star Nikulin. See page 169.

Alexander Nevsky Lavra, St Petersburg. One of Russia's grandest monastic ensembles is also one of its most sacred places. See page 203.

Smolny Cathedral. This masterpiece of baroque architecture stands upon St Petersburg's old tar yards. See page 203.

BEST REMNANTS OF REVOLUTION

Lenin's Mausoleum, Red Square, Moscow. Where else are you able to enjoy a private audience with a major world leader and be allowed to do all the talking? See page 151.

Muzeon Sculpture Gardens. Some Soviet-era statues were pulled down by Muscovites in the 1990s. They are displayed here alongside works commemorating victims of famines, purges and Gulags. See page 165.

Lenin Head, Ulan-Ude. Dominating the Buryat capital's main square,

this huge Lenin head is the biggest in the world and the city's main tourist attraction. See page 273.

Ploshchad Lenina. Just outside St Petersburg's Finland Station, a statue marks the arrival of Lenin from Finland in 1917. He issued a call to arms from this square. See page 189.

BAM Railway. This 'Soviet Hero Project of the Century' was completed just as the USSR collapsed, preserving the towns along its tracks as open-air museums of communism. See page 270.

BAM Railway train near Tynda.

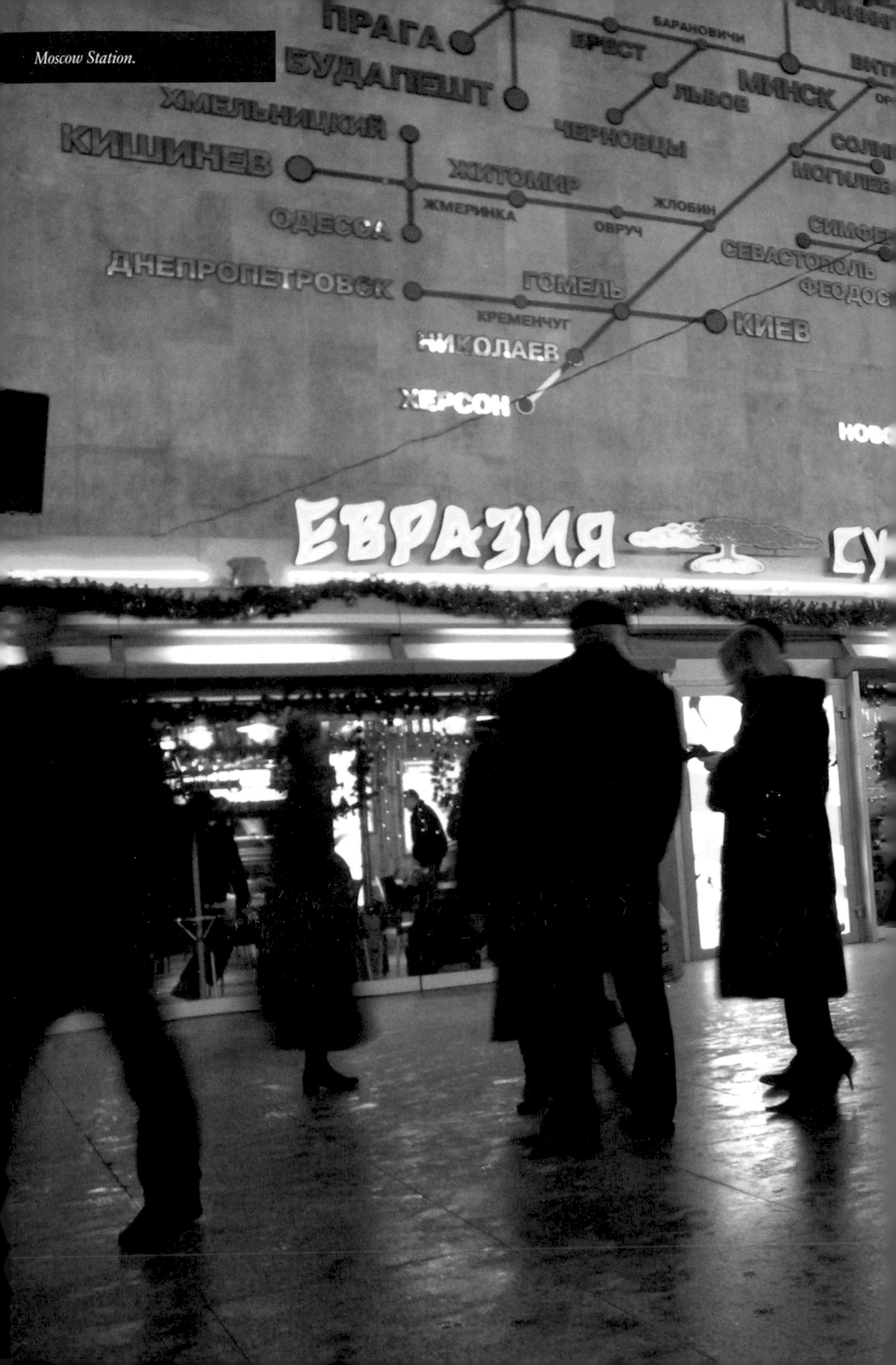

Moscow Station.

Typical wooden architecture in Listvyanka, Siberia.

A common mode of transport for
little ones; here in Veliky Novgorod.

THE RIDDLE OF RUSSIA

Stereotypes may have been broken down and tourists have found their way into Russia but some, it seems, would prefer a return to the past.

Lenin mural in Sochi.

Russia cannot be understood/ With the mind,/ Nor can she be measured/ By a common yardstick./ A special character she has:/ In Russia one can only have faith. (Fyodor Tyutchev, 19th-century poet)

Such understanding has never come easily to outsiders. "Russia is impenetrable," wrote the American historian Henry Adams in 1895, "and any intelligent man will deal with her better, the less closely he knows her." Sir Winston Churchill, trying to predict Russia's behaviour in 1939, coined the description: "a riddle wrapped in a mystery inside an enigma."

Mystery always fascinates, and since the collapse of Soviet communism in the late 1980s, tourists have poured into Russia, many of them venturing beyond St Petersburg and Moscow to find out what provincial and rural Russia is like. Just as Russians have discovered that foreigners are not, in the words of the poet Yevgeny Yevtushenko, "all spies with cameras in their buttons, radio transmitters in the heels of their shoes, and pockets full of Colorado beetles", so Westerners have had their own preconceived ideas overturned. Siberia, for example, is shedding its *Gulag Archipelago* image and revealing itself as a stunningly beautiful and diverse land with a budding tourism industry, especially around Lake Baikal.

Irkutsk, Siberia.

However, as most people around the world know, Russia isn't all good news these days. President Putin came to power in 2000 and quickly got the country functioning again after the chaotic 1990s. Order and stability, a functioning economy on the back of oil and gas exports and improving living standards made him a popular figure along with his party Yedinaya Rossiya (United Russia). A middle class emerged in the cities, business became possible and Russians began to travel, though in relatively small numbers compared to the West. But Putin it seems has another agenda – to use this economic strength to reclaim Russia's position as a superpower and to reconstitute the Soviet Empire in some form. Russia's short war with Georgia in 2008 was the first sign that Russia may be moving away from the path many had hoped it would take.

And then came Ukraine. Kiev's Maidan Revolution shattered Putin's hopes for a customs union between former Soviet Republics – his revenge has been severe. Russia's invasion of Crimea and East Ukraine have led to sanctions and isolation. The riddle for the West today is what to do about a problem like Russia.

The dense Siberian taiga.

A BOUNDLESS LAND

**To make sense of the immensity of Russia,
its varied and dramatic scenery and its diverse
climate, one must begin with the land itself.**

The vastness of Russia is hard for Westerners to grasp. The Russian Federation from Kaliningrad in the west to Kamchatka in the east covers 16.4 million sq km (6.3 million sq miles), 68 times larger than Great Britain and twice the size of Brazil. Russia ranges across 11 time zones. When citizens in westerly Kaliningrad are getting up in the morning, their fellow countrymen on the Pacific seaboard are home from work and thinking about going to bed. Train journeys in this country are measured in days rather than hours.

Russia reaches well into the Arctic. The world's largest polar city is Murmansk, built on the uppermost fringe of the Kola Peninsula at the point where the warm Gulf Stream licks the coast. Because it takes advantage of this geographical accident, Murmansk is Russia's only ice-free seaport in the north. But in the south, Russian territory extends into the balmy climes of the Black Sea.

Sunrise over St Petersburg during its white nights of June.

White nights of June

Russia's landmass is shaped like a great wedge, which has its point in the west. (This geopolitical fact alone helps to explain 500 years of Russian foreign policy: the further west Russia's borders lie, the shorter is its frontier and so the easier to defend.) The fatter, Eurasian end of the wedge extends to the north and east for 10,460 km (6,500 miles). Moscow is roughly on the same latitude as Glasgow in Scotland or Edmonton, Alberta in Canada. Consequently the days are long in summer and short in winter. Murmansk is in darkness round the clock from November to March, while St Petersburg has made an annual festival of its "white nights", a month-long celebration in June and July when the city is bathed in an eerie, nocturnal translucence, which makes it difficult to sleep.

The climate across Russia is continental: that is, short hot summers with long cold winters. Temperatures of -20°C (-4°F) are not unusual in Moscow in January, and the winters in Siberia are cold beyond description. The coldest inhabited place on earth is Oymyakon, in the diamond-rich uplands of Yakutia, where daytime temperatures of -70°C (-94°F) have been recorded. Around Lake Baikal winter temperatures of down to -40°C/F can be expected each year.

East-west divide

Only one geographical feature interrupts the great, level Eurasian plain between the Carpathians and the Far Eastern highlands. Like the spine of a book laid open on its face, the Urals run in a straight line for 1,930 km (1,200 miles) from the Barents Sea in the north, almost to the Caspian Sea in the south. These low mountains are the official boundary between Europe and Asia, and between European Russia and Siberia. But they are not a formidable natural barrier, and no invader was ever stopped by them. In fact, when travelling on the Trans-Siberian Railway most travellers don't even notice they have crossed the Urals.

The Russian south is like a thick ribbon of ripe yellow wheat under a blue band of sky. Here the main crop is winter wheat, sown in the autumn and protected from the cold by a layer of snow. Further to the north, all kinds of farming are to be found in the cleared expanses between the ancient forests: dairy, pigs and poultry, oats, root crops, flax and potatoes.

Tundra, taiga, steppe and forest

A satellite's eye view of the Russian plateau would show that, east of the Urals especially, it is divided east to west into four broad vegetational zones. Three of these zones are so distinctive that they are known to geographers by their Russian

The Ukok Plateau is a remote and pristine grasslands area in the Altai Mountains, southwestern Siberia.

TOXIC EARTH AND POISONED SEAS

For all its natural beauty, the former USSR is a land of ecological nightmares. The Chernobyl disaster of 1985 is symbolic of the dangers, but even that catastrophe pales next to the environmental damage that was done in earlier Soviet times. The nuclear installation at Chelyabinsk-65 in Siberia is a kind of serial Chernobyl. It has had several massive accidents, the worst in 1957. It is still spewing nuclear waste into Lake Karachai, officially the Earth's most radioactive place. Nuclear contamination is only part of the picture. Much of the pollution is the result of the Stalinist drive to industrialise at any cost. Until recently Lake Baikal, the largest body of fresh water on the planet, was in grave danger of irreversible poisoning from a paper-pulping plant on its shore and sewage from Mongolia still makes its way into these otherwise pristine waters. The acid rain which falls on the Kola peninsula, which has devastated thousands of hectares of forest, is the result of the gases released from nickel refineries. Environmental groups intent on solving Russia's environmental issues are now being dubbed agents of the West and intimidated, banned and driven out of the country. The latest example of this was the 30 Greenpeace activists who were jailed and then released in 2013 for a peaceful protest at an Arctic Gazprom oil platform.

names: the tundra, taiga and steppe. The fourth zone is the great swathe of mixed forest which has fed hunters and hindered farmers for generations.

The tundra is the northernmost belt. At its most extreme, in the Arctic, it is a cold, white, lifeless desert. A little further south a few stunted trees grow, but their roots are shallow because they cannot penetrate the permafrost. In spring, when the uppermost layer of snow melts, the moss and lichen burst forth and the ground is carpeted with bright and hardy flowers. Later in the year migratory birds pass through, and regiments of furry animals – silver foxes, wolves,

in the southern reaches of Siberia, the archetypal Russian birch. This dark kingdom is the habitat of the (now rare) sable, prized for its fur above all other animals, as well as of brown bears, lynx, and in Siberia elks and maral deers. In summer black swarms of bloodthirsty mosquitoes make the taiga almost uninhabitable for humans.

The taiga shades gently into a variegated stripe of mixed forest, where the trees are deciduous, such as oak, ash and maple. In European areas the trees have been systematically cleared for agriculture. East of the Urals the mixed forest covers an area far beyond Russia's borders. Animal spe-

Long, cold winters are a feature of the climate.

ermine, ferrets and lemmings – emerge from the southern forests. But as winter and darkness draw in again, the only animals that can survive the tundra are polar bears and seals.

The tundra gives way to the taiga, a gigantic and almost impenetrable belt which accounts for about a third of the world's forest. This zone is about 5,000 km (3,000 miles) long and 1,000 km (600 miles) wide. The insulating effect of such a density of trees means that in its deepest pockets the snow almost never melts and the ground below maintains permafrost.

The result is a "drunken forest" where over-tall spruce tilt at tipsy angles in the shallow top soil. The species of tree vary from region to region over this wooded ocean: there are pine, larch and,

cies unique to this zone include the last European bison, which live in conservation areas.

South of the forest the narrow strip of open grassland running from Romania to China is known as the steppe. It is easily traversed, and as such has served as the main highway for nomadic peoples travelling from Asia to Europe. The soil here is prone to erosion by the freezing winds of winter and the thunderstorms of summer.

In the Siberian steppe there is a sense of emptiness and desolation. Much of the native fauna – antelopes and wild horses – has been hunted to extinction. But in the air, the superb steppe eagle is still visible, and on the ground there are small and exotic rodents such as the bobak marmot, the five-toed jerboa and Chinese striped hamster.

Cape Dezhnev is the country's easternmost point – on a clear day you can stand on the shore of the Bering Strait and wave across to America.

Beyond the highlands of Yakutia and the now-abandoned Gulag zone of Kolyma is the eastern seaboard, where Russia is washed by the waters of the Pacific. The Kamchatka Peninsula, a strange proboscis on Russia's eastward-looking face which is dotted with active volcanoes, is located

Recent efforts to reverse the damage and restore the sea are slowly improving the ecosystem.

Before it was destroyed by overuse and chemical pollution, the Aral ranked as the fourth-biggest inland sea in the world; the biggest is the Caspian Sea on Russia's southern flank. In Siberia, near the Mongolian border, is the world's biggest (by volume) freshwater reserve and also the deepest freshwater lake, Baikal. It's actually not a lake at all, but a massive tear in the earth's crust which will one day become an ocean and divide Asia in two. On the map of Russia the lake looks small, but it holds more water than the

Cape Dezhnev, Russia's easternmost point.

here. Here, too, is the Chukotsky Peninsula, on the tip of which is Cape Dezhnev. This is where Russia's territory runs out.

Rivers and other riches

These four bands are criss-crossed by great, meandering rivers. In Siberia they flow from south to north. The longest of the Siberian waterways, at 5,700 km (3,360 miles), is the Ob, though the Yenisei and the Lena are both more than 3,200 km (2,000 miles) long.

In the 1970s there was a plan to reverse the flow of Siberian rivers to irrigate the cotton fields of central Asia and save the Aral Sea. Thankfully the madcap plan was abandoned, but then again the Aral was turned into a desert of poisonous dust.

entire Baltic Sea, and is home to over 1,500 species of animal found nowhere else in the world.

Mineral wealth

Beneath all this variety is a treasure chest of mineral riches. Western Siberia has vast deposits of coal and iron ore. The Urals are studded with emeralds, rubies, malachite, jasper and gold, and the diamond deposits in Yakutia are thought to be immense. But it's Siberia's huge supplies of gas and oil that have fuelled Russia's economy in recent years, especially with world prices high. However, with lower oil prices and most countries in Europe hunting around for other sources of gas following Russia's actions in Ukraine, this may be slowly coming to an end.

DECISIVE DATES

The First Russians

The Moskva and Volga rivers region was settled from prehistoric times by Finno-Ugrians, Indo-Europeans and Germanic tribes. Scythians inhabited the steppes.

AD 400–600

Eastern Slavs migrate into what is now Ukraine and western Russia.

800–900

Swedish Varangians (Vikings) under Prince Rurik advance southwest along the rivers establishing strongholds at Novgorod and Kiev.

900–1240

Kiev becomes the centre of the first Eastern Slav state, the Kievan Rus; trade flourishes with Byzantium.

988

Prince Volodymyr, ruler of the Kievan Rus, converts to Christianity and forces the entire population to do likewise.

The Mongol Yoke

1200–1300

While Alexander Nevsky defends Russia's western borders from Swedish attack, Batu Khan, grandson of Genghis Khan, invades from the east, conquers Moscow (1238) and sacks Kiev (1240). For the next 250 years, Russian princes are forced to pay tribute to the Golden Horde (Mongols).

1300–1400

Poland captures Belarus and Ukraine.

1328

Ivan Kalita ("Moneybags") is designated Grand Prince by the Khan. He moves from Vladimir to Moscow, where he fortifies the kremlin (fortress).

1380

Grand Prince Dmitry, grandson of "Moneybags", defeats the Mongols in the Battle of Kulikovo but cannot prevent them from sacking Moscow. The city recovers to become a symbol of Russian unity. The power of the Mongols begins to wane.

1462–1500

Ivan III, "The Great", refuses to pay Moscow's tribute to the Mongols, whose domination comes to an end. Russia succeeds Byzantium as the "Third Rome".

Catherine the Great.

The Rule of the Tsars

1547–84

Ivan IV (the Terrible), is crowned Tsar of All Russia. He defeats the Tatars at Kazan (and builds St Basil's Cathedral in celebration) and Astrakhan, colonises Siberia and sows the seeds of serfdom.

1584–1613

Anarchy and civil war prevail; Boris Godunov presides over The Time of Troubles.

1613

Tsar Mikhail Romanov restores stability. His dynasty rules until the revolution of 1917.

A Window on the West

1682–1725

The widely-travelled tsar, Peter the Great, introduces Western

Tsar Nicholas II.

ways, reforms the civil service and army, and builds a modern navy. He recaptures the Baltic coast from the Swedes and starts building his new city, St Petersburg, at the mouth of the River Neva. In 1712 the court moves to St Petersburg, which becomes the official capital of Russia.

1725–62

Under Peter's heirs the court becomes Westernised.

1763–96

Catherine II (the Great) ushers in a period of enlightenment. She reforms local government, liberalises the penal code, founds hospitals and invites leading architects to St Petersburg who give the city its classical look. Belarus and Ukraine are recaptured from Poland, Crimea is conquered and the mineral wealth of Siberia is exploited.

The Emperors

1796–1825

Catherine's son, the military dictator Paul I, is assassinated in 1801. He is succeeded by the more liberal Alexander I.

1812

Napoleon invades and occupies Moscow. The inhabitants set fire to the city. Napoleon withdraws.

1825

Decembrist Rising in St Petersburg is crushed by Nicholas I in 1825. The Decembrists are dispersed

Vladimir Lenin.

across Siberia where they spread education, culture and European ways.

1853–6

Nicholas I's reign of repression and stagnation comes to an end with Crimean War which pitted Russia against Britain, France and the Ottoman Empire.

1855–81

Alexander II liberates the serfs, 1861. He is assassinated by revolutionaries, 1 March 1881.

1881–94

Rapid industrialisation under the repressive rule of Alexander III leads to a huge increase in the size of the urban working class.

Abdication and Revolution

1894–1917

The last tsar, Nicholas II, is unable to contain the groundswell of discontent.

1898

Vladimir Lenin forms the Social Democratic Party.

1905

Bloody Sunday (9 January): 140,000 workers march to the Winter Palace. Troops open fire; 100 marchers are killed, hundreds wounded. The Tsar agrees to establish the Duma (State Assembly).

1914

Russia enters World War I against Germany.

1917

Russia is on the brink of economic and political catastrophe. Tsar Nicholas II abdicates. A provisional government is set up. On 25 October the Bolshevik Central Committee, under Lenin's leadership, seizes power in the Great Socialist Revolution. Lenin nationalises industries and radically reforms agriculture.

1918

Treaty of Brest–Litovsk ends war with Germany. The Tsar and family are murdered in Yekaterinburg. Civil war rages until 1922 when Lev Trotsky's Red Army declares victory.

Communists Take Control

1922–8

Lenin declares the Union of Soviet Socialist Republics (USSR); Moscow becomes the official capital. Lenin dies in 1924 and Petrograd is renamed Leningrad in his honour. Joseph Stalin wins power struggle and starts the first Five Year Plan of industrialisation and agricultural collectivisation backed up by a purge in which millions either die or are deported.

1941–5

The Nazis invade the USSR: around 25 million citizens die in what the Russians call the "Great Patriotic War". Victory over Germany is declared on 9 May 1945.

Satirical cartoon depicting the Bloody Sunday massacre of 9 January 1905 in St Petersburg.

1953

Stalin dies. Nikita Khrushchev emerges as leader and immediately denounces Stalin's crimes. A cultural thaw ensues.

1955

Eastern Bloc countries sign the Warsaw Pact declaring a military alliance.

1956

USSR intervenes in Hungary.

1964–82

Leonid Brezhnev partially reverses Khrushchev's reforms. He crushes the Prague Spring in Czechoslovakia (1968) in the name of protecting socialism, and invades Afghanistan (1979). The Cold War with the West and arms race with the US continue until détente and the Strategic Arms Limitation Talks (SALT) of the late 1970s.

Disintegration and Democracy

1985

Mikhail Gorbachev introduces reforms based on

Yeltsin's troops outside Parliament, Moscow 1993.

restructuring, openness, democratisation and a limited market. Satellite states agitate for independence.

1991

A failed coup d'état by hardline communists leads to the eclipse of Gorbachev, the collapse of communism and the disintegration of the USSR. A fragile federation of the republics, the Commonwealth of Independent States, takes its place. Russia under Boris Yeltsin becomes successor state to USSR.

1993

Political struggle between president and parliament turns violent. Street battles in Moscow. Yeltsin uses tanks to shell the parliament building. In the aftermath, the presidency is granted sweeping powers.

President Putin presents figure-skater Yulia Lipnitskaya with a national award after she wins gold at the Sochi Winter Olympics, aged only 15.

1996

Boris Yeltsin wins a second term as president.

1998

The rouble is devalued. Yeltsin appoints Yevgeni Primakov as prime minister to restore stability.

1999

Boris Yeltsin surprises the world by resigning on the last day of the millennium.

Putin's Russia

2000

Erstwhile KGB operative Vladimir Putin wins presidential election.

2001

Putin offers immediate support to the US after the 11 September attacks.

2002

In a siege inside a Moscow theatre over 100 people die in a bungled rescue attempt by the authorities.

2003

St Petersburg hosts tricentenary celebrations.

2004

Putin re-elected to second term. Over 330 people, many of them children, die in a school siege in Beslan (Russian Caucasus), the world's worst hostage crisis.

2007

Yeltsin dies and is buried in the first religious state funeral since the 1917 Revolution.

2008

Dmitry Medvedev becomes president, avoiding the need to change the constitution, which states a president can only serve two consecutive terms. Putin is free to return in 2012. Russia starts to intimidate neighbours, going to war with Georgia over South Ossetia and Abkhazia and cutting off gas supplies to Ukraine.

2012

As expected, Putin returns as president. Anti-Western rhetoric is accelerated in the state-controlled media. State repression of opposition and protests increases.

2014

Russia hosts the Winter Olympics in Sochi but this is overshadowed by the Maidan Revolution in Kiev which ousts Russian ally President Yanukovych. In response Russia invades Crimea and organises "referendum" on annexation. West accuses Kremlin of major role in subsequent war in East Ukraine that kills thousands and displaces millions. Sanctions slapped on Russian state companies and regime members by the West.

Tenth-century manuscript depicting the Russian cavalry ambushing the Bulgars.

BEGINNINGS

Of all the migratory groups to cross Russia in the Dark Ages, the Slavs and the Vikings were the most influential.

The 9th-century Viking conquest of hitherto stateless Slavs scattered across modern Russia, Ukraine and Belarus was traditionally made to sound like an act of high-minded charity. "Our land is great and rich but there is no order in it," the Slavs are reputed to have cried. "Come and rule over us." Prince Rurik of South Jutland in Denmark was ready to oblige. He made himself master of Novgorod, the most northwesterly Slav settlement, and within three years of his death in 879 his successors, who came to be known as Varangians, had extended their rule to include Smolensk and Kiev.

The invitation – such as it was – fitted in perfectly with the Varangian desire to monopolise the lucrative trade route between the Baltic and the Black Sea, which happened to pass through the allegedly rich but disorderly land in question. The main artery of this largely river-borne trade was the Dnieper (Dnipro) River, and of the settlements which the Varangians deigned to rule over, Kiev was the most valuable strategically. It was accordingly declared "the Mother of Russian cities".

Rurik I, the legendary 9th-century Viking prince who was invited by the Slavs to rule over them.

Kiev was only one, but by far the grandest, in a network of embryonic city-states which various Varangian princes established and fought over among themselves. The estate of Yuri Dolgoruky of Suzdal was the beginning of Moscow while Prince of Polotsk's settlement on the Dvina River was the nucleus of Belarus.

It was not until the Mongol invasions of the 13th century that the focus of Russia moved away from Kiev to the north. Viewed from the forests, the depopulated area around Kiev was seen as "Ukraine", meaning the borderland.

Ukraine was also referred to as "Black" land because of its dark rich soil, but it was common land on which the semi-nomadic population

had the right to roam on payment of a kind of licence fee to the ruling prince, and "Black" became synonymous with these property rights. "White Russia", on the other hand – the translation of "Belarus" – drew attention to the fact that the territory was not common land but subject to the feudal tenure which applied while it was, as we shall see, under Polish administration. The people living on it were tied serfs.

Three Russias therefore came about, even if the dividing lines were historically and geographically fluid: Great Russia, born of Muscovy and these days simply called Russia; Ukraine, which picked up yet another name, Little Russia; and White Russia (Belarus).

Cultural melting pot

To begin with, there were no ethnic or cultural divisions. Migration across the northern plain from Central Asia into Europe had long been taking place before Rurik and his Vikings sailed south. The Slavs who supposedly invited the Vikings to come and rule over them were relatively recent arrivals, mostly 5th and 6th century, who spoke kindred Slavonic languages. They followed in the wake of Finno-Ugrians who ended up in Finland and Estonia, Indo-Europeans who became Lithuanians and Latvians, and a host of Germanic tribes who, one

Princess Olga of Kiev converted to Christianity in 957.

way or another, became not only Germans but French and Anglo-Saxon English.

There was a high degree of fusion between the newly arrived Slavs and earlier inhabitants. The Lithuanians were spread across the plains and forests until, under pressure from the Slavs, they retreated to the marshy Baltic shores. The high cheekbones, darkish complexion and broad nose typical of some Russians are attributed to the Finno-Ugrians, obviously a far cry from notions of fair-haired, blue-eyed Scandinavians, a different group altogether. Some claim Russians may be more Finno-Ugric than Slav.

The Varangians did fit the Scandinavian model, but they were only a military elite and it was a case common throughout history of conquerors being assimilated by the numerically superior conquered. It is unrealistic to think of the Varangians as being anything other than bona fide Slavs quite soon after their conquest.

Cultural comparisons between modern Russians and the tribes who roamed the northern plain long before the Slavs are irresistible. Russians cheerfully admit to being a trifle xenophobic and, according to Herodotus, the ancient Greek historian, the Scythians, who inhabited the steppes in the 5th century BC, had "an extreme hatred of all foreign customs". Herodotus was sceptical about Scythian descriptions of people living even farther north. According to them, they had goats' feet, could turn themselves into wolves if the occasion arose, and slept for six months at a time like hibernating animals. He did not doubt, however, that the northern winters were so cold that the inhabitants could drive wagons across frozen rivers and lakes and if necessary make war on them. "The ground is frozen iron-hard, so that to turn earth into mud requires not water but fire."

The Empire moves east

The Scythians eventually had to make room for new migrants arriving from Central Asia, and it was the overflow of these northern tribes – notably Huns, Goths, Visigoths and Vandals – across the Danube that spelt the end of the Roman Empire in the West. With repeated sackings of Rome, the Empire was moved from west to east, specifically to the ancient Greek colony of Byzantium, nicely positioned at the narrow Bosphorus crossing to control what was becoming the greatest trade route in the world, the one between Europe and the East.

The Mediterranean provided the obvious connection between Byzantium and Western Europe, but it was plagued by pirates. Northern Europe had something special to offer the markets of Byzantium: precious stones, furs and honey from the Russian forests and fair-skinned slaves. It was this trade via the Dnieper and to some extent the Volga that attracted the Varangians.

By the time the Slavs had settled along the Dnieper, the transplanted Roman Empire had made Constantinople, the Christianised capital of the East, the richest and most glamourous city on earth, Greek in flavour rather than

Every spring a flotilla would sail down the Dnieper to the great city of Constantinople with its cargo of furs, honey and luckless slaves, in order to return with gold, silk, wines and spices.

Roman. Rome was degenerating into a run-down dump on a dirty river.

The Slavs arrived at the tail-end of the transition from Rome to Constantinople. They drifted in different directions on reaching Europe and

The main drawback to living on the plain was exposure to new and invariably hostile migrants arriving from Asia. The forests, on the other hand, were relatively safe. Furthermore, the natural products of the forest, notably furs, honey and wax, were so plentiful that the forest-dwellers generally had surpluses available for trade. It was their surplus wealth which the Vikings needed to trade with Constantinople.

In 957 Princess Olga of Kiev joined the Dnieper River traders to see the fabled sights of Constantinople and was so impressed that she defied powerful pagan traditions to be bap-

Tenth-century Varangian family.

later assumed regional characteristics, either due to division by considerable natural boundaries, like the Carpathian mountains, or because they were split by alien invaders such as the Finno-Ugrian Magyars, the founders of Hungary. The Slavs in the Balkans came to be recognised as Southern Slavs, or "Yugoslavs", while those in the West took on the national identities of Poles, Czechs, Sorbs and Slovaks. The future Great, Little and White Russians were lumped together as Eastern Slavs. The first split in the homogeneity of the Eastern Slavs was between those who elected to remain on the steppes, which were reminiscent of the grasslands they had left behind in Central Asia, and those who ventured into the northern forests.

tised as a Christian. She then tried to persuade her son, Svyatoslav, to follow her example but he was more interested in a military campaign which in due course added the Volga region to Kievan Rus. The question of the religious allegiance of the Eastern Slavs was passed on to his successor, Prince Vladimir, and he was not to be rushed either. Vladimir wished to hear not only from advocates of Byzantium and Rome but also those of Islam and Judaism. They were invited to state their cases, the lead being given to the Jewish representatives. Both they and the Muslims who followed made a poor impression by mentioning circumcision and abstention from pork and alcohol; while the Pope's emissaries, on broaching the subject of fasting, drew an unambiguous response from Vladimir: "Depart hence!".

Forewarned, the Byzantine Greeks launched into a history of the world, saving until last a painting which showed in terrifying detail just what an infidel could expect come the Day of Judgement. Vladimir was unsettled by this revelation, but reserved final judgement until emissaries could visit Constantinople and confirm that joining the Church would bring material benefits. They returned to say that the city was so magnificent they had wondered whether they were in heaven.

A byzantine mosaic of St Basil, Hosios Loukas Monastery, Greece.

Vladimir's alignment with Byzantium was formalised by his baptism at Kherson in 990 and cemented by marriage to Anna, the Byzantine emperor's niece. Christianity spread throughout the Eastern Slavic lands with fortress monasteries – outposts in the vast forests and steppes that would grow into cities and industrial centres – and later parish churches, the centres of learning and morality.

The alignment with the Byzantine church was to have an extraordinary influence on statehood and culture. More contemplative and less activist than the Western church – and not divided by the Reformation like the rest of Europe – the Russian Orthodox Church

became the thread that bound the royal families to the people they ruled, while providing both the inspiration and the setting for art, architecture and music over the course of the next millennium. It was also a conservative force that was to hold back social and political change. In its beginnings however, the church was a bridge that joined the Eastern Slavs with the great Christian civilisations.

The rise and fall of Kiev

Kiev built a cathedral, named after and modelled on St Sophia's in Constantinople, and numerous churches. It was more emphatically than ever the outstanding Slavic city of the age, but not for long. The eastern Mediterranean, long closed to traders by pirates and the Arabs who had taken over the Levant, was reopened by the success of the early Crusades. The sea route to northern Europe through the Strait of Gibraltar was longer, but it could take ships of any size and eliminated porterage. The value of the Dnieper route dwindled and so did Kiev's profits from it.

The Varangian princes were inclined to move north. Prince Yuri Dolgoruky, founder of Moscow, also acquired Kiev only to be told the city had become virtually worthless. "Here, father, we have nothing," his son said, "let us depart to Suzdal while it is still warm." The same son inherited Suzdal, and in 1169 he proved his point by sacking Kiev and casually tossing the princedom to a younger brother.

In both trade and religion, Russia's orientation had been towards Constantinople, but in 1204 the Fourth Crusade abandoned its avowed purpose of fighting the infidel Turk in the Holy Land in order to ransack Constantinople and put a hostile "Latin Emperor" on the throne of Byzantium. Baldwin, the emperor in question, was not long in office, but the reprieve became meaningless in the light of what was developing unseen thousands of miles away.

While Alexander Nevsky ("of the Neva") defended Russia's western borders from Sweden, a different threat was gathering force in the east, where Temuchin Bagatur, the chief of a Mongol tribe, had conquered China in nine years, a victory which prompted him to assume the name of Genghis Khan, "Ruler of the World". He meant to make that boast good by finding out what lay west of the Ural mountains and conquering it as well.

THE MONGOL YOKE

The Mongols – or Tatars – descended on
Russia like a whirlwind, and their reign
lasted for hundreds of years.

The Mongol onslaught took the Russian people completely by surprise. It was a vicious, bloody bolt from the blue. Even now, the folk memory of their bloody rule is an indelible scar on the national psyche. Russian mothers can still be heard invoking the name of a long-dead commander to frighten naughty children. "Eat up your greens," they say, "Or Mamai will get you."

The Russians' first encounter with these fearsome foreigners on horseback came in 1223, when an army was smashed at the Kalka River by a Mongol detachment which then melted back into the steppe. News of this strange catastrophe rippled through to the cities of Russia, but no more was heard of the dangerous horsemen from the east, whom the Slavs called Tatars.

The Kalka outriders were no more than an advance guard, sent by the Mongol Emperor Genghis Khan to investigate the rich pickings to the west. The real invasion came in 1236, under the command of Genghis Khan's own grandson Batu Khan, and this time the Mongols meant business.

Tatar onslaught

The Tatars were the most awesome fighting force the world had seen, not excluding their contemporaries, the Crusader knights. They were undeterred by the Russian winter, and in fact preferred to campaign when the earth and the rivers were frozen. The frost and the ice provided a hard surface for their ponies, which were trained to dig through snow to find grass.

Every Mongol warrior kept two or three ponies in tow, and this gave them remarkable speed and endurance. They never went into battle without first erecting dressing stations. Soldiers wore an undershirt of raw silk next to their

Genghis Khan, the Mongol emperor.

skin. This light vest sank in under the impact of an arrow, enabling the barbed head to be drawn out without aggravating the wound. Their small bows had a range far longer than the English long-bows used at the Battle of Crécy (1346), and could be fired from the saddle at a gallop.

The Tatars' preferred method was to pick off enemy strongholds one at a time and let the news of their victory travel ahead to weaken the resolve of the next target. The city of Ryazan, a small vassal state of Suzdal, was one of the first to fall.

Grand Prince Yuri of Ryazan tried to buy off Batu Khan with gifts, but laughed at the Khan's suggestion that he hand over his own wife as part of the tribute. Khan was not joking; he put the Grand Prince to death on the spot.

The Khan then laid siege to the city, breaching its defences just before Christmas 1237. "The pagans entered the cathedral church of the Most Holy Mother of God," recount the chronicles, "And there they put Yuri's mother, Grand Princess Agrippina, and her daughters-in-law and the other princesses to the sword. They consigned the bishops and the clergy to the flames and burned them in the holy church. They spilt much blood on the sacred altars. Not one man was left alive in the city. All lay dead together. And all this came to pass because of our sins."

Fighting the invading Tatars.

Moscow and, to the northeast, Suzdal and Vladimir were subdued in similar fashion. Veliky Novgorod was the next prize on the Tatars' path, but the city was spared by an unseasonal thaw. Novgorod became an island in a vast sea of mud, and the Tatars chose to turn back rather than attempt to wade through it.

Under the yoke

By 1241, the Tatars had conquered most of Hungary, Romania and Poland, and it seemed that nothing could stop them. But just as Europe lay within his grasp, Batu Khan learned that his uncle, the Emperor Ogedei, had died in the Tatar capital of Karakorum. Batu Khan decided to go home and fight his corner in the domestic power struggle.

> *Following the sacking of Vladimir in 1240 the Mongols moved south to attack Kiev, sparing only St Sophia's Cathedral and a few houses. A visitor to the scene five years later reported skulls and bones still littering the streets.*

This timely death, and the snap decision it drew from Batu Khan, saved Western European civilisation from a second Dark Age. But it was already too late for Russia. The country was now under the Tatar yoke, cut off from all the great advances of the Renaissance which were destined to take place in Western Europe over the next centuries. On the one hand, Western achievements in the sciences, the arts and in philosophy reached Russia later on, leading to a sense of inferiority or backwardness: much of subsequent Russian history – the frantic westernising of Peter, the uncritical embrace of Putinism in today's Russia – can be read as an attempt by the Russian state to catch up with all that it missed out on during this period. On the other hand, Mongol rule allowed Russian philosophical thought to develop, either independently – especially in the areas of culture and religion, where the Mongol overlords exerted no influence – or under the sway of Byzantium.

But this is to run ahead. When Batu Khan rushed home in 1241, he left his Russian domains in the charge of a detachment whose base, Sarai (encampment), was near the site of the present-day city of Volgograd. This particular detachment was known as the Golden Horde, and in time their name became synonymous with the Tatar regime.

The rise of Moscow

That regime, once its dominion was established, revolved around the business of tax-collecting. The Tatars were not interested in imposing their culture, and while only too happy to burn down churches to encourage prompt payment of tribute, they did not interfere with the religion of their subject peoples. Consequently, the Russian church became a focus of Russian nationhood, and the local vassal princes of cities such as Moscow found that they could still wield a good deal of power, just so long as they made sure they paid their tribute to the Golden Horde at Sarai.

All this time, no one in the West had the faintest idea, or expressed any interest in, what had become of Russia. Only cities such as Novgorod and Pskov, both beyond the Mongol orbit, kept links with the Baltic cities and the world beyond.

Behind this medieval Iron Curtain the insignificant but strategically placed city of Moscow (which together with its lands is known to history as Muscovy) was growing strong. Successive grand princes of Muscovy had gained favour with their absentee landlords, the khans of the Golden Horde, and in 1328 a prince named Ivan was put in charge of collecting and delivering all taxes and tributes. His skimming earned him the nickname "Kalita" ("Moneybags").

"Dmitry of the Don"). The Tatars came back and wreaked vengeful havoc on Moscow in 1382, but the story of the 100 years that followed is one of gradual decline for the Golden Horde. The Tatar yoke ended in anti-climax in 1480. Ivan III, the incumbent Grand Prince of Muscovy, had been withholding tribute for 20 years. However, when it came to a Kulikovo-style showdown, neither side had much of a stomach for the fight.

The Mongols turned their backs and retreated, and Ivan let them go. The Golden Horde decamped to the area south of the Don, and established a state of its own, the Khanate of

The Tatars' invasion of Moscow in 1382.

Moreover, troops of the Muscovy principality were used to crush revolts against the Tatars instigated by lesser princes. In this way the Moscow state slowly took on both the political authority and the methods of the Golden Horde.

Russian princes retaliate

Ivan Kalita's grandson, Grand Prince Dmitry, was the first Muscovite prince to feel strong enough to challenge the Tatars' demands in battle. In 1380 he met the Mongol host at the Field of Kulikovo on the River Don and, sensationally, he defeated them. This battle was Russia's Agincourt, a pivotal moment in the country's history. Dmitry's victory shattered forever the myth of Tatar invincibility (he was afterwards dubbed "Donskoi",

> Moscow's annual tribute to the coffers of the Golden Horde was 4,000 roubles compared with the more important city of Vladimir, which paid 85,000 roubles.

Astrakhan, which survived until it was conquered by Ivan the Terrible.

The Mongols' legacy, visible in the high cheekbones and slightly Asiatic features of many Russians, is a mixed one: the Mongols plundered cities and kept Russia from Western integration, but they also brought with them concepts of finance, of administrative order, that have left their mark on the Russian language.

THE FIRST OF THE TSARS

The new caesars ruled Russia with an iron hand, persecuting treacherous nobles and laying the foundations of serfdom.

A wandering German knight ventured into Muscovy some six years after Khan Ahmed had meekly brought 250 years of Mongol overlordship to an end. The report he made to the Holy Roman Emperor, Frederick III, was full of strange and fascinating things.

The title which anyone addressing the Grand Prince of Muscovy was required to know by heart was a measure of recent military successes. He was "Ivan, by the grace of God, Sovereign of all Rus, and grand prince of Vladimir and of Moscow and of Novgorod and of Pskov and of Tver and of Yugria and of Vyatka and of Perm and of Bolgary and of others". Frederick was impressed and sent word that as Holy Roman Emperor he was prepared to bestow on Ivan the title of king. "We have been sovereign in our land from our earliest fore-fathers," came the reply, "and our sovereignty we hold from God." Ivan III, who had played a crucial role in consolidating the Muscovite state, was in fact using the title tsar, a derivation of caesar, because the Russian Orthodox Church had proclaimed Moscow the third Rome after Byzantium. His son, Ivan IV, was crowned Tsar of all Russia in 1547.

Reports filtering through to the West, of Italian architects and engineers engaged in strengthening Moscow's defences and building churches and cathedrals, aroused enormous curiosity. In 1553 Sir Richard Chancellor, an English seaman, was looking for a northern sea route to China when storms forced him to land near Archangel in the White Sea. Local fishermen informed him that he had wandered into the realm of Ivan Vassilievich.

Chancellor travelled inland with a view to meeting this king, a journey which he described as colder and more uncomfortable than anything he had ever experienced at sea. It was only after

Ivan III unifies Moscow in the 15th century.

"much ado" that he came to Moscow, "the chief city of the kingdom and the seat of the king". The 12 days Chancellor spent waiting for an audience were an eye-opener. Moscow was larger than London, he thought, but "rude and without order". The nine churches in the Kremlin he considered "not altogether unhandsome" but he did not think the royal palace compared with "the beauty and elegance of the houses of the kings of England". The king, Ivan IV, he learned, commanded an army of more than 200,000 mounted archers, and what he heard about the system of government sounded like tyranny.

Chancellor was dazzled by the splendour of the court when at last he got to see it. A hundred courtiers were dressed in gold down to their ankles. The king himself, Chancellor reported, was not only dressed in gold but had a gold crown on his head and a gold sceptre inlaid with precious stones. All the tableware at the state banquet he attended was gold. He dined on roast swan and other dishes accompanied by copious quantities of mead. Ivan was clearly impressed by what Chancellor told him of England, so much so that he decided there and then that he wished to marry the English queen, the redoubtable Elizabeth I. Chancellor secured a favourable trade agreement for English merchants and said he would forward the proposal.

Ivan the Terrible, tyranny at large.

Russia, observed Richard Chancellor in 1553, was "a very large and spacious country, every way bounded by divers nations".

Ivan the Terrible

Chancellor's suspicions of tyranny at work were well-founded. Ivan IV (1530–84) came to be known in his own lifetime as "Ivan the Terrible", although it should be noted that "Awe-inspiring" is a more apt translation of the Russian.

Ivan IV succeeded to the throne when he was only three, and owed his early survival to the clever machinations of his mother and regent, the Polish Princess Elena Glinskaya. She was eventually poisoned by the lesser nobles *(boyars)*. Instead of murdering the young tsar at the same time, it suited the *boyars* to let him be. Ivan continued to live in the palace, but the *boyars* used it as a kind of playground, helping themselves to anything that caught their fancy, Ivan's toys included.

These experiences fired in Ivan a desire for revenge, but to begin with he participated lustily in the unbridled licence of palace life. He is reputed to have rollicked in the company of several hundred women before his 16th birthday, when it was thought he ought to get married. He chose Anastasia for his wife, the daughter of a minor noble family named Romanov.

Ivan's foreign policy was to win the remaining fragments of the Mongol Empire. He conquered the Kazan khanate on the Upper Volga in 1552, a victory he celebrated by building St Basil's Cathedral in Moscow. The capture of Astrakhan four years later made him master of the Volga from Moscow to the Caspian. These victories opened the way to the conquest of Siberia, a task entrusted to the Stroganov family of merchant-adventurers protected by the Cossack hero Yermak and his men.

With the Stroganovs energetically at work, Ivan looked west towards the Baltic, especially as the Turkish conquest of Constantinople in 1453 had made the Varangian trade routes down the Dnieper and Volga redundant. Ivan's Baltic ambitions ran into stiff opposition. The Teutonic Order of Knights had dug themselves into Estonia and were in possession of Narva, the port which was Russia's most obvious Baltic outlet. Neither Denmark nor Sweden were inclined to sit back and let the Russians encroach, and farther south Poland and Lithuania had united to become a powerful force.

At home Ivan reformed the legal codes and introduced local self-government. He grew increasingly ruthless in his determination to reduce the powers of the *boyars*. He confiscated *boyars'* estates, and installed his own placemen, called *pomeshchiki*, to run them. He ensured that the *pomeshchiki* had the labour they needed by confining the peasants to the land, thus laying the cornerstone of Russian serfdom. Peasants who risked the death penalty by running away often headed south to the steppes where they joined the growing number of footloose adventurers and fugitive slaves who together constituted the Cossacks.

To enforce his repressive measures Ivan instituted the *oprichniki*, a kind of cross between a Spanish inquisition and a palace guard. They were the first incarnation of Russia's secret police, and they set a precedent for many of Ivan's successors up to and including Stalin. The *oprichniki* wore black, rode black horses and on their saddles they carried a broom and a severed dog's head to symbolise their role as purifiers of the state and their ferocious loyalty to the tsar.

The worst example of Ivan's terror resulted from his conviction that Novgorod was seething with treachery. In 1570 he sentenced the entire

> Ivan the Terrible liked to play chess, but only according to his own rules. These eliminated the king from the board, so that the king could never be checked.

young man arrived with a Polish army swelled with Russians and Cossacks and claiming to be Dmitry, half-brother of Fyodor (who had died in mysterious circumstances in 1591), the nobles believed him. Following Godunov's death, the false Dmitry was installed as tsar.

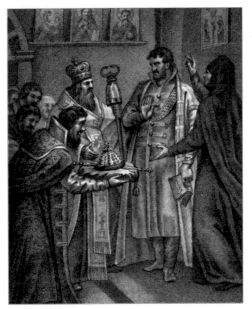

Boris Godunov is crowned Tsar in 1598.

The False Dmitry, mysterious interloper.

population to death and thousands of inhabitants were killed in the space of five weeks. As Russia braced itself for his next move, Ivan died.

Time of Troubles

Ivan's heir was his second son, the simple-minded Fyodor (he had accidentally killed his eldest son in a fit of anger) and so began Russia's "Time of Troubles", a bleak period of anarchy, civil war and invasion. Fyodor's regent and successor as tsar was Boris Godunov (1551–1605). While Godunov reformed the justice system and encouraged trade with Western Europe, he, too, had a ruthless nature and was swift to persecute anyone suspected of treason. In so doing he invoked the wrath of the *boyars*, and when a

The troubles came to an end with the advent of the Romanovs: Mikhail Romanov was elected tsar in 1613, mainly on the strength of his family's connection by marriage to Ivan the Terrible. His successor, son Alexei, began to open Russia to Western influences and so lay the foundations for the momentous reign of his son, Peter the Great.

Meanwhile, restrictions on the free movement of serfs imposed in the mid-17th century led to peasant rebellions. In 1670 Stepan (known as Stenka) Razin and his force of 7,000 Cossacks captured the Volga-Don region, including the towns of Tsaritsyn, Astrakhan and Saratov. Razin was finally defeated by the tsar's Western-trained army and was executed in Moscow. He lives on as a folk hero, immortalised in songs and stories.

Peter the Great, mastermind behind
the Westernisation of Russia in the
18th century.

WINDOWS ON THE WEST

Peter and Catherine both looked to the
West for ideas that would transform
Russia into a progressive nation.

Peter was in every sense a giant of a man:
not just in stature – though at 2 metres
(6 ft 7 in) he towered above his fellow
countrymen – but also in his titanic energy and
appetites, in his vast breadth of interests, in his
capacity for kingly generosity and in his bloodthirsty rages. But the biggest thing about Peter
was the scale of his ambition and the size of his
achievement. He set himself the task of hauling
Russia out of the thick mud of medievalism and
onto the paved highway of European civilisation.
He wanted his Russia to be a modern state and
a great power, and he did not care what it cost.

The child tsar

Peter was born in the Moscow Kremlin in 1672.
His mother, Natalya Naryshkina, was Tsar Alexei's second wife. At the age of 10, in 1682, he
was proclaimed tsar along with his sickly elder
half-brother, Ivan. But his ambitious and wilful
half-sister Sophia chose this moment to foment
a revolt among the Streltsy, the palace guard,
against the Naryshkin faction at court. The
coup turned into a frenzied bloodbath.

The boy Peter was spared, but many of his
relatives and courtiers were hacked to death
before his eyes. Later historians would cite this
as one of the main sources of Peter's hatred for
Moscow and its Byzantine palace intrigues.

Sophia was installed as regent and Peter, still
co-tsar, was sent into semi-exile to Preobrazhenskoye, a hunting lodge near Moscow. Here, in
the country, Peter was left largely to his own
devices. Guided by his own insatiable curiosity, he set up a "toy regiment" with his young
playmates. This game of soldiers soon became
deadly serious: Preobrazhenskoye was transformed into a barracks where Peter drilled
and trained with a small army of teenage

Catherine I, wife of Peter the Great.

men-at-arms, fully equipped with artillery, dark-
green uniforms and tricorn hats. Out of Peter's
adolescent experiments grew the Preobrazhensky regiment, for 200 years the proudest and
most elite unit in the Russian army.

Preobrazhenskoye also happened to be near
the "foreign suburb", the home of Western
merchants and specialists, many of whom had
come to Russia in the reign of Peter's father.
Peter spent days in this Little Europe, and saw
that the foreigners had all sorts of knowledge
that was new to him and to Russia. One of these
foreigners, a Dutchman, taught Peter to sail a
Western-style boat on the River Moskva. Peter,
already an accomplished carpenter, resolved to
learn the art of boat-building. Now the three

passions of his life were in place: a fascination with the West; a gift for waging war; a desire to build a navy.

As soon as he was old enough to do so, Peter put an end to the regency. After a brief power struggle, Sophia was confined to Moscow's Novodevichy monastery and Peter came back to the city. He continued to rule jointly with Ivan until the latter's death in 1696.

Peter's "year out"

As soon as he was sole and undisputed tsar, Peter did something so unprecedented, so radi-

Peter's travels were cut short by the news that the Streltsy had once again risen against him. The revolt had been put down by the time Peter got back to Moscow, but he was determined to deal with the rebels once and for all. There was an orgy of torture and public execution in which Peter personally took part. Red Square ran with the blood of the mutineers, and their corpses hung on the Kremlin walls for months after. Peter's vengeance for the massacre of his mother's family was complete.

Peter had come back from the West inspired to build a modern navy. To achieve this he

Peter the Great at Deptford Dock by Daniel Maclise.

cal, that it was perceived by many of his subjects as a downright blasphemy. He went abroad. No Russian tsar had ever left the country, but for more than a year Peter travelled round Western Europe. This was no ordinary diplomatic progress. Peter's aims were practical: he went to lectures on anatomy, made shoes, visited cannon foundries, but chiefly spent his days working as an apprentice in the shipyards of Holland and England under the transparent incognito of Peter Mikhailov. He felt that the way to learn any subject was to immerse oneself in the basics, and he applied this principle to his new civil service and remodelled army: everyone started at the lowest rank and worked their way up.

needed a port, and so he spent most of his reign in a protracted war with Sweden to win a stretch of Baltic coastline.

Building St Petersburg

Peter finally wrested the province of Kareliya from Swedish control, and on this marshy desolate piece of land, at the mouth of the River Neva, he built his seaport. The human cost of the construction is incalculable – thousands died of disease or mishap – but Peter got what he wanted: a modern city, a "window on the West", and a shop window in which the West might admire his achievements. He equipped it with the trappings of a civilised society: Western style palaces and ministries, a university, a library, museums. To symbolise the break with the old Byzantine ways of Moscow, he designated the new city the capital of Russia and named it Petersburg (Peter's city).

Meanwhile Peter sent hundreds of young Russians west to learn the technologies and skills which Russia lacked. He also invited a range of Western specialists to Russia. More radically still, he insisted that Russians adopt Western dress and manners, hence the tax on beards, which was Peter's way of declaring that the Westernising reforms were not just a passing whim.

By the time Peter died in 1725, at the age of 53, Russia had indeed changed irreversibly. No lesser personality could have shaken Russia out of its age-old slumber. Peter's successors could not turn the clock back, and some, notably Catherine the Great, made it their business to carry on the work of this remarkable man.

Six monarchs reigned over the next 37 years: Peter's wife Catherine I, his grandson Peter II, then his niece Anna, followed by Ivan VI, Elizabeth and Peter III (ineffectual great-grandson of his namesake). During this period, some of Peter's achievements were eroded or corrupted:

Count Potemkin, one of Catherine the Great's lovers.

Alexis Orlov, also one of Catherine's lovers.

THE LOVERS OF CATHERINE THE GREAT

Catherine was no great beauty, but she possessed an ability – part womanly instinct, part cold calculation – to inspire loyalty as well as passion in the men who wooed her. There were many such men in the course of her life, and for this her enemies dubbed her "the Messalina of the North". Among the first was Grigory Orlov, a leader of the coup that brought Catherine to power and the murderer of her demented husband. But before that, while Peter III was Emperor, she secretly had a son by Orlov. The infant was smuggled from the Winter Palace in the pelt of a beaver – *bobr* in Russian. In memory of this, the boy was named Alexei Bobritsky, and his descendants are still one of the proudest families in Russia. Before Orlov, there had been an assignation with Stanislaus Poniatowski, a Polish count. When Catherine tired of him she installed him as King of Poland, a typically Catherinesque conjunction of political and emotional convenience. But the great romance of her life came when she was 51. This was Grigory Potemkin, a shaggy, one-eyed giant of a man who conquered the Crimea for the love of his Empress. Catherine, for her part, was glad to surrender to so grand and untamed a personality. He was not her last love – she continued to take lovers into her sixties – but he was the one she always came back to, like a prodigal wife.

the court became Westernised to the extent that it was completely cut off from the world of the peasant masses, almost an alien ruling class; the nobility found ways round Peter's meritocratic rules, and reasserted its ancient privileges; the God-fearing lower classes began to forget the impossibly tall ruler who had made them shave their chins.

Catherine the Great

Peter III was deposed by his young German wife Catherine. In the coup that brought her to power Catherine showed the skills she was

Catherine the Great in her prime.

to exhibit throughout her life: a politician's instincts, a lack of sentimentality, an appetite for personal glory, and a habit of making her lovers her closest advisers and political allies.

Catherine's reign began in the spirit of the Enlightenment. As a Westerner herself, she was aware of the backwardness of her adopted land and, like Peter, she was determined to impose change for the better. She liberalised the penal code, introduced plans for primary education, reformed local government, founded hospitals and orphanages, expressed the view (in her correspondence with Voltaire as well as to her advisers) that rulers were called to serve the state. She invited the leading architects of the day to Russia, and it was during her reign that Petersburg first acquired its cool, classical character. These are some of the achievements that merit her title "the Great". Catherine was also possessed of an imperial acquisitiveness which would have made Peter proud. In her reign the Crimea was conquered, and Russia thus gained a port on the Black Sea at last. And at her behest, the vast riches of Siberia – the furs, the forests and the minerals – were exploited.

A turning-point in Catherine's reign was a peasant revolt of such scope and fury that it nearly tore the Russian state apart. The leader of the revolt was a Cossack, deserter Emelian Pugachev. In 1773 he appeared on the southern fringe of the Empire making the unlikely claim that he was Peter III, Catherine's murdered husband. Enough people chose to believe him – outlaws, disaffected Cossacks and Old Believers, Muslim Kalmuks and Tatars – for him to raise a ragbag army. Serfs flocked to him in their thousands: for what did they have to lose? Pugachev captured the city of Kazan and put it to the torch. The serfs of Nizhny Novgorod rose up and laid waste the entire region. As Pugachev's confidence grew, so did his ferocity. His shabby juggernaut rolled on, murdering and raping as it went.

A loyal army, hurriedly recalled from the war with the Turks, headed Pugachev off when he marched on Moscow. Pugachev turned south, and this retreat damaged his prestige. He was betrayed by his own lieutenants and handed over to Catherine's forces, who paraded him through the desolate provinces in a cage. He was put to a cruel death in Moscow.

After Pugachev, Catherine's rule slowly took on a darker hue. Her early intentions to abolish serfdom were abandoned, and in fact by the end of her reign the serfs were more numerous and more tightly bound than ever, the human property of the landowners.

Catherine's youthful plans and mature achievements were diminished still further after her death in 1796. Her son, the new Tsar Paul I, hated his mother, and set about undoing her legacy the moment he came to the throne. He introduced a Prussian-style military dictatorship, and heaped scorn on his mother's memory and accomplishments. But it did not last long. He was assassinated in 1801, strangled with his own nightshirt by supporters of his dreamy son Alexander. Russia's 19th century would continue to jolt from reform to bloody turmoil.

FIVE EMPERORS

The last five Russian autocrats were unable to control their wayward land. For a century the country zigzagged between repression and reform.

Russia began the 19th century in hopeful mood. Mad Paul was dead and the new tsar, his son Alexander, was a man of known liberal views. One of Alexander I's first acts as tsar was to abolish the secret police (they were soon reinstated).

These years were dominated for Russia, as for all Europe, by the problem of Napoleon. Alexander chose to make peace with the French Emperor at Tilsit in 1807. But a treaty did not put an end to the aggressor's ambitions, it merely bought a little time: France invaded Russia in 1812.

The war with Napoleon was a wrenching, destructive ordeal that roused Russia to righteous fury and would be called the Patriotic War. Ancient class enmities were forgotten as the nation rallied to the flag. When the French took the old capital, Muscovites put the city to the torch and rendered it uninhabitable. Napoleon had no choice but to turn back. His army was harried all the way by partisans, regular troops – and by "General January and General February", the merciless Russian winter. Of the 450,000 French troops who crossed the Niemen into Russia, barely 100,000 completed the long march home.

After the defeat of Napoleon, Alexander became increasingly distracted. He had always been weak and indecisive (the writer Alexander Herzen famously described him as "Hamlet crowned") and now he indulged his growing interest in religious mysticism, leaving the country in the hands of the deeply reactionary minister Count Arakcheyev.

The Decembrist uprising

Alexander died unexpectedly in 1825, and his death provoked a constitutional crisis which set the tone of Russian history for a century to come. A group of officers had been planning a coup

Alexander I presenting Russian troops to Napoleon.

against the tsar. They were all acquainted with life in the West – many had fought the French all the way to Paris – and they were convinced that Russia could take her place in the European family of nations if the autocracy were abolished and replaced with a constitutional republic. Alexander's death provided them with their opportunity.

On the day the army was due to take its oath of allegiance to the new tsar, Alexander's brother Nicholas, they led their troops onto Senate Square in St Petersburg, and faced up to the ranks of loyal guardsmen ranged on the far side. It was a freezing December morning, and for most of the day the two sets of troops stood eyeing each other in the cold and confusion. Most of the soldiers under the command of the plotters had no idea that they were the pawns in a revolt.

While negotiators rode back and forth across the square, the builders who were then working on the new St Isaac's Cathedral threw a few bricks from the scaffolding at the massed troops. As evening fell, there was a brief and bloody exchange of cannon fire, and then the revolt simply fizzled out.

All the plotters were arrested and interrogated by Nicholas personally. The ringleaders were executed and others were sent to Siberia. The incident became known as the Decembrist uprising after the month when it took place. It left Nicholas with a pathological dread of revolution which he passed on to his successors like a hereditary illness. Nicholas's own treatment for the revolutionary disease was to put the patient on ice.

For the 30 years of his rule, Nicholas was the cold, cold leader of a frozen country. He inaugurated a government department called the Third Section, the function of which was to extinguish any spark of dissent, indeed any sign of original thought. This department was headed by Count Benckendorff, another of those ideological policemen that Russia so often

Nicholas I's Life Guards; the tsar lived in fear of revolution.

STOLYPIN – TSARISM'S LAST HOPE

After 1905, Peter Stolypin was Russia's last hope of avoiding the catastrophe of revolution. He said he needed 20 years of stability to rescue Russia – he got five years of chaos. He was made prime minister in 1906, at a time when government officials were being murdered by terrorists at a rate of more than 100 a month. Stolypin answered violence with violence. He set up court-martials which tried and executed assassins so swiftly that they were often in their graves before their victims. Having crushed the revolution, Stolypin passed laws to liberate peasants from the rustic tyranny of the commune and from feudal practises such as strip farming. Peasants were invited to buy land, sow whatever crops they chose, and employ workers. (The able peasants who seized this opportunity were annihilated as *kulaks*, or exploiters, under Stalin.) Stolypin also presided over an industrial boom which made Russia an emergent economic superpower. He tried to work with the fractious Duma, but was hamstrung by the disapproval of the weak and stubborn tsar. Yet given more time and luck, Stolypin might just have steered the Russian state out of the path of disaster. His luck ran out in 1911: he was assassinated at the Kiev Opera in full view of his Imperial employer. His successors were well-meaning nonentities, and Russia blundered on into the abyss.

produces. Nicholas himself functioned as a kind of supreme government inspector, taking a minute interest in the day-to-day running of his unhappy empire – especially in matters of discipline. He sacked civil servants for scruffy dress, decided which university students should be awarded prizes, designed the buttons for bandsmen's uniforms, suggested changes to Alexander Pushkin's poems. His favourite architect, Carlo Rossi, transformed the city while the country's first railway was built (1837) and the first permanent bridge was put up across the Neva.

But the inadequacy of Nicholas's regime was exposed by the Crimean War. It was ironic that an empire run on strict military lines could not win a war on its own soil. It was a matter of intense humiliation for Nicholas personally that the British and French troops, with supply lines running right across Europe, were better armed and fed than the Russians fighting in their own back yard. Nicholas died – one might almost say he died of shame – before the war was declared at an end.

Alexander II frees the serfs

Nicholas's son, Alexander II, came to the throne convinced of the need for reform. The national disaster of Crimea, he understood, was due to Russia's backwardness, and in particular to the iniquitous institution of serfdom. Alexander signalled his good intentions by releasing the last surviving Decembrists from exile, and then set about the complex task of liberating his nation of peasant slaves. The emancipation of the serfs came in 1861, not without terrible problems and injustices, but nevertheless it came: no more would Russians sell their fellow countrymen like cattle.

Despite the changes for the better, or more likely because of them, revolutionary groups were more active than ever during the reign of the Tsar Liberator. These men (and women) were a different breed from the well-intentioned aristocrats and reformers of the past. They were anarchists and extremists, firm believers in assassination as a political weapon. Their chief target was, naturally, the tsar himself; there were many attempts on his life: a bomb in his train, another in the Winter Palace, a lone gunman who chased the emperor down the street. Each attempt on his life led to a crackdown, which in turn justified the next murderous attempt. And in the end they got him. On 1 March 1881, Alexander's legs were blown off by a suicide bomber as he rode in his carriage through St Petersburg. He bled to death in the Winter Palace. Later that day, he had been due to issue a promulgation granting Russia a limited constituent assembly. The announcement was cancelled.

> Nicholas I was renowned for his intolerance: he ordered imperial guardsmen to wear only black moustaches; other colours, he decreed, had to be painted black.

The 1905 Bloody Sunday massacre.

Return to repression

And so, in the now familiar rhythm, the pendulum swung back towards repression. The first days of the reign of Alexander III were especially brutal, marked by widespread semi-official pogroms against the Jews. In the years that followed, national minorities were forcibly Russianised, censorship was tightened, and access to education was restricted for the working classes. At the same time, the working classes were swelling as a result of the policies of Alexander's chief minister, Sergei Witte, who instituted an astonishingly rapid process of industrialisation. Thousands of miles of railway were laid (the Trans-Siberian railway was begun in 1891), a vast coal industry was founded in the Don basin, and foreigners queued up to invest in this new Russia. The process continued under the last tsar and his prime minister Peter Stolypin. But the combination of political repression and a large urban proletariat was dangerous: the revolutionary brew was beginning to bubble again.

Rasputin's gaze, said the French ambassador to Russia, "was at once piercing and caressing, naive and cunning, far off and concentrated." In conversation, "his pupils radiated magnetism."

The infamous Rasputin, whose domination of the tsarina led to his assassination by a group of nobles.

In 1894 Alexander III died in his bed – by now no mean achievement for a tsar. He was succeeded by his son, Nicholas, a devoted family man of limited intelligence and imagination.

The last tsar

The accession of Nicholas II was marred by a dreadful accident which set the tone for his entire reign. A crowd of half a million gathered to celebrate at Khodynka Field near Moscow, where they were plied with free beer in coronation mugs. At some point in the afternoon an urgent rumour circulated among the crowd that the beer was running out. There followed a drunken stampede for the booths, and thousands of people, mostly women and children, were crushed to death.

Khodynka was not the last pointless loss of life in Nicholas's reign. Far worse was to come. In January 1905, in the midst of war with Japan, a priest named Father Gapon led a demonstration of aggrieved workers to the Winter Palace. It was a huge but loyal gathering – many of the workers were carrying icons and portraits of the tsar. But when they reached Palace Square they were met by mounted guards, who panicked at the sight of so large a crowd and opened fire. The carnage was terrible, and it sparked a full-scale revolution. Within days the entire country was on strike. A new kind of workers' committee, dubbed a soviet, sprang up in the capital and other cities. The leader of the Petersburg soviet was a fiery young man named Lev Trotsky.

The 1905 revolution, which Lenin later referred to as the "dress rehearsal", was put down by a mixed policy of repression and concession. A kind of pale parliament, called the Duma, was set up to advise the tsar. But it was heavily weighted in favour of the land-owning gentry and deeply resented by Nicholas, who saw it as an affront to his God-given right to rule. It was, in any case, too late for parliamentary democracy.

By 1905 the autocracy was unreformable. The revolutionaries bided their time in foreign exile, and Nicholas gradually retired into the bosom of his beautiful family. The scandalous symptom of the rottenness of the regime was that Nicholas allowed a profoundly sinister peasant healer, Grigory Rasputin, to dominate his wife and dictate to his ministers.

Riot and revolution

The collapse of the autocracy, when it came, was an anti-climax. On a February day in 1917, hungry people queueing for bread began to riot. The troops who were routinely sent to disperse them were themselves peasant conscripts, and they joined the rioters. The rule of law simply evaporated in a moment.

Revolution spread through the land just as it had done in 1905, only this time nothing short of the tsar's abdication would placate the angry, tired masses. Nicholas gave in. With a weary flourish of his pen, he put an end to 304 years of rule by his family, with whom he went into exile. Eighteen months later came the Romanov dynasty's mournful postscript: gunsmoke, bayonets and a bloody end in a far-flung Siberian basement.

Tsar Nicholas II and his family.

Poster of Lenin directing the Revolution.

ИЗ РОССИИ
НЭПОВСКОЙ
БУДЕТ РОССИЯ
СОЦИАЛИСТИЧЕСКАЯ
(ЛЕНИН)

THE RISE AND FALL OF THE SOVIET EMPIRE

Russia's communist experiment is a central fact of 20th-century history and its consequences have endured well into the 21st century.

The fall of the Romanov dynasty in March 1917 was greeted by some with jubilation, but it did not solve Russia's political crisis. The war with Germany raged on, and at home the many fragmented political factions – Mensheviks, Socialist Revolutionaries, Constitutional Democrats, Liberals, Bolsheviks, Monarchists – were at each other's throats. A provisional government was established, but in the cities food was scarce, and the chance of popular unrest high. In the midst of the chaos and the infighting Lenin, the exiled leader of the Bolshevik faction, arrived back in Petrograd (St Petersburg).

Vladimir Lenin (1870–1924) had been a professional revolutionary all of his adult life. After the usual apprenticeship – expulsion from university followed by a string of terms in tsarist prisons – he had escaped to the West, where he spent his middle years organising congresses, publishing clandestine newspapers and writing theoretical pamphlets.

A Red Army soldier, with his distinctive budenovka hat.

The October revolution

Lenin's grand theory, the core idea of Bolshevism, was that the coming revolution must be led by a small band of dedicated activists, otherwise it was bound to become watered down into mere social reform. Lenin expounded this view with all the power of his great intellect. He possessed self-discipline to an awesome degree, and he devoted every waking moment to the cause (his only personal pleasure was chess, at which he was unbeatable). Yet he never expected to get the chance to put his ideas into practice. The February revolution took him, as it did everybody, by surprise.

Now that the revolutionary opportunity was there, the single-minded Bolsheviks were best placed to make the most of it. They struck in the autumn, seizing control of key institutions around Petrograd and arresting the provisional government in one night. It is this coup, not the popular uprising of the previous spring, which was for 74 years celebrated in Russia as the pivotal event in modern history, the Great October Socialist Revolution.

In the months that followed the Bolshevik putsch, the Cheka, the new secret police, began the long work of rooting out "counter-revolutionaries". Meanwhile Lenin withdrew unilaterally from the war with Germany. But peace did not come to Russia, as the country was plunged into a civil war. For three years the Bolshevik regime tottered, but did not fall.

By 1921 the country was, once again, in a state of utter ruin. At this moment Lenin made a bold move: he announced concessions allowing for a partial return to a market economy. Peasants were to be permitted to sell their produce for a profit; city-dwellers could set up and own businesses. Moscow and Petrograd filled up with Art Deco restaurants where jazz-age Russian yuppies celebrated the fact that the good times were back.

Many Bolsheviks in Lenin's own government were horrified by this "New Economic Policy" (NEP). For them, any kind of trade was un-Marxist and bound to lead down a slippery slope to petty-bourgeois capitalism. But Lenin saw it as an essential tactical retreat. The old devil of the profit motive was the only thing which could get the economy moving again. When the time came, they would stuff the devil back in its sack. It is not clear how long Lenin intended NEP to last. It was in full swing when he died in January 1924, having been incapacitated by a stroke more than a year before. The power struggle that followed was in the oldest Kremlin tradition. It lasted four years and was won by the rank outsider, Joseph Stalin.

Stalin's brutal regime

Stalin, unlike most of the top-ranking Bolsheviks, was not a middle-class intellectual. He was the son of a Georgian cobbler, and made his name in the revolutionary underground by leading "expropriations" – bank robberies – in the Caucasus. He played a very minor role in the October Revolution, but had since established himself as a good organiser.

At the time of Lenin's death, Stalin occupied the key post of general secretary, which meant that he had an overall control of appointments within the party. It was through this office that he levered himself into power, out-manoeuvring factions led by high-profile leaders such as Trotsky.

Once swathed in Lenin's mantle, Stalin, drawing on massive support among rank and file Party members, brought NEP to a halt and launched the first Five-Year Plan, a massive programme of state-led industrialisation

Trotsky as Commissar of Defence.

THE REVOLUTION'S SPURNED GENIUS

Lev Trotsky (1879–1940) was the haughty ringmaster of the Russian Revolution. He was the only thinker in the movement who could argue on equal terms with Lenin, and he was a writer of such polemical brilliance that he was known as "the Pen". As Menshevik chairman of the St Petersburg soviet (workers' committee) he played a leading role in the 1905 uprising, and this practical experience of revolution gave him huge authority. In 1917 he defected to Lenin's Bolsheviks, consigning his former Menshevik allies to the "dustbin of history". He garnered yet more influence as architect of the victorious Red Army in the civil war, and was seen as the natural successor to Lenin. But after Lenin's death, his feuds with the leader were disinterred and made to look like disloyalty. Moreover, his intellectual conceit did not make him a popular figure, and his long years as a Menshevik were held against him: the Bolsheviks were deeply snobbish about party pedigree. In 1927, Stalin expelled him from the party, then from the country. In exile, Trotsky railed eloquently but impotently against "the gravedigger of the revolution", while his own achievements – his very name – were expunged from Soviet history. Stalin had him murdered in Mexico City in 1940. Trotsky's books include *History of the Russian Revolution* and *Diary in Exile*.

intended to transform the Soviet Union into a modern power.

The parallel collectivisation of agriculture aimed to harness the country's productivity and bring it under state control. But the mass

> At the start of the war with Germany, Stalin locked himself away. It seems he had a nervous breakdown. Foreign minister Vyacheslav Molotov announced the news of war to the Russian people.

Khrushchev on a visit to a collective farm; he was fanatical about planting maize.

of peasants refused to be herded into collective farms; many killed their cows and sheep rather than hand them over. Stalin's response was brutal. He effectively declared war on the countryside. Millions were branded as *kulaks* (peasant exploiters) and driven into the burgeoning Gulag; millions more died in artificially engineered famines, particularly in Ukraine. Stalin said he was "liquidating the *kulaks* as a class".

The Great Terror

These measures were backed up by a purge of indescribable horror. The secret police, now renamed the NKVD, swept through the country, their task to arrest "enemies of the people". It was as if the vicious, pathological personality of Stalin had been magnified and unleashed against the entire nation. In blind terror, arrestees denounced everybody they could think of, thereby providing new crops of pseudo-enemies to be harvested. Others denounced neighbours and workmates out of sheer ideological zeal.

The Great Terror of the 1930s was a silent slaughter of millions upon millions of people; later entire nationalities such as the Chechens were deported. And through it all,

Leonid Brezhnev, guardian of the Cold War.

in factories and schools, happy workers and their children sang a favourite song of the era: "I know no other country where a man can breathe so free..."

After the Terror, disaster struck again: in 1941, Hitler invaded the Soviet Union – although here at least was an enemy one could openly disparage and hit back at. The Soviet people threw themselves into the fray, and yet more millions died in what Russians have called the Great Patriotic War. There were countless acts of epic heroism, particularly in Leningrad (Petrograd had been renamed to commemorate Lenin in 1924), which was besieged for 900 days but did not surrender. The entire western part of the country was devastated and 20 million people lost their lives.

As with the Mongol invasion centuries before, Russians felt that they had taken the full force of barbaric onslaught upon themselves, thereby saving the West from submission. The defeat of Germany in 1945 left Russian troops in the heart of Europe. In a way, this was a fulfilment of Peter the Great's dream: a Russian state at the heart of Europe, respected and even feared by its Western neighbours. Stalin's final years in office saw renewed mass paranoia. A grand purge aimed

streets of Budapest in 1956 proved, it had very definite limits – but it was never forgotten.

Nikita Khrushchev is fondly remembered in Russia for other reasons too. He increased state pensions, was fanatical about planting maize

Khrushchev's tombstone in Novodevichy cemetery is a bust of the man with one side of his head black, the other white. This symbolises his personality and achievements: part good, part bad.

Mikhail Gorbachev, the father of perestroika.

Boris Yeltsin, two-term president.

at Jews was in the pipeline when he died in 1953. His successor, after a power struggle, was Nikita Khrushchev.

Cultural thaw

Khrushchev's great achievement, the act for which he will forever have the gratitude of the Russian people, was to denounce Stalin's Terror. He declared the nightmare to be over, and it is a measure of his success that when he was subsequently deposed it was not thought necessary to liquidate him physically.

In the cultural thaw that accompanied "de-Stalinisation" Russians had a tiny intoxicating taste of freedom: to read, to speak, to criticise. It was not much – and as the tanks on the

(during the Khrushchev years, Soviet shops overflowed with cornflakes and popcorn), and he launched a massive and much-needed housing programme: the five-storey apartment blocks which abound in the suburbs of most Soviet cities are known in his memory as *khrushchevki*.

But Khrushchev made some terrible blunders: he brought the world to the brink of nuclear war by provoking the Cuban missile crisis; he quarrelled with China and so divided the world communist movement; he clowned around on the world stage, thumping tables at the UN with his shoe. It was to put a stop to these alarming and embarrassing escapades that he was removed by a conspiracy of cautious, faceless Party men.

The grip tightens

One of these Communist careerists – Leonid Brezhnev – replaced him. Brezhnev's tenure represented a return to a mild form of Stalinism. A monstrously bloated cult of personality grew up around this unappealing man, who unblushingly awarded himself high honours, including even the Lenin Prize for Literature. On the international stage, Brezhnev was a monumental disaster for his country. In 1968, he crushed the Prague Spring, Czechoslovakia's experiment with liberal socialism; and in 1979 he sent Soviet forces into Afghanistan, committing his country to an unwinnable war.

Under Khrushchev and Brezhnev the USSR dug itself deeper and deeper into the trenches of the Cold War. The arms race against America drained a Soviet economy crippled by the age-old sicknesses of indolence and absenteeism. Consumer goods were scarce, and became practically nonexistent by the 1980s. People queued for hours to buy frozen chicken, or left work and rushed to a shop where, rumour had it, there had been a shoe delivery. The black market became endemic, and in fact the only efficient part of the economy.

This decrepitude was covered in a thick blanket of lies. Brave individuals who spoke out were silenced, or worse, declared insane as psychiatry became a weapon of the KGB (secret police). Christians were oppressed; Jews were persecuted, but refused permission to leave for Israel or the US; the people were paralysed by cynicism.

The dawn of perestroika

This was the situation inherited by Mikhail Gorbachev in 1985. Gorbachev believed passionately in the communist ideal, but saw that the whole system was in need of a drastic overhaul; this project was given the slogan perestroika, restructuring. He knew he needed the genuine support of the people, and decided that the way to win it was to be honest about the country's problems. This part of the plan was called glasnost, usually rendered "openness", though a more accurate translation would be "frankness" because the Russian word implies publicly acknowledging a state of affairs that is already clear.

Perestroika was not intended to make the USSR more Western, still less to dismantle the communist system. It was all done under the banner of a "return to Leninist principles". At the same time, Gorbachev was careful to endear himself to the West: he put an end to some of the grossest human rights abuses of his predecessors (for example, he released the dissident physicist Andrei Sakharov from internal exile); he allowed the satellite states to pursue glasnost locally, though several of them such as Czechoslovakia and the GDR were deeply opposed to the policy; he talked seriously about disarmament and economic cooperation; all the while using his considerable charm to win dollar support for reforms.

Bust adorning Khrushchev's tomb in Moscow.

But Gorbachev had sown the seeds of his own downfall. The spotlight he turned on the Soviet system only revealed that it was rotten beyond repair. The limited debate under glasnost soon broadened into a discussion of the legitimacy of the entire regime. The peoples of East Europe, who had always viewed communism as the oppressors' tool, turned on their Communist leaders. In 1989, the Soviet sphere in Europe fell apart in a series of popular revolts and Gorbachev, to his credit, did not intervene. The USSR tottered on for two years. An attempted coup against Gorbachev in the summer of 1991 was the regime's death rattle. Gorbachev was sidelined: president of a geopolitical entity that was about to disappear. Power devolved to the new President: Boris Yeltsin.

Capitalism arrives

The new man in the Kremlin was master of a much-reduced and bankrupt domain. Yeltsin threw open the doors and invited capitalism in, rushing to sign in laws that would regulate the system. Within a year Russia had all the trappings of a free market economy, including a stock market; food and goods appeared but so did hyperinflation, organised crime and lawlessness.

A Moscow street vendor shows off a pair of matryoshka dolls depicting Russian Presidents Boris Yeltsin, left, and Leonid Brezhnev, right.

The market economy was never given the chance to stabilise. When the reactionary parliament opposed Yeltsin he sent tanks into Moscow and shelled their stronghold; he used similar strong-arm tactics, on a much bloodier scale, against the separatist republic of Chechnya. In his second term, as his democratic credentials wore thin, he looked less like a Westernising reformer in the tradition of Peter the Great (which is how he saw himself), and more like a sad repeat of Leonid Brezhnev: unaware, drunk and helpless.

On the final day of the 20th century, Yeltsin surprised the world by resigning from office and naming Prime Minister Vladimir Putin as acting president. A former KGB officer, Putin rode a wave of patriotic fervour after the renewal of the military campaign in Chechnya. He was elected president in 2000 and won a second term in 2004.

For a decade the West tolerated Putin's less than glittering human rights record as it seemed he was the man who would finally get Russia on its feet. The economy was buoyed up with oil and gas money, the oligarchs were sidelined by a centralising Kremlin and standards of living reached heights never seen before. But the background chatter had a different narrative, one that Western leaders either failed to pick up on, or intentionally ignored, distracted as they were by the world economic crisis. Armed with a law that gives the Russian state the right to protect ethnic Russians wherever they are in the world, the Kremlin began to pump propaganda and fear into areas with large "Russian" populations such as East Ukraine, Crimea, the Baltic States and Georgia with the apparent intention of destabilising the region.

Putin intervened in Georgia in 2008, effectively annexing two areas of the country (South Ossetia and Abkhazia) and his reaction to Ukraine's Maidan Revolution, which ousted pro-Russian president Yanukovych and set the country on a path to EU and NATO membership, was to invade Crimea and East Ukraine, though the Kremlin denies everything. This has awoken the West to Putin's real intentions – to use Russia's newfound wealth to resurrect the Soviet Empire. For its actions in Ukraine, Russia was kicked unceremoniously out of the G8 and selective sanctions have been imposed on regime bigwigs and state companies.

In 2014 oil prices nose-dived and took the rouble and the Russian economy with it. As living standards inevitably begin to decline it's expected President Putin will have to keep feeding the population his brand of nostalgic paranoia and anti-Western rhetoric to keep them onside. Despite everything, Putin enjoys incredible popularity ratings but in a traditionally unstable country like Russia, a power struggle could arise between groupings in the Kremlin, sweeping Putin away in a Soviet-style changing of the guard. What might come after Putin is anyone's guess.

It's all smiles as President Vladimir Putin visits the MAKS-2015 International Air Show.

LIFE TODAY

The last three decades have brought unexpected hardships, yet the Russian people remain remarkably resourceful in their ability to survive.

Life has never been easy in Russia. From the Mongol hordes to Stalin's terror and from the Nazi invasion to geopolitical adventures of today's Kremlin, it seems Russia has never had a prolonged period of peace and stability. This has left its mark on the Russian people, leaving them with less faith in the future, more susceptible to the alarm call of propaganda and less trustful of outsiders. But their history has also made them a hardy bunch, resourceful in times of trouble, survivors on the shifting sands of Eurasian history.

A land of diversity

The people of the Russian Federation are a diverse lot to say the least. Russia has incredibly ethnic diversity (see page 78), with over 180 different officially recognised nationalities within its borders. There are also huge variations within the Russian population spread out over 11 times zones from Kaliningrad to Kamchatka. A Siberian oil worker has a very different lifestyle to a Moscow market analyst; a resident of almost sub-tropical Sochi leads a completely different existence to a semi-nomadic Sami on the chilly Kola Peninsula. So what holds this vast land together? The bonds are surprisingly strong – the Russian language unites most of Russia's 143.3 million people, as does a sense of shared national culture and a love of Mother Russia.

Soviet influence

The Soviet era left a huge imprint on the peoples of Russia, both materially and culturally. Almost three decades after Communism began to crumble, it is still visible not only in the country's rusting Soviet infrastructure but in people's mentalities. Just as physical remnants of the old regime linger – Lenin's Mausoleum,

Shop assistant in a Matryoshka doll souvenir shop.

countless place-names, the occasional statue – so the effects of seven decades of stifling dictatorship are only slowly wearing off.

Communism taught people not to take the initiative in case they were blamed for mistakes. Factory workers grew lazy because they knew they would be paid regardless of the rate of production. This has spilled over into post-Soviet society, with a complex culture of subordination coupled with defiance now firmly established.

As a result, Russia has developed its own extreme breed of capitalism. Businesses have sprung up all over the place, but service is largely a foreign concept; the idea of free trade has taken off, but tax dodging is still a real issue.

While business in the major cities is conducted in a modern environment, it is bureaucratised and consequently labour-intensive. At times everything is up to international standards; at other times there seem to be no standards at all. Corruption is still a major problem across Russia, especially in universities, town halls and among the police. The government has launched half-hearted attempts to tackle the problem but with little effect. In 2014, Transparency International's Corruption Perception Index rated Russia 136th out of 175 countries, behind the likes of Mali, Colombia and Indonesia.

for whom friends and family – not to mention friends of friends and family – are everything. The "Russian spirit" is a great stereotype, but it is certainly true that Russians are very emotional and loyal towards those they love.

Russians love flowers. In winter, they are sold from glass display boxes warmed with candles to protect the petals from frost. Always give an odd number of flowers, even numbers are for funerals.

Moscow's Luzhkov Bridge is dotted with love-lock 'trees' and is popular with newlyweds.

Split personalities

The Russian is famous for having "two faces": that of the man or woman on the street, and that of the man or woman at home.

It is striking that Russians can be rather brusque when you meet them in any formal public situation, yet delightfully warm and generous in personal relationships. A hotel receptionist might glower and hiss at you for asking a perfectly reasonable question by Western standards and shop assistants will sit sulkily filing their nails as you try to catch their attention; when you finally succeed, you are greeted with a surly "What d'you want?"

But in their private life, these same people are transformed into big-hearted individuals

Another celebrated feature of the Russians is their hospitality. An invitation to dinner will entail not only elaborate and abundant food, but also numerous vodka toasts to "friendship", "reunions" and "health".

The dichotomy between public and private life is difficult for outsiders to understand. There is probably no single explanation, but it is likely that years of communist corruption have taught Russians not to trust anyone they do not know. As the proverb goes, "You don't really know a man until you've eaten a sack of salt with him". Above all, the bluntness of Russians is a relic of the Soviet era that may fade with time, its roots possibly to be found in the country's long history as a peasant nation.

Peasant roots

It should not be forgotten that until the middle of the 20th century Russia was inhabited almost entirely by peasants. During the 1930s the country was transformed, within a single generation, from a nation of illiterate agricultural workers to an educated proletariat, thanks to Stalin's massive industrialisation drive which was radical on many fronts: politically, economically and socially.

This incredibly rapid change has meant that people's peasant roots are still fairly strong, and are reflected in their clan-like tendencies:

Russia as "our" country, in the collective, conjuring up a real sense of a united people, history and culture; equally, they will refer to peoples of the former USSR as "ours".

Nowhere is this patriotism expressed more starkly than in Russians' defence of the "motherland", time and time again. The degree to which Russians have suffered for their country is remarkable, and perhaps unsurpassed by any other nation – you need only to reflect that the period of the "Great Patriotic War" of 1941–45 saw the deaths of between 20 and 30 million people. Their tremendous resilience

Honey vendors at St Petersburg's Kuznechny Market.

firm loyalty and boundless generosity towards those they know, severe mistrust and hostility towards those they don't. Certainly Russia's vulnerability to attacks from the east and west have spawned a wary attitude towards foreigners.

A manifestation of this mentality is found in Russians' fierce patriotism, which has an unfortunate tendency to extend to other republics of the former Soviet Union. Leaders and philosophers who look to the West have only served to reinforce this, leading to a nation defensive of its national culture, traditions and history.

Russians' attachment to their country reminds one of a child's relationship with its parent: the parent can be stern, severe, even harsh, but is still adored by the child. A Russian will refer to

Before setting out on a journey, Russians traditionally assemble their suitcases in the hallway and sit on them together for a moment to collect their thoughts. It's said to bring good luck on the journey.

has served them well, under Tsarism and serfdom, revolution, civil war, Stalin's purges, "Wild East" capitalist chaos and today's uncertain geopolitical and economic situation.

Loss of Empire

Psychological adjustment to the break-up of the USSR has been very difficult for Russians, many of whom considered its entire expanse to be their homeland. The entry of Latvia, Lithuania and Estonia into the European Union in May 2004, and the 2014 pro-European Maidan Revolution in Ukraine evoked mixed feelings, to put it mildly. Despite the fact that Russia is still the world's largest country, and although it was widely recognised that the Soviet Union could not have survived unchanged indefinitely, the Russian people feel impoverished by the loss of their empire, an enormous, and enormously powerful union of which they were proud. President Putin has tapped into these emotions, hence the lack of effective opposition to wars in Georgia and Ukraine and his destabilising policies in other former Soviet republics.

Education and training

As a rule, Russians are highly trained and one of the nation's biggest assets is its human capital. It is in danger of losing this, however, if people cannot afford to study – getting through university can require large bribes. The country has a high proportion of professionals such as doctors, scientists and academ-

Anti-government demonstration, Moscow 2015.

RUSSIAN BANYAS

A *banya* is the Russian equivalent of the Finnish sauna, the main difference being that the heat is wet rather than dry. Every town has a *banya* and cities have several. During the long winter nothing gets the circulation going better than exposing the body to steaming heat followed by the shock of the icy plunge pool (or a quick roll in the snow). More invigorating still is the tradition of first covering the body in honey to smooth the skin, then beating it with a *venik*, a bunch of damp birch twigs. It is inadvisable to eat during a *banya*, but Russians quench their thirst with beer (never vodka) as it is believed to prevent dehydration.

ics, and every year new institutes award degrees and diplomas to thousands in the professions of the modern age – such as management, public relations and law.

The Russian education system relies heavily on rote learning and can be criticised for its rigidity. Certainly there is little room for independent thought, but children are left with a thorough knowledge of their town or region's history, of literature, mathematics and the sciences. What is more, the range of opportunities on offer – with specialised dancing, music, sports and foreign-language schools – is astounding. It is not uncommon for chess, karate and skating to be part of the everyday school curriculum. Only history is a problematic subject – from a discussion with anyone who has been through the Soviet/Russian school system it becomes clear that the "version" of history taught in Russian schools differs wildly from that in other countries, even other former Soviet republics. Even today Russian schoolchildren are already reading in text-books that the Maidan Revolution in Ukraine was a coup funded by the US.

Leisure and the great outdoors

The pursuit of these interests was encouraged by the communist policy of making theatre,

Young Muscovite.

ballet and classical music affordable for all. Every large city had its own companies, and an evening at the opera was as commonplace as a trip to the cinema. Books, too, were extremely cheap to buy, although hard to find.

Sadly live entertainment has been largely usurped by television and its onslaught of low-grade pop-music shows, reruns of US serials and badly dubbed films. In the cities, nightclubs and bars have mushroomed and cater for all tastes in music, from garage to jazz. Many attract a trendy clientele. Most young Russians are fashion conscious and women especially are always smartly turned out and carefully made-up.

Outdoor recreation is widely enjoyed, as Russians love nothing better than an excursion to

their *dacha* (country cottage) to pick wild berries or mushrooms. *Babushki* (grandmothers) returning to the cities with loaded baskets are a common sight, as *dachas* and their vegetable plots have become a vital source of subsistence for many, especially the elderly. Winter sports include sledging and cross-country skiing, at which most Russians are quite accomplished. Those who are brave enough (nicknamed "walruses") even swim, cutting holes in the ice for a quick winter dip.

Russians adore animals and transport their dogs out to the dacha for some exercise at week-

Cold War chess set for sale in a souvenir market, St Petersburg.

ends. It is prohibited to take them on the Metro, however, so they hide them in their handbags or blanket-covered baskets.

High-rise homes

The vast majority of city-dwellers in Russia live in small flats in enormous high-rise blocks. Indeed, in some parts of the country, entire cities are made up of row upon row of these bleak, dispiriting buildings. While Westerners may associate such structures with crime, poverty and social deprivation, in Russia they do not carry the same connotations. These living conditions can be cramped – many families of three live in two-room flats and it is not uncommon for extended families to share living and sleeping quarters – but new "elite" apartment buildings going up everywhere provide more space and additional services. A small number of *komunalki* (communal flats) still exist, too. Made famous by the novelist Fyodor Dostoyevsky, these are reserved for the very poorest. Whole families live in a single room, sharing the kitchen and bathroom with their fellow tenants. However these are being slowly phased out.

The cost of living

The phenomenon of the extended family, largely eroded in the West, is one of Russia's

Reminders of the Soviet era: high-rise blocks and Lada car.

most valuable resources: communal bills are lower if the flat is registered in a pensioner's name, and grandparents provide free childcare for working parents. The young and the old have a special place in Russian society. Children are adored and utterly spoilt, while pensioners and war veterans are treated with great respect.

Indeed one of the most attractive aspects of Russian society is its supportive and generous social networks, which go a long way to explaining how millions of Russians today manage to get by on what appear to be impossibly small sums of money.

Whereas prices of food and clothing are virtually the same as those in the West, at times even outstripping them, wages and state benefits remain at a low level. It is almost impossible to conceive that the average teacher's salary, for example, is a fraction of that of his or her counterpart in the West, while officially a Russian doctor earns less in a month than most doctors in the West earn in a day. Similarly, the ordinary pension is many times lower, while the student grant has all but disappeared. Rent, heating and water are all subsidised by the state yet these bills still swallow up a substantial part of Russians' meagre wages.

On the other side of the coin, salaries for the middle classes in the private sector have grown, especially in Moscow, and avid shoppers routinely fill the supermarkets and malls at weekends.

New Russians

As a result of current uncertainty, many people have reverted to spending what they have when they have it, because who knows what it will all be worth tomorrow? But the highly visible wealth on the streets of the big cities – in the form of powerful cars and fur coats – belongs to the class of so-called "New Russians": rich, flashy biznesmeny and corrupt officials with money to burn. They have the cash to splash out on trips abroad and other luxuries, like cars, properties abroad and private education for their children in England and Switzerland. They inhabit a different universe to the Irkutsk schoolteacher or the Kaliningrad shop assistant, but while there is some resentment of these social differences, it has yet to boil over into any meaningful political movement.

GUM shopping mall: where Moscow's New Russians spend their rubles.

THE WOMEN OF RUSSIA

The concept of motherhood has always been central to Russian culture, yet women still have a long way to go to achieve an equal status in society.

The word "Russia" has a feminine gender in the Russian language and according to Russian tradition the country itself has a feminine soul. The myth of "mother Russia", deriving from the divinity of "mother earth" is central to the history of Russian culture from pre-Christian times to the present day. This is reflected in Russian fairytales, folklore, art and social structures.

Until the 13th century many Russian women had a certain status, power and even equality in some spheres of life, including military affairs. The situation changed when Eastern Slavic civilisation moved from Kiev to Moscow. With the introduction and growing influence of Byzantine religion and the militarisation of Muscovite society, particularly during the Tatar invasion, the status of women diminished and the Christian doctrine of "female impurity" spread to Russia. Women from the upper classes were confined to the realm of domestic life and their status there was the lowest.

In rural areas, in peasant communities, women continued to have some freedom and power. They worked in the fields with the men, and often ruled the roost at home, particularly if their husbands were serving in the army. They could even become starosta, the head of a rural community.

Female achievers

Russian history is full of outstanding women who played key roles in the political, cultural and social life of the country.

Catherine the Great, who ruled Russia from 1762 to 1796, extended the territories of the country, introduced new liberal laws and improved educational institutions. Her foreign policy made Russia one of the

Mother and daughter cooks in a fishing camp in the Kamchatka Peninsula.

greatest European countries. Her friend Catherine Dashkov (born Vorontsova) was the first woman in the world to become the head of an Academy of Sciences, an institution which she herself founded, together with the Russian Academy of Arts.

Other outstanding figures include Vassilisa Kozhina, who led the peasant army during the Napoleonic War, and Sofia Kovalevskaya, a mathematician, astronomer, physicist and writer. The first female astronaut, Valentina Tereshkova, was also Russian.

In the 19th century, Russian women were more prominent as instigators of social and political change than women anywhere else in

Europe. They campaigned for equal education of the sexes, organised charity fairs for women from a lower social background and worked as nurses in the Crimean War. They fought for social justice and equality on the barricades of the Paris Commune and in the underground terrorist groups in St Petersburg.

Many of them were educated in Europe. Thousands of women belonging to *Narodniki* (Populists) walked down muddy country tracks to take literacy and social consciousness to the peasants. Equality of the sexes was a popular concept, particularly among the urban intelli-

Babushkas are loved and feared in equal measure.

gentsia. The women who supported the cause were known as *Ravnopravki* (women for equal rights). They organised small ventures, providing jobs for other women, and published newsletters and journals.

Opportunities open

In 1917 feminist ideas were swallowed up by socialist ideology. However, a decade later, Russian women again achieved a certain equality and social status. Besides the right to vote, which was guaranteed by the new Soviet Constitution, the state provided a child day care system, free abortion and a new marital law which made husbands provide child support in cases of divorce. Marriage and divorce became very

easy and the ideas of free love were expressed and supported by a prominent Bolshevik and feminist leader, Alexandra Kollontai.

Stalinist industrialisation and militarisation of the Soviet state put a new demand on women to produce more soldiers and workers for the Motherland. A special tax for childless families was introduced and abortion became illegal in 1936. Divorce procedure in court became far more complicated. As well as fulfilling the role of mother, Soviet women were also expected to work in factories and collective farms, as well as in professional spheres.

During World War II women fought alongside men on the battlefields, serving as doctors, surgeons and nurses. There were women pilots and women snipers in both the artillery and among the marine troops. Women formed the overall majority of the workforce in the plants and factories producing arms and military equipment, and constituted the bulk of labour in the collective farms.

During the Soviet period Russian women enjoyed increased success in professional spheres – a little over half of the labour force were women, and it was the same proportion who achieved higher education, such as university teachers, doctors and lawyers. But since the family tradition was and still is very patriarchal, women were also supposed to carry the double burden of domestic chores and childcare. Equality was harder to achieve in reality than on paper.

The late Soviet period, marked by the declining economy of the state, was especially hard on Russian women. Poor household equipment (lack of washing machines, vacuum cleaners and no dishwashers), a poor (though cheap) system of childcare, and a deteriorating medical service, made Soviet women resent the achievements of "emancipation".

Perestroika ushered in new aspirations for social and political change. However, it didn't improve the position of women. If anything, their situation became worse than before. In the preceding period women were guaranteed 33–34 percent of parliamentary seats. The first election in the democratic period left women with 5–6 percent of seats in the Russian parliament and in all local governing bodies. Today the situation is slightly better with female MPs making up 12 percent of the Duma. But the gender gap in Russian politics is still huge: out

Among the fairytale images of feminine strength are Rusalki, the virgin mermaids with powers of witchcraft; Baba Yaga, a witch with a wooden leg, and Vassilisa Premudraya (Vassilisa the Wisest), a woman who is far wiser and cleverer than any man.

of 31 ministers in the Russian government only two are women.

A multiplicity of roles

For a while, the idea of equality was illogically associated with the rejected ideas of Communism, and therefore considered misguided and wrong; the former concept of woman-comrade, and woman-friend was being replaced by woman-wife and woman-mother. In the 1990s a new phenomenon arose, prompted by the pseudo-Westernisation of Russian society through advertisements and films – the image of woman as a sex-object.

Women's response to these developments is not simple. Some believe that their place is in the home as wives, mothers and carers. Others are struggling for the economic survival of their children and themselves in an often difficult economic reality, and have proved to be very adaptable – opening small businesses or holding down several part-time jobs, learning a language and going to night school. Those who are active socially and politically are operating in a changed society.

Even after more than two decades of "freedom" the experience of building a civil society still feels new to Russia, but women are playing an active role. They have formed various political, social, environmental and cultural groups, associations of women in business, single mothers and widows. There are professional unions of women writers, women journalists and university educated women. Notably, one of the greatest voices speaking out against the war in Ukraine has been the Soldiers' Mothers of Russia – its leader was arrested for 'fraud'.

Russia's women have a growing desire to express themselves – like their 19th-century predecessors, they are striving to maintain and improve their social and political status and are reluctant to give in to conservatism. Despite the growing difficulties of everyday life, Russian women still form the majority among the producers and consumers of cultural values. In museums and theatres, in libraries and exhibitions you will still see more women than men.

In cities and villages it is the women who do the shopping and take care of the children, it is the women who help the poor; it is the women who perform the duties of social workers and run the churches. The battle to achieve real equality and status for women in Russian society might be long, but the evidence of Russian history, the strength and great abilities of the women themselves, are proof that change is possible.

A hen party in Moscow.

WOMEN VS PUTIN

Women have so far played a key role in the opposition movement to the increasingly autocratic Putin regime. Members of the Pussy Riot punk band were famously imprisoned for their anti-Putin protest in the Cathedral of Christ the Saviour, one ending up in a penal colony in Siberia. Although founded in Kiev and now based in Paris, the Femen protest group has launched numerous bare-breasted attacks on members of the Kremlin elite, getting very close to Patriarch Kirill and Putin himself. Anna Politkovskaya was a journalist critical of the Kremlin's war in Chechnya – she paid with her life for her views.

RUSSIA'S ETHNIC DIVERSITY

Many assume Russia to be inhabited by the stereotypical fair-haired Slav, but Russia's broad sweep of geography has given its population many faces.

From ethnic Germans to nomadic Arctic reindeer herders, Siberian Poles to Kamchatka's Chukchi tribes, the Russian Federation is a place of incredible ethnic diversity, almost unknown outside of the country itself. Imperial Russia swallowed up entire countries and cultures, and when the Cossacks claimed Siberia for the tsar in the 17th century, they weren't conquering a land devoid of human habitation. Numerous tribes eked out an often stone-age existence on the steppe and in the taiga, worshipping their spirits and living a hunter-gatherer life as they had for century after tranquil century. Nomadic lifestyles still exist in Russia, especially in Siberia and the Arctic.

A praiseworthy work documenting Russia's various ethnicities is *The Red Book of the Peoples of the Russian Empire* which was published in 1991 in Estonia. It lists over 80 different peoples, though focuses only on those groups whose numbers are below 30,000. Many more such as the Buryats of Siberia and the Tatars are not included – in fact over 180 ethnicities are officially recognised as living within Russia's borders.

The Russian melting pot

The Soviet Union was the ultimate ethnic melting pot, a swirling concoction of peoples from across Eurasia bound together by a political entity if little else. It's not uncommon to find Estonians and Lithuanians in the Far East, Tatars and Tuvans in Kaliningrad and Ukrainians just about anywhere. Intermarriage, the attraction of the "long rouble" in Siberia (wages were higher in Siberia than in the European part of the USSR), exile, ethnic strife and absurd government policy (officials and

Multi-ethnic hotel staff in Ulan Ude, eastern Siberia.

other employees were often sent thousands of kilometres away to take up posts) saw Eurasia's gene pool stirred gently for seven long decades and the process continues to this day.

Of course no discussion of Russia's ethnic groups can be had without the mention of the word "russification". The Soviet Union pretended to celebrate its diversity with various folk festivals and ethnographic museums. But in general local culture was suppressed in favour of the one-size-fits-all Slavic standard. Since the collapse of the Soviet system, this has been relaxed and ethnic identity has seen a real upsurge. Some damage is irreversible (Russian remains the dominant language of the cities) but places like Tatarstan, Buryatia and Tuva have reclaimed a strong sense of nationhood. It remains to be seen how far an increasingly autocratic President Putin will allow them to go down that road.

Europe

While the populations of many former communist countries in Europe, such as the Czech Republic and Poland, became largely homogenous after World War II when many minorities such as the Jews and ethnic Germans were wiped out or deported, this was never the case with European Russia. While

Caucasus flooded into the capital to work on construction projects, adding to the ethnic ruckus.

Caucasus

Looking at the map of the Caucasus region it would seem every valley has its own resident ethnicity. There are seven different republics in this region of Russia each containing many different peoples. Chechnya is the best known of these for all the wrong reasons – Karachay Cherkassia, Karbadino-Balkaria and Kalmykia may not be such familiar names. Hardly any

Singers from Kazan in traditional dress.

white Slavic Russians make up 81 percent of the population of the Russian Federation, in the European part there are large Ukrainian, Tatar (Tatarstan), Bashkir (Bashkortostan) and Chuvash (Volga region) minorities. Smaller numbers of Mordvins, Mari, Belarusians, ethnic Germans, Jews and Roma make up the bulk of the rest.

Naturally Moscow forms the country's biggest ethnic jumble with people from every corner of the former communist world living and working there. A Muscovite describing his- or herself as Russian might have four grandparents from the four corners of the Soviet empire. During the years of economic boom in Moscow, many workers from the

RUSSIA'S POLES

One now almost invisible ethnic group in Siberia are the Poles. Thousands of Poles found themselves exiled to Siberia over the course of the 18th, 19th and 20th centuries and many of them stayed. There were an estimated 20,000 Poles living in Siberia in 1860, a considerable share of the population. Western Slavic surnames and the odd Gothic Catholic church are the only evidence of their existence as they have assimilated into the Russian majority. However some "Russians" may still have "Pole" entered into their passport – it's estimated that almost 50,000 people across the Russian Federation consider themselves Polish.

of these republics have homogenous populations but are split and split again into tiny ethnic minorities each with their own language and customs, making the political map of the region look like someone has taken an

> The Evenks of Siberia live in wooden tepees called chums. When moving from one herding ground to another, only the leather and fur lining is transported and fresh timber cut at the new site.

partially nomadic lifestyle in the taiga, herding reindeer and collecting berries.

The Buryats are another huge ethnic group though unlike the Evenks they have their own republic – Buryatia. Buryats are essentially ethnic Mongolians (they gave the world Genghis Khan's mother) and mostly practice Tibetan Buddhism. Buryats can also be found on the western side of Lake Baikal but here they are shamanists.

The fascinating Republic of Tuva was an independent country between the wars and was only sucked into the USSR in 1945. Russians

Young Buryat woman.

A warmly dressed fish seller in Yakutsk's Christian Market.

axe to it. On top of this are the three former Soviet Republics of Georgia, Armenia and Azerbaijan, themselves containing several ethnic minorities and spilling over into the Russian Federation.

Siberia and the Far East

Siberia is where you will find Russia's most fascinating ethnic diversity. Although indigenous peoples are outnumbered by Russians in all but one republic (Tuva), Eastern Siberia in particular is where the ethnic voice speaks loudest and where the flame of Russian Slavic culture is at its dimmest.

Evenks still scatter the vast expanses of northern Siberia, some still leading an entirely or

are in the minority here and Tuvan is the dominant language. Tuva has a unique and absorbing culture, producing some of the best throat singers in Asia.

In the Far East the Yakuts inhabit their own gargantuan diamond-rich republic with its capital at Yakutsk.

Siberia, like Moscow, has seen incomers in the past two decades. Chinese workers flooded across the border in search of work during building booms in Siberia's cities. Most have returned home but some remain, often illegally. Omsk has a large Kazakh population and across Siberia and the Far East myriad peoples from the Caucasus have arrived to work in various industries.

A TASTE OF RUSSIA

**Hearty dishes are firmly back on the menu as Russian
restaurants showcase the best of traditional cooking.**

The popular belief that Russians survive on a diet of potatoes and beetroot alone, with a healthy portion of *ogurtsi* (cucumbers) and home-distilled vodka to aid the digestion is not actually that far from the truth – these are indeed national favourites and a reflection of the peasant life most Russian led until fairly recently. However, with a little less prejudice and a desire to discover the truth, your stay in Russia can be enriched and your palate educated by the wealth of cuisines from across the former USSR on offer. From Ukrainian borshch, delicious beetroot soup, normally served with *petrushka* and *smetana* (fresh parsley and sour cream), to *sibirskie pelmeny*, a small boiled pastry parcel of meat, mushrooms or potatoes, the national cookbook is as comprehensive as the former empire was big.

The years since perestroika have seen a renewal of the European influence in every walk of Russian life, including the kitchen. The sunny summer streets of towns buzz with outdoor cafés, and with hip bars below street level. In addition to foreign fads such as sushi and pizza, there has been a noticeable revival of traditional Russian restaurants catering for every budget, from modest self-service canteens serving basic but filling local dishes for a few roubles to luxury gourmet restaurants for Russia's super-rich elite offering ingredients airfreighted in fresh from around the globe.

In the 19th century, Russia was obsessed with all things French, and borrowed from Paris not only its food, but also its theatre, poetry, architecture and fashion in hats. The French influence is felt in the fondness for rich sauces to accompany meat, in the love of complicated salads, and in the huge variety of cream-filled tortes eaten at the end of

Ready to entertain.

the meal with *chai* (tea). One such cake is the *ptiche moloko* (bird's milk), so called because it is supposed to be so fine that it couldn't possibly be created by humans.

Today, a plethora of restaurants introduce visitors to the spectrum of Russian cuisine, from simple home-cooking to revived aristocratic dishes, and updated Asian- and European-influenced classics.

Tempted by *zakuski*

The glory of Russian cuisine is the genuine desire of the host to see his or her guests fed and watered to capacity – a desire that springs from the quintessence of the Russian soul: generosity and pride. It is the tradition to load the dinner table in advance with a vast variety of *zakuski* (hors d'oeuvres).

The *zakuski* plays an important role in the process of dining in Russia, and can save the inexperienced from certain disaster when drinking with the locals. Russians may have a big heart, but their capacity to consume alcohol is certainly tremendous. As a guest in a private home you will be treated in style to the best your host has to offer. However, don't expect any leniency when it comes to drinking, you will have to imbibe your share. Toasting is as important, and here, too, you

Every host prides themselves on their culinary creations and might even claim a recipe handed down through the generations. Popular favourites include *seledka pod shuboi*, literally, "salted herring in a fur coat", which is a combi-

> *Russians seem to be able to add dill to almost every dish, sometimes in copious amounts. A tongue-in-cheek Facebook group called Dillwatch documents some of the worst cases of dill contamination.*

Street food stall in Kazan.

Mussels, Siberian style.

won't be let off the hook with a moderate "cheers". Toasts can last for minutes and are a science of their own. The formula to remember is: your host, the women present and the spread in front of you. If you are teetotal, the only way out is to claim an inability to drink "for health reasons".

In fact, the *zakuski* are the main event of the meal, and it is an experience as daunting as it is appetising to look on a table laden with red and black caviar, a selection of cold meats, garlic sausage, smoked sturgeon, salmon, an array of potato salads, mushrooms in sour cream, pickled cabbage, beetroot vinaigrette, goat's cheese, as well as the usual liquid ensemble of deep-chilled vodka, *shampanskoye*, and fruity wines.

nation of fish, beetroot, boiled (and grated) egg and mayonnaise; and *domashni piroshki* (home-made pies), which can be stuffed with cabbage, meat, mushrooms or apricots. By the time the second course arrives, most diners are already too full to lift a fork. Pace yourself!

Asian specialities

Russians can also call on some spicy southern, almost sub-tropical traditions in food. The cuisines of Armenia, Georgia and Azerbaijan, as well as Uzbekistan, Kazakhstan and Kyrgizstan – which make liberal use of typical Asian ingredients such as coriander leaf, fruit and meat together, walnuts, vine leaves, chillies, beans and flavoured breads – can be found in the Russian home as well as on the menu in restaurants. Meat in these Asian countries will more often than not be boiled – with the tasty exception of *shashlik*, which is normally made from lamb and pork and grilled over glowing embers. This much-loved dish is known throughout the former USSR and the chef, more often than not the man of the house, will be passionate about the preparation and cooking of what some may simply call a barbecue.

Meat in a pastry case puts in an appearance wherever you are in Russia: Siberia has its

Tea time in the dacha.

pelmeny – made in vast quantities and frozen for the winter; Central Asia and the Trans-caucasus boast the large, flat, fried *cheburek*, the Republic of Buryatia has its golf-ball-sized *buuzy* which are known as *manti* in Kazakhstan – a more wholesome version in Georgia is known as the *khinkali*.

Some or all of these may be found on the *zakuski* section of the menu, and the most expensive restaurants will have them waiting on the table when clients arrive. Other *zakuski* include *zhulien* (julienne – a creamed mushroom dish), slices of smoked and non-smoked red and white sturgeon and *kolbasa* (salami-like sausages). *Salat* (salad) is often simply tomatoes and cucumbers, but can be an elaborate and complicated melange.

Traditional dishes

The Russian cookbook may now be as cosmo-politan as any other, but the traditional meals as eaten during the reign of the tsars would have been very different. *Kasha* (a porridge of oats, buckwheat or wheat) was the basis of most meals and was eaten with savoury and sweet foods alike. *Shchi*, a soup made from *kislaya kapusta* (sauerkraut) and meat or fish, would probably feature in every main meal of the day.

The fruits of Russia's abundant forests have long been harvested. Berries such as *brusnika*, *chernika*, *klyukva*, *zemlinika*, *golubika*, *oblipikha*, *malina*, and *yeshevika* (foxberry, bilberry, cran-berry, wild strawberry, blueberry, thornberry, raspberry and blackberry) were gathered and used to make preserves, jams, desserts and

VODKA – NOT THE ONLY DRINK

Russians are great chai (tea) drinkers and make as much fuss over their *brews* as the British. Before the onslaught of imported flavoured teas, Russians would eagerly add mint, cherry and currant leaves to their tea. Green tea is also a favourite, especially in Siberia where it is taken with milk.

Some pre-Revolutionary *napitki* (drinks) have been experiencing a comeback, including *kvas*, made from rye bread, currants, and spices; *medovuka* or *med*, a mixture of fermented and spiced honey, yeast and hops; and *sbiten*, a hot drink made from honey, spices, hops and a variety of herbs.

Other alcoholic drinks include *nastoiki*, which tend to be bitter and made from berries and herbs and, on occasion, chilli peppers; and *nalivki*, which are sweet and aromatic. The common element is vodka – no less than 40 percent! Armenian cognac should be taken chilled with slices of lemon to complement the rich, smooth flavour. *Shampanskoye* (champagne) should be *polusukhoye* or *polsladkoye* (semi-dry or semi-sweet). A bottle of *Sovietskoye* is the classic drink on New Year's Eve.

Pivo (beer) is Russia's second tipple and the market has been growing for years. Baltika is the main national brand but there are numerous local brands available, too.

drinks – as indeed they are still today. Root vegetables such as *rediska* (radish), *markov* (carrot) and *chesnok* (garlic) were staple foods, too.

Still traditional today is the *blin* (pancake), which is eaten both as a savoury and sweet dish. *Bliny* with lots of honey, *smetana* or red caviar are natural choices for hungry Russians. *Bliny* are most commonly eaten at *Maslinitsa*, the week leading up to the *veliki post* (great fast of seven weeks) before Easter, which in turn is celebrated at the end with a *kulich*, a light, Easter cake similar to the Italian Christmas *panettone*. A delicious sweet dish, *paskha*, synonymous

> Beluga, osetrina and sevruga are translated as one, "sturgeon", and produce black caviar. Far cheaper red caviar comes from salmon.

with the celebration of Easter is prepared from *tvorog* (curds) with dried fruits and sugar.

The upper echelons of society would have known a different menu, one which shocked many visiting dignitaries with its richness and quality. Carp in *smetana*, baked *osyotr* (sturgeon) and *okorok* of ham (baked leg of ham in pastry with fruit and spices) were some of the dishes served to important visitors and the ruling class. Great pies of fish and meat, *zapikanky* (bakes) of rice, *smetana*, eggs and sugar and *kulebyaki* (more pies) with fillings of cabbage, mushrooms and meat, or fish, were common for those that could afford it. *Khren* (horseradish sauce) was often the only addition to the natural juices that the dish was cooked in. *Kholodets*, or aspic is another favourite method of preparing meat and fish.

Welcome treats

Possibly the greatest sign of respect that can be shown to a guest is the giving of a *karavai*, an intricately decorated bread shaped like a cake, which is presented, normally at the border of a village or as the guest enters the house, and is accompanied by a small pot of salt. This ritual symbolises the wealth of the village, or host. One is expected to break off a corner, dip it in the salt and taste it before advancing. Today this is normally only reserved for visiting dignitaries and party bigwigs at regional airports, but can also be seen at weddings.

The *grib* (mushroom) is at the heart of a national pastime: whole families spend their weekends together in the country gathering mushrooms to preserve for the rest of the year in various concoctions of vinegar, spices and herbs. The culture of mushroom-gathering is one instilled from an early age and most Russians will be able to recite a lengthy list of edible, and deadly, sorts.

The marinading of *griby* and *ogurtsi* (mushrooms and cucumbers) is another culinary passion of the Russians and, it is to be said, one of the few occasions when Russian men will

Ochpochmak, a Tatar speciality, are parcels of pastry filled with minced beef, onion and potatoes.

gladly roll up their sleeves and help out in the kitchen.

A real treat when visiting Russia is tasting the *ikra* (caviar) which comes in (rare) *chornaya* and *krasnaya* (black and red) and is sold by the kilo to the rich and in little tins to everyone else.

Red caviar is best eaten on white bread spread with a generous layer of butter, and black caviar from little egg-baskets (made from the white of hard-boiled eggs, carefully cut into a basket form). Overfishing and poaching have depleted the sturgeon, so they are no longer a bargain. But a shot of freezing vodka followed by a bite of caviar is a gastronomic delight everyone should try once.

Memorial to Tsar Nicholas II and his family in Ganina Yama; their bodies were moved here after their mass execution.

...лизи сей шахты
...июле 1918 года
...гнём и серною
...истотою
...ыли уничтожены
...естные тела
...ятых Царственных
...мучеников и их
...верных слуг

НЕ ПОЩАЖУ его
ИБО ОН ПЕРЕЖЕГ
КОСТИ ЦАРЯ
ЕДОМСКОГО
В ИЗВЕСТЬ

Амос 2.1

RELIGION IN RUSSIA

Though the relationship between Church and State was never an easy one today the Kremlin and the Orthodox Patriarch rule as one.

The gradual rehabilitation of churches since the late 1980s, together with the congregations they attracted and the growing number of novices entering the priesthood, constituted something of a religious revival in Russia. Some saw it as a triumphant repudiation of the propaganda drummed into Russians over four generations by State organs such as the Society of the Militant Godless. Others drew comparisons with the rise of Islamic fundamentalism in the Asian republics of the former Soviet Union, a manifestation of confused societies dredging through their past for some kind of cultural anchor. That revival can now be declared complete and the wealthy Russian Orthodox Church now enjoys privileges and power it could only have dreamt of two decades ago.

Religion in Russia should not be equated with, say, Roman Catholicism in Poland, which itself underwent a renaissance in the two decades after the fall of communism. The latter is a more political and intellectual force at loggerheads with everything atheistic Communism represented. Russian Orthodoxy, on the other hand, was never intellectualised as Christianity in the West was by the likes of Thomas Aquinas in the 13th century. The Russian faith was and is rooted in worship, not scholastic theology, and it is not inconceivable that it could have contrived a *modus vivendi* with Communism as it did with tsarist absolutism.

Who goes to church

Visitors to a Russian Orthodox service will be struck by the highly orchestrated ritual. There are no books in evidence, but almost everyone seems to know the procedure. Even those who don't can cross themselves and bow at

Buying candles at Bogoyavlensky Church, Irkutsk.

almost any time. The air is thick with incense, the richly coloured icons hold pride of place, and there is close interaction between clergy and congregation, communicating with one another through the medium of splendidly sonorous chant. Anyone familiar with the Greek Orthodox liturgy can see their common Byzantine source.

Anyone who visited Russia in Communist times will not fail to notice not only the large number of churches now open across the country, but also the age range of the worshippers. One or two Moscow churches even provide a carpet and toys for children. Even in less accommodating churches, people feel free to come and go. Closer acquaintance will reveal that nearly all middle-aged and younger Christians, at least in the cities, are well-educated, while poorer, working-class people are to be found only in the few churches that undertake serious social involvement, such as prison visiting and distribution of food and clothing. In addition, there are the sometimes bossy *babushkas* (grandmothers) and other elderly people who have been faithful through the decades of persecution.

Of course, the enthusiasm for getting baptised, a craze which started in the late 1980s, has produced many nominal Christians who no longer go to church; some of these, in particular, are inclined to look back to times before Bolshevism, with a view to reliving past glories of the Russian Empire. Russian culture is closely interwoven with Orthodox values and symbols. But nostalgic fantasy can lead to alarming ideas. One of these is a desire to restore an absolutist monarchy. A small minority of Orthodox church-goers are monarchists.

The role of Church and State

The Russian Church had a peculiar role in society, because it never went through the process which eventually separated Church and State to varying degrees in the West. Ivan the Terrible directed arbitrary horrors against the church in the 16th century (for which he undertook exaggerated penances), but the Church was not subjugated until the early 18th century, as part of the Westernising reforms of Peter the Great. Peter abolished the office of patriarch, replacing it with the Holy Synod. The synod was an organ of the State, presided over by a government official who had power to appoint and move bishops, and parish priests were even required to report to the police things heard in private confessions. When their time came, the Russian Communists regarded themselves as the ultimate spiritual authority, in exactly the same way as they assumed command of the armed forces.

The messianic manner in which the Bolsheviks presumed to convert the whole world to Communism was uncannily reminiscent of the phenomenon of Moscow as "the Third Rome". Constantinople became "the Second Rome" after Rome was overrun by barbarians in the early 5th century. The fall of Constantinople to the Turks in 1453, just as Russia had emerged from the Mongol yoke, was a devastating blow to the Russian Church, and Ivan III decided it was Moscow's sacred duty to become "the Third Rome", the beacon of the True Faith. This mission ultimately led to what were in large part religious wars with Roman Catholic Poland in which the latter was no less determined to win Russia for the Pope and Rome. Today many again speak of Russia's special role as the "Third Rome" – a country with a unique fate and a special spiritual mission in the world. This has recently come sharply to the fore as Russian volunteers heading to the war in East Ukraine often declare they are fighting

Procession in Pyatigorsk.

GREGORIAN CALENDAR

The Russian Orthodox Church observes the Julian calendar, known as "old style". This means that church festivals are 13 days later than in the West – so, for example, Christmas Day is on 7 January rather than 25 December. The Church Council of 1918–19 decided to follow the State and adopt the Gregorian calendar ("new style"). Every diocese had to lose the 13 days simultaneously, but State persecution and the arrest of bishops prevented it from being announced. Any suggestions for change always meet strong resistance from the mass of churchgoers who fear any "Westernising" influence.

a "crusade against the West" and that Donetsk is the "New Jerusalem".

Old Believers

In the mid-17th century Russia was plunged into a religious dispute, which, unlike the Reformation, was about ritual rather than doctrine. Nikon, a peasant monk who was a close friend of the Romanov Tsar Alexei Mikhailovich, became patriarch in 1652. He decided to bring Church ritual into conformity with contemporary Byzantine practice – in effect this meant people crossing themselves with three fingers rather than two – and eliminate errors copyists had brought to the texts. But these minor changes in spelling, prayers and rituals were opposed by conservatives within the Russian Church who came to be known as "Old Believers".

Nikon was an authoritarian and uncompromising character, and persecution was fierce and even cruel in some places. It continued into the reign of Peter the Great when the Old Believers refused to surrender their beards in the interest of bringing Russian society into line with Western Europe, where men were in the habit of shaving. Old Believers fled to remote areas such as Buryatia in southern Siberia.

Many Old Believers sects exist to this day. Some are in communion with the Moscow Patriarchy, but other groups chose to remain isolated even when official persecution ceased. They became famous for their hospitality, although in some communities if the visitors were not Old Believers any plates or glasses they used had to be smashed afterwards. Guests were expected to leave money for replacements. In other places they have become something of a tourist attraction.

Monasticism

Russian monks could claim much of the credit for opening up vast tracts of the Russian interior. Taking after the desert fathers of Syria and Egypt, they went deep into virgin forests to find sites for secluded monasteries. The tireless energy with which they made these remote areas habitable was their undoing because they were trailed by peasants pleased to exchange their labour for the right to settle on the monastic lands as tenants. These arrangements were preferable to serfdom, and led to

the monasteries becoming the biggest and richest landowners in Russia. Many monks were content to capitalise on their enterprise and become landlords, but others preferred to push the frontiers ever outwards and start all over again. The cycle repeated itself until monasteries ringed the White Sea and encroached on the fringes of Siberia.

St Sergius of Radonezh (14th century) is the best known and most revered of the monks who simultaneously Christianised and colonised Russia. His tomb is venerated at Sergiev Posad Monastery, 50 km (30 miles) outside Moscow,

Icon and candles at Ganina Yama.

probably the holiest shrine in the country. It resembles a walled fortress and contains seven churches and one of the Orthodox Church's theological seminaries. There is also provision for visitors, with a museum and shops.

The Church under Communism

The Tsar's abdication in February 1917 was welcomed by the Church, which saw its opportunity to break free from State control and to restore the office of patriarch after a gap of two centuries. Patriarch Tikhon, who had been metropolitan archbishop in North America, was elected. Some people welcomed the Bolshevik revolution and Lenin's decree of 23 January 1918 which separated Church from State and schools from Church. This separation turned out to be rather one-sided as the State took over all Church property, and placed obstacles in the way of free association and travel.

This was before serious persecution began. The famine of 1921–23 persuaded Patriarch Tikhon to hand over much of the Church's gold and silver plate, stipulating only that sacred vessels be melted down by Church authorities and handed over in the form of bullion. This was done, raising enormous sums, but accounts show that all the money went into Party funds, and none, apparently, to the

St Elizabeth Feodorovna, the Duchess who became a nun.

famine victims. The Party, or often just local officials, wanted to take everything. Tikhon issued an appeal to resist the theft of Church property, and the result was 1,500 "bloody conflicts", followed by exile to Siberia or execution for the culprits. Tikhon was also arrested and ecclesiastical Communist sympathisers usurped his position. They declared the patriarchate void and called on "every faithful churchman…to fight with all his might together with the Soviet authority for the realisation of the Kingdom of God upon earth…and to use all means to realise in life that grand principle of the October Revolution."

The faithful proved to be unmoved by the call and stayed loyal to the patriarchate rather than the alternative "Living Church" offered to them. The Living Church derived from sincere moves for reforms within the Church dating back to the 1880s. There was a general desire for change, but little agreement on detail. Various groups amalgamated and the Communists saw this as an opportunity to split the Church. They favoured the Living Church with privileges, including free travel, while restricting everyone else. Gradually, believers saw through this trap and deserted the group, unfortunately leaving to this day the suspicion that moves for change are tainted with Bolshevism.

> A statue was unveiled in London's Westminster Abbey in 1998 to commemorate St Elizabeth Feodorovna, one of Russia's most famous martyrs of the Communist era of religious persecution.

Tikhon was arrested and urged to repent in order to resume his duties. "I was filled with hostility against the Soviet authorities," he said on his release in 1923. "I repent of all my actions directed against the government." Tikhon's confession reaffirmed the traditional solidarity of Church and State.

The Church moves underground

More serious was the statement made by Tikhon's successor, Patriarch Sergei in 1927, although the content was very similar to that of Tikhon, his predecessor. Assuming that both these confessions had been made under duress, elements of the Church went underground. Taking their cue from the Communist cell system, they used passwords to make themselves known to one another. Priests in plain clothes would pop up unannounced in villages, administer to the faithful, and as suddenly disappear.

In 1927, the year in which the first Five-Year Plan commenced, intellectuals and Christians were denounced as enemies of the revolution. Over the next 15 years historians estimate that hundreds of thousands of church priests, monks and nuns were killed. Tax collectors swooped on churches and, if the sum demanded was not met, they were boarded up. Teaching religion to children under 18 was forbidden except in private houses and to groups of no more than three children at a time.

Stalin relaxed the ban on Church activities during World War II in an attempt to lift morale. The Germans were allowing churches to open in territories they occupied, and after they withdrew the churches remained open by popular demand. When the war was over, however, controls were reimposed in the form of intense anti-religion propaganda in schools and general intimidation of anyone who aired religious convictions.

Under Khrushchev and Brezhnev, many believers served terms in prison for holding prayer meetings or conducting baptisms – not because they were crimes as such, but because they constituted anti-Soviet agitation. The few officially registered places of worship were infested with KGB informers. Bibles and other religious texts were unavailable except on the black market.

Persecution intensified in the early 1960s, and more churches were closed under Khrushchev than had been under Stalin. The Communist state went to great lengths to discourage religious observance. For example, at Easter, the high point of the Orthodox calendar, state television would schedule a rare night of rock music. Those who went to midnight mass would encounter police whose job was to stop anyone under 40 from entering the church. They were not forbidden to enter, but it was made clear that names of those attending "cult events" would be noted by the authorities.

When Gorbachev introduced perestroika in the 1980s, Christians of all denominations sensed freedom, and took every opportunity to come into the open. The millennium celebration of Russian Christianity, held in 1988, was a big international event. The present Russian constitution makes an official separation between Church and State, but today all major political events are attended by the clergy, and all major religious holidays are attended by the political elite.

Other faiths and denominations

All religions suffered repression and persecution under Communism. The Baptists, an active (though not numerous) union of Protestants who trace their origins in Russia to 1870, were in turn tolerated and persecuted like the members of the Orthodox Church. Roman Catholics, who were granted freedom by Peter the Great, were totally suppressed. Islam had a

marginally easier time because most Russian Muslims live in communities that are ethnically not Russian, and less easy to control from Moscow. Buddhism has seen a huge revival (even bigger than that of the Orthodox Church) in places like Buryatia and the Republic of Tuva, and shamanism, virtually wiped out during the decades of Communism, is thriving across Siberia. Pentecostal churches draw large crowds in many parts of Russia, and missions from Mormons and other sects also have limited success.

Under pressure from right-wing nationalists, and with some support from the patriarchate,

Buddhist temple (Datsan) in Buryatia.

laws were passed which curb the religious activity of "non-traditional" denominations. The pendulum is swinging back towards intolerance and persecution of religious minorities as "Orthodoxy" is accepted as the *de facto* State religion. For instance, the government actively interferes in property conflicts, solving the problem in favour of the Orthodox Church, while it smothers other Christian denominations with bureaucracy. The patriarch has amassed enormous power and influence over Putin, say some sources, because the president sees the church as a foundation for the nation. The Orthodox Church has certainly not stayed silent when it has come to recent events in Ukraine, towing the Kremlin line to the letter.

*The Last Day of Pompeii
by Karl Bryullov.*

The Entombment (anon.).

ART AND INSPIRATION

Early Russian icon painting was to have a profound influence on the avant-garde work of the 20th century.

Russia's art and culture was for 700 years – from the official adoption of the Orthodox faith in 988 until the time of Peter the Great – largely derived from Byzantium. After the Roman Emperor Constantine, the first Christian emperor, moved the capital from Rome to Constantinople, now Istanbul, in 323, civilisation and Christianity prospered in this new Byzantine Empire for a millennium.

Soon after the Turks captured Constantinople in 1453, Moscow declared itself "the Third Rome", the presumed heir to Rome and Byzantium. All art produced in Russia served the one ideal of a Christian, theocentric view of the universe. Byzantine art – and hence Russian art – was subject to strict canons regarding what could be depicted and how, in keeping with the dogma of the Orthodox religion. We should not seek to apply Western humanistic criticism to icon painting: in doing so we are seeing things that were not necessarily intended and not seeing other things that were. The austere spiritual power that radiates from icons is a reflection of a universe with God at its centre. Their painterly language and use of colour and line are powerfully expressive; so much so that icon painting was to exert profound influence on the avant-garde at the beginning of the 20th century, and in turn have a vital effect on 20th-century painting worldwide.

Pre-15th century

Both wall paintings and icons survive from before the 15th century, but most painters at this time were either Greek masters invited to Russia, or their Russian pupils working faithfully in the Byzantine tradition. The most famous, and probably one of the last of these

The Rider by Karl Bryullov.

Greek painters to make his career in Russia, was Theofan, called "the Greek", who arrived in Veliky Novgorod around 1380. Few works have survived which can be positively attributed to him. A panel showing the Transfiguration in the Tretyakov Gallery in Moscow is probably by him or a pupil.

In 1240 the fire-worshipping Tatars took Kiev, and there followed a period of occupation which lasted well into the 15th century. Only the far north of Russia, including the merchant city state of Novgorod, remained unaffected by the Tatars. Cut off from Constantinople until the late 14th century, the icon painting of Veliky Novgorod and the northern monasteries, to which learned Slavs from much of occupied Russia fled, was for a time forced to fall back on its own resources. These icons are markedly provincial yet highly expressive, with their vivid colours and unsubtle, folkloric designs. They are best seen in Novgorod's Museum of Architecture and Ancient Monuments.

One superb example is the mid-15th-century *Battle of the Novgorodians with the Suzdalians*, an unusual work in that it is not based on a biblical event, but commemorates a battle that took place in 1169. The subject matter and its treatment reveal much about

Copy of The Mother of God of Vladimir, a national treasure.

its Novgorodian creators; this town of merchants, a member of the international Hanseatic League, was a place of down-to-earth people, interested in concrete facts and simple storytelling set out in a decorative and easily comprehensible manner. The painterly language derives from Byzantium, but the bold and rhythmic use of reds and whites in the work owes much to folk traditions. Later the Novgorodians were not "helped" by this icon; Moscow defeated Novgorod in 1471, and a century later the city fell completely under the dominance of Moscow.

Theofan, Rublyov and Dionisius

In the 15th century, Moscow became the dominant political centre in Eurasia as the Tatar kingdoms began to weaken; obvious in both its imperial aspirations and also in its painting style. Theofan, who moved from Novgorod to Moscow some time before 1400, worked on the iconostasis of the Annunciation Cathedral in the Kremlin together with a young Russian monk, Andrei Rublyov. We know the latter's name from references in contemporary documents, but it was not until 1904, when his famous *Holy Trinity* (now in the Tretyakov Gallery, Moscow) was cleaned for the first time, that scholars were able to get an idea of his style. The panel was painted for the Trinity-St Sergius monastery outside Moscow, in memory of its founder, St Sergius of Radonez (*circa* 1314–92). Rublyov, who had entered the monastery as a monk and then left to paint icons in other places, was asked to return in 1422 in order to decorate the

---

AN ICON WITH MIRACULOUS POWER

The Mother of God of Vladimir is the greatest miracle-working icon of Russia. According to Orthodox tradition, it is one of three likenesses of the Virgin Mary that were painted by St Luke during her lifetime. Legend states that in the 5th century the icon was taken to Constantinople, where it remained until the 12th century (in fact, research suggests it was painted in Constantinople in the early 12th century). It arrived in Kiev in the 1130s and was placed in a convent in Vyshgorod. In 1155 Prince Andrei Bogolyubsky took the icon north on a campaign. As he crossed the River Klyazma, the horses carrying the icon were unable to go forward. Taking this as a sign, the prince built a

church there, in the village of Bogolyubovo ("loved by God"). The icon was later placed in the prince's new church at Vladimir and it went on to play an important role in Russian history: tsars were crowned in its presence; it accompanied Prince Andrei Bogolyubsky to victory against the Volga Bulgars (it supposedly sent out fiery rays to protect the prince's soldiers); and it is credited with saving Moscow from the Tatars on two occasions, and from the Poles on another. The fame of the icon was such that it was copied all over Russia and all icons of this type are known as *The Mother of God of Vladimir*. It is housed in the church attached to the Tretyakov Gallery in Moscow.

new stone church. It was at this time that he painted the *Holy Trinity*.

It is difficult to imagine a greater contrast in styles than that between the nervous, expressionistic Theofan and Rublyov. But it was Rublyov who had the greater influence over the next half-century. A late 15th-century *Entombment* (in the Tretyakov Gallery) by an anonymous master uses a combination of mathematics, music and rhythm to achieve a devastating harmony. The theme of the icon is grief, but whereas a European painter would have expressed the grief through facial expressions, the Orthodox painter does not concern himself with private feeling. The grief in this icon is that of the loss of Christ, the son of God, and even the mountains grieve. Christ's body, bound in white, is laid out, a horizontal, long note, against which a small rhythm of hands and faces is constructed, slowly fading as it moves towards His feet; behind is a rhythm of colour and rhetorical gesture, reaching a high point with the scarlet-robed Mary Magdalene's outstretched arms. Even nature submits itself and inclines towards the dead Christ.

The last major figure in classical icon painting is Dionisius (1450–1508). Again, little can be firmly attributed to him, and the main basis for an evaluation of his style is a cycle of frescoes in the Ferapontov Monastery, 570 km (350 miles) north of Moscow. He deployed a delicate colour scheme, applying pale, translucent washes of paint over fine, precise drawing, to achieve an elegant solemnity. In the Tretyakov Gallery, one can see biographical icons of the sainted metropolitans of Moscow, Peter and Alexei, which exude a dignified mysticism.

When Ivan the Terrible killed his son in 1581, he put an end to the dynasty that had ruled Muscovy since its beginnings. The early 17th century brought military defeat and, for the first time, ideological confrontation with the Catholics to the west. The Poles overran Moscow in 1605 and 1610, and despite the coronation of Mikhail Romanov in 1613, Polish influence and Catholic claims in Russia continued well into the century.

Russia could no longer live behind closed borders, protected from the pervasive culture of the Germano-Latin West. Forced to seek help first from Sweden, and then from England and Holland in order to overcome the

military threat posed by Poland, Russia opened herself up to Western trade; it was not long before Dutch engravings, and Piscator's Bible in particular, found their way to Russia, and this inevitably had an effect on icon painting. The best icons were now produced in the tsar's workshops in the Armoury Palace of the Moscow Kremlin.

The 17th century was a period of transition; as so often happens when a culture begins to lose its way, ornament and decoration preoccupied the new generation of painters. Elaborate, jewel-encrusted silver covers that obscured the

Harvest Time: Summer by Alexei Venetsianov.

image, miniature paintings to rival those of Persia, fine gold decoration; and, to the horror of those who upheld tradition, naturalism. According to Avvakum (c.1620–82), champion of the Old Believers, Christ was portrayed in the new icons "with a plump face, red lips, curly hair, fat arms and muscles... which altogether make him look like a German, big bellied and fat." Theological arguments aside, the golden age of icon painting was dead.

Secular themes

Peter the Great began an enforced Westernisation on an unwilling population. He moved the capital to St Petersburg, a new city without the history and religious baggage of Moscow, inviting foreign artists and craftsmen to come and work and to teach Russians. St Petersburg was to be the cradle of the new secular art, while Moscow remained a holy city, a city of icons and incense. By the end of the 18th century there were a number of good portrait painters (Levitsky, Rokotov, Borivikovsky) influenced by French and German painters, and an embryonic school of history painting. The Romantic Orest Kiprensky (1782–1826) spent most of his unhappy life in Italy, and is remembered for his classic portrait of Pushkin in the Tretyakov Gallery.

The Appearance of Christ to the People by Alexander Ivanov.

Painting recaptured its Russian voice again at the beginning of the 19th century, with Alexei Venetsianov (1780–1847). While the fashion, in Russia and elsewhere, was for neoclassicism, Venetsianov turned his attention away from Ancient Greece and Rome and focused on Russian peasant life. *Harvest Time: Summer* in the Tretyakov Gallery shows a girl in a traditional, colourful costume, breast-feeding her child while work continues. It is a simplified, rather than an idealised, vision of peasant life, for the idealisation is only in the deliberate beauty of the scene, and the bright, calm colours of the Russian countryside.

The second quarter of the 19th century was dominated by Karl Bryullov (1799–1852)

and Alexander Ivanov (1806–58). Each is well known for one monumental work (Bryullov's *Last Day of Pompeii* and Ivanov's *Christ's Appearance before the People*, and they were both instrumental in raising the social standing of the artists, who had hitherto served, but not been part of, society. Bryullov, who is alleged to have refused to paint Nicholas I's portrait because the latter turned up late for the first sitting, lived in Italy for many years, and it was there that he painted his masterpiece. Its allegorical allusion to the collapse of antiquity and, by extension, the old regime, has perhaps been overplayed by Soviet critics, but the canvas, for its sheer size and drama, made Bryullov famous all over Europe.

The bourgeoisie

Nicholas I was a severe man, conservative and of bourgeois tastes, and his reign marked a departure from neoclassicism and romanticism, towards genre painting and realism. During the 1840s and early 1850s, Pavel Fedotov (1815–52) painted canvases depicting the bourgeois: the gestures and expressions are often so exaggerated as to be amusing, and social criticism is never far from the surface. During the next decade Vasily Perov (1834–82) produced more serious works; humour was now more bitter, and during the Soviet period, anyone who idealised the pre-Revolutionary past was shown Perov's paintings: drunkenness, poverty, peasant backwardness and the corruption of the Church were among his favourite themes.

By the 1870s, painting and campaigning for social reform had become so intertwined that the Society for Travelling Art Exhibitions, known as the Wanderers, was formed. They took it upon themselves to tour the Empire with their exhibitions, which were intended to educate the population and press for social reform.

The Wanderers are best represented by Russia's greatest realist, Ilya Repin (1844–1930). Repin lived a long, productive life, but his reputation was made with large-scale canvases such as *The Volga Bargehaulers* and *The Zaporozhie Cossacks Writing a Mocking Letter to the Turkish Sultan*. These monumental paintings have a photographic quality that makes a direct appeal to the viewer. They greatly impressed the people who had never come into contact with painting before. The historical paintings of Vasily Surikov (1848–1916), Vasily Vereshchagin (1842–1904) and Viktor Vasnetsov (1848–1926), also executed on a huge scale, were similarly didactic. Landscape painting also enjoyed a revival in the second half of the 19th century. Ivan Aivazovsky (1817–1900), an extremely prolific painter of seascapes, achieved enormous fame in Russia and abroad for his dramatic canvases. Among the best is *The Ninth Wave*.

The years between 1885 and 1925, saw the most extraordinary explosion of cultural life

of demons, which he painted in great quantity, and died in an asylum. He was perhaps the first to break the mould of the Wanderers' legacy, and to return to painting as an end in itself, rather than as a vehicle for social comment. His genius lay in the twin powers of draughtsmanship and imagination.

Vrubel's break with tradition encouraged others to follow his example. One who did so was Valentin Serov (1865–1911). Again, Serov's outstanding characteristic is his sure draughtsmanship; he had the ability to render a face, a figure or an expression in just a

The Zaporozhie Cossacks Writing a Mocking Letter to the Turkish Sultan by Ilya Repin.

in Russia, during which Russian art – not only painting, but also music and literature – was among the most exciting in the world. Instrumental in this was the railway tycoon Savva Mamontov, who gathered young talent about him at his Abramtsevo Estate, near Moscow. Many of the most gifted artists spent time there, and the estate became a hothouse of activity in many media – sculpture, ceramics, architecture and art history – with a particular inclination for the study and revival of Russian folk art.

Mikhail Vrubel (1856–1910), a painter whose genius was so extraordinary that he does not fit comfortably in any movement, came to the colony in 1890; he became obsessed with visions

few fluid lines. His portrait of the dancer *Ida Rubinstein* (Russian Museum, St Petersburg) is outstanding.

Art for art's sake

The year 1898 saw the founding in St Petersburg of the *World of Art* magazine by a group of intellectuals who shared an idealisation of the past and an interest in "art for art's sake". Their worldly outlook now seems both decadent and prophetic. This was the pictorial accompaniment to Alexander Blok and the "Silver Age" of Russian poetry. Leon Bakst (1866–1924), one of the founders of the group, became famous in the West as a costume designer for Diaghilev's Ballets Russes in the 1910s, but he is second only to Serov in his abilities as a portraitist. Another member, Nikolay Roerich (1874–1947), explored the theme of ancient Rus in his brightly coloured work. Konstantin Somov (1869–1939), the most "decadent" of all, was fascinated by harlequins, fireworks and ladies in 18th-century costume, which he meticulously rendered on canvas. Boris Kustodiev (1878–1927) joined the group late, in 1911; his work, which sometimes borders on caricature, celebrates the larger-than-life world of the provincial Russian merchant class; enormous ladies at

Portrait of Chaliapin by Boris Kustodiev.

tables straining under the weight of samovars, pots of jam, and pies stuffed with sturgeon, buckwheat, boiled eggs and rice. It is a world familiar to readers of Gogol. Among his best paintings are pictures of fairs, but he was also a fine portraitist. One of his finest canvases is an enormous portrait of the singer *Chaliapin* (Chaliapin Museum, St Petersburg).

The years 1906–11 witnessed the formation of dozens of groups, splinter groups and exhibitions. Two of the most active figures were Mikhail Larionov (1881–1964) and his wife, Natalia Goncharova (1881–1962).

Together with Pavel Kuznetsov (1878–1968), they formed the Blue Rose Group in 1906. Kuznetsov's main preoccupation was with

colour, and from Symbolist beginnings, influenced by Puvis de Chavannes, he reached his artistic peak in the 1910s and 1920s, when he painted a series of mystical landscapes of the Caucasian steppes. Goncharova drew her inspiration from Russian folk art and icon painting, and her best work, with its strong linear rhythms and striking colour scheme, reworks Byzantine draughtsmanship.

Larionov delighted in the unexpected and the shocking. Close in spirit to his contemporaries, the Futurist poets, he was the first Russian neo-primitivist, and produced a series of paintings

> Two influential, early 20th-century collectors of Impressionist paintings, Sergey Shchukin and Ivan Morozov, opened their doors once a week to allow Muscovites to view these important works.

of soldiers in which anatomy is deliberately distorted; in 1913 he turned to semi-abstract painting, having devised a system known as Rayism, by which he painted not objects but the rays emanating from objects, which by their intersection could define space.

Moscow's avant-garde

In 1910, Larionov helped to organise the first exhibition of the Knave of Diamonds group, which included works by foreign artists, and four compositions by Vassily Kandinsky (1866–1944). It was an important event in the history of the avant-garde, for it generated an independent Moscow-based group: the Russian avant-garde would change art all over the world.

Kandinsky can be considered the first true abstract painter; his brand of expressionism was concerned primarily with spirituality, and to achieve it he used explosions of colour and line, often including traces of figurative elements. Kazimir Malevich (1878–1935), meanwhile, began his career with Symbolist paintings, moved on to neo-primitivist works inspired by Larionov, but towards 1912 was beginning to develop a style of his own, which he called Suprematism. This was an attempt to break from representation of the visible world, to concentrate on space and through painting to forge a link with absolutes of everything and nothing. The supreme symbol of this period is his painting *Black Square* (1914), which is everything its name suggests.

A similarly uncompromising attitude towards art and the public is found in Vladimir Tatlin's work (1885–1953). His legacy is Constructivism: a type of semi-abstraction by which he sought, often with the help of relief, to penetrate the essence of objects, and then of material itself. Among his greatest works, however, is a self-portrait of 1911 in the Russian Museum. Painted in tempera, it recalls icon painting in its use of curved lines and highlights.

Tretyakov Gallery contains several outstanding examples of his work, including *The Bathing of the Red Horse* (1912).

This frenzy of artistic activity took place against a background of political intrigue, World War I, the Revolution and finally the Civil War. Many avant-garde artists greeted the new society with open arms, applying their talents to propaganda and public information art. The works of the photographer Alexander Rodchenko (1891–1956) and the poet-artist Vladimir Mayakovsky (1893–1930) were to define international poster and book design

The Bathing of the Red Horse painted by Kuzma Petrov-Vodkin in the early 20th century.

The dream like world of Marc Chagall (1887–1985) is represented by early paintings in the Tretyakov and Russian Museums. He was the youngest of the avant-garde painters, spent most of his life abroad, and other than a penchant for neo-primitivism had little in common with his contemporaries.

Kuzma Petrov-Vodkin (1878–1939) also sought to use the language of icon painting: his large canvases are built of areas of strongly contrasting colours, usually including a brilliant, almost luminous red. He deliberately manipulated space to give an impression of flatness, and played with shadow and highlight in such a way that his figures seem, as in icon painting, to be illuminated from within. The New

effectively until the 1980s. But disillusionment set in, and while some artists chose exile, those who remained and sought to practise their art were finally brought down by an official decree of 1934, which established Socialist Realism as the only acceptable form of art.

Now began a strange period during which many talented artists applied some of the more acceptable discoveries of the avant-garde to utopian paintings on Soviet subjects. Some confined themselves to the new heroes of proletarian society – the workers and peasants, sportsmen and women, students at the new literacy colleges – but others went still further, producing vast works showing Lenin and Stalin, Party Congresses and political meetings.

This was a time for huge public commissions, for works of art to fill skyscrapers, for paintings, mosaics, for metro stations, creating palaces for the people. Many of these Stalinist buildings and their interiors survive, a symbol of the utopian euphoria which reigned, and socialist realist paintings are now sought out by collectors.

But there was no "underground" at this time: the underground was a post-war, post-Stalin phenomenon. Artists such as Pavel Filonov (1883–1941) and Vladimir Sterligov (1904–1973) continued to work throughout the 1930s and 1940s, but were not allowed to exhibit.

Two Ovals by Vassily Kandinsky, 1919.

They designed book covers and scenery, taking one or two students, to whom they passed on the knowledge that they alone possessed.

With the "thaw" of the 1950s and 1960s, a flood of artists who propounded "formalist" – non-representational – theories emerged, tolerated but not accepted by the authorities. The true divide between official and unofficial became clear at the end of the 1960s. While "acceptable" painters such as Andrey Mylnikov and Boris Ugarov produced bland, non-controversial pictures of Pushkin, of power stations, of Moscow as the symbol of a contented Soviet Union – but without the inspirational mood of the 1930s – the underground came into its own. Artists like Dmitry Plavinsky, Vladimir

Veysberg and Oskar Rabin pushed art in vastly different directions, from expressionism to formalism. Secret exhibitions were held in apartments. Artists became more radical, and in 1974 they showed their works publicly – which resulted in the bulldozing of a whole exhibition in Moscow in that year.

Searching for direction

But with the 1980s and perestroika, the relaxation of controls, and the massive explosion in exhibitions – public exhibitions, not cramped in small apartments – Russian art found itself facing a crisis. Despite the massive popularity of Russian art abroad, the lesser artists of the underground had made their reputations on opposition, on the expression of dissent. Once the point of opposition was removed, Russian art had to learn to see itself not as a political statement, but as an expression of intellectual and artistic aims.

> The Soviet era was a time of opportunity for the willing artist. Painters such as Samokhvalov and Deineka represent the best official art of the period. Their works are now valuable pieces of collectable art.

Moscow and St Petersburg, which still dominate the art scene, have emerged from the crisis. St Petersburg remains a city of painting, sculpture and creativity. Timur Novikov's New Academy of Arts propagandises a return to the values of pre-Revolutionary art, to beauty, to neoclassicism. Meanwhile Moscow has become the centre of a vibrant arts scene, particularly noted for the use of new media, such as performance and video. Moscow has held five Biennales of Contemporary Art, bringing artists from many countries to the city for the festival. Perhaps contemporary Russian art is still in its growing stage, where experimentation and innovation trump artistic vision. However art lovers will be delighted to see that it is not only confined to museums, but also to be found in the country's growing number of galleries and salons. In recent years the Kremlin has had little to say about art in general, though in the current climate it may only be a matter of time before some level of censorship is reintroduced.

Effigies of Russian authors Nikolai Gogol, Fyodor Dostoyevsky, Vladimir Mayakovsky, Alexander Pushkin and Anton Chekhov parading at Moscow city day celebration.

LITERATURE

Russia's literary heritage is one of the greatest in the world. At every step it reflects the tragic, comic, glorious history of the country.

Russian literature is rooted in an ancient oral tradition which lives on in the national passion for jokes, elaborate toasts, proverbs, fairytales and aphorisms. The literary tradition began with the *byliny*, folk tales told by minstrels in the courts of Kiev over 1,000 years ago, and continued with *The Lay of Igor's Host*, a kind of 12th-century Russian *Beowulf*. The opening words of this long saga are known to every educated Russian, and even in pale translation can send a shiver up the spine: "Is it not fitting, o my brothers, to begin with the old songs, the hard tales of Igor, son of Svyatoslav, and his battles..."

Literary genius

But the man held to be the founder of modern Russian literature is Alexander Pushkin. He was born in 1799, in an age when French was still considered the only language suitable for literary expression, and Russian was the lingo of the kitchen and the farmyard.

Pushkin's work took Russian to new and undreamed-of heights. His instinctive feel for the cadences of the Russian tongue, acquired at the knee of his peasant nanny, was transmuted by his genius into deathless lyric poetry, prose, verse novels and plays. It is present, too, in the long poem, *The Bronze Horseman*, and the verse novel *Evgene Onegin*.

Pushkin's place in Russian literature cannot be overstated; he is not just its source, but the landscape against which its story unfolds. He set the pattern for Russian men of letters in other ways, too: he was harassed by the authorities (Tsar Nicholas I acted as his own personal censor), and he met a tragic end, killed in a foolish duel at the age of 37.

Pushkin's immediate heir was Mikhail Lermontov. He circulated a bitter poem immediately

Poet Yevgeny Yevtushenko, New York 1967.

after Pushkin's death blaming the philistine court of Nicholas I for the loss of Russia's great poet. The authorities paid Lermontov the compliment of exiling him to the Caucasus, and, not for the last time, official punishment boosted a young writer's reputation. In the dramatic mountains of the south, Lermontov wrote poetry which developed the existential idea of the "superfluous man", the view that in Nicholas's Russia, indeed in the world at large, there is no outlet for the energies of men of talent and feeling, so life consists of frittering away time on meaningless diversions such as love and war, and in taking what solace there is in nature. This philosophy is expressed with deep eloquence in his novel, *A Hero of Our Time*. Lermontov lived by the idea, breaking hearts and picking fights until he, too, was killed in a duel. He was 26.

A very different light was cast on Russia by Ukrainian-born writer Nikolai Gogol, the third great literary talent of Russia's first flowering. Gogol's gift was for the grotesque. His hilarious short stories (*The Two Ivans*, *The Nose*, *The Overcoat*) are populated with pompous provincials, uppity civil servants, and all sorts of shallow, greedy gargoyles. But beneath the surface runs a dark seam of fear: perhaps his clownish world is not a burlesque, perhaps humanity really is that ugly. Gogol himself certainly came to believe

by contemporaries to be a vicious caricature of a revolutionary idealist; but modern readers see a well-meaning man whose rational world is thrown into turmoil when he falls in love with a beautiful widow. Turgenev's portrayal of women is one of his strengths; he is also masterful and compassionate when portraying the oppressed: his first book was *Hunter's Sketches*, short stories about the lives of serfs, and many readers think it is his best.

Turgenev was a "Western" writer: moderate, restrained and economical. Dostoyevsky was the opposite: his books are full of madly excit-

Maxim Gorky and his literary circle.

so. One senses it in his farce, *The Government Inspector*, and in the novel *Dead Souls*, written as he descended into a private hell of religious mysticism and inexplicable guilt.

Great storytellers

The next generation comprises the three giants of Russian letters: Ivan Turgenev, Fyodor Dostoyevsky and Leo Tolstoy. All three dealt with the burning issues of their day – serfdom, Russia's Asiatic and European heritage, the revolutionary movement. But what makes all three of them great is that their works rise above the issues that inspire them. They are all marvellous storytellers. For example, Turgenev's Bazarov, the hero of *Fathers and Sons*, was interpreted

able people given to passionate ideas and dizzying swings of emotion, people who are buffeted by sin and repentance, who are, in a word, "Russian". Dostoyevsky used this gallery of tortured souls to explore the biggest questions: good and evil, freedom and responsibility, salvation and damnation. His mature novels – *The Brothers Karamazov*, *Crime and Punishment*, *The Devils* – are strong meat, difficult reads and profoundly absorbing works of art.

While Dostoyevsky's doleful gaze was fixed on the dark vortices of the Russian soul, Leo Tolstoy could not tear his eyes from the great, gaudy pageant of Russian society. Tolstoy the Preacher wanted to condemn its frivolity, but Tolstoy the Artist could not resist glorying in it all. This tension is at the heart of both *War and Peace* and *Anna Karenina*, either of which might justifiably be named the greatest novel ever written. *War and Peace*, a vast panorama of the Napoleonic era, is the more ambitious work. Its scope is as deep as it is broad. The focus zooms in and out, alighting at one moment on the daydreams of a teenage girl, at another on great armies in battle. To read the book is like climbing a mountain: it takes stamina and dedication to get there, but the view from the summit is worth it.

Tolstoy, like nearly all Russian writers since Pushkin, was a nobleman by birth. At the turn

Soviet letters. To his credit, he used this position of authority to protect young writers from the excesses of the Stalinist regime.

Immediately before the Revolution Russian poetry re-asserted itself. Never before had so many gifted and varied poets arisen at one time. There were the Symbolists who elevated poetry to a kind of mystical religion of which they were the high priests; there were the Futurists, bold experimenters who refused "to cling to Pushkin's coat-tails", as Vladimir Mayakovsky put it, and who wanted to remake the language as the Revolution would remake the country;

Anton Chekhov.

Fyodor Dostoyevsky.

of the 20th century, the voice of the bourgeoisie made itself heard in the stories and plays of Anton Chekhov. The boredom and sense of failure that hangs around his heroes can be seen as a reflection of the political impotence and shallow roots of the middle classes, soon to be uprooted and borne away on a tidal wave of revolution.

Poets and proletarians

The future belonged to the working masses, whose authentic coarse tones resound in the vibrant, colourful works of Maxim Gorky (his play *The Lower Depths* and his autobiographical sketches *Childhood, Apprenticeship and My Universities*). He was the first truly proletarian writer, and later became a kind of godfather of

there was the rowdy peasant Sergei Yesenin whose life and poetry are a long lament for the doomed Russian countryside; there were the Acmeists, exquisite craftsmen who saw poetry as a refined verbal architecture; and there were poets who either stood apart from these movements or transcended them: Alexander Blok, Boris Pasternak, Anna Akhmatova.

Prose came back into fashion in the 1920s, and dramatic accounts of the revolutionary upheaval vied for attention with joyful comic writing, much of it hailing from the south: Babel's *Odessa Tales* and *Red Cavalry*, Sholokhov's *And Quiet Flows the Don*, the anecdotal short stories of Zoshchenko and Zamyatin, Ilf and Petrov's *Twelve Chairs*.

Promoting the cause

In the 1930s Stalin's grip on the arts tightened. Henceforth literature was to be harnessed for the socialist cause. It was still a high calling because writers are, said Stalin, "engineers of the human soul", and as such a vital element of the production line which turns out right-minded Soviet citizens. This mandate was, of course, a death sentence on real literature. Indeed, it led directly to the death of many writers: Yesenin and Mayakovsky had already committed suicide in despair; Osip Mandelshtam, Nikolai Gumilev and Isaak Babel were swallowed up by the Ter-

Anna Akhamatova by Natan Altmann, 1914.

ror. Of the first rank of writers only Pasternak and Akhmatova survived. Akhmatova's poetic account of those years, *Requiem*, is a monument of world literature and a testament to her dignity.

The novelist Mikhail Bulgakov once wrote that "manuscripts don't burn", meaning that the impulse to create and consume literature is made stronger when it is attacked. Stalin failed in his attempt to amputate the human spirit, and the Soviet people's hunger for books was made all the sharper. This is why it was common in the USSR to see queues of people waiting to buy some slim volume of civic verse or collection of short stories. Bulgakov was himself one of the writers who satisfied Russians' spiritual hunger. *The Master and Margarita*, his tale of how the devil visits Moscow

Five Russian writers have won the Nobel Prize for Literature. They are Ivan Bunin, Mikhail Sholokhov, Boris Pasternak (who was forced to refuse it), Alexander Solzhenitsyn and Joseph Brodsky.

and wreaks havoc, is one of the most profound (and funny) novels of the century, savoured and quoted by Russians of all ages.

A brief thaw

The Master and Margarita was published only in 1965, 25 years after Bulgakov's death. This was the time of the Thaw, the heady period under Khrushchev when many banned works saw the light of day. The key event of the Thaw was the publication of *One Day in the Life of Ivan Denisovich*. This short story, a pitilessly truthful snapshot of Gulag life, was the debut work of Alexander Solzhenitsyn. It made him famous overnight and led to a flood of camp memoirs as "rehabilitated" writers unburdened themselves of their terrible experiences.

Poets also benefited from the Thaw. There appeared in the 1960s a group of young poets – Yevgeny Yevtushenko, Andrei Voznesensky and others – who chose to declaim their verse to an audience. Some of them set their poems to music, and the best – Bulat Okoujava, Vladimir Vysotsky, Alexander Galich – were hugely popular because their subjects were so often taken from humdrum Soviet reality and the eternal themes of love, honesty and happiness.

As the Brezhnevian winter set in, many freethinking writers found themselves out of favour with the censors. Popular works passed from hand to hand in typewritten copies, a homemade method of publication known as *samizdat* ("self-publishing", a pun on the state publishing organisation, Gosizdat). Works by banned Westerners and Russian emigrés – George Orwell, Vladimir Nabokov, Aldous Huxley, Joseph Brodsky – were all read in the 1970s, but secretly.

In search of a modern Tolstoy

By the time of glasnost, officially approved literature had grown stagnant, and the best writing of the Soviet period was banned or bowdlerised by the censor. Even politically harmless classics were unavailable. In this absurd situation, all Gorbachev had to do to win sympathy from the intelligentsia was to let them read whatever they wanted. He did just that, and for a couple of years there was a reading frenzy, as eager *intelligenty* devoured the poetry of Marina Tsvetaeva, the satires of Aksyonov and Zinoviev, and (at long last) the novel *Doctor Zhivago*. There was a simultaneous boom in new works, of which the best was *Children of the Arbat*, Anatoly Rybakov's memoir of a Moscow childhood.

The post-Communist era, by contrast, was initially marked by a descent into pulp with cheap, low quality detective thrillers. However, there are serious writers whose work is both popular and provocative. The most famous of these are Victor Pelevin and Vladimir Sorokin; the latter's *Golobuye Salo (Blue Lard)* book was the object of a court action by a pro-Kremlin youth movement Iduishii Vmeste (Moving Together) due to its descriptions of homosexual acts between Stalin and Khrushchev. Russians are also reading foreign fiction in translation. So far, however, the era has not produced its Pushkin, Tolstoy or Bulgakov. Perhaps more years are needed for writers to assimilate the enormous changes and influx of information of past decades – Russian readers look forward to that day.

Alexander Solzhenitsyn in Vladivostock, upon his return from exile in the US in 1994.

VOICES OF DISSENSION

Russia has had dissidents for almost as long as it has had books. One of the first was Alexander Radishchev, whose account of serfdom under Catherine the Great, earned him long years in Siberia. A more sinister precedent was set when the 19th-century philosopher Peter Chaadayev was declared insane for criticising the tsarist regime. But dissidence is now associated with the Soviet era, especially its last years when the system was oppressive enough to punish free thinkers, but not so despotic as to murder them. The leading anti-Soviet writer of this time was Alexander Solzhenitsyn. His novels *Cancer Ward* and *First Circle*, and his history of the camps *The Gulag Archipelago*, were all published abroad. He was exiled in 1970, but returned home to see his work printed in his native land. Solzhenitsyn was the godfather of dissidence, but there was never a unified movement. Indeed, dissidents often objected to each other as much as they did to the state. *Inakomysliye* (thinking otherwise) covered all kinds of writing and opinions: Marxist historian Roy Medvedev, religious poet Irina Ratushinskaya, human rights activist Andrei Sakharov, Nobel laureate Joseph Brodsky, *samizdat* heroes Sinyavsky and Daniel, and comic novelist Vladimir Voinovich. All are worth reading for their own sake, as well as for what they have to say about the repressive regime.

A bell ringer at the Sabantui Festival in the village of Mirny, Tatarstan.

THE MUSIC MAKERS

Influenced by their early folk and ecclesiastical traditions, the country's musicians have created, to worldwide acclaim, an authentic Russian sound.

Russian music is often said by those outside the country to have dated from the 1830s and 1840s, when Mikhail Glinka became the first Russian composer to obtain European recognition. In fact, the country has a rich musical tradition that originated in the folk songs of the eastern Slavs who settled in the region about 1,300 years ago. This folk music, which celebrated all events of life from working in the fields to weddings and festivals, served as the foundation for the great Russian classical musical tradition that burst forth in the mid-19th century.

The first professional musicians (*skomorokhi*) appeared in the 11th and 12th centuries in the courts of the Russian princes in Kiev and Novgorod. *Skomorokhi* were travelling troupes of actors who played a variety of instruments unique to Russia, such as the *gusli* (stringed instrument), *rozhok* (wind instrument) and *volinka* (wind instrument akin to the bagpipes). The Orthodox Church also played a strong role in the development of Russian music from the 10th century when it became the national religion. Its liturgical monotone and style of singing had a powerful impact on the Russian composers of the 19th and 20th centuries.

But the Church had a negative effect, too. It taught that only the human voice could be used in divine worship, and for a long time secular performers were regarded by the Church as "messengers of the devil who turn people's minds from God with songs and trumpets and games". This was, in fact, a fairly accurate depiction of the bawdy and irreverent *skomorokhi*. The only instrument permitted by the Church were bells, and the Russians developed bell-ringing to a sophisticated level. Today, after 70 years of silence under Communism, the art of

Accordionist in traditional costume, Kazan.

bell-ringing is enjoying a revival; the resonant pealing can be heard on Saturday evenings and Sundays before services.

Despite the dominance of the Church, Tsar Ivan III created a secular court choir in the 15th century. Towards the end of the 16th century, as contact with the West increased (Elizabeth I, for example, sent an organ and virginals to Ivan the Terrible), even church music began to move with the times. By the 17th century, five-line notation, polyphony and major and minor keys were gradually introduced to the liturgy, allowing it to obtain a richer sound and effect.

With the foundation of a court theatre during the reign of the enlightened Alexis

Mikhailovich (1645–76), a secular musical tradition grew from the seeds sown by Ivan III, but it was during the reign of Peter I (the Great) that the greatest innovations occurred. By moving the capital from Moscow to his new city of St Petersburg in 1712, Peter transformed conservative, pious Muscovy into the modern state of Russia at a stroke. Along with all the architects and craftsmen imported to modernise his backward country came foreign musicians to play in the new military bands and sing in the new state choir. Music soon became an integral part of everyday court

soon became the rage among the aristocracy, thanks largely to the patronage of the imperial family. Indeed, opera became so popular in the 18th century that wealthy landowners such as Count Sheremetev (whose enchanting miniature theatre can be visited at Ostankino) were soon setting up their own companies and orchestras on their estates, using serfs as well as foreign artists as performers.

Glinka marks a turning point

It is customary to view Mikhail Glinka (1804–57) as the first genuinely Russian composer.

Mikhail Glinka, 19th-century opera composer.

Music-making in the 18th century was dominated by enthusiastic nobles whose expertise left much to be desired, yet there was a great deal of talent around, particularly in composition.

life. Yet Peter was not very musical himself, so music-making remained entirely foreign in origin. For the vast majority of the population, hearing music meant either going to church or listening to folk songs.

By the mid-18th century the Russian court had its own orchestra, and a special theatre was built for the performance of opera, which

But the achievements of 18th-century composers such as Dmitri Bortnyansky, Maksim Berezovsky and Yevstignei Fomin (who was originally a serf musician) and their successors Alexander Alyabev and Alexei Verstovsky should not be overlooked, even if their Italian training meant that their music did not sound very Russian. They were the first Russian musicians to compete with foreign counterparts on their own level, and they did much to raise musical standards.

Peter the Great's relentless westernising encouraged the nobility to regard Russian culture with contempt, but the upsurge of patriotism which followed Napoleon's defeat in 1812 swelled hearts with national pride. A new generation of artists, musicians and writers appeared on the scene who were anxious to create a genuinely Russian culture.

Among them was Glinka, whose two operas marked a turning point in the history of Russian music. Both *A Life for the Tsar* (1836) and *Ruslan and Lyudmila* (1842) combined Western techniques of composition with music that was clearly inspired by native folk sources. They were profoundly Russian works.

Glinka's operas are traditionally considered to be the cornerstone of classical Russian music. His musical plays laid the foundation for the

Pyotr Tchaikovsky, composer.

Russian symphonic school, and his vocal compositions are the first examples of the Russian romance. Alexander Dargomizhsky (1813–69) continued the search, begun by Glinka, for a national Russian musical style.

Since opera was government-funded in tsarist Russia, the conservative tastes of the St Petersburg aristocracy for foreign music in particular continued to determine what works were performed and when. Public concerts, held on a regular basis since from the end of the 18th century, were not held during the four great religious fasting periods, when all theatres and concert halls closed their doors as well. There was still no professional training available for budding Russian musicians.

A distinctly Russian sound

Anton Rubinstein (1829–94), the virtuoso pianist and composer who did the most to change this situation during the liberal years of Alexander II, was more concerned with raising general standards of musicianship than with promoting specifically Russian music. He founded the Russian Musical Society in 1859 (the first organisation that was allowed to hold concerts throughout the winter season) and the St Petersburg Conservatory in 1866. Similar institutions were founded in Moscow by Rubinstein's brother

> Under Nicholas I thousands of roubles were spent on the resident Italian opera troupe, while the Russian Opera had to struggle to make ends meet.

Nikolai. Not all Russian musicians favoured Rubinstein's reforms.

In particular, the group of Slavophile composers which gathered around Mily Balakirev in the 1860s vigorously opposed the professionalism of the Conservatory training and its classical Western orientation. In an attempt to keep Russian music free from foreign contamination and preserve its independent status, Balakirev (1837–1910) started a rival Free School of Music.

Together with Alexander Borodin (1833–87), who earned a living as a well-respected chemist, Nikolai Rimsky-Korsakov (1844–1908), who forged a successful career in the navy, Modest Musorgsky (1839–81) and César Cui (1835–1918), Balakirev set about promoting a native Russian musical tradition, believing that art belonged to the people and should be realistic in style.

It is to these composers that Russian music owes much of its distinctive sound. Drawing on the melodies of native folk song and Eastern music, they sought inspiration in the legends of Russian history and literature. Borodin based his opera *Prince Igor* (1874) on a 12th-century epic poem, Musorgsky turned to Pushkin for his masterpiece *Boris Godunov* (1874), and Rimsky-Korsakov created magical operas that had their source in Russian fairytales.

A contemporary of the "Five" was Pyotr Tchaikovsky (1840–93), one of the first students at the St Petersburg Conservatory. Besides the six major symphonies, the piano concertos and the ever popular ballets, Tchaikovsky is also best remembered for his operas, which drew on the works of Pushkin and Gogol. *Evgene Onegin* and *The Queen of Spades* are perhaps his greatest works in this genre. The Moscow Conservatory now bears his name.

By the end of the 19th century, Russian music was being performed regularly, and the conservatories of St Petersburg and Moscow were producing composers, conductors and performers of great talent. With the exception of the Impe-

after the Revolution. Scriabin formed close links with the mystical Russian Symbolists who emerged in the early years of the 20th century and forged a musical idiom that would greatly influence composition throughout the world.

Nikolai Rimsky-Korsakov shaped the musical life of St Petersburg at this time. It was his students, including the music professors Anatoli Lyadov (1855–1914) and Alexander Glazunov (1865–1936), who in turn influenced two of the leading Russian composers of the 20th century – Sergei Prokofiev (1891–1953) and Dmitri Shostakovich (1906–75).

Dmitri Shostakovich playing with the Glazunov Quartet in 1940.

rial theatres, the government had little control over musical life.

The brightest stars at the turn of the century were the singer Fyodor Chaliapin and the composers Sergei Rachmaninov (1873–1943) and Alexander Scriabin (1872–1915), the most famous graduates of the Moscow Conservatory where they studied with Sergei Tanyeyev (1856–1915), a composer, pianist and musical theorist who had been Tchaikovsky's student.

Rachmaninov, best known for his major contributions to the piano repertoire (but also a composer of some magnificent symphonic works), was himself a highly accomplished pianist, and was able to earn a good living on the concert platform during his long years of exile

Composers of the 20th century

Igor Stravinsky (1882–1971) and Sergei Prokofiev became the real innovators in the field of composition. Stravinsky, one of the great musical giants of the 20th century, came to world prominence when Diaghilev staged his ballets, *The Firebird* (1910) and *Petrushka* (1911), in Europe as part of his famous "Ballets Russes" seasons. His *Rite of Spring* (1913) was considered so modern when it was first performed that it caused uproar all over Europe. Stravinsky continued to blaze new paths in music for the rest of his long career, his eclectic works transcending narrow national boundaries. Like Rachmaninov, he lived in exile after 1917, visiting his homeland only in 1962.

Prokofiev completed his studies, as Stravinsky had, at the St Petersburg Conservatory with Rimsky-Korsakov; but he too left the country in the wake of the Revolution, leaving Russia bereft of its greatest talents. He returned in the mid-1930s.

The Soviet muse

While the 1917 Revolution had a cataclysmic effect on musical life in Russia, with theatres closing and concert series abandoned, it also injected it with energy. The years just after the Revolution were a time of experimen-

Vladimir Ashkenazy conducting in 2013.

tation. Many people attended the opera for the first time and vast musical and dramatic spectacles were organised to commemorate the events of 1917.

Music became an important weapon for propaganda purposes. But until new composers appeared who could write morally uplifting socialist music, the Bolsheviks were content for the old repertory to be performed. Innocuous opera titles were often changed for ones that were more politically charged.

The greatest period of artistic tolerance came during the 1920s. Two rival musical organisations formed in 1923: the avant-garde and modernist Association of Contemporary Music, which favoured experimentation, and the

Russian Association of Proletarian Musicians, which was the more militant of the two, dismissing all past music as bourgeois and alien.

The period from the 1920s to the 1940s was the heyday of the composer and music teacher Nikolai Myaskovsky (1881–1950), who wrote 27 symphonies, among other works. Other talented composers to appear during the 1920s were Nikolai Roslavets (1881–1944), later a victim of the purges, whose major contribution to the development of atonal music is now beginning to be recognised, and Alexander Mossolov (1900–71), whose famous

> In the 1940s and 1950s much Western music was banned from the concert platform and in the classroom was denounced as "decadent" and "reactionary".

orchestral work full of mechanical sound effects, *The Iron Foundry* (1926), is a testament to the early years of Soviet industrialisation.

By far the most gifted composer to emerge during the early years of Soviet power was Dmitri Shostakovich (1906–75), whose *First Symphony* was first performed in 1926 when he was just 20 years old, and followed by another masterpiece, his opera *The Nose* (1928), based on Gogol's short story.

For a time, Leningrad (as St Petersburg became known) vied with Berlin to be the centre of musical experimentation, but towards the end of the 1920s, as ideology came to play a bigger role in artistic life, the freedoms enjoyed by Soviet artists gradually disappeared.

Music for the masses

In 1932, the Union of Soviet Composers was formed and music was placed under direct government control. Composers were told that they had to write music according to the doctrine of socialist realism. In other words, music had to be understandable to the masses and nationalistic in character. It was to depict "reality in its revolutionary development".

It was not until 1936, however, that composers really came under pressure to conform. Shostakovich's great operatic masterpiece *Lady Macbeth of Mtsensk* was first performed in Leningrad to great acclaim in 1934, but things started to go wrong following a Moscow performance in January 1936 attended by Stalin. The next day an editorial entitled "Muddle Instead of Music" appeared in *Pravda*. Shostakovich's opera, and avant-garde music in general, was subjected to a merciless attack. He responded with his *Fifth Symphony*, a darkly ambiguous work subtitled "A Soviet Artist's Reply to Just Criticism". His relationship with the authorities was ever after to be tortuous and complicated. It determined the content of the music he was to write over the next four decades. But while Shostakovich paid lip service to the ideology of the Soviet regime, of atonality, dissonance and disharmony", which reflected the "decay of bourgeois culture".

Khrushchev's accession to power heralded the thaw in cultural life, symbolised by the great success of Shostakovich's *Tenth Symphony* in 1953. Restrictions began to be slowly relaxed and contacts with the West were cautiously resumed.

Stravinsky was allowed to return to Russia in 1962 and visits made by Western musicians such as Leonard Bernstein, Glenn Gould and Aaron Copland made a huge impact on the new generation of music students. It came as something

The Song and Dance Ensemble of the Russian Army performing in Moscow.

beginning with his *Fourth Symphony*, he carried out subtle resistance to the established order, as did most composers.

Accusations of decadence

The attack on Shostakovich in 1936 signalled the beginning of a systematic destruction of the Soviet musical intelligentsia. After the temporary hiatus caused by World War II, the purges intensified. During the first Congress of Composers held in 1948, Shostakovich, together with Prokofiev, Aram Khachaturian, Myaskovsky, and a number of others, was found guilty of "formalism". By refusing to write music filled with bright, optimistic melodies, these composers were accused of following the "cult

of a shock for these young Russians to hear the music of Schoenberg and Webern for the first time. The thaw was a brief one. Another bleak period of isolation and repression followed Khrushchev's removal from power in 1964. In the musical sphere it was spearheaded by Tikhon Khrennikov, who presided as head of the Union of Composers from 1948 until its collapse in the aftermath of the 1991 coup.

The Soviet conservatories, however, produced an array of outstanding talents, among them the pianist Svyatoslav Richter, the conductor Gennady Rozhdestvensky and the violinists David and Igor Oistrakh. Young Soviet musicians and conductors took gold medals in international competitions.

The opera and ballet troupes of the Bolshoi Theatre (Bolshoy Teatre), the symphonic orchestra under Mravinsky and Svetlanov, as well as numerous other talented musicians successfully made tours to the West to great acclaim. And in Moscow, the International Tchaikovsky Competition has enjoyed great prestige since its inception in 1958.

Despite all these glittering successes, many greatly gifted artists, including the cellist Mstislav Rostropovich, the violinist Gidon Kremer and the pianist Vladimir Ashkenazy, were forced either to emigrate abroad or defect. Meanwhile,

"official" composers continued to churn out leaden operas and orchestral works, and were rewarded for their efforts with trips abroad and privileged lifestyles, while avant-garde composers such as Alfred Schnitke (1934–98), Sofia Gubaidulina, Nikolai Karetnikov (1930–93) and Edison Denisov (1929–96) made a living in the best way they could, knowing that their works could never be performed to the public. Their music, which represented a defiant and triumphant statement of the values they steadfastly continued to believe in, also faithfully reflected the troubled times in which they lived.

DJs in Kazan.

THE POP-ROCK SCENE

Russian pop stars are generally unknown in the West. One exception to this is the group Tatu who made headlines outside of Russia. Some other pop stars to look out for are Alsu (a female singer from Tatarstan), Ivanushki International and Slivki. Russian rock enjoyed its heyday in the period in and around perestroika. Groups from this period such as Kino, DDT and Akvarium continue to be popular to this day. Other recent popular acts include Mummi Troll, from Vladivostock, and Zemfira, from Ufa. Live music is still very popular in Russia and new, and not so new, bands can be seen playing live in clubs.

Together with a growing interest in the musical avant-garde, one of the leading figures of this era was Giorgi Sviridov (1915–98) who embodied the national musical traditions. From the 1960s to the 1980s, Sviridov's creative talents were especially prevalent in choir and vocal-symphonic genres.

A new flowering

All this changed when Mikhail Gorbachev came to power in 1985. With glasnost came an explosion of Soviet cultural life, as artists and writers were allowed to travel abroad freely, and previously forbidden works were published and performed. Rostropovich and Ashkenazy both made much-publicised return visits to Russia, concert repertoires widened and Russian music started to become popular in the West.

Today, the St Petersburg school of music is best represented by Galina Ustvolskaya, Lucian Prigozhin (1926–94), Sergei Slonimsky, Boris Tishchenko, Yuri Falik, Alexander Knaifel, and their younger colleagues. Notable musicians from the Moscow school include Boris Tchaikovsky (1925–96), Vyacheslav Artemov, Eduard Artemov, Vladimir Martinov, and the husband-and-wife team of Dmitry Smirnov and Elena Firsova.

After the economic crisis in Russia, which left musicians, orchestras and musical institutions struggling to survive financially, musical life began to thrive and is now enjoying a period of strong revival. The number of symphonic and chamber orchestras has grown, and new music festivals and competitions have become an inherent part of the music scene.

Opera and ballet companies such as the Mariinsky (formerly Kirov) Theatre tour abroad and Russian conductors and musicians are much sought after internationally. All this goes to show that Russia has retained its status as a music superpower.

Female throat singing group Tuva Kyzy inside a wooden yurt in Aldyn Bulak, Republic of Tuva.

TUVA'S TRADITIONAL MUSIC

If you thought music in the Russian Federation was all *balalaikas* and military choirs, then head to Siberia's Republic of Tuva for a real world music treat. Tuva has a musical tradition all of its own, one similar to neighbouring Mongolia. Throat singing is the local speciality, a technique whereby a range of sounds are produced in the throat – interesting when heard recorded, mind-boggling when experienced live.

The republic also has a number of traditional stringed instruments such as the *igil* and the *doshpuluur* and songs reflect the age-old life of the nomads on the grasslands of this forgotten part of Asia – many echo the beat of horses' hooves. The Tuvan National Orchestra (www.tuvanorchestra.ru) are the undisputed masters of Tuvan music and often tour outside Russia, but there are lots of other ensembles such as Alash, Chirgilchin and Huun Huur. All of them can be found at the new Centre for Tuvan Culture in the Tuvan capital Kyzyl where they take turns to put on concerts. You can also sneak into rehearsals or book a throat singing lesson.

The festivals of Naadym (July and or August) and Ustuu Khuree (July) are also good times to hear the eerie burp and whistle of Asia's most unusual music genre.

RUSSIAN CINEMA

Russia's film industry has emerged revitalised from its silent battle with the censors and the creative lull of the 1990s thanks to its variety of new genres.

We consider film the most important art form of all, said Lenin. Indeed, the Soviet Union built up a powerful film industry that was useful in shaping the mentality of the new socialist man, as well as providing entertainment in a drab world. Cinemas were built in every town. Cheap tickets and a limited choice of other forms of entertainment meant that large crowds were always assured. Massive state subsidies, however, meant not only the mass production of social realist films but also, in Moscow and St Petersburg, the establishment of film schools that were to be creative powerhouses.

Talent in the grip of the censors

Beginning with the masterpieces of Sergei Eisenstein, such as *Battleship Potemkin*, and to the present day, Russia has produced an impressive number of high quality films and nurtured a constellation of talented directors and actors. Some of them, like Arsenii Tarkovsky, have been forced to emigrate because their art was considered subversive and too conceptual by the establishment – all forms of dissent were severely punished. To preserve their artistic integrity many film makers had to develop a cinematic language of their own that the state control did not comprehend. In the early 1970s Nadezhda Kosheverova released *The Shadow*, followed in 1988 by Mark Zakharov's *To Slay The Dragon*; both films were based on the plays by Eugene Shwartz who was a victim of Stalinist purges. Their subject is the corruptive action of an absolute power in a totalitarian state, but the stories are set in a fairytale land. Others had to restrict themselves to portraying everyday life minus its political and social issues.

The short time between the start of perestroika and the collapse of the Soviet Union afforded filmmakers a brief respite: censorship

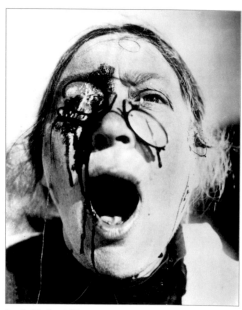

Battleship Potemkin.

was relaxed and funds still available. As a result, previously forbidden topics were thrown up for discussion and films were made that openly dealt with drugs, organised crime and prostitution – among them *Assa* (1987) by Sergei Soloviyov and *The Needle* (1989) by Rashid Nugmanov.

However, the Soviet period wasn't all doom and gloom. From the 1960s to the 1980s the USSR's film studios churned out superb farcical comedies to lift the mood of the masses. Many of these paint a picture of Soviet life that was closer to the actual reality for ordinary people and provide an insight into the USSR of the Krushchev and Brezhnev eras. For the sunnier side of Soviet film, it's worth seeking out movies such as *Kidnapping Caucasian Style* (1967), the fast-moving *Ivan Vasilievich Changes Profession* (1973), the superb New Year favourite *The Irony of Fate* (1975), the cult classic *The Diamond Arm* (1968), the ever popular *Office Romance* (1979) and the Leningrad comedy *Autumn Marathon* (1979) to name just a few.

The post-Soviet wave

After the collapse of the Soviet Union, Russian film struggled to find its bearings. Eldar Ryazanov, a former mainstream director, made *The Promised Heaven* (1991), a highly sarcastic take on the Soviet reality. The subject of Stalinist

contemporary cinema's only themes. As many as 70 films are now produced annually, with the highest-grossing film of all time a 2004 Russian sci-fi film, *Nightwatch* (and *Daywatch* in 2006) by Timur Bekmambetov, which surpassed even The Lord of the Rings at the Russian box office.

Contemporary directors such as Nikita Mikhalkov, Alexander Sokurov and Alexander Rogozhkin have adjusted successfully and produced some fine works. Mikhalkov's *Burnt by the Sun*, a chilling film about Stalin's era, won the 1995 Academy Award for Best Foreign Film. Rogozhkin's *Peculiarities of the National Hunt*

Leviathan (2014), set on the outskirts of a small coastal town in the Barents Sea.

purges and their consequences, previously taboo, was broached in *Cold Summer of 1953* (1987) by Alexander Proshkin. However, the economic crisis of the 1990s meant that these were two of just a handful of new films made during those years.

In the past decade, all that has changed. Mainstream cinema, after a period of fascination with Russian mafia-themed films and TV series reflecting the dog-eat-dog reality of the early 1990s – such as *Brigada* (2002) – embraced a wave of films marked out by a renewed patriotism, nationalism even, that neatly coincided with Putin's arrival in power. Innumerable films glorifying the Russian Army's successes in wars, from World War II to the Afghan and Chechen wars, continue to be made. However, these are not Russian

(1995), a comedy about Russian hunters and the national character, is a rare example of a financial blockbuster. Less commercially successful, but a favourite with critics was Sokurov's *Russian Ark* (2002). Its 96-minute journey through Russia's history was shot in a single take and includes all the rooms of the Hermitage.

Films from this decade worth looking for are *Elena* (2011), an appraisal of contemporary Moscow society by one of Russia's best post-Soviet directors Zvyagintsev; the black-and-white *Hard to be a God* (2014) by Aleksey German; *Leviathan* (2014), another picture by Zvyagintsev dealing with life in modern Russia (this time corruption); and the Arctic drama *How I Ended this Summer* (2010) by director Aleksei Popogrebsky.

THE TRANS-SIBERIAN RAILWAY

The Trans-Siberian Railway is one of the epic journeys. It takes over a week to travel its length, and the route runs through Russia's dark heart.

A trip across Russia on the Trans-Siberian Railway is more like an ocean voyage than a train ride. The cities of Siberia are strung along the route like islands, and each one is like a new port of call. Half the fun of getting to them lies in the empty stretches between landfall as you get to know your fellow-travellers.

The Trans-Siberian is also the best way to *feel* the immensity of the Russian hinterland, as for day after day the train ploughs its chugging furrow over the often featureless steppe. The journey is perhaps more spectacular in winter, when the snow fields extend to the horizon and the glare from this great unruffled white blanket is blinding. In summer, Siberia is hot and dusty, though the longer days mean there are more hours in which to soak up the view, fewer to spend in your muggy compartment playing cards.

The classic Trans-Siberian route will take you to Vladivostok – "Conqueror of the East" – on Russia's Pacific seaboard. From there it is a short hop in a plane to Japan. But another option is to dip south along the Trans-Mongolian, skirt the shining banks of Lake Baikal, and strike out across the Gobi Desert to China. Either way, at the end of a week you will be a seasoned train-dweller: for days after you will continue to feel the rhythmic hammering of the wheels beneath your feet.

The restaurant cars are of unpredictable quality. Be sure to take plenty of dry and canned food with you, to be on the safe side.

Travelling through the steppe. Some trains come all the way from Beijing via Mongolia.

It is worth making friends with the conductress, who will then keep you supplied with tea and gossip.

Vladivostok is the last stop. Once a closed city, it is now a boom town doing more business with Tokyo than with Moscow.

THE IRON ROAD TO THE EAST

The Trans-Siberian Railway was one of the great engineering projects undertaken during the period of rapid industrialisation under the last two tsars. It was begun in 1890, and its primary purpose was to link European Russia with the new city of Vladivostok, which had been founded only 30 years before, but had grown rapidly into a major port. Like the great railroads of the American West, the Trans-Siberian also had the effect of opening up the land for urban adventurers. All the old towns on its route – Yaroslavl, Yekaterinburg, Krasnoyarsk, Irkutsk, Khabarovsk – grew bigger when they became staging posts along the iron road. The railway was finished in 1905, just in time to serve as a supply line in the Russo-Japanese war. In 1918 it carried the tsar and his family on their last journey to Yekaterinburg. The railway played a military role once again in 1941, when thousands of factories in European Russia were rapidly dismantled and shipped wholesale down the line to Siberia, where they churned out tanks and guns beyond the reach of the advancing Germans. Today it is still Russia's number one piece of infrastructure, the girdle of steel that holds the Russian Federation together.

Many imagine there is one Trans-Siberian "Express" but there are in fact numerous trains that ply sections of the line. Only the Rossiya, Russia's premier train service, makes the entire trip from Moscow to Vladivostok. Other less illustrious services might make the run from Novosibirsk to Khabarovsk or just Ulan-Ude to Irkutsk. These are working trains with three classes of sleeping car. Most travellers opt for second class with compartments sleeping four. Bring lots of food as there's often none on board.

Stops are a chance to stretch your legs. But do not stray too far from the train: they do not always stick to the timetable, and have been known to leave early.

One can often buy food en route. But in hard times shops close when the train arrives, so that travellers do not clean them out.

Compartments for two are small but cosy. They are neatly designed to convert daily from bedroom to sitting room and back.

ІНУ И КНЯЗЮ ПОЖАРСКОМУ
РОССІЯ. ЛѢТА 1818

On the Yaroslavl–Vologda train.

INTRODUCTION

A detailed guide to the entire country, with principal sites clearly cross-referenced by number to the maps.

Stained glass in the Moscow Metro.

Russia's brand is a strong one and everyone has an image of Russia in their heads. That might be golden onion domes or a Soviet tower block, the vast steppes or magnificent Baroque palaces of the imperial age, the ice-bound landscape or a Red Square military parade. Russia is all these things and much more – above all it's a fascinating place to explore.

Until now Russia has been on developmental fast-forward. The major cities have been transformed from drab and lifeless utilitarian places to vibrant, flashy metropolises, with sushi bars and luxury cars, extending from Kaliningrad to Vladivostok. Today Moscow feels like it never has before, with most Muscovites enjoying a standard of living their parents could only dream of. Provincial towns have begun to modernise, and there are now good hotels and restaurants almost everywhere. But virtually all the trappings of the consumer society and tourist industry date only from the late-1990s, and there are still pockets of under-development and moments of inconvenience.

Hikers, Altai Mountains.

Russians say that Moscow is not Russia, but it is the centre of the country's cultural, political and artistic life. Here you can find all Russia's history on the streets and in its museums, and experience the New Russia in raucous nightclubs, gourmet restaurants, and glitzy shopping centres. The city is surrounded by the Golden Ring – ancient Russian cities that have preserved the glories of the religious past. Imperial St Petersburg is truly magnificent, but nearby Pskov and Novgorod, two of Russia's most ancient and beautiful cities, are also worth a visit. For a different experience, take a boat trip along the slow Volga, lined with industrial towns and woodlands. The Russian South is another world altogether, with the ancient, non-Slavic cultures of the rugged Caucasus; and the sub-tropical Black Sea coast.

The Ural Mountains mark the border between Europe and Asia, and offer many delights for outdoor enthusiasts. Siberia is a place of extraordinary beauty and history. Unesco-listed Lake Baikal would be a major international tourist attraction were it not in the eastern reaches of Siberia. Russia's Far East is an even less-travelled land of snow, ice and volcanoes.

Of course Russia today is not the place it was a decade ago. The old antagonism of the Cold War seems to have returned, and Putin's reaction to Ukraine's Maidan Revolution has made Russia an international pariah once again. Hopefully Russia's return to autocratic rule will not hinder visitors to journey around this vast and beautiful land.

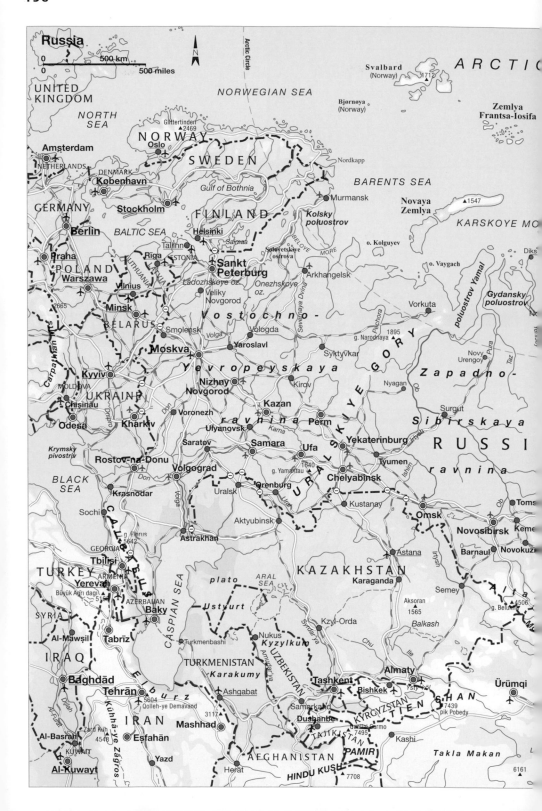

Russia

0 ___ 500 km
0 ___ 500 miles

UNITED
KINGDOM

NORTH
SEA

NORWEGIAN SEA

Svalbard
(Norway)

ARCTIC

Bjørnøya
(Norway)

Zemlya
Frantsa-Iosifa

Amsterdam
NETHERLANDS

DENMARK

Kobenhavn

GERMANY

Berlin

Praha

POLAND

Warszawa

Glittertinden
▲2469

Oslo

NORWAY

SWEDEN

Nordkapp

BARENTS SEA

Murmansk

Novaya
Zemlya

▲1547

KARSKOYE MO

Gulf of Bothnia

Stockholm

BALTIC SEA

FINLAND

Helsinki

Tallinn

Riga

Vilnius

Kolsky
poluostrov

o. Kolguyev

o. Vaygach

Diks

LITHUANIA

ESTONIA

Sankt
Peterburg

Saimaa

BELOYE
MORE

Solovetskiye
ostrova

poluostrov Yamal

Gydansky
poluostrov

Ladozhskoye oz.

Veliky
Novgorod

Onezhskoye
oz.

Severnaya Dvina

Arkhangelsk

Vorkuta

Minsk

BELARUS

Smolensk

Volga

Vologda

Yaroslavl

V o s t o c h n o -

Pechora

1895
g. Narodnaya

GORY

Novy
Urengoy

Zapadno-

Moskva

Kyyiv

MOLDOVA

Chisinau

Odesa

UKRAINE

Kharkiv

Y e v r o p e y s k a y a

Nizhny
Novgorod

Voronezh

Don

Ulyanovsk

Kazan

Kirov

r a v n i n a

Kama

Perm

Syktyvkar

URALSKIYE

Nyagan

Ob

Surgut

S i b i r s k a y a

Yekaterinburg

Irtysh

R U S S I

Saratov

Samara

Ufa

Tyumen

r a v n i n a

Rostov-na-Donu

Volgograd

Don

Volga

g. Yamantau
1640

Chelyabinsk

Ishim

Ob

Toms

BLACK
SEA

Krasnodar

Sochi

Uralsk

Orenburg

Ural

Kustanay

Omsk

Novosibirsk

Keme

g. Elbrus
5642

Astrakhan

Aktyubinsk

GEORGIA

Tbilisi

TURKEY

ARMENIA

Yerevan

Büyük Ağrı dağı
5165

AZERBAIJAN

Baky

KAVKAZ

CASPIAN SEA

plato

Ustyurt

ARAL
SEA

KAZAKHSTAN

Astana

Karaganda

Aksoran
1565

Semey

Barnaul

Novokuzi

▲4506
g. Belukha

Alta

SYRIA

Al-Mawşil

Tabrīz

IRAQ

Baghdād

Tehrān

Elburz

5604
Qolleh-ye Demavand

IRAN

Mashhad

Kühhā-ye Zāgros

Zard Kuh
4548

Esfahān

Al-Basrah

KUWAIT

Yazd

Al-Kuwayt

Turkmenbashi

TURKMENISTAN

Karakumy

Ashgabat

3117▲

Nukus

Kyzylkum

Amudarya

UZBEKISTAN

Syrdarya

Kzyl-Orda

Chu

Balkash

Ile

Semey

Balkash

Samarkand

Tashkent

Bishkek

KYRGYZSTAN

Dushanbe

TAJIKISTAN

g. Garmo
7495

PAMIR

Almaty

Ysyk-Köl

TIEN

7439
pik Pobedy

SHAN

Kashi

Takla Makan

Ürümqi

Dilah

Al-Furat

AFGHANISTAN

Herāt

HINDU KUSH

▲7708

6161

L

A colourful restaurant in Moscow.

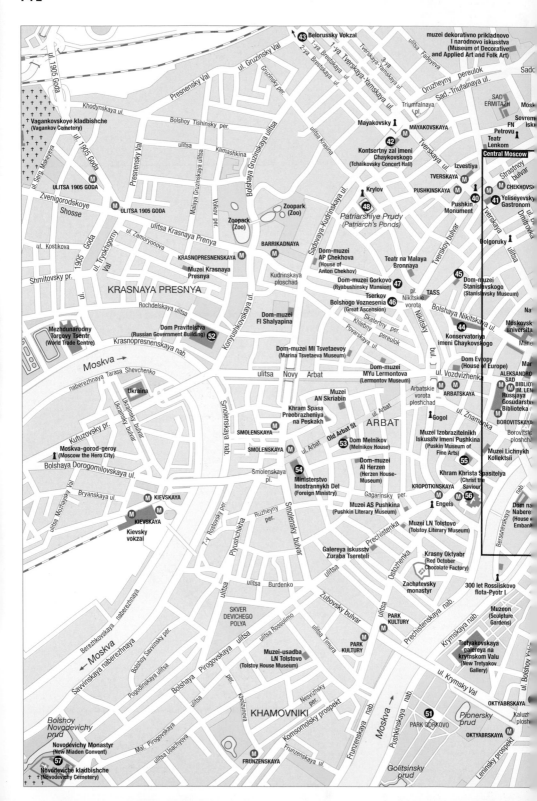

43 Belorussky Vokzal

muzei dekorativno prikladnovo I narodnovo iskusstva (Museum of Decorative and Applied Art and Folk Art)

SAD ERMITAZH

Mosk

Sovrem
FN
iski

Petrovu

Teatr
Lenkom

Central Moscow

Mayakovsky

MAYAKOVSKAYA

42 Kontsertny zal imeni Chaykovskogo (Tchaikovsky Concert Hall)

Izvestiya

TVERSKAYA

Strastnoy
bulvar

CHEKHOVS

Krylov

PUSHKINSKAYA

40

41 Yeliseyevsky Gastronom

Vagankovskoye kladbishche (Vagankov Cemetery)

Khodynskaya ul.

Bolshoy Tishinsky per.

48 Pushkin Monument

Dolgoruky

ULITSA 1905 GODA

ulitsa Klimashkina

ULITSA 1905 GODA

Patriarshiye Prudy (Patriarch's Ponds)

Zvenigorodskoye Shosse

Zoopark (Zoo)

Tverskoy bulvar

Zoopark (Zoo)

ul. Kostikova

BARRIKADNAYA

Dom-muzei AP Chekhova (House of Anton Chekhov)

Teatr na Malaya Bronnaya

45 Dom-muzei Stanislavskogo (Stanislavsky Museum)

Shmitovsky pr.

KRASNOPRESNENSKAYA

Muzei Krasnaya Presnya

Kudrinskaya ploschad

Dom-muzei Gorkovo (Ryabushinsky Mansion) **47**

pl.
Nikitskie
vorota

TASS

Na

KRASNAYA PRESNYA

Tserkov Bolshogo Voznesenia (Great Ascension) **46**

Bolshaya Nikitskaya ul.

Moskovsk
universita

Rochdelskaya ulitsa

Dom-muzei FI Shalyapina

Skateriny Per.
Khlebny pereulok

44 Konservatoriya imeni Chaykovskogo

Mane

Mezhdunarodny Torgovy Tsentr (World Trade Centre)

Dom Pravitelstva (Russian Government Building) **52**

Povarskaya ul.

Dom Evropy (House of Europe)

Mar

ALEKSANDRO
SAD

Krasnopresnenskaya nab.

Dom-muzei MI Tsvetaevoy (Marina Tsvetaeva Museum)

BIBLIO
IM. LEN

Moskva →

ulitsa Novy Arbat

Dom-muzei MYu Lermontova (Lermontov Museum)

ul. Vozdvizhenka

Russjaya
Gosudarstv
Biblioteka

Ukraina

Arbatskie vorota ploshchad

ARBATSKAYA

BOROVITSKAYA

Kutuzovsky pr.

Muzei AN Skriabin

ul. Arbat

ARBAT

ul. Znamenka

Borovitsk
ploshcha

Moskva-gorod-geroy (Moscow the Hero City)

Khram Spasa Preobrazheniya na Peskakh

Gogol

Muzei Izobrazitelnikh Iskusstv imeni Pushkina (Puskin Museum of Fine Arts)

Muzei Lichnykh Kollektsii

Bolshaya Dorogomilovskaya ul.

SMOLENSKAYA

Old Arbat St

53 Dom Melnikov (Melnikov House)

55

Bryanskaya ul.

SMOLENSKAYA

ul. Arbat

Dom-muzei AI Herzen (Herzen House-Museum)

Khram Khrista Spasitelya (Christ the Saviour)

KIEVSKAYA

Smolenskaya pl.

54 Ministerstvo Inostrannykh Del (Foreign Ministry)

KROPOTKINSKAYA

56

KIEVSKAYA

Gagarinsky per.

Engels

Dom na
Nabere
(House
Emban

Kievsky vokzal

Muzei AS Pushkina (Pushkin Literary Museum)

Prechistenka

Muzei LN Tolstovo (Tolstoy Literary Museum)

Krasny Oktyabr (Red October Chocolate Factory)

Galereya iskusstv Zuraba Tsereteli

Ostozhenka

Zachatevsky monastyr

300 let Rossiiskovo flota-Pyotr I

ulitsa Burdenko

Zubovsky bulvar

Muzeon (Sculpture Gardens)

SKVER DEVICHEGO POLYA

PARK KULTURY

Prechistenskaya nab.

Moskva

Berezhkovskaya naberezhnaya

PARK KULTURY

Tretyakovskaya galereya na krymskom Valu (New Tretyakov Gallery)

Muzei-usadba LN Tolstovo (Tolstoy House Museum)

ul. Krymsky Val

Moskva

KHAMOVNIKI

Komsomolsky prospekt

OKTYABRSKAYA

Kaluzh
plosh

Bolshoy Novodevichy prud

51

Pionersky prud

Novodevichy Monastyr (New Miaden Convent)

57

PARK GORKOVO

OKTYABRSKAYA

Novodeviche kladbishche (Novodevichy Cemetery)

Golitsinsky prud

Leninsky prospekt

FRUNZENSKAYA

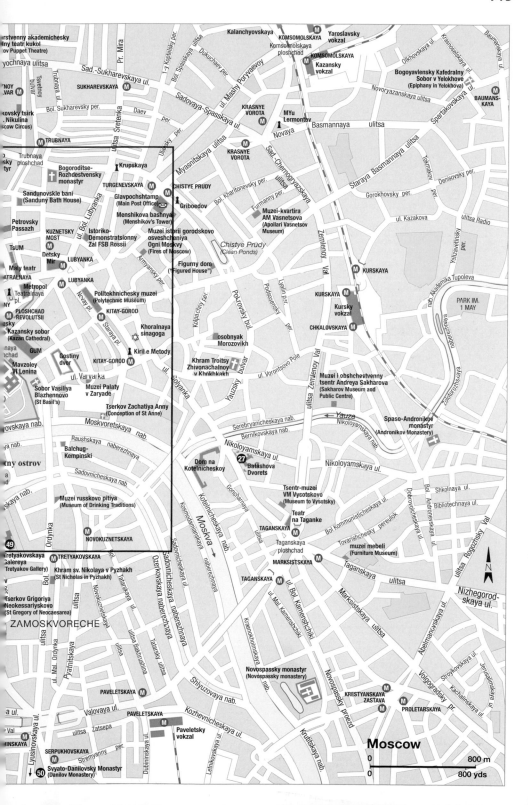

rstvenny akademichesky
ny teatr kukol
ov Puppet Theatre)

yochnaya ulitsa

Sad.-Sukharevskaya ul.

Ⓜ SUKHAREVSKAYA

Trubnaya
bulvar

Tsvetnoy

Ⓜ

'NOY
VAR

ovsky tsirk
. Nikulina
scow Circus)

Bol. Sukharevsky per.

Ⓜ TRUBNAYA

Kalanchyovskaya

KOMSOMOLSKAYA **Ⓜ**

Yaroslavsky
vokzal

Komsomolskaya
ploshchad

KOMSOMOLSKAYA **Ⓜ**

Ⓜ Kazansky
vokzal

Bogoyavlensky Kafedralny
Sobor v Yelokhove
(Epiphany in Yelokhova)

Novoryazanskaya ulitsa

Ⓜ BAUMANS-
KAYA

1-y Kopteisky per.

Bol. Spasskaya per.

Dukuchaev per.

ul. Mashy Poryavevoy

Spartakovskaya ul.

Olkhovskaya ul.

Krasnoselskaya ul.

Baumanskaya ul.

Sadovaya-Spasskaya ul.

KRASNYE
VOROTA

MYu
Lermontov

Novaya

Basmannaya

ulitsa

Staraya Basmannaya ulitsa

Tokmakov

Denisovsky per.

Gorokhovsky per.

ul. Kazakova

ulitsa Radio

Yalizavetinsky
per.

Pr. Mira

Trubnaya
per.

Daev

Sretenka

ulitsa

Ulansky
per.

Myasnitskaya ulitsa

Sad.-Chernogryazskaya
ulitsa

Zemlenoy
Val

Trubnaya
ploshchad
sky
tyr

Bogoroditse-
Rozhdestvensky
monastyr ✝

☦ Krupskaya

Ⓜ TURGENEVSKAYA

Ⓜ CHISTYE PRUDY

Bol. Kharitonevsky per.

Fumanny per.

Muzei-kvartira
AM Vasnetsova
(Apollari Vasnetsov
Museum)

Sandunovskle bani
(Sanduny Bath House)

Ⓜ KRASNYE
VOROTA

Petrovsky
Passazh

Glavpochtamp
(Main Post Office) ✉

✝ Griboedov

KUZNETSKY
MOST

Ⓜ

Menshikova bashnya
(Menshikov's Tower)

TsUM

Istoriko-
Demonstratsionny
Zal FSB Rossii

Muzei istorii gorodskovo
osveshcheniya
Ogni Moskvy
(Fires of Moscow)

Chistye Prudy
(Clean Ponds)

Detsky
Ⓜ Mir

LUBYANKA

Maly teatr

ATRALNAYA

Figurny dom
("Figured House")

Metropol
Teatralnaya
pl.

Ⓜ LUBYANKA

Ⓜ

KURSKAYA

Lyalin per.

Podsosensky
per.

KURSKAYA **Ⓜ**

Kursky
vokzal

nab. Akademika Tupoleva

NY

PLOSHCHAD
REVOLUTSII **Ⓜ**

esky

Politekhnichesky muzei
(Polytechnic Museum)

Nizvy per.

Staraya pl.

Armyansky per.

Pokrovsky bul.

Kolpachny per.

CHKALOVSKAYA **Ⓜ**

PARK IM.
1 MAY

Khoralnaya
sinagoga ✡

osobnyak
Morozovikh

Kazansky sobor
(Kazan Cathedral)

GUM

Gostiny
dvor

Kiril e Metody ☦

Ⓜ KITAY-GOROD

Khram Troitsy
Zhivonachalnoy
v Khokhkakh

Solyanka

ul.

Yauzky

bulvar

ul. Vorontsovo Pole

ulitsa Zemlenoy Val

Muzei i obshchestvenny
tsentr Andreya Sakharova
(Sakharov Museum and
Public Centre)

Zolotorozhsknab

Mavzoley
VI Lenina

ul. Varvarka

Muzei Palaty
v Zaryade

Sobor Vasiliya
Blazhennovo
(St Basil's)

Tserkov Zachatiya Anny
(Conception of St Anne)

Moskvoretskaya nab.

Serebryanicheskaya nab.

Bernikovskaya nab.

Nikoloyamskaya ul.

Nikoloyamskaya nab.

Yauza

Spaso-Andronikov
monastyr
(Andronikov Monastery) ✝

ovskaya nab.

ya nab.

Raushskaya naberezhnaya

Balchug-
Kempinski

Sadovnicheskaya nab.

Dom na
Kotelnicheskoy

27

Balashova
Dvorets

Nikoloyamskaya ul.

Shkolnaya ul.

Bol. Andronevskaya

Bibliotechnaya ul.

ny ostrov
a
d

Muzei russkovo pitiya
(Museum of Drinking Traditions)

Tsentr-muzei
VM Vysotskovo
(Museum to Vysotsky)

Teatr
na Taganke

Bol. Kommunistichesky pereulok

Tovarishchesky pereulok

Dobrovolcheskaya ul.

49

Ⓜ NOVOKUZNETSKAYA

Kotelnicheskaya nab.

Goncharnaya

Moskva

TAGANSKAYA **Ⓜ**

Taganskaya
ploshchad

muzei mebeli
(Furniture Museum)

Taganskaya ulitsa

Nizhegorod-
skaya ul.

Ⓜ Tretyakovskaya
Galereya
(Tretyakov Gallery)

Ⓜ TRETYAKOVSKAYA

Khram sv. Nikolaya v Pyzhakh
(St Nicholas in Pyzhakh)

MARKSISTSKAYA **Ⓜ**

TAGANSKAYA **Ⓜ**

Bol. Kamenshchiki

Marksistskaya ulitsa

Abelmanovskaya ul.

Stroykovskaya ul.

Volgogradsky pr.

Kachalinskaya ul.

Yerusalimskaya ul.

v

Tserkov Grigoriya
Neokessariyskovo
(St Gregory of Neocaesarea)

Novokuznetskaya

ulitsa

Mal. Kamenshchiki

Krasnokholmskaya

N ↑

ZAMOSKVORECHE

Pyatnitskaya

Bol. Ordynka

Mal. Ordynka

Tatarskaya ulitsa

Ozerkovskaya naberezhnaya

Sadovnicheskaya naberezhnaya

Krasnokholmskaya naberezhnaya

Novospassky monastyr
(Novospassky monastery)

Novospassky proezd

Krutitskaya nab.

PAVELETSKAYA **Ⓜ**

KRESTYANSKAYA
ZASTAVA **Ⓜ**

Ⓜ PROLETARSKAYA

a ul.

Valovaya ul.

PAVELETSKAYA **Ⓜ**

ulitsa Zatsepa

Shlyuzovaya nab.

Kozhevnicheskaya nab.

Ⓜ

Paveletsky
vokzal

Dubininskaya ul.

Lyusinovskaya ul.

Val ul.

Ⓜ

NSKAYA

SERPUKHOVSKAYA

Stremyanny per.

Letnikovskaya nab.

50

Svyato-Danilovsky Monastyr
(Danilov Monastery)

Moscow

0 | | 800 m

0 | | 800 yds

MOSCOW

Russia's capital beckons exploration.
Here domed cathedrals, Baroque palaces and
towering Soviet edifices compete for attention
amid the bustle of modern city life.

Moscow's first mention in historic chronicles is a brief note written in 1147 indicating that there was a small settlement surrounded by small hills on the banks of the Moskva River. Such limited mention is not surprising: Moscow lay on the extreme borders of the Suzdal Knyazhestvo (principality), the centre of which was far to the southwest in Kiev. When Prince Yuri Dolgoruky arrived in 1156, Moscow must have been no more than a cluster of wooden huts. However, he saw its potential as a trading outpost and ordered a kremlin (fort) to be built.

Historians believe the name Moskva derives from an old Slavonic word meaning "wet", probably an allusion to the marshy countryside that surrounded the site. The broad Moskva River winds through the city and used to be swelled by a number of smaller streams and rivers, so the site was ideal for a fortress. However, the Tatars still torched it at regular intervals, even after Grand Prince Ivan Kalita ("Moneybags") built stone walls around the settlement in the early 14th century. The walls were made of limestone and earned Moscow the name "belokamennaya" (literally "of white-stone").

As Ivan Kalita's power and prestige grew, so did Moscow. But his real coup

was managing to persuade the Russian Metropolitan to move the Holy See from Vladimir to Moscow. As chief centre of both religious and secular power, Moscow was on the map. The city blossomed during the reign of Ivan III, in the late 15th century. Ivan dealt with the Tatars effectively and was the first prince to take the title "tsar", the Russianised form of Caesar. To match his new status, he imported Italian architects to create a new kremlin. Many of the cathedrals and walls they built still stand.

Main Attractions

Kremlin
Red Square
St Basil's Cathedral
Bolshoi Theatre
Tretyakov Gallery
Gorky Park
Arbat
Cathedral of Christ the Saviour

The entrance to Red Square.

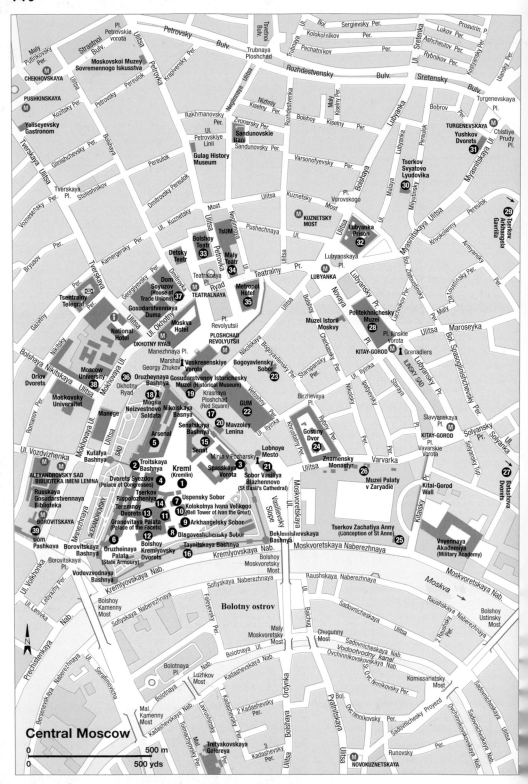

Central Moscow

Pl.
Petrovskie
vorota

Maly
Putinkovsky
Per.

Strastnoi
Bulv.

Petrovsky
Bulv.

Tsvetnoi
Bulv.

Trubnaya
Ploshchad

Bol.
Sergievsky Per.

Kolokolnikov
Per.

Lukov Per.

Ashcheulov
Per.

Prosvirin.
Per.

Rybnikov
Per.

Kostiansky Per.

Ulansky Per.

PUSHKINSKAYA

Moskovskoi Muzey
Sovremennogo Iskusstva

Kozitsky Per.

Petrovka

Krapivensky Per.

Rozhdestvensky

Bulv.

Sretensky
Bulv.

Turgenevskaya
Pl.

Chistiye
Prudy Pl.

Yeliseyevsky
Gastronom

Tverskaya
Ulitsa

Glinishchevsky Per.

Pereulok

Rakhmanovsky
Per.

Ul.
Petrovskiye
Linii

Ul. Kuznetsky

Nizhniy
Kiselny Per.

Zvonarsky Per.

Maly
Kiselny Per.

Bolshoy
Kiselny Per.

Lubyanka

Bobrov
Per.

TURGENEVSKAYA

Yushkov
Dvorets

31

Tserkov
Arkhangela
Gavriila

29

Dmitrovsky Pereulok

Gulag History
Museum

Sandunovsky Per.

Sandunovskie
Bani

Varsonofyevsky
Per.

Pl.
Vorovskogo

Ul.

Tserkov
Svyatovo
Lyudovika

30

Milyutinsky

Tverskaya
Pl.

Stoleshnikov
Per.

Kamergersky Per.

Detsky
Teatr

Bolshoy
Teatr
33

TsUM

Maly
Teatr
34

Pushechnaya

Ul.

Pl.
Vorovskogo

KUZNETSKY
MOST

Lubyanka
Prison

32

Lubyanskaya
Pl.

LUBYANKA

Politekhnichesky Per.

Krivokolenny

Armyansky

Tserkov
Svyatovo
Lyudovika

Voznesensky
Per.

Bryusov
Per.

Georgievsky Per.

Dom
Soyuzov
(House of
Trade Unions)
37

Teatralnaya
Pl.

Ryad

TEATRALNAYA

Metropol
Hotel
35

Novaya
Pl.

Lubyansky Pr.

Bol. Zlatoustinsky Per.

Maly

Zlatoustinsky Per.

Loussinsky Per.

Zirz

Maroseyka
Ulitsa

Tsentralny
Telegraf

Gosudarstvennaya
Duma

Ul. Okhotny

Moskva
Hotel

Pl.
Revolyutsii

PLOSHCHAD
REVOLYUTSII

Muzei Istorii
Moskvy

Politekhnichesky
Muzei
28

Pl. Ilinskie
vorota

Ilinsky sad

Bol. Spasoglinishchevsky Per.

National
Hotel

OKHOTNY RYAD

Manezhnaya Pl.

Marshal
Georgy Zhukov

Voskresenskiye
Vorota

Nikolskaya

Bogoyavlensky
Sobor
23

KITAY-GOROD

Grenadiers

Slavyanskaya
Pl.

Orlov
Dvorets

Moscow
University
38

Oruzheynaya
Bashnya
36

Okhotny
Ryad

Gosudarstvenny Istorichesky
Muzei (Historical Museum)
19

Bogoyavlensky Per.

Staropansky Per.

Cherkassky Per.

Ul. Ilyinka

Nikolsky

Ipatievsky Per.

Slavyanskaya
Pl.

KITAY-GOROD

Moskovsky
Universitet

Manege

Mogila
Neizvestnovo
Soldata
18

Nikolskaya
Basnya

Krasnaya
Ploshchad
(Red Square)
17

GUM
22

Birzhevaya
Pl.

Gostiny
Dvor
24

Vavarsky
Vorota

27

Bashova
Dvorets

Arsenal
5

Senatskaya
Bashnya

Senat

Mavzoley
Lenina

Znamensky
Monastyr
26

Kutafya
Bashnya

Troitskaya
Bashnya
2

Minin v Pozharsky

Lobnoye
Mesto

Varvarka

Ulitsa

Muzei Palaty
v Zaryadie

Kitai-Gorod
Wall

ALEXANDROVSKY SAD
BIBLIOTEKA IMENI LENINA

Dvorets
Syezdov
(Palace of Congresses)
4

Kreml
(Kremlin)
1

Spasskaya
Vorota
3

Sobor Vasiliya
Blazhennovo
(St Basil's Cathedral)

Beklemishevskaya
Bashnya

Tserkov Zachatiya Anny
(Conception of St Anne)
25

Voyennaya
Akademiya
(Military Academy)

Russkaya
Gosudarstvennaya
Biblioteka

BOROVITSKAYA

Tserkov
Rispolozheniya
14

Teremnoy
Dvorets
13

Uspensky Sobor
7

Kolokolnya Ivana Velikogo
(Bell Tower of Ivan the Great)
10

Arkhangelsky Sobor
9

Vasilievsky
Slope

Moskvoretsky
Most

Dom
Pashkova

39

Granovitaya Palata
(Palace of the Facets)

Borovitskaya
Bashnya

6

Oruzheinaya
Palata
(State Armoury)

Bolshoy
Kremlyovsky
Dvorets

Blagoveshchensky Sobor

Taynitskaya Bashnya
16

Kremlyovskaya Nab.

Moskvoretskaya Naberezhnaya

Bolshoy
Moskvoretsky
Most

Moskva

Bolshoy
Ustinsky
Most

Uom
Pashkova

Borovitskaya
Pl.

Vodovzvodnaya
Bashnya

Kremlyovskaya Nab.

Sofiyskaya Naberezhnaya

Raushskaya Naberezhnaya

Sadovnicheskaya Naberezhnaya

Ul. Volkhonka

Ul. Lenivka
Nab.

Bolshoy
Kamenny
Most

Bolotny ostrov

Maly
Moskvoretsky
Most

Chugunny
Most

Vodootvodny kanal

Ovchinnikovskaya Nab.

Komissariatsky
Most

Prechistenskaya Naberezhnaya

Serafimovicha

Sofiyskaya Naberezhnaya

Bolotnaya
Pl.

Luzhkov
Most

Kadashevskaya Naberezhnaya

Sadovnicheskaya Ul.

Bol.
Pyatnitsky Per.

2 Raushsky
Per.

Bersenevskaya Naberezhnaya

Mal.
Kamenny
Most

Bolotnaya Ul.

Lavrushinsky Per.

Kadashevskaya Nab.

Tolmachevsky Per.

Ordynka

Bol.
Ovchinnikovsky Per.

Sadovnicheskaya Ul.

Tretyakovskaya
Galereya

2 Kadashevsky
Per.

Ulitsa

Runovsky
Per.

NOVOKUZNETSKAYA

0   500 m

0   500 yds

The Kremlin

When the Italian architects Fioravanti, Ruffo and Solari had finished their job in 1495, praise was effusive and another "eighth wonder of the world" was added to that already lengthy list. But the accolade was not entirely undeserved. The imposing red-brick walls running around the **Kremlin ❶** (www.kreml.ru; Fri–Wed 10am–5pm) are 2,230 metres (7,316 ft) long, 20 metres (66 ft) high and 6 metres (20 ft) wide in some places. It has four gates and 20 towers. Inside, the Italians created three stone cathedrals to replace the more humble structures that existed before. These came to symbolise tsarist power: the Uspensky was used for coronations, the Blagoveshchensky for baptisms and weddings, and the Arkhangelsky for funerals.

The main entrance for visitors is the **Troitskaya Bashnya ❷** (Trinity Tower) that crosses Alexandrovsky Gardens and the Neglinka River (which was channelled into a large stone underground pipe in the 19th century). In pre-Revolutionary times this gate was used for regal entrances. Napoleon, in 1812, obviously didn't know this – although his army entered the Kremlin this way, he used the **Spasskaya Vorota ❸** (Spassky Gate). He is supposed to have lost his famous tricorn hat in the process, making it unlucky, according to popular lore, to pass through the Spassky Tower wearing a hat.

At one time the Kremlin was considered almost impregnable. Its southeastern side is protected by the Moskva, and a deep moat, which once linked the Moskva and Neglinka rivers, takes care of the remaining walls. The **Arsenalnaya Bashnya** (Arsenal Tower) had its own well, which fed a secret reservoir and an underground passage to the Neglinka River. During long sieges, the garrison could thus come and go as they pleased.

Although the Russian tricolour now flutters above the Kremlin, the symbols of Soviet power are still apparent in the red stars topping five of the towers. These have been there so long (since 1937) that most Muscovites just accept them as part of the structure. Another Soviet relic is the steel and glass **Dvorets Syezdov ❹** (Palace of Congresses) that was planted in the middle of the Kremlin in 1961. Once the venue for Party congresses, it is now used for operas, ballets and the city's most lavish concerts. In 2008 Deep Purple put on a bash for the oil giant Gazprom with Vladimir Putin and big fan Dmitry Medvedev in the best seats.

Several ancient monasteries inside the Kremlin walls were demolished in Soviet times, but the complex retains its ancient beauty. The former **Arsenal ❺** buildings were constructed by Peter the Great between 1701 and 1736 and its facades are hung with Napoleonic military trophies. The **Oruzheinaya Palata ❻** (State Armoury) at the foot of the **Borovitsky Bashnya** (tower) houses the oldest Kremlin museum and is perhaps the highpoint of any visit. It contains lots of armour, but pride of place goes to the valuables

FACT

Trams, buses and trolleybuses operate from 5.30am to 1am. You'll need a talon (ticket), obtainable in strips from street kiosks, the conductor or the driver.

Rush hour outside the Kremlin.

The Cap of Kazan, made for Ivan the Terrible in the 16th century to mark his victory over the Tatars in Kazan, features in the Armoury Museum collection.

Bell Tower of Ivan the Great soaring behind the red-brick Kremlin wall.

accumulated by the Russian tsars, in particular diamonds and jewellery. You'll need a separate time-specific ticket to enter the Armoury, which you should buy at the Kremlin gates.

The three original cathedrals still dominate the heart of the Kremlin, with the grandiose **Uspensky Sobor** ❼ (Cathedral of the Dormition), built by Fioravanti, as centrepiece. This is a prime example of European Renaissance building combined with Byzantine traditions. Inside is a remarkable collection of frescoes devoted mainly to the Virgin Mary, in addition to the famous 14th-century Trinity icon. It is here that the city's bishops and patriarchs were interred.

To the south is the contemporary **Blagoveshchensky Sobor** ❽ (Cathedral of the Annunciation), which was built as a private church for Moscow's Grand Princes. The cathedral started life as a three-domed, galleried building in the Pskov style (Ivan III had opted for Russian rather than foreign stonemasons for this particular project). As this was essentially a private church, the builders set it on a very

high foundation so that its entrance would be accessible from the second floor of the royal palace. Over the centuries more chapels and cupolas were added, giving the church an eclectic appearance. The extended porch, called the Ivan the Terrible steps, was added so that the tsar could hear services after he was banned from entering – a punishment for having so many wives and concubines.

Built on the site of a wooden structure of the same name, it inherited the original church's iconostasis, painted by two of the greatest names in Russian iconography: Feofan the Greek and Andrei Rublyov. Its floor is tiled with agate and jasper, a gift from the Shah of Persia. Portraits of the Grand Princes hang alongside biblical fathers and Greek and Roman luminaries such as Aristotle, Plutarch and Virgil.

Next to the Annunciation is the **Arkhangelsky Sobor** ❾ (Archangel Cathedral), a 14th-century church rebuilt in the early years of the 16th century by Venetian architect Alevisio, nicknamed Novy (the new), because an Italian of the same name had worked in Moscow before him. It was here that the princes and tsars were buried until Peter the Great built his new capital in 1712. Ivan the Terrible's tomb is hidden behind the iconostasis.

The Kremlin's focal point is the **Kolokolnya Ivana Velikogo** ❿ (Bell Tower of Ivan the Great). Started by Ivan, it was augmented by Boris Godunov. At 81 metres (265 ft), it is still the tallest structure in the Kremlin. It carries the inscription: "By the grace of the Holy Trinity and by order of the Tsar and Grand Prince Boris Fyodorovich, Autocrat of all Russia, this temple was finished and gilded in the second year of their reign." The tower's 21 bells, including the 64-tonne Resurrection Bell, are rung on religious holidays. Inside you'll find a 21st-century interactive exhibition on the Kremlin's architecture.

Ivan III was a prolific builder. The **Granovitaya Palata** ⓫ (Palace of the

Facets) is perhaps the most fabulous of the secular buildings he initiated. Unlike any other structure in Moscow, the palace is a pure example of Italian Renaissance architecture, designed by Ruffo and Solario. It was here that the tsars received foreign ambassadors and other dignitaries and the whole place was decorated as a showpiece. The frescoes are painted on backgrounds of gold, and you'll even find a portrait of Ivan the Terrible in the guise of the "Just Knight" in the Hall of Facets.

These are the oldest buildings in the Kremlin, but over the centuries myriad others have been erected between them. Until the modern Palace of Congresses was built, the most recent was the 700-room **Bolshoy Kremlyovsky Dvorets** ⑫ (Great Kremlin Palace) built by Konstantin Ton, architect of the Cathedral of Christ the Saviour. The first floor of the palace is devoted to the royal family's private chambers (including one for the Russian president that is off limits to visitors). The two-storey high second floor has the Kremlin's most luxurious state halls, where presidents are sworn in and the most important ceremonies held. These halls were returned to their pre-Revolutionary glory under Boris Yeltsin. Just in front is the spectacular **Teremnoy Dvorets** ⑬ (Terem Palace), now sadly closed to the public. Built along the lines of traditional wooden houses, it was first occupied by Mikhail Romanov's family. The first of his line, Mikhail (1613–45), and later his son Alexis, used this palace to conduct state affairs. It was meant to convey the power and unity of the Russian state so the interiors are lavish indeed.

Tucked between the Uspensky and Palace of the Facets is the tiny **Tserkov Rizopolozheniya** ⑭ (Church of the Deposition of the Robe), which was commissioned by Patriarch Geronty in 1480. The church was built by masons from Pskov. Initially, it served as a private chapel for the Russian patriarchs, but it was requisitioned by the Romanovs for their own use in 1653. Now it houses a small exhibition of icons and religious wooden sculpture.

The Patriarch's Palace and Church of the Twelve Apostles (Patriarshie palaty i Tserkov Dvenadtsati apostolov) was

Inside the Armoury Museum.

*The iconic St Basil's
Cathedral at night.*

completed in 1656 and now houses
a Museum of 17th-Century Life and
Applied Art, with religious treasures
and a room reconstructed to be a medieval boyar's (nobleman's) chambers.

The eastern side of the Kremlin
is reserved for government buildings. The main structure is late 18th-
century and was designed by Matvei
Kazakov for the Moscow Department
of the Senate, which was then located
in St Petersburg. After the Revolution,
Moscow became the capital and the
top floor of the **Senat** ⑮ was used by
Lenin as an apartment building from
1918 to 1923. It's now the epicentre of
Russian state power.

Although the buildings inside the
Kremlin are the main attractions,
some of the 20 towers that line the
walls are worth mentioning. The oldest, **Taynitskaya Bashnya** ⑯ (Tower
of Secrets) in the southern wall, has
fascinated scholars for centuries. It has
an underground passage to the river,
but it is also thought to have been
the site of Ivan the Terrible's famous
library. The collection was started by
his grandmother, Sofia Paleologue,

who brought a wealth of manuscripts
to Moscow as part of her dowry. Some
believe the library is still hidden
beneath the Kremlin walls, probably
under the Arsenal Tower overlooking the Alexandrovsky Gardens. The
newest tower (1680) is the small Tsar's
Tower where Ivan the Terrible reput-
edly watched life on Red Square.

Another of the towers that shouldn't
be missed is the **Spasskaya Bashnya**
(Spassky Tower) located by the Spasskaya Vorota. Built in 1625, its Gothic
and Renaissance splendour served
as a fitting background for the state
entrances of the tsars. In the 20th century, the guard of honour for Lenin's
mausoleum passed through here on
the choreographed march to the revolutionary's tomb.

Red Square

Touching the wall as you leave the
Kremlin is supposed to bring you luck
and ensure your return. **Krasnaya
ploshchad** ⑰ (Red Square) adjoins
the eastern side of the Kremlin, but to
get there you have to leave the Kremlin through Trinity Gate and walk
through **Alexandrovsky Gardens**,
with its lime trees and remarkable
19th-century grotto in the Kremlin's
wall, past the **Mogila Neizvestnovo
Soldata** ⑱ (Tomb of the Unknown
Soldier) – a popular spot for wedding
pictures – and turn right. The turreted
red-brick building on your left is the
Gosudarstvenny Istorichesky Muzei
⑲ (Historical Museum; Wed and Fri–
Mon 10am–6pm; last entry one hour
before closing time), which houses a
rare collection of artefacts tracing Russian history up to the present day.

Red Square started life as the eastern
moat protecting the Kremlin, but this
was eventually filled in and the resulting square was cobbled in the 15th century. For much of its history the square
was crammed to bursting point with
wooden market stalls where merchants
from all over the world set up shop.
The whole place formed a major fire
hazard and the Great Fire of Moscow

that destroyed much of the old city in 1737 started here.

The **Mavzoley Lenina** ⓴ (Lenin Mausoleum; Tue–Thu, Sat–Sun 10am–1pm), which partially obscures the red Kremlin wall, still houses the great man's embalmed body – join the queue to see his waxen features but put your camera away or risk a ticking off from the strict guards. The building itself was designed by Shchusev in 1930.

The area of the Kremlin wall between the Nikolskaya and Senatskaya towers is the burial place of top Soviet statesmen, public figures and military leaders. Here lie such names as Leonid Brezhnev, Maxim Gorky, Lenin's wife Nadezhda Krupskaya; first cosmonaut Yuri Gagarin, nuclear physicist Igor Kurchatov, and John Reed, the American journalist whose book on the birth and early years of the Russian Revolution, *Ten Days That Shook the World*, was a revelation to subsequent generations of Marxists throughout the Western world. It describes Western governments' attempts to undermine and destroy the Revolution, and until the 1960s seemed to explain and even justify the burgeoning paranoia and suspicion of the young Soviet state.

Sobor Vasiliya Blazhennovo ㉑ (St Basil's Cathedral; daily 11am–5pm) is to Moscow what the Eiffel Tower is to Paris, or Big Ben is to London. It is essentially Muscovite, a fantastic swirl of shapes, colours, textures and patterns that dominates the square and symbolises the extravagance of the Russian spirit. Ivan the Terrible commissioned St Basil's, more properly known as the Church of the Intercession on the Moat, to commemorate major victories over the Tatars. Every victory (nine in all) added a new chapel to the structure, each one dedicated to the saint on whose day the victory was won. The whole golden-domed complex became known as St Basil's when one of the chapels was dedicated to Basil the Blessed, a holy man revered by the tsar.

In the 17th century, Red Square became a centre of political debate and was the venue for many popular uprisings. The **Lobnoye Mesto** (a raised circular platform in front of the cathedral) was used for religious services and for reading tsarist decrees. Later the leader of the 1671 peasant revolt, Stenka Razin, was executed here and in 1648 the Streltsy mutineers and supporters of Tsarina Sofia, Peter the Great's half-sister, also met their deaths on Red Square. But for most of its history, the square was the trading centre of the capital city, covered with wooden booths that sold everything to be found in the vast kingdom.

It's hard to judge just how the wooden city of Moscow looked because Muscovites put it to the torch in order to frustrate the imminent arrival of Napoleon and his troops in 1812. By the time Napoleon arrived he found the buildings in flames and anybody who was anybody, and a lot who weren't, gone.

In retrospect, you could say Moscow should be grateful to Napoleon. The reconstruction transformed the

For a few roubles, you can have your picture taken next to a 'Soviet general' in Red Square.

Tomb of the Unknown Soldier, a popular spot for wedding pictures.

The 40-ton bronze Tsar Cannon was cast in a Moscow foundry in 1586. The biggest cannon in the world, it was once positioned in Red Square to repel enemy attacks, but never fired a shot.

The colourful domes of St Basil's Cathedral.

city from a medieval warren of small alleys and streets into an elegant capital whose main streets and quarters were dominated by stylish mansions. In charge of the massive project was an architect called Osip Bovet. He restored the Kremlin wall and rebuilt the shopping galleries that lined the eastern side of Red Square. These were later replaced by the still magnificent **GUM** ㉒ building, with its pastel interiors and ornate fountain. GUM opened in 1893, was nationalised in 1921 and celebrated its centenary by returning to the private sector following an auction of the retail units that make up what was once the most up-market shopping mall in Russia. In the late 19th century another red-brick building was added to the northern end of Red Square, just opposite the Historical Museum. It housed the city's Duma or council until the Revolution. After Lenin's death it became a museum devoted to the father of the country and housed the city legislature, both of which have now moved to other locations.

On Manezhnaya Square, just off to the right of Red Square, is the **Voskresenskiye Vorota** (Resurrection Gate) a replica of the 1680 gateway rebuilt in 1995. The original was pulled down by Stalin to make way for the tanks that used to roll across Red Square on revolutionary holidays. Next to the gate is the **statue of Marshal Georgy Zhukov**, who led the Soviet Army to victory over Germany in 1945.

Moscow's ring roads

The Kremlin and Red Square may have been the heart of the original city, but its arteries were the old quarters that clustered around them. The city was built in rings, with main roads to important towns, such as Smolensk, Tver and Kaluga, radiating in a wagon-wheel pattern that still exists today. Not surprisingly, these roads became major thoroughfares and until the Revolution were simply named after the places they led to. Since 1917 they have had different names – Kalininsky prospekt (now Novy Arbat), ulitsa Gorkogo (now Tverskaya) and Leninsky prospekt respectively. In day-to-day

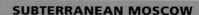

speech and on street signs most of them have reverted back to their original names. Other street names are clues to the trades and businesses once conducted there, e.g. Meshchanskaya (Petty Bourgeois Street), Zhivoderka (Abattoir Road) or are derived from a monastery or church.

The Kremlin formed the central ring, and was followed by the former **Kitay-Gorod wall**, which bordered the Kremlin to the northeast. This wall was 2.5 km (4 miles) long and had 14 towers and several gates. Built in the mid-16th century around the original marketplace, its name may be derived from the Mongolian word for "middle", i.e. middle fortress or from the word *kita*, meaning "wattle". These walls have not survived, but remains can be seen on Teatralnaya ploshchad, close to the Metropol Hotel, and on Kitaisky prospekt in Zaryadye.

The third ring accounts for Moscow's reputation as the "white city". These walls ran 9 km (5 miles) along what is now the **Bulvarnoye Koltso** (Boulevard Ring), had 10 gates and 17 blind towers, and were built of white stone. They were constructed in the early 16th century and served as a sturdy defence for the outskirts of Moscow until they were eventually demolished in the late 18th century.

The final ring, **Zemlyanoy Val** (Earthern Wall), was constructed at the end of the 16th century and was really a rampart. Two hundred years later it was replaced by gardens which gave their name to a whole area: the **Sadovoye Koltso** (Garden Ring) follows the course of the original ramparts.

Moscow of merchants and nobles

Many of the old streets of Kitay-Gorod lost a lot of their original charm at the same time as the old walls were demolished. This was one of Moscow's liveliest quarters and runs due east from the north end of Red Square. **Nikolskaya** was known as the "street of enlightenment" as the city's first higher education facility, the Slavonic-Greek-Latin Academy, was located at Nos 7–9. Further up the street on the same side is a magnificent Russian Gothic building with a sundial adorning its

GUM, Moscow's upmarket shopping centre.

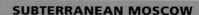

SUBTERRANEAN MOSCOW

Moscow has a secret which the Kremlin regime now keeps very secret indeed: an underground city with one section beneath the suburb of Ramenki about 6 km (4 miles) southwest of Red Square. It was designed to accommodate up to 30,000 party élite and their families for as long as 30 years in the event of a nuclear war. Ivan the Terrible laid the foundations of subterranean Moscow to give his *oprichniki* militia secret access from his palace to various parts of the city. The KGB, the de facto successor to the *oprichniki*, built a tunnel to ferry prisoners from prison to their headquarters. But these efforts were nothing compared to the refinements of Leonid Brezhnev in the 1960s and 1970s. The Ramenki complex was built on several levels over 202 hectares (500 acres) with streets wide enough to take cars. It has its own metro linking it to central Moscow and Vnukovo airport. There are cinemas and swimming pools, and warehouses filled with food.

As for the old jest about Moscow's "wedding-cake" ministry buildings being perilously close to the breaking strain of the earth's crust, it seems that they are almost as deep underground as they are tall, and each has its own stop on the private "Metro 2" and other concealed links with Moscow's underground warren.

facade. Built in 1814 as the Orthodox Synod's printing house, it printed the first books in Russian. Today, it is the History and Archives Institute.

Turning right into **Bogoyavlensky Pereulok** you'll see the magnificent **Bogoyavlensky Sobor** ㉓ (Church of the Epiphany) on your right, parts of which are 13th-century, but whose main facade is a typical example of 17th-century Moscow Baroque. It was founded in 1296 by Prince Daniel Nevsky, the same man who built a string of fortified monasteries, including the Danilov, around the city. Ilyinka used to be the Moscow equivalent of Wall Street, but during the Soviet era the bank buildings and the Mercantile Exchange (at No. 6) were confiscated and turned into public offices – the Exchange became the Soviet Chamber of Commerce and Industry. Contemporary photographs show a lively commercial street cluttered with bright advertisements. Today, state buildings overshadow the narrow street.

If you go right into **Ilyinka ulitsa** you'll see the **Gostiny Dvor** ㉔ (Old

Ilyinka ulitsa.

Merchant Arcade), another of the city's famous shopping arcades. When it was completed in 1805 by the Italian architect Quarenghi it was considered a major accomplishment. Its elegant, white Corinthian pillars still retain their original magic. The building, which was warehouse space for decades, has now been restored to its original glamour.

Parallel to Ilyinka is ulitsa **Varvarka**. Little remains of the old street. Around 20 tiny churches and a number of houses were demolished to make way for the staggering **Rossiya Hotel** complex, an eyesore the city tore down some years ago. But a stretch of the old Kitai-Gorod wall is still extant, along with the small **Tserkov Zachatiya Anny** ㉕ (Church of the Conception of St Anne), which was built at the time of Columbus's voyage to America.

To the right you'll see the Vasilievsky Slope running down to the **Bolshoy Moskvoretsky Most** (Bridge), which German teenager Matthias Rust used as a landing strip on his extraordinary flight to Moscow in the mid-1980s.

The world held its breath when it was revealed that a teenager in a light plane had managed to dodge Soviet radar. As detente was well established and the Cold War beginning to thaw, most people thought Rust would be sent home with a slapped wrist. In the event, the Soviets imprisoned him for a short period before quietly letting him go home – on a scheduled flight, of course.

The humble-looking white-stone, wooden-roofed building is the **Old English Court** (4 ulitsa Varvarka; Tue, Sat–Sun 10am–6pm, Wed, Fri 11am–7pm), where English merchants ran their businesses. Next door is the **Znamensky Monastyr** (Monastery of the Sign), with its five domes. Started in 1684, the belfry was added in 1789. The building beside it (No. 10) was the home of Mikhail Romanov, the first tsar of the dynasty that ruled Russia for more than three centuries. The house had fallen into disrepair, but in the late 19th century it was restored. Now a museum, the **Muzei Palaty v Zaryadie** ㉖ (Thu–Mon 10am–5pm, Wed 11am–6pm), shows how the ancient Russian nobility lived. The interiors are simply stunning.

Slavyanskaya ploshchad runs northwest and if you cross it at its southern end you turn right onto **ulitsa Solyanka** (Salt Street). For centuries, this eastern quarter was the centre of the artisans' guilds and it became notorious in the 19th century for prostitutes, brothels and criminals. The central marketplace at the top of **Podkolokolny Pereulok** was known as the Khitrovo, and the pickpockets who thrived there were said to be so clever that they once stole a bronze cannon from the grounds of the Kremlin. To escape public disgrace, the Governor-General of Moscow ordered his men to find the cannon at all costs. As usual, the local police set up a meeting with the criminal bosses and the cannon was back in its place the next day. But there's a twist to the tale. It was discovered that the returned cannon had itself been stolen from the opposite side of the Kremlin wall; the first cannon was never recovered.

You can easily spend a couple of hours in this picturesque quarter

The Mayakovsky Museum, 3/6 Lubyansky proezd, is devoted to the life of the poet Vladimir Mayakovsky, who worked here before his suicide in 1930 (open Fri–Tue 10am–5pm, Thur 1–8pm).

Old English Court.

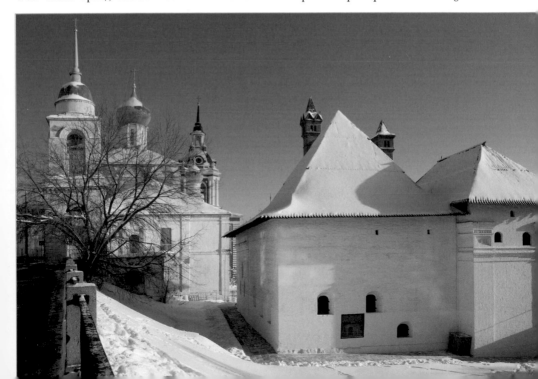

The imposing Polytechnic Museum is devoted to technological advances in such fields as mining, electronics and space travel.

The Kotelnicheskoy apartments in Taganskaya.

which is bordered by the Yauza River whose embankment makes a pleasant walk up to the **Yauza Boulevard**, the starting point of the Boulevard Ring. Solyanka and the main thoroughfares in the vicinity were popular residential streets for the nobility. Most of their mansion homes have either disappeared or have been turned into institutes or academies. The former home of the Naryshkin family at 14a is now the Obstetrics Institute. Peter the Great's mother was a Naryshkin and the family liked to remind everyone of its royal connections, so the palace they built (all gone now) had more than its share of pomp and circumstance. The Court of Wards erected in the 1820s and the 18th-century Foundling Hospital at Nos 14 and 16 are now the buildings of the Academy of Medical Science. Solyanka runs into Yauzskaya and ends up in **Taganskaya**. Worth seeing is the former **Batashova Dvorets ㉗** (Palace) at No. 1, another aristocratic legacy. Now the 23rd City Hospital, the palatial building set back off the street in its own landscaped gardens is a real jewel.

On Slavyanskaya ploshchad, you could opt to walk up Lubyansky Proyezd and turn right onto **ulitsa Maroseika**. To your left in the central garden you'll see the **monument to the Grenadiers** killed at the battle of Plevna during the Russo–Turkish War in 1887. At the top of the square is the **Politekhnichesky Muzei ㉘** (Polytechnic Museum), which was built between 1874 and 1907. It houses more than 40,000 exhibits tracing the development of Russian technology and science but has been closed for years for renovation work (a new museum has been promised for 2018).

The old embassy quarter

A walk along ulitsa Maroseika, which runs into Pokrovka, takes you into the old embassy quarter. Numerous embassies can still be found here and in the area around **Chistiye Prudy** (Clean Ponds). Like most old cities, certain quarters of Moscow came to be associated with particular nationalities. In Ivan the Terrible's day, much of the land behind the Clean Ponds was owned by German merchants. To the northwest, the French set up shops in the streets around Malaya Lubyanka; the English and Poles gravitated to Myasnitskaya Street. By the end of the 17th century, Moscow's wealthy *boyars* had bought up much of the land and built opulent palaces.

A cluster of noble dynasties dominated the area – the Dolgoruky family lived on Kolpachny Pereulok 1, the Lopukhins at Starosadsky 5, and the Botkins at Petroverigsky Pereulok 4 – all to the southwest of Chistiye Prudy. Their grand palaces are overshadowed by the splendid **Tserkov Arkhangela Gavriila ㉙** (Church of the Archangel Gabriel) on Archangelsky Lane. Grand Prince Menshikov had the church built in the early 18th century and the tower still bears his name. Menshikov's aim was to top the Kremlin Bell Tower. It was the tallest building in Moscow and an old tsarist decree prevented the erection of anything

higher. The Grand Prince was something of a favourite with Peter the Great, but when the tower was struck by lightning in 1722 no one lifted a finger to put out the ensuing fire which consumed the giant bronze statue of Gabriel mounted on top. The disaster was seen as a sign of God's displeasure with the tsar's favourite. Muscovites had good reason to be angry with the tsar – he had moved the capital to St Petersburg some years earlier, relegating Moscow to provincial status. Another church worth seeing is **Tserkov Svyatovo Lyudovika** ❸⓿ (St Ludovic's; Lubyanka Malaya 12). It's a working Catholic church founded by the French in the early 19th century.

Myasnitskaya to Lubyanka

The corner of ulitsa Myasnitskaya and Turgenevskaya ploshchad is dominated by what remains of the grand **Yushkov Dvorets** ❸❶ (Palace), built in the late 18th century by architect Vasily Bazhenov, when most of the aristocracy became interested in philanthropy and art collections. The Yushkov family were famous for their elegant parties. It is said that one Yushkov scion held a soirée that lasted three days – it ended only when the whole district had become disrupted by the crowds that had come to gape at the fireworks, music and the gorgeously dressed guests. Since 1844 the Yushkov Palace has housed the Academy of Art and Sculpture.

Next door is an amazing looking building that was constructed in the late 19th century for the tea-merchant Perlov. He was hoping to entertain the Chinese emperor's ambassador during Nicholas II's coronation celebrations so the classical three-storey house-cum-tea-shop was topped by a Chinese pagoda. The envoy never turned up, but the pagoda still graces the roof.

A statue of Felix Dzerzhinsky, Lenin's closest associate and founder of the KGB, once cast a stony stare over Moscow's citizens in Lubyanskaya ploshchad. It was one of the first to go following the unsuccessful coup against Mikhail Gorbachev and his reformers in 1991. The busy square now has its old name back, although it also has some creepy connotations.

Lubyanka, former KGB headquarters.

Lubyanka Prison ㉜ in the headquarters of the Federal Security Service, formerly the KGB, on the northeast side of the square can still send shivers up spines. It goes without saying that no part of the building is open to the public. The square is also a popular meeting place for Moscow's die-hard communists.

The city's shopping centre

If you walk westwards down ulitsa Okhotny Ryad you'll come to **ulitsa Neglinnaya**, in the city's main shopping centre. Neglinnaya takes its name from the river which used to flow down to the Moskva on this site but has long since been channelled deep underground. The area became a mecca for shoppers in the last century when it was noted for its French fashion stores. Russia's first department store (now **TsUM**) was built in the late 19th century on **ulitsa Petrovka** behind the Maly Teatr. Nearby is the **Gulag History Museum** (16 ulitsa Petrovka; Tue–Sun 11am–6pm, Thu until 8pm) where guides dressed as guards take visitors through the

The newly renovated Bolshoi Theatre dazzles once again.

history of the Gulag and describe the horrors of camp life.

At 1st Neglinny Pereulok is the famous **Sandunovskie Bani** (daily 8am–10pm), the oldest public baths in the city. They are elaborate and decadently luxurious structures. Taking a bath in Russia is a social event and traditionally you would drink kvas, a home-brewed non-alcoholic drink resembling root beer, while steaming yourself clean.

At Trubnaya ploshchad (Pipe Square), Neglinnaya crosses the Boulevard Ring and runs into **Tsvetnoi** (Flower) **Boulevard**, now famous for the main circus building. In the old days, its park was best known as a shelter for the homeless. At Trubnaya, you may opt to turn right and walk a block to the busy ulitsa Sretenka, running northeast.

Sretenka terminates at **Sukharevskaya ploshchad**, which was named after the tower that stood here until the 1930s. Sukharev was the only officer who remained loyal to Peter the Great during the Streltsy rebellion and the grateful tsar erected the tower in Sukharev's honour. Later on, the

square's associations were less lofty: it hosted an officially recognised weekly market for stolen goods. Permission for the market was granted by Governor Rostopchin following the great fire of 1812. When the wealthy Muscovites returned home, they found their homes stripped bare and scoured the market in the hope of retrieving their valuables.

This is also the location of the **Sklifasovsky Hospital**, which was founded by the noble Sheremetyev family. Sheremetyevo, Moscow's international airport, is built on what was once one of their country estates. Turn left at Trubnaya, and walk along Petrovsky boulevard. Where this meets ulitsa Petrovka you'll find the **Moskovskoi Muzey Sovremennogo Iskusstva** (Moscow Museum of Modern Art; 25 ulitsa Petrovka; Tue–Wed and Fri–Sun noon–8pm, Thu 1–9pm) a collection of 20th-century works with some pieces by Chagall and Kandinsky. There are also paintings and sculptures by 1950s and 1960s artists whose work was deemed nonconformist by the Soviet authorities. From the museum, take Strastnoi Boulevard to ulitsa **Tverskaya**, the city's main street. Tverskaya leads to the Kremlin, with Teatralnaya ploshchad on the left.

Teatralnaya ploshchad

Two main thoroughfares come together on Teatralnaya – Neglinnaya and Petrovka (named after the Vysoko-Petrovsky monastery built by Prince Ivan Kalita). The world-famous **Bolshoy Teatr** ❸❸ (Bolshoi, meaning "big" Theatre; Mon, Wed and Fri one-hour tours in English 12.15pm) dominates the northern side of the square. Formerly known as the Grand Imperial Theatre, it was built in 1825 and restored and remodelled following a fire some years later. Between 2005 and 2011 the entire building was renovated at huge cost – the theatre needed shoring up to remedy serious structural flaws that had developed. The result is astounding and the

theatre has been given a new lease of life. Once again it is Moscow's main theatre, employing over 900 actors, dancers, singers and musicians. A performance here is a highlight of any visit to Moscow and tickets are not as expensive as you might imagine, especially for matinees.

The Bolshoi's near neighbours are the **Maly Teatr** ❸❹ (Maly, "little", Theatre), the oldest drama hall in the city, and to its left, the Detsky Teatr (Central Children's Theatre). The Detsky opened in 1921 and was Moscow's first professional theatre for children.

Across from the Bolshoi Theatre in the centre of the square is a stolid statue of Karl Marx, who seems to be emerging from an angular piece of rock. The inscription reads "Proletariat of all countries, unite!".

Famous hotels and mansions

The eastern side of Teatralnaya ploshchad is home to the glamorous fin-de-siècle **Metropol Hotel** ❸❺, designed by a Scottish-Russian team, William Walcott and Leo Kekushev. Restored

TIP

When in the vicinity of TsUM, check out Petrovka 38, an imposing classical building that has housed the Moscow police department since the Revolution.

The opulent interior of the Bolshoi.

to its original glory, it is once again the best and most exclusive hotel in town. It is worth having a coffee in one of the ornate lounges if the room prices are beyond your reach. Opposite is the site of the **Moskva Hotel**, which in a true Russian manner was pulled down in 2004 and replaced with an exact replica containing all modern conveniences and 600 fewer rooms. Opened as the Four Seasons Hotel Moscow in 2014, some guestrooms overlook the Kremlin, a luxury the KGB had forbidden in the original design.

Okhotny Ryad ❸❻ was once a big covered market place where hunters would trade game, rabbits and such. Small stalls selling meat, fish, fruit and vegetables made it one of the dirtiest places in Moscow.

On the corner of Okhotny Ryad and ulitsa Bolshaya Dmitrovka is a green-painted, white-colonnaded former mansion. Once the Nobles' Club, it is currently the **Dom Soyuzov** ❸❼ (House of Trade Unions). The mansion originally belonged to Prince Vasily Dolgorukov, the city's military commander in the early 1780s. In 1783 it was sold to the newly established Assembly of the Nobles, who started a very exclusive club in the building. Said to be the most beautiful house in Moscow, the interior is stunning, but the building is only open to the public when the white and gold **Kolonny Zal** (Hall of the Columns) is used as a concert venue.

Directly in front of the Moskva Hotel is the small underground **Archaeological Museum** (Tue, Thu, Sat–Sun 10am–6pm, Wed and Fri 11am–7pm; closed for renovation but should reopen in 2017), which exhibits the artefacts dating back to the 12th century that were found during the excavations of Manège Square – the vast expanse fronting the Kremlin wall. In the centre of the square is an up-market underground mall called **Okhotny Ryad** (Hunters' Row; daily 11am–10pm). The mall, topped with glass domes, and the park above it, were designed by Zurab Tsereteli. Part of the Neglinnaya River has been released above ground to flow amid sculptures of fairy-tale characters and, during the summer, fountains.

The theatre district around the Bolshoi.

Along the Kremlin walls are the Alexandrovsky Gardens, where you can pay a visit to the **Tomb of the Unknown Soldier**, which was dedicated in 1967 on the 25th anniversary of the Battle of Moscow. There is an eternal flame above an unidentified soldier of the Great Patriotic War with the inscription: "Your name is unknown, your deed is immortal". A bit farther down towards the Manège is a **Grotto** (also known as the Ruins) built into the Kremlin wall, and the obelisk dedicated in 1913 on the 300th anniversary of the Romanov dynasty, transformed by Lenin into the Monument to Revolutionary Thinkers.

The oldest building of **Moscow University** ❸ is on the west side of the square. Set slightly back from the street and fronted by a small garden, the classical yellow mansion was constructed between 1776 and 1793 by Matvei Kazakov and restored by Domenico Gilardi after the 1812 fire.

In the centre of the square is the former Manège, whose construction commemorated Russia's victory over Napoleon in the 1812 Patriotic War.

After a fire razed it in 2004, it was rebuilt and is now an exhibition hall.

If you follow Okhotny Ryad down to the river, you'll see the white marble **Russkaya Gosudarstvennaya Biblioteka** (Russian State Library, formerly the Lenin Library; Mon–Fri 9am–8pm, Sat 9am–7pm), which holds an impressive 30 million books in 247 languages. To the right is an astounding palace, **Dom Pashkova** ❸ (Palace; open only to Russian State Library card holders). Built in the time of Peter the Great by the son of one of his administrators, Peter Pashkov, the palace was designed to vie with the Kremlin in magnificence and style. The money to build this gloriously Baroque mansion had come from Pashkov's father Igor, who had made a fortune by investigating the bookkeeping of the governor of Siberia, Prince Matvei Gagarin. Pashkov claimed the prince was lining his own pockets on the proceeds of lucrative diamond and grain deals. Although he was well liked by the Siberians, Matvei was hanged and a great deal of his wealth and estates, along with a

Moscow University.

few thousand serfs, passed to the punctilious Pashkov and his family. The last of the Pashkovs presented the palace to Moscow University, which, in its turn, gave it to Count Rumyantsev to house his collection of art and manuscripts. After the Revolution, the art works were removed to the Pushkin Museum (see page 167), but the books remained and the mansion now forms part of the state library.

Tverskaya ulitsa

Moscow's best-known street is **Tverskaya ulitsa**, the main thoroughfare since the early 19th century when wealthy nobles began building new palaces and imposing mansions in Moscow. Tverskaya was the main road to St Petersburg, so the road was called the Tsar's Road and was the entry point to the city from the northern capital. The triumphal arch that once stood near the Belorussian train station was dismantled and moved to Kutuzorsky prospekt. The most incredible things were done to Tverskaya in the 1930s as part of Stalin's master plan to create a communist capital of awe-inspiring

Arriving at Belorussky train station.

proportions. First, it was straightened and widened. Several major buildings were moved deeper into the existing blocks of houses, including the former Governor General's residence which housed the Moscow Council of Deputies after the Revolution and is now the Mayor's Office; it also gained two storeys in the process.

The **Pushkin Monument** ⓬, about a third of the way up the street, was moved from one side of the boulevard to the other, into the small square in front of the Pushkin Cinema, venue for film festivals and premieres; the majestic Strastnoi Monastery was knocked down to accommodate the cinema. The building at No. 14 Tverskaya housed one of Moscow's biggest food stores. It was bought in 1898 by an entrepreneur called Yeliseyev who owned a chain of grocers. The "supermarket", **Yeliseyevsky Gastronom** ⓭, on the ground floor amazed even sophisticated Muscovites. The shop, which always had some food, even in the grim Soviet era, now has shelves stocked with exclusive imported groceries and luxury items. Just past the square to the north is the former English Club, now the **Muzei Sovremennoi Istorii Rossii** (Museum of the Modern History of Russia; Tverskaya ulitsa 21; Tue–Sun from 10am). Modern is a bit of a misnomer as the exhibition documents Soviet history from the early 20th-century revolutions to the 1980s and is a pleasingly retro experience. Look out for the collection of Soviet propaganda posters, some by famous artists of the day.

About halfway up Tverskaya, is **Triumfalnaya ploshchad**. The **Kontsertny zal imeni Chaykovskogo** ⓮ (Tchaikovsky Concert Hall) was built in 1940 to mark the centenary of the composer's birth. It has a giant 20-tonne pipe organ with 7,800 pipes and is a venue for the state symphony orchestra. Across the square is the old Stalinistera **Pekin Hotel**, once again a four-star establishment after extensive restoration work. At the end of Tverskaya is

Belorussky Vokzal 43 (station), the terminus for trains from Western Europe and the start of the road to Sheremetyevo International Airport.

Parallel to Tverskaya is **Bolshaya Nikitskaya ulitsa**. Once called a "museum of classicism" for its lovely mansions. Today some can still be found amid the up-market shops and restaurants. The **Orlov Dvorets** (Palace), at No. 5, is typical of 18th-century classical architecture. At No. 11, the former home of the Kolychev *boyars* is now the voice department of the Moscow Conservatory.

The **Ekaterina Romanovna Vorontsovoi Dvorets** (Palace) is at No. 12. Ekaterina (1744–1810) was one of the first patrons of the arts in Russia. A great friend of Catherine the Great, Voltaire and Diderot, she developed into a true philanthropist and spent her fortune on sponsoring students, lectures and literary publications. She was head of the Russian Academy of Sciences from 1783 until 1796. After her death, the palace was bought for the Moscow Conservatory of Music, **Konservatoriya imeni**

Chaykovskogo 44. Tchaikovsky, Glier and Neuhaus taught Rachmaninov and Scriabin here and the Great Hall is a venue for the International Tchaikovsky Competition held every four years. The Lesser Hall presents chamber music and recitals.

Across the street from the conservatory is the pretty little church of the Little Ascension, beautifully restored inside. The arts are celebrated in the Mayakovsky Drama Theatre (No. 19) and the Gelikon Opera Theatre (Nos 19 and 16).

Theatre buffs should head for the **Dom-muzei Stanislavskogo** 45 (Stanislavsky Museum; Thu, Sat–Sun 11am–6pm, Wed, Fri, 2–8pm), just up the street and round the corner to the right at No. 6. Stanislavsky transformed theatrical practice, and in particular the business of rehearsal. He made his actors literally live their part: they stayed in costume and in character day and night in order to achieve an understanding of the role. The desired result was a theatre which was convincing because it was realistic, rather than moving because it was

Concert at the Tchaikovsky Conservatory.

mannered and rhetorical. The Stan-islavsky approach has had a lasting influence on Hollywood, where his ideas were developed by Lee Strasberg of the Actors' Guild, and practised by followers of his such as James Dean, Marlon Brando and Robert De Niro.

At the same corner, Nikitskaya is crossed by Nikitsky (formerly Suvo-rovsky) Boulevard – the building on your right belongs to the **ITAR-TASS** news agency. If you cross Nikitsky here, Nikitskaya continues on the opposite side of the boulevard but twists off to the left, turning into Malaya Nikitskaya. The church on your left is the **Tserkov Bolshogo Voznesenia** ㊻ (Church of the Great Ascension), where the poet Alexander Pushkin married Natalya Goncharova in 1831. They are immortalised in a fountain on the square.

Turn right onto Spiridonovka to find the side entrance to the fabulous Art Nouveau **Dom-muzei Gorkovo** also now known as the **Ryabushinsky Mansion** ㊼ (Gorky House Museum; Wed–Sun 11am–5.30pm), which fronts Malaya Nikitskaya.

Patriarshiye Prudy, Patriarchs' Ponds.

The house was commissioned at the turn of the 20th century by the merchant Stenka Ryabushinsky. Its architect, Fyodor Shekhtel, was the most exciting of the day and he finished the lyrically imposing building in 1902. It is one of the finest examples of an Art Nouveau interior in Russia – or indeed anywhere in Europe. The centrepiece of the house is the magnificent curved limestone staircase called The Wave. Writer Maxim Gorky lived here from 1931 to 1936, and his modest belongings, plus his extensive book collection, share this impressive and quite unique space.

Follow Spiridonovka to the next corner on the right and turn down Spiridonievsky Pereulok. This will bring you to Malaya Bronnaya. Turn left and the street leads to **Patriarshiye Prudy** ㊽ (Patriarchs' Ponds), where Mikhail Bulgakov set the opening scene of his famous novel *Master and Margarita*. This attractive neighbourhood is full of shops and cafés.

In 2002 there was an attempt to erect monuments to Bulgakov near the pond, as well as to carry out

extensive reconstruction of the area. Both of these plans were met with strong resistance from local residents: many people felt that the pond itself served as a good enough monument to *Master and Margarita* and that any redevelopment of the area was unnecessary. In the end the residents were victorious, and the pond, albeit after being drained and refilled, remained as it was before.

South across the river

The area opposite the Kremlin on the south side of the Moskva River, between the bridges of Kamenny and Moskvoretsky around the **Tretyakovskaya Galereya** ㊽ (Tretyakov Gallery; see box), comes as something of a surprise after the appalling 20th-century urban planning generally apparent in the old heart of the city. **Zamoskvorechye** (literally "beyond the Moskva River") was the artisan centre in the 18th century, hence street names such as Kadashevskaya (barrel-maker) and Novokuznetskaya (blacksmith). Wealthy merchants moved in during the 19th century and built palaces and

mansions. Today, it is embassy country, and the classical 19th-century buildings, with their Chantilly stucco, give an idea of what Moscow must have been like before the Revolution.

Pyatnitskaya ulitsa is the best street for shopping, but it is pleasant to stroll along the narrow surrounding streets, lined with churches and manor houses.

When Prince Daniel Nevsky built his string of fortified monasteries in the 13th century, he dedicated the best and most beautiful to his patron saint. The **Svyato-Danilovsky Monastyr** ㊿ (Danilov Monastery) still stands today, enclosed by its white walls, due south from Moskvoretsky Most (Bridge) at the end of ulitsa Bolshaya Ordynka. The Orthodox Church restored the complex to its former gold-domed splendour even before the end of communist rule, and the patriarch has had his official residence here since the late 1980s.

While south of the river, don't miss **Park Gorkovo** ㉛ (Gorky Park). It surrounds the landscaped Neskuchny Garden (literally "not dull") created

The surreal staircase at the Gorky Museum.

Tretyakov Gallery.

TRETYAKOV GALLERY

On the south bank of the Moskva River, opposite the Kremlin, is one of the greatest collections of Russian art in the country. The fully renovated **Tretyakovskaya Galereya** (Tretyakov Gallery; Lavrushinsky Pereulok 10; Tue–Sun 10am–6pm, Thu–Fri until 9pm) spans 1,000 years of Russian art, from early icons to 20th-century works. The building itself is in the Russian style – an urban interpretation of a *boyar*'s mansion built in 1900 to house the collection accumulated by the brothers Pavel and Sergei Tretyakov in the late 19th century. The two men, who had made their fortunes in textiles, later donated their collection and palace to the state. On the gallery's ground floor, the remarkable icon collection includes the Byzantine *Mother of God of Vladimir* and Andrei Rublyov's 15th-century *The Trinity*. You'll find 17th- and 18th-century portraits upstairs, along with treasures of Russian realism and grand historical canvases.

A short walk to the west brings you to the **Novaya Tretyakovskaya Galereya** (New Tretyakov Gallery; Krymsky Val 10; same hours), housing Soviet and post-Soviet art. The newly renovated **Muzeon Sculpture Gardens** next door (daily 9am–8pm) display more than 600 statues including Soviet monuments that were pulled down in 1991.

Gorky Park is a favourite place of relaxation for Muscovites, with its amusement park and Disney-style rides. It lies southwest across the Moskva River from the Kremlin.

Strolling along Old Arbat.

by the millionaire industrialist Demidov on the south bank of the Moskva in the mid-18th century, the name of which derives from the fantastic collection of plants that lined the pathways. Today, Demidov's mansion is home to the Academy of Sciences. Leninsky prospekt, along the south side of the park, is known as the Avenue of Soviet Science because more than 30 research centres are here. The park itself is very popular among Muscovites wanting to escape the city's urban sprawl and features many attractions and that rare commodity in Moscow – grass.

West to Old Arbat

Walking westwards up ulitsa Vozdvizhenka from the Manege on Okhotny Ryad, you can't miss the broad eyesore of ulitsa **Novy Arbat** starting at Arbatskaya ploshchad and ending near the **Dom Pravitelstva** ❷ (Russian Government building) overlooking the Moskva River. In the 18th century, the Romanov, Naryshkin and Sheremetyev families all had houses on this part of the street.

Novy Arbat is dissected by Nikitsky Boulevard at Arbatskaya ploshchad and to your left is the beginning of the **Old Arbat**. The name derives from the Turkic word for caravan – *rabat* – and once housed traders from the south.

In the 18th century the Arbat was popular with the city's artists and writers, who immortalised the charming crooked lanes of the neighbourhood. The Russian writer and revolutionary Alexander Herzen called it Moscow's St Germain, and true to its reputation the Arbat again became a mecca for artists when glasnost began. Satirical and political cartoonists, painters and sculptors, who couldn't get access to official art galleries, began exhibiting their work on the pedestrianised street. It has subsequently become something of a tourist trap, but in spite of that, the cafés, buskers and souvenir sellers make it lively and fun.

One building you shouldn't miss is the **Dom Melnikov** ❸ (Melnikov House), tucked down a side-street off the Arbat in Krivoarbatsky Pereulok, about halfway along the pedestrian street to the south. Konstantin

Melnikov was a founder member of the avant-garde arts movement that flourished in the first decade after the Revolution. Along with artists such as Kandinsky and El Lissitsky, he formulated a new and iconoclastic approach to the arts. But the movement which influenced the Bauhaus and De Stijl schools was short-lived in Russia. Stalin decided that the proletariat should have neoclassical facades on their apartment blocks, but Melnikov built himself a family home, a white cylindrical structure with lozenge-shaped windows. Finished in 1929, this constructivist masterpiece was the only private home in the city during the Soviet years. The house is closed, as Melnikov's heirs battle out their rights in court.

The Arbat ends on Smolenskaya ploshchad (Square), an enormous road junction which is dwarfed by the **Ministerstvo Inostrannykh Del** ⑤ (Foreign Ministry). There are seven of these Stalinist "wedding cakes" in the city: all were built in the late 1940s and 1950s, partially inspired by American skyscrapers and meant to

be a symbol of the USSR's recovery after the war.

The Pushkin Museum

Following the lead of Peter the Great, the nobles of the 18th century began taking the kind of Grand Tour that had created the fabulous aristocratic art collections amassed in other parts of Europe. The great Russian collectors, the Rumyantsevs, Golenishchevs, Shchukins and Morozovs, were both catholic and discerning in their tastes, as well as immensely wealthy. Their collections were nationalised by Lenin in the early 1920s and brought together in the **Muzei Izobrazitelnikh Iskusstv imeni Pushkina** ⑤ (Pushkin Fine Arts Museum; ulitsa Volkhonka 12; Tue–Wed and Fri-Sun 10am–7pm, Thu 10am–9pm).

The museum was founded in the late 19th century as a school of art, and incorporated copies of major sculptural works from around the world. It holds a wealth of original works, ranging from ancient Egyptian art to a collection of Impressionists and Post-Impressionist paintings,

Art students at the Pushkin Fine Arts Museum.

including those by Cézanne, Gauguin, Matisse and Van Gogh. The latter have been moved to a new branch next door, the **Gallery of European and American Art of the 19th & 20th Centuries** (Volkhonka 14; same hours as main building).

A temple to communism

Opposite the museum is the **Khram Khrista Spasitelya**  (Cathedral of Christ the Saviour) famously rebuilt in the 1990s and opened in time to mark Moscow's 850th anniversary in 1997. The church is a copy of the original, which was erected between the 1830s and 1880s. It soon became the outstanding symbol of the city – it was not just a church, it was also a monument to the Russian victory over Napoleon, a symbol of the idea that, with God's help, Russia could overcome any catastrophe. However, to the new Soviet regime the cathedral was little more than an ugly reminder of the autocratic regime.

In 1931, to the horror of Muscovites, Stalin had the cathedral dynamited. In its place he planned to erect a gigantic skyscraper, which would be the largest in the world. It was called the Palace of Soviets, and it was in effect a temple of communism. It was to be crowned with a statue of Lenin so colossal that its upper half would have been permanently lost in the clouds – it's claimed Lenin's forefinger would have big enough to hold a cinema! But the megalomaniac plan was never realised – the skyscraper could not be made to stand up, and the gaping hole of the foundations was turned into the Moscow open-air swimming pool.

Resurrecting the past

The demolished cathedral became a forbidden topic in the USSR, a non-building. But when communism collapsed, the resurrection of the church became a cause célèbre. The then mayor of Moscow, Yuri Luzhkov, took up the baton. It was built in the astonishingly short space of three years and stands as much as a monument to Luzhkov's tenure of office as a place of divine worship. In 2007 Boris Yeltsin's funeral was

The Peter the Great Monument – you can't miss it.

SCULPTURE IN THE CITY

Walking around Moscow, you cannot escape the sight of a curious structure in the middle of the Moskva River between the Cathedral of Christ the Saviour on the north bank and the New Tretyakov Gallery on the south bank. The giant sculpture of a figure on a sailing boat is Peter the Great. It is one of the many creations of Zurab Tsereteli, Moscow's most controversial sculptor. Tsar Peter I, founder of St Petersburg, is known to have detested Moscow, and it is a bizarre twist of fate that this sculpture has found a home here. According to Tsereteli's critics, it was originally intended to represent Christopher Columbus and had been commissioned by the United States for the 500th anniversary celebrations of the discovery of North America. The us is said to have rejected it on first sight. The 60-metre (200-ft) bronze body had to be disposed of somehow and Tsereteli subsequently won a commission from Moscow's mayor, Yuri Luzhkov. The reincarnated statue raised an outcry in Moscow, but has so far survived a massive public campaign for its removal as well as a demolition attempt. You can sample other works by Tsereteli studded around Moscow, including interiors of the Cathedral of Christ the Saviour and his animalistic forms in the Okhotny Ryad shopping mall.

held here, the first religious service since 1917. Recently it hit the news again when the Russian female punk band, Pussy Riot, famously staged an anti-Putin protest there in 2012. The members' trial and imprisonment caused international outrage until they were released by President Putin in time for the Sochi Winter Olympics in 2014.

Before the 1917 Revolution, Moscow was celebrated for its "forty times forty" churches, whose golden, blue and wooden cupolas adorned the city's skyline. The campaign against religion in the early years of the Soviet era was responsible for the destruction of most of the churches. They were turned into warehouses, dormitories, film studios or offices – or simply torn down, their gold and silver vessels stripped of jewels and melted down, and their icons either tossed onto dumps or sometimes sent to museum storage halls.

Since the fall of the Soviet regime in 1991, most of the city's churches have been returned to the Patriarchate and have been re-consecrated for services. Unfortunately, where there were once rich frescoes and ancient icons, there are now whitewashed walls and a few modern icons.

However, through the efforts of individuals and business interests, the exteriors of most of the city's churches have been restored and the cupolas re-gilded. One of the delights of strolling through the city is discovering a small parish church tucked away in the middle of a housing estate or between two Stalinist-era skyscrapers.

Novodevichy Convent

Perhaps one of the most beautiful religious complexes is the **Novodevichy Monastyr** ⑤⑦ (New Maiden Convent; Wed–Mon 9am–5pm). To the southwest of the Kremlin, strategically placed on a bend in the river, the convent was founded by Vasily III in 1524. Some of the buildings became a museum in 1922, but today much of what you see is once again a working monastery.

From a distance the white walls topped by red roofs and 16 golden domes look picturesque, but the convent's history is chequered. The strong walls and fortified towers were used as a prison for potentially troublesome female nobles. A string of well-born women from influential families ended up imprisoned here, including Irina Godunova, the widow of Tsar Fyodor and the sister of Boris Godunov; Peter the Great's first wife Evdokia, and his half-sister Sofia, after she attempted to take the throne.

While you are at the convent take the time to visit the **Novodevichy Cemetery** (daily 9am–5pm) where the biggest names of Russian music and literature are buried. Chekhov, Gogol, Bulgakov and Mayakovsky, Shostakovich, Prokofiev and Rostropovich lie buried the near graves of such leaders as Nikita Khrushchev (buried here and not at the Kremlin wall like other Soviet leaders) and Boris Yeltsin. Rostropovich and Yeltsin were buried here within days of each other in April 2007.

Novodevichy Cemetery covered in snow.

The entrance to the Novodevichy Convent.

THE MOSCOW METRO

Muscovites are extremely proud of their metro system, and they have every right to be. It is clean fast, efficient, cheap – and spectacular to look at.

In most cities the metro is a dull way to get around: there is not much for a visitor to look at 20 metres (65 ft) under the ground. In Moscow, on the other hand, the metro is something of a tourist attraction. The stations are well known for their sumptuous and unique decoration. Where else in the world is the rumbling approach of the train heralded by a delicate tinkle of chandeliers?

The metro is a good way to travel for practical reasons, too. During the Russian winter, it makes sense to do your waiting in the damp warmth of the underground rather than at a freezing bus stop. Throughout the cold months armies of *babushkas* (grandmothers) are employed to mop up the slush which passengers carry into the station vestibules on their winter boots.

The metro has its own very definite etiquette. When it comes to boarding a train it is every man or woman for themselves, and in rush hour it is a scrum between the people getting on and those getting off. But once on the train, invalids, pensioners, pregnant ladies and people with children have an indisputable right to seats. This right is in the "Rules For The Use of the Metro", a Soviet-era document which is displayed in every train. The first rule of the metro states, in true bureaucratic fashion, that passengers must obey the rules.

Mayakovskaya, with its elegant arches, is true Art Deco chic.

Many metro stations were built in the war years and used as shelters. Park Pobedy, opened in 2003, is the deepest station in the world and features two enamelled panels depicting the Great Patriotic War.

The grand mosaics at Kievskaya tell the 'happy story' of Russian-Ukrainian relations: two peoples working to the same communist goal.

Komsomolskaya is one of the busiest stations because it serves three railway terminals. It is also one of the most ornate, with its giant chandeliers and a terrace round the platforms.

DIGGING TUNNELS FOR SOCIALISM

The building of the metro was the centrepiece of the first Five-Year Plan. Like many of the industrial undertakings of the 1930s it was a symbolic project, intended to show that socialism could achieve anything capitalism could. The first line to be built was the red one, which runs to the southwest of Moscow. The stretch from Palace of Soviets station (now Kropotkinskaya) to Frunzenskaya was opened with much pomp in 1935. Kropotkinskaya itself is one of the most beautiful and restrained stations. It is lined with marble taken from the facade of the demolished Cathedral of Christ (now reconstructed nearby). It was only later, in the 1940s and 1950s, that it became fashionable to build in a style that one might call Soviet Baroque. Newer stations are mostly utilitarian. In the suburbs, metro stations are lined with blank, easy-to-clean tiles. To enjoy the gaudy architecture of the metro, stay inside the Circle Line.

The names of stations are not always obvious, so visitors should listen for the recorded announcements: "Doors closing, next stop…"

The escalator at Kurskaya–Koltsevaya station.

Now that Socialist Realist statuary is out of fashion, Ploshchad Revolutsii (Revolution Square) is one of the few places you can see monumental Soviet art.

THE GOLDEN RING

The princely towns of the Golden Ring reached their zenith before Moscow was even conceived. Here, beneath gilded onion domes, is the historic centre of ancient Muscovy.

The Golden Ring (Zolotoe Koltso) comprises a dozen medieval towns northeast of Moscow that once formed Russia's political, spiritual and cultural heartland. Despite heavy Soviet destruction, these towns have managed to retain many of their architectural features and, together with Moscow and St Petersburg, top the list of Russia's most popular tourist destinations. While Suzdal and Sergiev Posad are the most visited towns – because of their proximity to the capital – other smaller, more remote towns are equally attractive for their peaceful rural charm.

Sergiev Posad

Situated 70 km (44 miles) north of Moscow on the Yaroslavl road, **Sergiev Posad ❶**, makes for a perfect day-trip from Moscow. It is built around the **Trinity Monastery of St Sergius** (daily 5am–9pm) founded in the mid-14th century by St Sergius of Radonezh – a holy man revered for his role in uniting Russia against the Tatars. Today, the remains of St Sergius are kept in the white stone **Troitsky Sobor** (Trinity Cathedral), also noted for its splendid icons painted by Russia's celebrated master Andrei Rublyov and his school of icon painters. A rolling service goes on here throughout the day. Behind Trinity Cathedral, the **Riznitsa** (Vestry;

Wed–Sun 10am–5.30pm) displays the lavish gifts amassed by the monastery over the centuries.

The **Uspensky Sobor** (Cathedral of the Dormition), resplendent with its deep-blue domes dusted with gilded stars, was completed on the orders of Ivan the Terrible in 1585. A modest tomb outside the west door contains the remains of Tsar Boris Godunov, the only Russian leader not buried in Moscow or St Petersburg. The pretty **Nadkladezhnaya Chasovnya** (Chapel-at-the-Well) nearby was

Main Attractions
Sergiev Posad
Rostov Veliky
Yaroslavl
Kostroma
Suzdal

The Trinity Monastery of St Sergius.

Rostov's exquisite Kremlin walls and Cathedral of the Dormition.

built over a spring where pilgrims now queue to collect holy water. The five-tier bell tower once had as many as 42 bells. Along the southern wall, the bulky 17th-century **Trapeznaya Tserkov Sv Sergeya** (Refectory Church of St Sergius), once a dining hall for pilgrims, now holds morning services in winter when the Assumption Cathedral is closed.

Pereyaslavl-Zalessky

This small town on the main road between Moscow and Yaroslavl, 50 km (30 miles) northeast of Sergiev Posad, was founded in 1152 by Prince Yuri Dolgoruky and is famous for being the birthplace of Alexander Nevsky. The highlight of **Pereyaslavl-Zalessky ❷**, whose name means Pereslavl Beyond-the-Woods, is the Kremlin with its solid **Spaso-Preobrazhensky Sobor** (Cathedral of the Transfiguration of the Saviour; Wed–Sun 10am–5pm), one of the oldest edifices in Russia, built in the mid-12th century. A bust of Alexander Nevsky stands across the square together with three other churches, including the **Tserkov**

Orthodox priest at the Holy Trinity Lavra St. Sergius.

Petra Mitropolita (Church of Peter the Metropolitan), built in 1585. On the banks of Lake Pleshcheevo, a young Peter the Great built a mock flotilla and thus laid the foundation of the Russian Navy. The history of this fleet is told in the **Botik Museum** (Tue–Sun 10am–5pm) on the southern bank of the lake. The museum's treasure is the *Fortuna*, one of a pair of Peter the Great's ships which have survived to this day. Southwest of the Kremlin, the pretty **Goritsky Monastery** (May–Oct 10am–6pm, Nov–Apr 9am–5pm) was founded in the early 14th century, although today its oldest standing buildings date from the 17th century. It is worth a visit and has a small **museum**.

Rostov-Veliky

Sleepy, somewhat forgotten **Rostov-Veliky ❸** is one of the Golden Ring's most atmospheric towns with its rustic Kremlin and monasteries dotting the landscape. Situated 220 km (137 miles) northeast of Moscow on the shores of Lake Nero, Rostov-Veliky is also the Golden Ring's

The Golden Ring

oldest town. It was first mentioned in chronicles dated 862 and by the end of the first millennium AD it was one of the biggest spiritual and trading centres in all of Russia. Entering the town from the south offers a fairy-tale panorama of the **Kremlin** (daily 10am–5pm) and the **Monastery of St Jacob** across Lake Nero. The town has retained much of its pre-Revolutionary charm, and has been relatively untouched by the building boom marring the rest of the country. Founded in the 12th century on the shore of the lake, the breathtaking Kremlin is framed by a 1-km (0.5-mile) -long wall and has a large central square which is full of flowers during the summer.

The 16th-century **Uspensky Sobor** (Cathedral of the Dormition), behind the Kremlin's northern wall, is magnificent despite its dilapidated state. Its five domes symbolise Christ and the four apostles. Next to it towers the great 17th-century belfry and 15 bells, each with its own name, the biggest weighing 32 tons. Bells are the symbol of Rostov-Veliky and

locals say that the Kremlin's bells can be heard for 18 km (11 miles). The two imposing gate-churches **Tserkov Voskreseniya** and **Tserkov Ionna Bogoslova**, and the **Tserkov Spasa-na-Senyakh** (Church of the Saviour-over-the-Galleries) have bright 17th-century frescoes but are open only from May to October to protect them from the cold. The former **law court** flanking the north gate has an interesting museum of *finift*, Rostov's traditional hand-painted enamelware, while the **Krasnaya Palata** (Red Chamber) and the **Belaya Palata** (White Chamber) in the south section house a museum of sacred antiques and a picture gallery.

Yaroslavl

Yaroslavl ❹, 250 km (155 miles) northeast of Moscow, is by far the largest town on the Golden Ring with more than 620,000 inhabitants. In 1010, Kyivan prince Yaroslav the Wise founded a fort in a small locality on the banks of the Volga called **Medvezhy Ugol** (Bear Corner) and is said to have gained the locals'

Seventeenth-century frescoes adorn Tserkov Ionna Bogoslova (Church of St John the Evangelist) in Rostov's Kremlin.

Yaroslavl street detail.

The Founding of Yaroslavl Monument along the frozen Volga River.

allegiance by killing a bear with an axe. The bear became the town's emblem and figures to this day on Yaroslavl's coat of arms.

As Yaroslavl grew into a major trading centre, rich merchants eager to compete with Moscow donated huge sums for the construction of churches all over the city. One of Yaroslavl's finest churches is the redbrick **Tserkov Bogoyavlenia** (Church of the Epiphany), built in the 17th century just off Bogoyavlenskaya ploshchad. Used as a storage facility for decades, this elegant church is decorated with the city's traditional hand-painted ceramic tiles and has rich frescoes and a carved iconostasis.

The 12th-century **Spaso-Preobrazhensky Monastyr** (Monastery of the Transfiguration of the Saviour; monastery grounds: daily 8am–8pm; museums: Tue–Sun 10am–5pm) encloses the imposing **Preobrazhensky sobor** (Cathedral of Transfiguration) dating from 1516, which contains rare 16th-century frescoes. The north section of the cathedral once housed the monastery library

where Russia's literary treasure, *Slovo o Polku Igoreve*, a kind of Russian *Beowulf* written in the 12th century, was discovered in the late 18th century. The spiky golden globes on the bell tower, which you can climb for a sprawling view of the city, were added in the 19th century.

All the monastery's churches are closed between October and May to preserve their frescoes.

Another of Yaroslavl's highlights is the graceful **Tserkov Ilyi Proroka** (Church of Elijah the Prophet; daily 9.30am–7pm) with its tall, candle-shaped bell tower, built in the mid-17th century by wealthy brothers who dealt in fur and jewellery. Located on Sovietskaya ploshchad, it contains splendid frescoes painted in just three months.

A walk along the picturesque Volga embankment will take you to the **Museum of Music and Time** (Volzhskaya naberezhnaya 33A; daily 10am–7pm; tours in English available) packed with the fascinating collection of old clocks, musical instruments, bells and samovars

ABRAMTSEVO'S ARTISTS

Early in the 19th century the Abramtsevo country estate, 60 km (37 miles) northeast of Moscow, was owned by the novelist Sergei Aksakov and frequented by Nikolai Gogol and Ivan Turgenev. In the 1870s it was purchased by industrial tycoon Savva Mamontov, who put it at the disposal of some of the country's leading artists in order to preserve its national heritage. It became the cradle of the neo-Russian style – the Russian variation of the Romantic and nationalist movements that swept Europe in the 19th century, and strove to preserve Russian folkloric traditions and skills. Abramtsevo attracted painters such as Ilya Repin, Mikhail Vrubel, Isaak Levitan, Valentin Serov and Viktor Krasnetsov. Russia's legendary opera singer Fyodor Chaliapin made his debut here. Today it houses a Museum of Literature and Art.

gathered by the eccentric actor and magician John Mostoslavsky.

Kostroma

Located 70 km (44 miles) east of Yaroslavl, **Kostroma** ❺ was once a key cultural and trading centre on the Golden Ring, but a devastating fire in 1773 and economic difficulties have made it an impoverished town with a struggling tourist industry. Still, this somewhat run-down city does not lack charm and is well worth a visit if only for its wonderful **Ipatevsky Monastyr** (Monastery of St Ipaty; daily 9am–5pm) on the broad Kostroma River – a tributary of the Volga. According to legend, a Tatar ancestor of the Godunov dynasty founded the monastery in the 14th century after recovering from a severe illness. The monastery was handed over to the Romanovs in the 17th century. The splendid **Trinity Cathedral** built by the Godunovs in 1652 has some of the Golden Ring's most vibrant and best-preserved 17th-century frescoes as well as a magnificent Baroque carved iconostasis; it also houses a museum of icons. The large building across the courtyard is the Romanov Chambers, which house a **Museum of Romanov Relics**.

Suzdal

Some 100 km (65 miles) south of Kostroma, **Suzdal** ❻ was first chronicled in 1024 and became the capital of Yuri Dolgoruky's Rostov-Suzdal principality in the early 12th century. Established on fertile soil on the banks of the Kamenka River, it was always a wealthy town with a thriving trade.

In the 19th century, the railway constructed between Moscow and Nizhny-Novgorod bypassed Suzdal, sparing it from industrialisation. Today the town has over 100 architectural landmarks dating from the 13th to the 19th century over an area of just 9 sq. km (3 sq. miles). This picturesque town is very tourist-friendly and filled with shops, cafés and sights, making it the best day trip from Moscow.

One serene delight is the working **Pokrovsky Monastyr** (Intercession

TIP

Suzdal is one of the better places to stay. It is well served by hotels, including the traditionally furnished wooden *izby* (peasant cottages) around Pokrovsky Monastery.

The courtyard of the Monastery of St Ipaty and the golden domes of Trinity Cathedal.

Convent), founded in 1364. The convent's history is retraced in a museum on the left of the main entrance. The three-domed **Pokrovsky Sobor** (Cathedral of the Intercession) was built in the early 16th century (monastery grounds: always accessible; museum: Fri–Tue 10am–6pm).

Further north, the **Spaso-Yevfimevsky Monastyr** (Saviour Monastery of St Euthymius; Tue–Sun 10am–6pm) is Suzdal's biggest monastery. Built in the 14th century to protect the northern flank of the town, its fortress-like red-brick walls contain countless churches, museums, bell towers, dungeons and ecclesiastical chambers.

In the city centre, the 11th-century **Kremlin** (Wed–Mon 10am–6pm) includes a few streets and several churches, its highlight being the **Rozhdestvensky Sobor** (Nativity of the Virgin Cathedral) with its blue and gold cupolas, magnificent 13th- and 17th-century frescoes, and two rare 13th-century Damascene doors of gilded copper. It took 12 years of restoration works to get the cathedral back to mint condition. The Archbishop's chambers are home to the **Suzdal History Museum** (Wed–Mon 10am–5pm).

South from the Kremlin across the river is the open-air **Muzei derevyanovo zodchestva i khrestyanskogo byta** (Museum of Wooden Architecture and Peasant Life; May–Oct Thu–Tue 9am–7pm, Nov–Apr 9am–4pm) exhibiting traditional peasant log houses and wooden churches built without using a single nail.

Vladimir

Vladimir ❼, a city of 340,000 some 35 km (22 miles) south of Suzdal and 190 km (113 miles) northeast of Moscow, was founded by Prince Vladimir Monomakh in 1108 on the banks of the Klyazma River but is thought to be much older. As Kiev's authority began to fade in the 12th century, Vladimir became the capital of medieval Russia, a status that was brought to an end in the 13th century by the Mongol invasion and the rise of Moscow.

Little remains of Vladimir's ancient roots, but the city nevertheless makes for a pleasant stopover on the way to other, more picturesque Golden Ring towns.

The interior of the imposing yet graceful **Uspensky Sobor** (Assumption Cathedral) are adorned with precious frescoes of the Last Judgement painted by Andrei Rublev and Daniil Chorny in 1408.

Nearby, the white-stone facades of the exquisite **Dmitrievsky Sobor** (Cathedral of St Dmitry), built between 1193 and 1197, are carved with a multitude of animals, plants and hunting scenes.

Vladimir's 12th-century **Zolotye Vrata** (Golden Gates) were built as replicas of Kiev's Golden Gates and are a mix of triumphal arch and fortress. The gates now house a **Museum of Military History** (Fri–Wed 10am–6pm).

*Suzdal in the
winter sun.*

Cathedral of St Nicholas – Russian Baroque at its best.

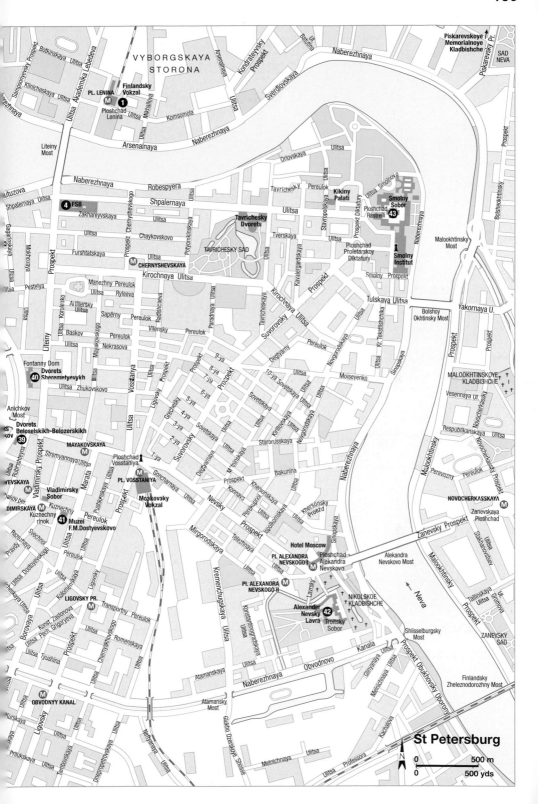

VYBORGSKAYA STORONA

Piskarevskoye Memorialnoye Kladbishche

SAD NEVA

Botkinskaya Prospekt

Samsonevsky Prospekt

Klinicheskaya Ulitsa

Ulitsa Academika Lebedeva

PL. LENINA ①

Finlandsky Vokzal

Ploshchad Lenina

Mikhailova

Komsomola

Naberezhnaya

Arsenalnaya

Liteiny Most

Kondratevsky Prospekt

Arsenalnaya

Sverdlovskaya

Batilina Ul.

Naberezhnaya

Piskarevsky Pr.

Prospekt

Bolsheokhtinsky

Kutuzova

Naberezhnaya

Robespyera

Shpalernaya

Orlovskaya

Ulitsa

Ulitsa

Pereulok

Kikiny Palati

Smolny Sobor

Ulitsa Smolnyo

Maloohktinsky Most

Shpalernaya

Gagarinskaya Ulitsa

④ **FSB**

Zakhareyvskaya

Tavrichesky

Ulitsa

Tverskaya

Prospekt Diktatury

Ploshchad Rastrelli ㊸

Smolny Institut

Smolny Sobor 1

Mokhovaya

Chernyshevskogo Prospekt

Ulitsa

Chaykovskovo

Potyomkinskaya

TAVRICHESKY DVORETS

Kavalergardskaya

Ploshchad Proletarskoy Diktatury

Smolny Prospekt

Furshtatskaya

Ulitsa

TAVRICHESKY SAD

Kirochnaya Ulitsa

CHERNYSHEVSKAYA Ⓜ

Pestelya

Maneznyy Pereulok

Ulitsa

Ryleeva

Paradnaya

Tavricheskaya

Kirochnaya Ulitsa

Suvorovsky

Prospekt

Kirochnaya Ulitsa

Novgorodskaya

Tulskaya Ulitsa

Bolshoy Okhtinsky Most

Yakornaya U.

Bolsheokhtinsky Most

Prospekt

Prospekt

Al.Ilmersky Ulitsa

Korolenko

Saperny

Pereulok

Radishcheva

Vilensky

Pereulok

Degtyarny

Pereulok

Kr. Tekstilshchika

Sinopskaya

MALOOKHTINSKOYE KLADBISHCHE

Vesennaya Ulitsa

Baskov

Mayakovskogo

Pereulok

Nekrasova

Ulitsa

Liteiny

Prospekt

9-ya

8-ya

7-ya

10-ya Sovetskaya Ulitsa

Sovetskaya

Moiseyenko

Novocherkasskaya

Novocherkassky Prospekt

Republikanskaya

Ulitsa

Fontanny Dom

Dvorets Sheremetyevykh ㊵

Ulitsa Zhukovskovo

Vosstaniya

Ulitsa

Ligovsky Prospekt

Grechesky Prospekt

6-ya

5-ya

4-ya

3-ya

2-ya

Suvorovsky

Sovetskaya

Kirillovskaya Ulitsa

Novgorodskaya

Degtyarnaya

Starorusskaya

Naberezhnaya

Novocherkassky

Perevozny

Pereulok

NOVOCHERKASSKAYA Ⓜ

Anichkov Most

Dvorets Beloselskikh-Belozerskikh ㊴

MAYAKOVSKAYA Ⓜ

Stremyannaya Ulitsa

Vladimirsky Prospekt

Rubinsteyna

Vladimirsky Sobor

Pushkinskaya

Marata

1-ya

Gonchamaya

Ploshchad Vosstaniya 1

PL. VOSSTANIYA Ⓜ

Moskovsky Vokzal

Minskaya

Mirgorodskaya

Bakunina

Prospekt

Konnaya

Khersonsky Proezd

Sinopskaya

Zanevsky Prospekt

Zanevskaya Ploshchad

VLADIMIRSKAYA Ⓜ

Zvakov per.

DIMIRSKAYA Ⓜ

Kuznechny rinok

㊶ **Muzei F.M.Dostyevskovo**

Pereulok

Svechnoi

Ulitsa Dostoyevskogo

Pravdy

Zagorodny

Razezhaya

Pereulok

Kolokolnaya Ulitsa

Nevsky

Prospekt

Ploshchad Alexandra Nevskovo

Hotel Moscow

PL. ALEXANDRA NEVSKOGO I Ⓜ

Alekandra Nevskovo Most

Neva

Maloohktinsky Prospekt

Tallinskaya Ulitsa

Stakhanovtsev Ulitsa

Ul. Gromova

Prospekt

ZANEVSKY SAD

LIGOVSKY PR. Ⓜ

Transportny Pereulok

Kremenchugskaya Ulitsa

Telezhnaya

Konstantinogradskaya Ulitsa

PL. ALEXANDRA NEVSKOGO II Ⓜ

Lavrsky

Alexander Nevsky Lavra ㊷

Troitsky Sobor

NIKOLSKOE KLADBISHCHE

Shlisselburgsky Most

Prospekt Obukhovskoy Oborony

ZANEVSKY SAD

Konst. Zaslonova

Pech. Grigoryeva

Boroyaya

Ulitsa

Romenskaya

Zmyakhovskogo

Ligovsky

Ulitsa Tyushina

Prilutskaya Ulitsa

Tambovskaya Ulitsa

OBVODNYY KANAL Ⓜ

Kurskaya

Prospekt

Atamanskaya Ulitsa

Naberezhnaya

Atamansky Most

Gukto Dzerzinsky Shosse

Kanala

Obvodnovo

Melnichnaya

Glinyanaya Ulitsa

Melnichnaya Ulitsa

Kachalova

Ulitsa Professora

Ulitsa

Prospekt Oborony

Finlandsky Zheleznodorozhny Most

Nefyanaya Ulitsa

Ligovsky Prospekt

Dnepropetrovskaya Ulitsa

St Petersburg

N

0 — 500 m

0 — 500 yds

The Winter Palace – in the winter.

ST PETERSBURG

St Petersburg is Russia's cultural capital, a stately city of islands, bridges and classical 18th-century palaces on the northern shores of the Baltic.

Sankt Piterburg, Sankt Peter-burg, Petrograd, Leningrad, Saint Petersburg – just as the city's name has changed over the centuries, so has its fortune. The history of St Petersburg has been one of continued struggle, destruction, and rebirth. Perhaps it is this constant tumult that has made it a living inspiration to some of the world's greatest cultural figures.

St Petersburg rose out of a swampy backwater on the Neva River delta at the beginning of the 18th century when Peter the Great realised his dream to build a new capital, a "Window on the West", that would open the way to European enlightenment and raise Russia out of its medieval past. Peter named his new capital using the Dutch pronunciation, Sankt Piterburg: he was enthralled with all things Dutch as he considered its civilisation to be the most advanced. Bringing "civilisation" to Russia, however, came at a medieval price. Historians estimate that at least 100,000 people died of exposure and disease while building the new capital. But by the end of the 19th century, when the city was called "Piter" by its inhabitants, it had indeed become great as the tsar-founder had envisaged and was a leading European cultural and scientific centre.

Frozen river and docks.

A change of name

When World War I began in 1914, anti-German sentiment convinced Tsar Nicholas II, a cousin of the German Kaiser Wilhelm, to change the capital's name to the more Russian sounding Petrograd. Then in March 1918, the Bolsheviks, who had seized power in a *coup d'état* in October 1917, moved the capital back to Moscow while the German armies advanced on the "cradle of the Revolution".

As the Communist order established itself, it, too, wished to honour

Main Attractions

Gosudarstvenny Ermitazh
Palace Square
Isaakievsky Sobor
Khram Spasa na Krovi
Mariinsky Dvorets
Russky Muzei

FACT

The winter climate in St Petersburg is harsh, with strong winds and snow between November and late March. In summer, from the end of May to early July, there is an air of festivity due to the extraordinary White Nights, when the sun sets for no more than two hours.

its heroes. In 1924, Petrograd's name was changed to commemorate the recently deceased founding father of the new Russian state. The city of Peter became the city of Lenin: Leningrad.

By 1924, a decade of world war, civil war, famine, class strife, and finally the forces of nature – the city was hit by a devastating flood in that year – had left the former imperial capital in ruins. The magnificent buildings remained, but gone was the soul of a great civilisation as the cream of its society was either dead or had left the country in exile. With the onset of World War II the city experienced yet more suffering and destruction.

Undaunted, the people of Leningrad worked once again to rebuild their city into an important cultural, industrial and scientific centre. With the collapse of the Soviet Union in 1991, many of these accomplishments were swept away by the winds of change. Nevertheless, the new freedom allowed the city to win back its historical name and memory. St Petersburg celebrated its 300th anniversary in 2003 and many long-awaited repairs were made.

Busy Nevsky Prospekt.

A beautiful misfit

From the beginning, St Petersburg has been something of an anomaly, a beautiful misfit, and a showpiece city. Peter the Great's vision of building a capital to rival the great cities of Europe seemed foolhardy to many, but in the end the great and stern tsar had the last laugh.

Peter gave his European designers – mostly Italian, German and French architects – a huge amount of space to play with. Hence the city's layout of massive perspectives and boldly symmetrical lines. Squares are laid out around monuments with buildings that draw the eye towards the architectural highpoint. The skyline is "horizontal" – low stone and pastel-coloured buildings punctuated by the golden spires of the Admiralty, the Peter and Paul Cathedral, and St Isaac's Cathedral.

However, the grid-like layout is not at all monotonous. The city is set on 44 islands surrounded by winding canals and rivers that are spanned by decorative and fanciful bridges. St Petersburg, so unlike the traditional Russian cities

that grew up around a fortress, has a special beauty and charm.

Tsarist tastes

Of course, Peter the Great is not directly responsible for the St Petersburg that we see today, and few examples of the buildings of his era remain. His taste was simple and sparse. The preferences of his daughter, the Empress Elizabeth (1741–61) were much more fanciful. Her favourite architect, Bartolomeo Rastrelli, liked colours and tended to decorate buildings as one would a cake for a great occasion, with piping and swirls. Catherine the Great (1762–96) favoured classicism, but buildings were nevertheless grand in scope, and became even more so in the reign of Alexander I (1801–25) when they were designed to reflect the glory of Russia's victory over Napoleon and increasing foreign expansion.

Commerce and industrialisation before the Revolution brought the first railways, which linked Moscow and St Petersburg in 1851. Fine examples of Art Nouveau sprang up at the turn of the 20th century. Following the Revolution, the architecture of Stalin in the 1930s and 1950s was kept to the outskirts. One outstanding feature of Stalin's time was the construction of the Leningrad metro, which started running in 1955. Besides the metro decorations (particularly impressive on the Kirov-Vyborg line) there is little art of the Soviet period in the centre of the city. However, around 100 statues and busts to Lenin still stand. Some are in public places, but most are at factories and institutes. You will find a huge statue of Lenin outside **Finland-sky Vokzal ❶** (Finland Station).

Despite extensive damage to older buildings during World War II, most of them have been rebuilt and faithfully restored to their original state. Since Saint Petersburger Putin came to power, the city has benefited from large amounts of investment, and many buildings have been renovated.

Literary connections

Architecture tells us much about a city, but equally revealing, particularly in St Petersburg, are the impressions of its famous writers whose works

Lenin statue outside Finlandsky Vokzal.

CITY OF ISLANDS

St Petersburg is Russia's largest seaport and second largest city with an official population of just under five million. It lies 60°N, on the same latitude as Alaska, Hudson Bay, the southern tip of Greenland and Oslo. While the city originally straddled 101 islands at the mouth of the River Neva, which sweeps majestically through its centre, many have since disappeared as the rivers, streams and canals have been filled in. Today, the city is situated on 44 islands linked by 432 pedestrian, car and rail bridges. Twenty of these are drawbridges, some of which rise each night between around 2am and 5am, from April to the end of November, to allow the passage of seagoing ships. The schedule is posted around the city so there's no excuse for getting stranded on the wrong side of the river. The Neva flows westerly from Lake Ladoga, 74 km (46 miles) to the east, into the Gulf of Finland. Here, where it branches into three arms, separating the Petrograd Side and Vasilievsky Island from the mainland, the main channel is 400 metres (437 yards) wide.

Today, granite embankments contain the 68 rivers, canals, channels and streams which separate the islands. These waterways, Lake Ladoga and the sea freeze over in winter and icebreakers have to be used to keep the port open throughout the year.

Peter the Great is usually represented as a young man, but in the grounds of the Peter and Paul Fortress there is a sculpture by Michael Chemyakin portraying him in later life.

The sprawling Peter and Paul Fortress.

have immortalised many of its sights. Alexander Pushkin (1799–1837) depicted St Petersburg's forbidding aspect in his poem *The Bronze Horseman*. The statue of Peter the Great, located on the river side in front of Isaakiyevsky Sobor (St Isaac's Cathedral), is known as the Bronze Horseman. In Pushkin's poem it comes to life and bears down on an enfeebled and terrified clerk called Evgeny. Pushkin also describes St Petersburg high life in his poem *Evgeny Onegin*. The hero, one of literature's great dandies, becomes bored and disillusioned by an endless round of balls, restaurants and women.

Tolstoy takes up the same theme in his novels *War and Peace* and *Anna Karenina*, contrasting the spontaneity and simplicity of Moscow life with that of St Petersburg, which he saw as false, artificial and corrupt. Dostoyevsky, in marked contrast, wrote of low life and the poor. Ukraine-born Gogol arrived in Sankt Piterburg in 1828 and wrote many of his latter works there, but this damp, dark city probably drove him mad.

In the poem The Twelve, Alexander Blok found in the 1917 Revolution a vision of the city's rebirth and the Second Coming of Christ. But he quickly became disenchanted with the barbarity of the Bolshevik regime, and died an untimely death in 1921.

Yevgeny Zamyatin, in his short story *The Cavemen*, compared post-Revolutionary St Petersburg to a society of cave-dwellers, whose civilised values are subverted when the protagonist is forced to beg and then steal firewood in order to exist for just one more day.

A city under siege

Records of the city's suffering also exist in living memory. The older generation remembers the Siege of Leningrad (in Russian *blokada*) during World War II when the city was completely cut off from the outside world for almost 900 days. The Germans invaded Russia in July 1941 and reached Leningrad in August of that year. The city was encircled and cut off from September, when mass bombing began. Soviet troops finally broke through the blockade in

January 1943 and provisions reached the city through Finland Station, but the siege did not end until January 1944 when the Germans were beaten back. Victory left nearly one million dead, most from starvation. Some 470,000 victims of the blockade are buried at the **Piskarovskoye Memorial Cemetery** on the northern outskirts of the city. The sheer size of this cemetery, with the dead buried in mass graves, gives a more chilling impression of the loss of life than any statistic.

Sts Peter and Paul Fortress

The most appropriate place to begin a tour of St Petersburg is **Petropavlovskaya Krepost ❷** (Peter and Paul Fortress; fortress grounds: Thu–Tue 8.30am–8pm; museums: Tue 10am–5pm, Thu–Mon 11am–6pm), built during the time of the Great Northern War, 1700–21. The first stone was laid on 16 May 1703 Old Style (Russia still used the Julian calendar, which was 13 days behind the Gregorian).

The fortress, built on **Zayachy Ostrov** (Hare Island) according to plans drawn by Peter himself, was designed to stave off the enemy, occupying as it did a strategic position at the dividing point of the Neva into the Malaya (Small) and Bolshaya (Big) Neva. It became a notorious prison – the Bastille of tsarist Russia. In 1917 the **Kommandantsky Dom ❸** (Commandant's House) was one of the Bolshevik command posts for the storming of the Winter Palace. But today such an infamous place has become a favourite area for relaxation, and many city-dwellers flock to the beach in front of the fortress on pleasant days. Though it is forbidden to swim there, many do, even in winter. There are various buildings to see within the fortress, as well as temporary exhibitions. The major features are **Petrovskie Vorota** (Peter's Gates), built by Domenico Trezzini, who also designed the cathedral. The gate, originally built in wood and later in stone (1717–18), has hardly changed since it was built. The bas-relief above the tsarist emblem of the double-headed eagle depicts the Apostle Peter overthrowing Simon the Magus, an allegory of Russia's victory over the Swedes.

Petropavlovsky Sobor (SS Peter and Paul Cathedral) is rectangular in layout and quite unlike a traditional Russian place of worship. It bears a tall spire standing at 122 metres (400 ft), which was the tallest building in the city until the Television Tower (316 metres/1,036 ft) was built. On the top is an angel carrying a cross. In 1830, Pyotr Telushkin, a roofer, climbed to the very top, with the aid of just a rope, to repair the cross which had been struck by lightning.

Inside the church are the white marble tombs of most of the Romanov emperors and empresses, as well as grand dukes. Peter the Great's tomb lies in the far right-hand corner. The remains of the last Russian tsar, Nicholas II, his wife, three of their children, and four servants were buried here in 1998 having been transported from Yekaterinburg in the Urals where they were murdered in 1918. Their grave is in **Yekaterinsky Pridel** (St Catherine Chapel), which is to the right as you enter through the main cathedral entrance. The last ruling Romanovs have been consigned to this private chapel for two reasons: Nicholas II renounced the throne; and commoners are buried with the royal family. The tombs of Alexander II, the tsar liberator who freed the serfs but was none the less blown up by leftist terrorists, and his wife are in great contrast to the others. Theirs are the only ones not made of marble, but made instead from Altai jasper and Urals rhodonite.

In 1717 the fortress became a prison for political prisoners and the cells are now open as a museum in the **Trubetskoy Bastion**. One of its first prisoners, who was later beaten to death, was Peter the Great's son Alexei, who was falsely accused of plotting against his father. Other distinguished inmates were Fyodor Dostoyevsky; Alexander Radishchev, author of *A Journey from St Petersburg to Moscow*, in which he criticised autocracy and serfdom; Nikolai Chernyshevsky, a Revolutionary democrat and author of *What is to be Done?*; Lenin's elder brother, Alexander Ulyanov, who was executed for taking part in the plot to murder Alexander III, and the socially orientated writer Maxim Gorky, who wrote

Peter and Paul Cathedral, where Russia's tsars lay to rest.

a Revolutionary proclamation calling for the overthrow of the monarchy. The prison is named after another of its inmates – Prince Sergei Trubetskoy – one of the organisers of the Decembrist revolt.

In the Soviet period, political prisoners were taken to the **KGB headquarters** ❹ (now FSB) on Liteiny prospekt in a building nicknamed the "Big House", and not without reason: it is the tallest, biggest building in the city centre.

Peter and Paul Fortress has six bastions, one named Gosudarev (Ruler's) in honour of Peter the Great, and the rest named after his closest companions who supervised the construction of the fortress. A cannon shot is fired every day at noon from the **Naryshkinsky Bastion**.

On the banks of the Neva

On the river banks on the other side of Troitsky Most stands **Domik Petra Velikogo** ❺ (Peter the Great's Wooden Cabin), which is now a museum (Wed–Mon 10am–5.30pm; closed last Mon of month). Although protected by stone on the outside, inside there is a perfectly preserved, two-roomed hut. It was made out of rough pine over a period of three days in 1703. Peter lived here for six years while overseeing the building of the city.

Normally moored in front of the blue **Nakhimovskoye Uchilishche** ❻ (Nakhimov Naval Academy) on Petrogradskaya Embankment – designed in the style of Petrine Baroque and completed in 1912 – is the cruiser **Kreyser Avrora** ❼ famous for its part in the 1917 Revolution. At 9.45pm on 25 October 1917, the Aurora fired a blank round, the signal for the Bolshevik forces to storm the Winter Palace, the seat of the provisional government. Prior to this, between 1904 and 1905, it served the tsarist government at the Battle of Tsu-Shima against Japan. Today, the cruiser once again flies the tsarist-era naval flag of St Andrew whose blue diagonal cross on

a white background is common in St Petersburg, home of the Russian fleet. In 2013 the ship was re-commissioned as the flagship of the Russian Navy. It is currently undergoing a refit but should be back at its mooring in 2016.

On the opposite side of the river is the tsar's modest **Letny Dvorets** ❽ (Summer Palace; May–Oct Wed–Mon 10am–6pm) built by Domenico Trezzini in 1710. It has retained most of its original features, occupying two floors of identical layout, one for the tsar and one for the tsarina. Its simple exterior was later decorated with terracotta panels depicting scenes from mythology – including allegorical portrayals of the Northern War. The palace was undergoing extensive renovation work at the time of writing.

Letny Sad (Summer Garden) in which the palace stands is the oldest garden in the city. Much of the work was done by the architect Jean-Baptiste Le Blond. It was originally a formal garden with many rare plants and trees, an aviary and a grotto, but its appearance has changed over the years as Venetian statues were

The St Peter and Paul Fortress also contains a Museum of Cosmonautics and Rocket Technology.

The cruiser Aurora outside the Nakhimov Naval Academy.

FACT

The Metchet (Mosque), built on Kronversky prospekt in 1912, is the main mosque in the city.

The Alexander Column stands proudly in front of the Winter Palace.

commissioned and buildings such as the **Chainy Domik** (Tea House) and a statue of Ivan Krylov (1768–1844), the author of children's fables, have been added, but it is still one of the city's most peaceful and shady places.

The path through the centre of the gardens leads as far as the Fontanka Canal and the red **Mikhailovsky Zamok** ❾ (St Michael Castle, also known as Engineer's Castle; Mon 10am–5pm, Wed and Fri–Sun 10am–6pm, Thu 1–9pm). The castle was built by Catherine the Great's son, Tsar Paul I, with strong walls and a moat to prevent any attempt at assassination, the fate which had befallen his father, Tsar Peter III, at Catherine's hands. But such efforts proved in vain: military officers bribed the guards and murdered Paul just 40 days after he had taken up residence. The castle acquired its current name when it became a school for engineers in 1819. Its most famous student was Dostoyevsky. It has several beautifully restored rooms and temporary exhibitions of works from the vast Russian Museum collection, of which it is a branch.

The Hermitage

The **Gosudarstvenny Ermitazh** ❿ (State Hermitage; Tue –Sun 10.30am–6pm, Wed until 9pm; last ticket one hour before closing, free admission last Thu of the month) consists of five buildings, **Zimny Dvorets** (Winter Palace), the Small Hermitage, the New Hermitage, the Old Hermitage and the theatre. Architect Bartolomeo Rastrelli started work on the Winter Palace in 1754, during the reign of Empress Elizabeth. He built it, to use his own words, "solely for the glory of all Russia". The palace was home to the imperial family, with the exception of Paul I, until 1917, when it became seat of the provisional government.

The **Hermitage Collection** was originally the private collection of Catherine the Great. She collected in earnest, instructing her ambassadors in Europe to buy not just individual pictures, but entire collections. She housed them in her retreat ("Hermitage") and only a select few were permitted to see them. The museum was not open to the public until 1852. During the siege in the 1940s, most

of the artworks were successfully evacuated. Although renowned for its collections of Western European art, including early 13th-century Italian works, French Impressionists, Flemish masters and modern art, the Hermitage has other important departments, notably those of prehistoric cultures, Oriental and classical antiquities, as well as an exhibition of Scythian gold treasures that are among the finest in the world.

Of equal interest is the architecture of the interior: the Jordan Staircase, Great Hall, Large Throne Room and Gallery of the 1812 War, to name a few (see page 208).

Palace Square

Behind the Hermitage is the impressive **Dvortsovaya ploshchad** ⑪ (Palace Square), with its towering **Alexandrovskaya Kolonna** (Alexander Column) designed by August de Montferrand to commemorate the victory of Russian armies in the Napoleonic War during the reign of Alexander I. It is made from a granite monolith transported from the northern shore of the Gulf of Finland. This 47.5-metre (156-ft) column is held together entirely by its own weight. On the south side of the square is the curved, sprawling, neoclassical **Generalny Shtab** (General Staff building; Tue–Sun 10.30am–6pm, Wed until 9pm), designed by Carlo Rossi (1775–1849). Its arch is decorated with a chariot of victory and statues of warriors, and inside you will find a branch of the Hermitage exhibiting some of its vast collection of Impressionists as well as temporary exhibitions, usually with a contemporary twist.

Rossi designed many buildings in St Petersburg, most of which are painted pale yellow as opposed to the pale greens and blues preferred by Rastrelli. Before the Revolution many of the government buildings with the exception of the Admiralty – were painted dark red (for example, the General Staff building, the Winter Palace and the Senate and Synod).

At the corner of Palace Square is Millionnaya ulitsa (Millionaires Street), which runs behind the Hermitage to the Field of Mars. At the beginning

Masterpieces at the Hermitage.

of Millionnaya ulitsa the porch of the New Hermitage building is supported by figures of Atlas designed by a German architect, Leo von Klenze (1784–1864). At the end of the street is the **Mramorny Dvorets** ⑫ (Marble Palace; Mon, Wed and Fri–Sun 10am–6pm, Thur 1–9pm). It is faced with marble, which is a rarity in this city of plaster facades. The palace was commissioned by Catherine the Great for one of her favourites, Grigory Orlov, and the task of designing it went to the Italian architect Antonio Rinaldi (1709–94). Before the Revolution the palace was the home of various grand dukes, but in 1937 it became the city's Lenin Museum. Now it belongs to the Russian Museum and houses the Ludwig Museum collection of contemporary art, which was a gift to the Russian Museum from Germany's Ludwig Foundation, and other fine and applied arts.

The tsar used to review his troops in **Marsovo Pole** ⑬ (Field of Mars). It was redesigned after the 1917 Revolution by Lev Vladimirorich Rudnyev, who later built the skyscraper of

Moscow University. Some communists who fought and died in the Revolution and Civil War are buried here, where an eternal flame burns.

Decembrists Square

Along the embankment west of the Hermitage is the city's most famous statue: **Medny Vsadnik** ⑭ (The Bronze Horseman), depicting Peter the Great on a rearing horse. It was cast by the French sculptor Etienne Falconet and completed in 1782. The head of Peter the Great was designed by Falconet's pupil, Marie Collot, who never earned the recognition she deserved for this particular work.

The square in which the statue stands contains the **Senat i Sinod** ⑮ (Senate and the Synod), a building designed by Carlo Rossi between 1829 and 1832 which now serves as the Constitutional Court.

Nearby stands the golden spire of the **Admiralteystvo** ⑯ (Admiralty). This was one of the first buildings of the city, built in 1705, then replaced between 1806 and 1823 by the present neoclassical structure designed

Celebrating the 85th anniversary of Russia's Airborne Assault Troops in the Field of Mars.

by Andrei Zakharov. It was used as a naval headquarters and shipyard. At the top of the spire is a weathervane in the form of a ship, the emblem of the city. From the Admiralty the main streets of Nevsky, Gorokhovaya and Vosnesensky stretch out like a fan. The fountains in front of the Admiralty are surrounded by statues of Russia's cultural heroes, including the writers Nikolai Gogol and Mikhail Lermontov, the composer Mikhail Glinka and the poet Vasily Zhukovsky. The building is now a naval academy and off limits to tourists.

St Isaac's Square

Isaakievsky Sobor ❶ (St Isaac's Cathedral; Thu–Tue 10.30am–6pm; colonnade: 11am–6pm) stands in the square behind the Admiralty. It was built over a period of 40 years in the first half of the 19th century by the French architect Auguste de Montferrand. The dome is covered with 100 kg (220 lb) of pure gold. Forty-three types of stone and marble were used to decorate the lavish interior, including the lapis lazuli and malachite columns of the iconostasis. Among the general surfeit of visual splendour is a statue of the architect carrying a model of the cathedral in his hand. Montferrand very much wanted to be buried here, but his wish was denied by the tsar because of the Frenchman's Catholicism. In the middle of St Isaac's Square stands a statue of Nicholas I on a prancing horse, by Pyotr Klodt. Some 262 steps lead up to the *kolonnada* (colonnade) which runs around the dome affording wonderful city-centre views.

Mariinsky Dvorets ❶ (Mariinsky Palace), on the south side of the square, is now home to the city's Legislative Assembly. It was built between 1839 and 1844 by Andrei Stakenschneider, making it the last neoclassical palace to be built in St Petersburg. The building was a gift from Nicholas I to his daughter Maria and is sometimes known as the Maria Palace. The bridge in front, crossing the River

Moika, is **Siny Most** (Blue Bridge) and is the widest in the city. Further along the Moika in the direction of **Novaya Gollandia** (New Holland) is **Yusupovsky Dvorets** ❶ (Yusupov Palace; tours 11am–5pm) at No. 94, home of Rasputin's chief assassin, Prince Felix Yusupov. Rasputin was murdered here in 1916 and a visit to the cellar where he was poisoned, beaten and shot is part of the excellent guided tour. The palace survived the centuries with much of the furnishings intact, and includes a magnificent "home" theatre.

Theatre Square

The Moika turns a bend along the Kryukova Kanal, bordering **Teatralnaya ploshchad** (Theatre Square), home of the Mariinsky (formerly Kirov) Theatre and, opposite, the **Rimsky-Korsakov Conservatory**. Named after Maria wife of Alexander II, the **Mariinsky Teatr** ❷, rebuilt in 1883–96, is where many of Russia's operas and ballets were first performed, including Musorgsky's *Boris Godunov* (1874) and Tchaikovsky's

St Isaac's Square and the gilded dome of St Isaac's Cathedral.

Model of the Mariinsky Theatre inside the box office.

The red Rostral Columns on Vasilevsky Island were formerly used as lighthouses.

Sleeping Beauty (1890). Dancers such as Kschessinska, Pavlova and Nijinsky made their debut here. The new millennium has been a troubled one for the theatre; in 2003 a fire swept through a storage annexe several blocks from the theatre destroying the costumes and many of the sets. Though it evoked great controversy, a modern wing – the Mariinsky II – opened in 2013. Opponents tried to the get the design changed so as not to disrupt the historical character of the area but to no avail. Beside Kryukova Kanal in **Nikolskaya ploshchad** (St Nicholas Square) is the blue and gold **Nikolsky Sobor** ㉑ (Cathedral of St Nicholas), also known as the "Sailor's Church". This cathedral is often compared with Rastrelli's Smolny Cathedral, and is considered one of the finest examples of Russian Baroque.

Vasilievsky Island

On the other side of the river, facing the *Bronze Horseman*, is one of the oldest parts of the city, **Vasilievsky Ostrov** (Vasily's Island).

At the western end of the island you'll find the **Muzei sovremennogo iskusstva Erarta** (Erarta Museum of Contemporary Art; ulitsa 29-ya Liniya 2; Wed–Mon 10am–10pm), arguably Russia's best contemporary art museum, with over 2,000 works from the 1950s onwards as well as temporary exhibitions. It's a must for anyone interested in underground art of the Soviet period.

One of the island's more "modern" buildings overlooking the river is the **Akademiya Khudozhestv** ㉒ (Academy of Arts; Wed–Sun 11am–7pm), built by Catherine the Great in 1757 as a training ground for professional painters, architects, sculptors and engravers. Repin, Bryullov and Losenko all studied here, and the museum shows some of their work as well as pieces by many other former students. In front of it, on a granite pier, stand two **sphinxes** which date from the 13th century BC. They were brought to St Petersburg from Egypt in 1832. The **obelisk** standing on the eastern side of the Academy commemorates Russia's victory over the Turks under Field-Marshal Rumyantsev in the 18th century.

The next building is the **Menshikovsky Dvorets** ㉓ (Menshikov Palace; Tue–Sat 10.30am–6pm, Sun 10:30am–5pm), now a branch of the Hermitage Museum. Alexander Menshikov was a friend and close associate of Peter the Great. As Menshikov's palace was finished before Peter's, it was used for large-scale entertainment. It has been meticulously restored and is a fine example of Dutch-inspired Petrine architecture.

Walking east along the embankment, the terracotta-coloured building is called **12 Kollegi** ㉔ (Twelve Colleges). Peter housed his *kollegia* (ministeries) here; it is now part of St Petersburg University. The building's construction, in which a number of architects, including Rastrelli, participated, was set as a competition – Russia's first. Construction took 19 years and was completed in 1741. To its east, the **Akademiya Nauk** ㉕ (Academy of Sciences) was built to house the expanding collection of the **Kunstkamera** (Chamber of Curiosities; Tue–Sun 11am–7pm) and a museum of anthropology and ethnography. Inside, beneath the dome, there is a collection of genetic abnormalities, embryos and human organs, which Peter the Great hoped would "cure" his people of superstition.

Vasilievsky Island's easterly "spit" offers one of the best views of the city. Many newlyweds come here to be photographed. Before the Revolution the magnificent building which dominates the spit was the Stock Exchange. Until the 1880s this point of Vasilievsky Island was the city's port. The red Rostral Columns were the lighthouses; they are decorated with the prows of boats representing four Russian rivers: the Volga, Dnieper, Neva and Volkhov.

Nevsky prospekt

The 4.5-km (3-mile) **Nevsky prospekt**, which runs southeast from the Admiralty to Alexander Nevsky Most (bridge), is the most famous street in the city. Apart from the splendid architecture of Nevsky prospekt, it is the city's main shopping street and filled with cafés, restaurants and night spots. It is almost always jam-packed with residents and tourists, especially on sunny days.

Starting from **Admiralteisky prospekt**, the first important street which crosses the Nevsky is **Malaya Morskaya**. Gogol lived at No. 17. Here he wrote the first chapters of *Dead Souls*. Pyotr Tchaikovsky died at No. 8. The next street is the once-fashionable **Bolshaya Morskaya**, home of the famous Fabergé shop (No. 24), still a jeweller's, but having lost its former glory.

The Nevsky crosses the River Moika where, on the right-hand side stands the red and white mid-17th-century **Stroganovsky Dvorets** ㉖ (Stroganov Palace; Wed and Fri–Mon 10am–6pm, Thu 1–9pm), home of one of Russia's leading families. Designed by Rastrelli, its exquisite period interiors, restored to the original glory, now form part of the Russian Museum.

Crossing Nevsky Prospekt.

The next street on the left, **ulitsa Bolshaya Konushennaya**, leads to the former stables. The residents of No. 13 Bolshaya Konushennaya included the Russian writer Ivan Turgenev and, later, the ballet dancer Nijinsky. The composer Rimsky-Korsakov lived at No. 11. A short distance along Nevsky prospekt, on the right, stands the majestic **Kazansky Sobor** (Kazan Cathedral; daily 8.30am–7.30pm) with its 90-metre- (295-ft)-high dome and 96 columns, designed by the architect Andrei Voronikhin in the first decade of the 19th century. In the square in front are statues of the heroes of the 1812 war, M.I. Kutuzov (who is also buried here) and M.B. Barclay de Tolly. From the 1930s, the cathedral was a Museum of the History of Religion and Atheism but today it is a working church once again. Opposite, at No. 28 Nevsky prospekt, is the Art Nouveau pre-1917 Russia head office of the Singer Sewing Machine Company.

As you cross the **Griboyedov Kanal**, the multi-coloured domes of **Khram Spasa na Krovi** (Church of the

Resurrection; Thu–Tue 10.30am–6pm), also known as the Church on the Spilled Blood, are visible. Built on the site of Alexander II's assassination, this is St Petersburg's most attractive church and boasts a wonderful mosaic interior. It took almost three decades to complete restoration work here, which began in the 1970s.

Two interesting bridges by the same architect, W. Traitteur (1825–6), cross the Griboyedov as it flows away from Nevsky prospekt to the right. The first is **Bankovsky Most** (Bankers' Bridge) on which stand guard two golden-winged griffins. The bridge is so named because the large building in front, housing the Institute of Finance and Economics, used to be the Russian Central Bank in tsarist times. Most of the country's gold supply was stored here; in ancient mythology, griffins stood guard over gold. Further down is **Lvinny Most** (Lion Bridge) where two lions hold the suspension cables of the bridge in their mouths.

Continuing eastwards along the Nevsky prospekt, on the left-hand side

Kazan Cathedral and New Year tree.

in ulitsa Mikhailovskovo is the luxurious **Grand Hotel Europe** ❸⓿. The street on which it stands leads into **ploshchad Iskusstv** (Arts Square), the home of the Russian Museum.

The yellow classical building of the **Russky Muzei** ❸❶ (Russian Museum; Mon 10am–5pm, Wed and Fri–Sun 10am–6pm, Thu 1–9pm) was built by Rossi between 1819 and 1825 for the Grand Duke Mikhail, Alexander I and Nicholas I's younger brother. Unlike the Hermitage it houses only Russian art and is a smaller, more manageable museum. The exhibits span almost 1,000 years of the history of Russian art, from a magnificent icon collection through works by avant-garde artists such as Malevich and Kandinsky to contemporary work.

Also in ploshchad Iskusstv stands the **Sankt Peterburzhskaya Filarmoniya** ❸❷ (St Petersburg Philharmonia) and the **Maly Teatr operi i Baleta imeni Mussorgskogo** ❸❸ (Small Musorgsky Theatre of Opera and Ballet). In the middle of the square is a statue of Pushkin by one of the city's leading sculptors, Mikhail Anikushin.

Back on the Nevsky prospekt, with ploshchad Iskusstv behind you, notice the long yellow and white facade of **Gostiny Dvor** ❸❹ on the right-hand side. This is one of St Petersburg's largest department stores. Two blocks along the Nevsky on the left-hand side, at No. 58, is **Yeliseyevsky** ❸❺, a food shop with an extravagant Art Nouveau interior, built by the rich merchant Yeliseyev and once the grandest delicatessen in St Petersburg.

Sadovaya Ulitsa runs beside Gostiny Dvor to **Sennaya ploshchad** (Hay Square), a traditionally seedy area. Raskolnikov, in Dostoyevsky's *Crime and Punishment*, wandered here, where "types so various were to be seen that no figure, however queer, would have caused surprise".

To the right just after the junction of Sadovaya ulitsa and Nevsky is **ploshchad Ostrovskogo**, a huge square with a statue of Catherine the Great surrounded by her most prominent court officials, some of whom were her lovers. This square is named after the playwright Alexander Ostrovsky. Its buildings include the **Rossiskaya**

Deep winter in the city.

Natsionalnaya Biblioteka ㊱ (Russian National Library; not open to the public) and the **Alexandriinsky Dramatichesky Teatr** ㊲ (Alexander Theatre of Drama), with its white Corinthian columns.

Behind the theatre, leading away from the right-hand corner of the square, is **ulitsa Zodchegvo Rossi** (Architect Rossi Street). This street has perfect proportions with the width of the street equalling the height of the buildings. Among its buildings is the **Vaganova Ballet Academy** ㊳, the training ground for some of the greatest names in ballet, including Pavlova, Nijinsky, Nureyev, Makarova and Baryshnikov.

Back on Nevsky prospect again, the next canal is the **Fontanka** with its impressive **Anichkov Most** (Anichkov Bridge). The horses which decorate the bridge are the work of sculptor Pyotr Klodt; during World War II they were buried underground in the nearby gardens of the **Dvorets Yunikh Pionerov** (Palace of Young Pioneers), as were many of the city's other famous statues.

Behind Anichkov Bridge stands the dark-red **Dvorets Beloselskikh-Belozerskikh** ㊴ (Beloselsky-Belozersky Palace), built by Stakenschneider in 1847–8 for Prince Beloselsky-Belozersky.

To the left, on the banks of the Fontanka, is the yellow **Dvorets Sheremetyevykh** ㊵ (Sheremetyev Palace; Thu–Mon 11am–7pm, Wed 1–9pm), built by Chevakinsky between 1750 and 1755. It houses a magnificent collection of musical instruments from the 19th and 20th centuries. One of its outbuildings, the **Fontanny Dom**, houses the **Muzei Anni Akhmatovoi** (entrance at 53 Liteyny prospekt; Tue and Thu–Sun 10.30am–6.30pm, Wed noon–8pm), the literary museum of Anna Akhmatova, one of Russia's greatest poets who lived here between 1924 and 1952.

At the next junction, Liteiny prospekt, is the famous second-hand bookshop, **Bukinist** (No. 59). To the right, **Vladimirsky prospekt** leads to a side street, Kuznechny Pereulok, where the **Muzei F.M. Dostyevskovo** ㊶ (Dostoyevsky Museum; Tue and Thu–Sun 11am–6pm, Wed 1–8pm) is at No. 5/2.

Anichkov Bridge and one of its famous horse statues.

At the very end of Nevsky prospekt is **ploshchad Alexander Nevskogo**, where the **Hotel Moscow** stands. Here is the **Alexander Nevsky Lavra ㊷** (grounds 6am–11pm), the oldest and most beautiful monastery complex in the city. Alexander Nevsky crushed two separate invading Swedish and German armies in the mid-13th century and was later canonised. His remains are buried inside the Lavra.

There are several cemeteries inside the Alexander Nevsky Lavra, where some of Russia's most famous citizens are buried. In the **Lazarus Cemetery** (daily 9.30am–9pm) where Peter the Great's sister, Natalya Alexeyevna, lies, you will find the graves of famous architects, including Carlo Rossi and Andrei Voronikhin. The composers Mikhail Glinka, Pyotr Tchaikovsky, Modest Musorgsky and Nikolai Rimsky-Korsakov are buried in the **Tikvin Cemetery** (same opening hours) opposite, together with Fyodor Dostoyevsky. Today, most famous people from the arts world are buried in the **Volkhov Cemetery**, a short drive away from the Lavra complex.

Smolny Cathedral and Institute

Another religious building not to be missed is **Smolny Sobor ㊸** (Smolny Cathedral; Thu–Tue 10.30am–6pm), situated northeast of Nevsky prospekt. Designed by Rastrelli, this pale blue and white building in the shape of a Greek cross seems to float rather than stand on the horizon. Smolny means "tar" and the site of the cathedral was used as a tar yard until 1723. Although construction began in the mid-18th century, the cathedral was not finished until the end of the 19th century.

In 1764 Catherine the Great created an institute next to the cathedral "for the education of well-born young ladies", the first of its kind in Russia. The **Smolny Institut** was housed in the yellow, neoclassical building designed by Giacomo Quarenghi between 1806 and 1808. In August 1917 this building became the headquarters of the Bolshevik Central Committee, and it was from here that Lenin led the uprising in October of that year.

Opposite the cathedral, two blocks along **Shpalernaya ulitsa**, are the

Dostoyevsky's grave in Alexander Nevsky Monastery Cemetery.

Kikiny Palati (Kikin Palace) and **Tavrichesky Dvorets** (Tauride Palace; 8am–10pm). Kikin was an associate of Peter the Great and although the palace has been rebuilt, the basic structure dates from 1714. The Tauride Palace was built between 1783 and 1789 for Grigory Potemkin, remembered for annexing the Crimea (called Tavria) in 1783. The building is closed to visitors, but the lovely gardens and lake are delightful for strolling around.

Out-of-town palaces

A visit to St Petersburg is not complete without a trip to one or more of the palaces around the city. Petrodvorets, the Catherine Palace at Pushkin (Tsarskoye Selo), and Pavlovsk attract the most visitors. They have been almost fully restored following the devastation of German occupation in World War II. The palaces at Oranienbaum and Gatchina have also undergone major and painstaking restoration work.

Petrodvorets (Peterhof; grounds: Tue–Sun 9am–8pm; Grand Palace:

Tue–Sun 10.30am–6pm), Peter's summer palace, is situated on the Gulf of Finland, 29 km (18 miles) west of the city. One of its most striking features is its fountains. The original palace was built by Peter the Great in 1725 to the design of Jean-Baptiste Le Blond. It was much simpler than the version that now stands, which was embellished and enlarged by Empress Elizabeth. They chose the magnificent site on a natural slope – a Versailles by the sea – and were responsible for the intricate fountains, a major feat on land consisting of marshy clay.

Looking at pictures of Petrodvorets after the ravages of World War II, one wonders how it was ever rebuilt. Some, but by no means all of its treasures were smuggled out in time to escape bomb damage. The Grand Cascade is the focal point of the water gardens in front of the **Grand Palace**, with the famous statue of Samson rending apart the jaws of a lion. There are 144 fountains in the 607 hectares (1,500 acres) of park, all operating without a single pump.

The gardens contain three pavilions. The first, the **Hermitage**, was where Peter entertained, helped by a "dumb waiter" device – a section of the round table which was lowered below ground for clearing and replenishing. The **Marly** is built in a simple Dutch style and **Monplaisir**, at the water's edge, became Peter's favourite retreat; he could see the sea from his bed.

Inside, his taste is reflected in the beautiful oak staircase, oak study and the elaborate throne room, where his original throne sits. Catherine the Great later introduced such rooms as the Portrait Gallery, with its portraits of 368 women in different costumes.

About 12 km (7 miles) along the coast is **Oranienbaum** (Wed–Mon 10.30am–6pm), built by Alexander Menshikov. It was the construction of Oranienbaum that inspired Peter the Great to build Petrodvorets. The **Chinese Palace**, built by Catherine, has a

Peterhof – 'Versailles by the Sea'.

rococo interior and a baroque exterior both designed by Antonio Rinaldi.

The Tsar's Village

Pushkin (formerly Tsarskoye Selo, the Tsar's Village) can be reached by train from St Petersburg's Vitebsk Station. This station is well worth seeing for its splendid Russian Art Nouveau interior. It was the first Russian station and the line between here and Tsarskoe Selo was the first Russian railway (1837).

Peter the Great's wife, Catherine I, chose the site for a stone country house, built as a surprise for her husband while he was away in Poland. It seems to be the fate of each royal palace to be altered by successive monarchs and Peter's daughter, the Empress Elizabeth, decided to build a new and more opulent palace here in 1741. She asked Rastrelli to model it on Versailles. It was enlarged by subsequent rulers, particularly by Catherine the Great, whose architect, the Scotsman Charles Cameron, gave the palace a more stately feel, but above all it is Elizabeth's own creation. The

extravagant, baroque design is symbolic of the mood which dominated during her reign. In 1941 Tsarskoye Selo was occupied by the German Army, which left the town and palace in ruins.

The interior of the restored **Bolshoi Yekaterinsky Dvorets** (Catherine Palace; Wed–Sun 10am–6pm, Mon 10am–9pm;), like its exterior, is a mixture of styles by different architects: for example, the baroque of Rastrelli and the classicism of Cameron. The Great Hall, with its massive mirrors, wood carvings and glistening gold is perhaps the most sumptuous of all. The palace is famous for its amber room, though what today's visitors see is a reconstruction, the original amber panels having been carted off by the Nazis. Their fate remains a mystery.

There is a great deal to see in the park, including the Upper and Lower Baths, the Hermitage, the great pond, the fountain of the milkmaid with the broken pitcher, inspired by one of La Fontaine's fables, and the Caprice. When visiting a palace that has been so highly restored, it is important to

Catherine Palace, the summer residence of Russian emperors.

The opulent Amber Room in the Catherine Palace.

THE AMBER ROOM MYSTERY

Of all the works of art that disappeared from St Petersburg's palaces during World War II, few have captured the imagination of historians and treasure hunters as much as the Amber Room. This priceless 18th-century masterpiece was created by German craftsmen in the early 1700s for the Prussian King Friedrich I's palace in Charlottenburg, Berlin, and his son gave it to Peter the Great in 1716.

In 1754 the Amber Room was mounted in the Catherine Palace at Pushkin, and German and Russian artisans expanded the original panels to fit the larger space. It comprised six large oak wall panels, covering 55 sq. metres (592 sq ft), inlaid with six tons of amber, wall mirrors, and Italian mosaics containing precious stones. The room prompted one 18th-century British ambassador to call it the Eighth Wonder of the World.

In 1941 the Nazis removed it to the German city of Königsberg (now the Russian city of Kaliningrad). What happened to it afterwards remains a mystery to this day, but it's generally thought it was destroyed along with the city in the RAF raids of 1944. In 1979 Russian craftsmen began work on recreating the room at the Catherine Palace, and reconstruction work lasted over 20 years. The room was re-inaugurated in 2003. The project cost a whopping $18 million with the German government and private investors footing a substantial part of the bill.

see the ruins, so a visit to the **Chinese Palace** is also recommended. In the grounds stand the **Alexander Park and Palace** (Wed–Mon 10am–5pm). This smaller, more classical palace was presented to Alexander I by his grandmother, Catherine the Great, on the occasion of his marriage.

A gift for Paul and Maria

The next stop on the Electric Railway, some 4 km (2 miles) further, is **Pavlovsk**. The palace at Pavlovsk (daily 10am–6pm), much smaller than the others, was built by Catherine the Great for her son Paul and his wife Maria Fyodorovna. The architect, who was also commissioned to redesign the palace gardens in accordance with the then fashionable English style, was again Charles Cameron. Later, an Italian architect, Vincenzo Brenna, was brought in. The land was originally chosen for the royal hunt, on account of the abundant elk and wild fowl. The rooms inside the palace reflect the personalities of Paul and his wife. Paul's militaristic interests can be seen in the Hall of War, Throne Room and

The Apollo Colonnade at Pavlovsk.

Hall of the Maltese Knights of St John. His wife's Hall of Peace forms a pleasant and intended contrast.

The tapestries in the Carpet Room represent motifs from Cervantes' *Don Quixote*. There is a lot of French furniture on display, embroidered French curtains in the Greek Hall, and in the Hall of Peace a tripod-vase of crystal and red-gold produced in the St Petersburg glass factory in 1811. In Maria Fyodorovna's boudoir stands a piano imported from London. There is also a large collection of Sèvres porcelain pieces and a clock in Paul's study presented to him by Pope Pius VI.

The most important features of the large gardens are the Temple of Friendship (the friendship between Maria and her mother-in-law), the Centaur Bridge, the Cold Baths, the Apollo Colonnade and the Pavilion of the Three Graces. In time Paul transferred his affections to the palace at **Gatchina**, 45 km (28 miles) south of St Petersburg (Tue–Sun 10am–6pm), which was designed by Rinaldi and completed in 1781. It has since undergone extensive restoration.

Church of the Resurrection, St Petersburg's most attractive church.

THE HERMITAGE

The Hermitage Collection of Old Masters, sculptures, antiquities and archaeology remains a powerful symbol for St Petersburg and Russia.

Art has always been political in Russia. Catherine II bought her first collection of 225 paintings in 1764 to get one up on Frederick of Prussia, who could not afford them. She went on to purchase vast national collections one after another – the Campana collection in Italy, the Crozat collection in France and the Walpole collection in England – until she had more than 4,000 paintings and 10,000 drawings. The sale of these works of art to Russia aroused storms of disapproval and political censure but, in each case, it also proved Catherine's wealth, power and cunning in the international arena.

The 19th century added rich archaeological collections – archaeology being a patriotic and political science important in proving the glory of the Russian land – and more paintings and applied art. All this came to the Hermitage, heir to the imperial collections, along with thousands of confiscated works including, after 1917, those of the Impressionists. During the Soviet era the Hermitage collection was a symbol of Soviet learning and magnificence, and today, with its 3 million pieces, it remains a great source of pride to Russians everywhere. In 2014, the Hermitage opened a new wing dedicated to contemporary art which spurred on much controversy.

Masterpieces by Rembrandt such as The Sacrifice of Isaac, Return of the Prodigal Son, The Holy Family and Descent from the Cross fill almost a whole room.

Rastrelli's Baroque palace (1754–62) dominates the immense Palace Square. It is most beautiful at night, when richly lit.

The Madonna Litta by Leonardo da Vinci, aquired by tsar Alexander II for the Hermitage.

The stunning display of Impressionist and Post-Impressionist canvasses includes Ladies of Arles by Van Gogh (above), as well as work by Monet, Sisley and Pissaro.

AN IMPERIAL RETREAT

Catherine the Great inherited Rastrelli's new Winter Palace when she came to the throne in 1762. She wanted a more intimate space, however, and added a small pavilion to be a "Hermitage", with room for her art, and tables for private dinners. She then added a second pavilion and galleries, forming the Small Hermitage (1764–67), and a Large Hermitage along the waterfront (1771–87). Here she hung her fast-growing collection, played billiards, and, after the addition of the theatre (1783–87), allowed guests to wander around after performances. In the 1830s Nicholas I decided to open the museum to the public. The New Hermitage opened in 1852. The Winter Palace was added to the museum after 1917, although for some years it was a Palace of Culture, showing films and lectures to the masses.

Visit the magnificent collection of gold, from 6th-century BC Scythian and Ancient Greek items to Oriental daggers and jewellery.

Once ambassadors ascended the Jordan staircase to be received at court. Today visitors can admire the stunning white marble and gold interior.

Picasso is well represented at the Hermitage. Below are his Woman with a Fan and Dance of the Veils.

Arkhangelsk is famous for its wooden architecture.

THE EUROPEAN NORTH

The North of Russia is a land of great beauty, of harsh winters and summer "white nights", where the life, traditions and architecture of old Russia can still be experienced.

Main Attractions

Vologda
Kargopol
Solovetsky Islands
Petrozavodsk
Kizhi
Vyborg
Veliky Novgorod
Staraya Russa
Pskov
Pushkin Estate

Russians often say that the medieval city of Vologda, 500 km (310 miles) east of St Petersburg, is the gateway to the north, an area stretching from Finland in the west to the Urals in the east, and north to the Beloye More (White Sea) and Barents Sea.

The importance of the north dates from medieval times. When Kiev came under the Mongol yoke, many of its inhabitants fled north, taking their skills with them. Monks settled the region and founded monasteries which grew into important cultural centres. By the end of the 15th century, with the formation of a single Russian state under Muscovite rule, the northern border needed defending. A series of fortresses was constructed, often in the form of monasteries and with the active help of the monks such as at Solovki.

A rich heritage

In 1553 Sir Richard Chancellor, an Englishman, opened up the northern waterways to foreigners and merchants sailed along the rivers Sukhona and Severnaya Dvina (Northern Dvina) en route to Moscow. Arkhangelsk (Archangel) was founded as a trading port and flourished, along with other towns such as Veliky Ustyug. Huge fairs attracted goods and traders from both East and West, from England, Holland, Greece, Armenia, China and Persia. There was a large community of English merchants in Arkhangelsk and an English wharf in the port. Local crafts – niello metalwork from Ustyug, carved ivory from Kholmogory – were valued all over Russia.

The north is rich in wooden churches, reflecting the wealth of the area between the 16th and 18th centuries, when the church was the centre of social and administrative life in a community. Indeed, the social

Sunrise in Veliky Novgorod.

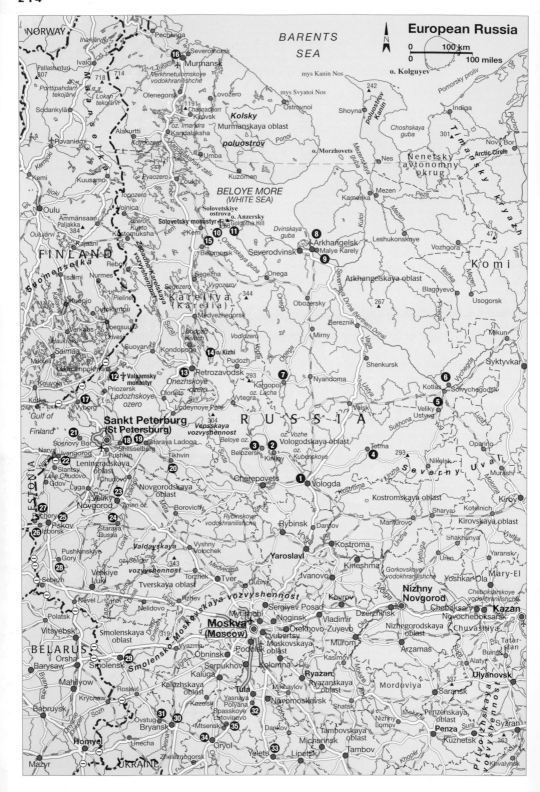

significance of churches was so great that the *trapeznaya* (narthex) was often larger than the church itself – in the case of the church of St Nicholas in the monastery of Muyezero, four times its size.

Peter the Great was in part responsible for the decline of the area when he ruled that the Gulf of Finland would be Russia's "Window on the West" and not Arkhangelsk as was previously. With the foundation of St Petersburg in 1703, the glorious days of the Russian north were suddenly over. Peter westernised his country by looking west rather than north. For 150 years the region was isolated from the mainstream of Russian life and the fairs and markets waned for lack of goods. Towns and villages dependent on trade declined to provincial status.

What may have seemed to be a tragedy was, in ethnographical terms, the area's salvation. When the north was rediscovered in the late 19th century by ethnographers, then by artists, they found a society which was living in the past. Not only were there hundreds of stone churches and monasteries set in magnificent landscapes, but there was a wealth of wooden buildings, religious and secular. What's more, the population had maintained age-old traditions, preserving fairytales, folk songs and customs which had already disappeared from much of Russia.

Artists flocked to the region. Nationalist composers such as Balakirev and Rimsky-Korsakov collected folk songs, incorporating the melodies in numerous compositions. Their art and music opened up the north to the world. For today's traveller who wants to get close to traditional Russian life and architecture, to understand how people lived in the past, this is one of the best places to go.

Gateway to the north

Ivan the Terrible fortified **Vologda** ❶, building a **Kremlin** (fortress) to strengthen control over the north which became an important trade route with Europe during his reign. He received Chancellor here on his memorable voyage, and from here a Russian envoy was sent to England. The chronicles record how Ivan personally oversaw the building of **Sofiysky Sobor** (Cathedral of St Sophia; Wed–Sun 10am–6pm), 1568–70, though, according to legend, when a red tile fell on his head as he walked round his new church the irate tsar set off for Moscow leaving the cathedral unconsecrated for 17 years.

The cathedral stands on the high bank of the River Vologda, in the centre of what was once the Kremlin. Its late 17th-century frescoes combine medieval monumentality and the contemporary decorative manner. The archbishop's residence, an attractive huddle of buildings by the cathedral, includes the Baroque **Palati Iosifa Zolotovo** (Palace of Joseph the Golden), 1764–9. What remains of the Kremlin is now the **Vologodsky oblastnoi krayevedchesky muzei** (Vologda Regional Museum; Wed–Sun 10am–5pm) which relates the history of the city. Just across from

Vologda's Kremlin.

the Kremlin stands the city's **Muzei Kryzheva** (Lace Museum; Wed–Sun 10am–5pm).

Vologda itself is a charming city best seen from the river with its 18th-century churches and secular buildings running along the embankment. Of particular note are the **Tserkov Svyatikh Konstantin i Yelena** (Church of SS Constantine and Helen), 1690, with its typical tent-shaped, free-standing belfry and, among the secular buildings, the **Dom Admirala Barsha** (Admiral Barsh Mansion), the neoclassical **Skuliabinskaya Bogadelnaya** (Skuliabin Almshouse) and the wooden **Dom Levashova** (Levashov House), as well as the enchanting wooden **Dom Zasetskikh** (Zasetsky House), 1790–5. Another place worth seeking out is a tiny museum called **Mir zabytykh veshchey** (World of Forgotten Things; Wed–Sun 10am–5pm) a quaint collection illustrating the 19th-century life of a local family.

Monasteries of the north

Some 4km (2.5 miles) north of Vologda, on the road to **Beloye Ozero**, is the **Spaso-Prilutsky Monastyr** (Monastery of the Saviour on the Bend). To get the best view climb the steep wooden staircase under the roof of the Water Tower. From here you can see the oldest and most typical northern building in the complex: the stone **Spassky Sobor** (Cathedral of the Saviour), 1542, the jumble of buildings around it and, over the walls, the Sofiysky Sobor. During Napoleon's invasion of Russia, treasures from the Kremlin and many Moscow monasteries were stored here.

Buses and sometimes pleasure boats travel from Vologda to the **Kirillov-Belozersky Monastyr** (St Kirill-Belozersky Monastery), which stands on the edge of Siverskoye Ozero (Lake Siverskoye), 120 km (72 miles) to the north. The boat winds past wooden windmills and churches before arriving at **Kirillov** ❷, where the monastery emerges from behind the trees, its white stone buildings and domes reflected in the water. The monastery was founded in 1397 and by the 17th century was one of the richest foundations in Russia, largely due to the sale of salt. Vasily III, tsar of Russia in the early 1500s, came here to pray for a child by his apparently barren wife, Elena, and the following year they were blessed with a son, who became Ivan the Terrible.

There are a number of 15th- and 16th-century churches, but the star is the **Uspensky Sobor** (Dormition Cathedral), which has superb frescoes and 17th-century iconostasis. Twenty kilometres (12 miles) northeast from the St Kirill-Belozersky Monastery is the **Ferapontovsky Monastyr** (Monastery of St Therapont) on the banks of **Borodavskoye Ozero** (Lake Borodava). Its main claim to fame lies in the frescoes in the **Rozhdestvensky Sobor** (Cathedral of the Nativity of the Virgin), painted in the first few years of the 16th century by Dionisius and his sons. The superb cycle, devoted to the life of the Virgin, is regarded as Dionisius' swan song. A romantic local

Vologda Regional Museum display.

legend attributes his appearance this far north to the death of his beloved wife and his subsequent desire to find peace in the monastery.

The town of **Belozersk** ❸, 40 km (25 miles) north of Kirillov, retains much of its wooden 19th-century appearance, plus the symbols of its wealthy past: the massive **Uspensky Sobor** (Dormition Cathedral), 1553, devoid of ornament; the heavy **Preobrazhensky Sobor** (Cathedral of the Transfiguration), 1670s, and the jolly **Vsemilostivovo Spasa** (Church of the Most Merciful Saviour), 1723. Most impressive of all are the remains of the ancient fortress, the high earthen ramparts which run around the old town.

Totma ❹, 200 km (124 miles) east of Vologda, is an attractive small town with superb 18th-century churches displaying fine monumental brickwork. Oddly enough, Totma was the starting point for several 18th-century expeditions, and is the birthplace of Ivan Kuskov, the explorer who established the Russian settlement of Fort Ross in California. The **Dom-Muzei**

Kuskov (Kuskov House Museum) examines his life.

Veliky Ustyug ❺, 250 km (155 miles) north of Totma, is now a sleepy provincial centre. Once it was one of the great market towns of the north, it is now renowned as the home of Ded Moroz – Grandfather Frost – complete with a touristy Yuletide theme park. The 17th-century **Uspensky Sobor** (Dormition Cathedral) houses a museum of religious art and vessels. Of particular note are the **Tserkov Zhyon-Mironosets** (Church of the Holy Women), 1714–22, the Baroque **Tserkov Simeona Stolpnika** (Church of Simeon the Stylite), 1725–65, and the **Mikhailo-Arkhangelsky Monastyr** (Monastery of the Archangel Michael), not to mention the wealth of 18th- and 19th-century mansions such as the **Dom Shilova** (Shilov House) on the embankment. It is an easy walk across the old town.

The Stroganov Masters

One of the richest periods in the history of Russian art is linked with the

Aleksander Nevsky Church, Vologda.

St Kirill-Belozersky Monastery.

Fine Arts Museum, Arkhangelsk.

Rush hour in Arkhangelsk.

so-called Stroganov Masters, artists employed by the wealthy Stroganov family, who made their fortune from the salt mines along the Severnaya Dvina River. The Stroganovs settled in **Solvychegodsk**  80 km (48 miles) north of Veliky Ustyug, and founded many fine churches, such as the fortress-like **Blagoveshchensky Sobor** (Annunciation Cathedral), 1560–79, which was the Stroganovs' own church, treasury and citadel, standing adjacent to their grounds. The cathedral is still rich in icons and frescoes.

They also founded the **Yavleniya Bogorodtsi Monastyr** (Monastery of the Presentation of the Virgin), 1689–93, its carved white stone details set off against the red brick and coloured tiles. The local museum contains many more icons and pieces of applied art linked with the Stroganovs and the town still has plenty of picturesque wooden buildings. Solvychegodsk is also a well-known health resort, with salt and mud baths, particularly good for the relief of rheumatism.

Arkhangelsk region

In the region bordering the White Sea is the small church-filled town of **Kargopol**, 427 km (257 miles) south of Arkhangelsk, yet another point on the important trading waterways of the north. Its key position on the River Onega led to a boom between the 16th and 17th centuries, manifested in the **Khristorozhdestvensky sobor** (Cathedral of the Nativity). The opening up of the northern trade route created the need for a port near the mouth of the Severnaya Dvina on the White Sea. In 1584 the town of Novye Kholmogory was founded; it later became known as **Arkhangelsk** (Archangel). By the beginning of the 18th century this was the centre of Russian shipbuilding. Now it is a big timber-logging and fishing area, known to the West through centuries of foreign trading links and the area's occupation by anti-Soviet Allied European and US troops immediately after the Revolution (1918–19). The great Russian scientist and poet Mikhail Lomonosov was born close to the town. The highlight here is the **Severny morskoi muzei** (Northern Naval Museum; Tue–Sun 11am–7pm) which looks at all aspects of life at sea in the region.

Some 25km km (16 miles) southeast of Arkhangelsk is the open-air **Muzei-zapovednik Derevyanova Zodchestva** (Wooden Architecture Museum Reserve; Wed–Mon, summer 10am–5pm, winter 10am–3pm) at **Malye Karely**. The forests make an effective backdrop for wooden churches, *izby* (cottages) and outhouses, many of them superbly decorated with carved window surrounds, eaves and crests running along the roof. The museum also holds concerts and provides a home to craftspeople.

Solovetsky Islands

Arkhangelsk is a departure point for the **Solovetskiye Ostrova** (Solovetsky Islands) in the White Sea, familiarly known as Solovki.

This name has a particular ring to those whose relatives were imprisoned or died in the Solovetsky Special Purpose Camp in the village of **Solovetsky**, one of the camps the writer Solzhenitsyn called the "gulag archipelago". You can visit the former gulag barracks housing the **Solovetskie lagerya i tyurma osobogo naznacheniya** (Solovetsky Forced Labour Camps and Prison), which conveys an honest look at the camp system here and its development. The **Solovetsky Monastyr** ❿ (Solovetsky Monastery) was a medieval fortress and major border post, and this can be seen in its grim, grey aspect, defensive walls and towers rising above the White Sea. The high windows recall embrasures, and the two 16th-century cathedrals were once linked by secret underground passages containing huge vaults for food and a hidden water supply in case of siege. Political and religious opponents were despatched here from the Middle Ages onwards. They were held in cells in the walls and towers and beneath the cathedrals.

The area is of outstanding natural beauty and this particular part of the White Sea has a comparatively moderate climate. You can take a tour on a small boat around the islands. The church on **Golgotha Hill** ⓫ on **Ostrov Anzersky** (Anzersky Island) is a good place from which to look over the whole archipelago.

Exploring Kareliya

The western side of the region, northeast from St Petersburg, is the Republic of **Kareliya**, with its richly forested, flat landscape dotted with lakes. To see what the area has to offer, take a five-day trip on a river boat. Tours start from St Petersburg (longer cruises from Moscow) and take in the Valaam islands on Ladozhskoye Ozero (Lake Ladoga), Petrozavodsk (capital of Kareliya) and Ostrov Kizhi (Kizhi Island). On the boat tour, the **Valaam Islands** come into view early on the second morning. Energetic passengers can walk the 5 km (3 miles) through the woods to **Valaamsky Monastyr** ⓬ (Valaam Monastery). Returned to

Typical wooden church in Malye Karely.

the Orthodox Church's possession in 1990, the monastery is an active religious community, with a farm and workshops, and many pilgrims. The buildings, outlying cells and chapels have been fully restored: major damage to the frescoes in the **Preobrazhensky Sobor** (Cathedral of the Transfiguration) was caused by over-officious guardians covering them with Perspex, thus trapping moisture and causing the paint and plaster to flake off.

The capital of Kareliya, **Petrozavodsk ⓭**, on the banks of Onezhskoye Ozero (Lake Onega) was founded in 1703 to serve a cannon foundry nearby. Despite the destruction wrought during World War II, Petrozavodsk is an attractive town, built on a series of plateaux rising from the water. The neoclassical **Kruglaya ploshchad** (Round Square, official name Lenin Square) is the epicentre of the neoclassical town centre.

About 70 km (43 miles) north of the town of Petrozavodsk is **Vodopad Kivach** (Kivach waterfall), the best of many on the River Suna, set in the midst of a vast nature reserve.

Petrozavodsk is the ideal springboard for striking out into the northern reaches of Lake Onega and in particular to the stunning island of **Kizhi ⓮**, a fabulous open-air museum of wooden architecture. One of Russia's greatest and most photogenic attractions, the 30-domed **Preobrazhenskaya Tserkov** (Church of the Transfiguration), dating back to 1714, are made entirely of wood and without the use of nails. The iconostasis inside the church is also of interest, not least because it is curved rather than straight. There are many other timber houses, workshops and churches here, too, many of the interiors looking pretty much as they did when they were still home to local peasants. Hydrofoils from Petrozavodsk run to Kizhi up to five times a day in summer.

Murmansk and the far north

Heading north, you come to **Belomorsk ⓯**, from where it is possible to take a trip to the Solovetsky

Kizhi Island's 22-dome Transfiguration Church and 9-dome Intercession Church, both built exclusively of wood.

islands. If you are intending to go to **Murmansk** ⑯, the journey north takes in some stunning scenery at any time of the year. And if one should be brave enough to go during the cold, dark winter months, you might be lucky enough to see the Northern Lights. To members of the older generation, Murmansk is equated with the Allied Forces who defended the town and port during World War II. It was through here that supplies from the West reached the rest of Russia. The port was founded in 1916 with British assistance (even the first houses were brought over from the UK) on the Barents Sea, which does not freeze thanks to the North Cape Stream. It rests between two low hills by the mouth of the River Kola and it is here, 68.5° north, that you really appreciate the meaning of a long winter night: the sun does not rise for two weeks. The **Atomny ledokol Lenin** (Lenin Nuclear Icebreaker) was the world's first nuclear-powered ice breaker, but is now a museum where a daily guided tour shows you the ropes.

The Leningrad region

The area around St Petersburg, still known as the **Leningrad region**, is well worth exploring if you get the chance. Northwest of the city, between (Lake Ladoga) and the Gulf of Finland, the landscape is dominated by country houses *(dachas)* belonging to residents of St Petersburg. Part of the region belonged to Finland until 1940, and some of the best houses here were Finnish built. Now the area is dotted with sanatoria and wooden houses, often huddled round picturesque lakes. It is an ideal region for cross-country skiing in winter.

The last town on the Russian side of the border is the Swedish-Finnish medieval city of **Vyborg** ⑰. This area changed hands many times between the 13th and 20th centuries. It may not seem very Russian, for many of its buildings are left over from Finnish rule and it's also a popular destination for Finns searching for their past and cheap vodka. **Vyborgsky Zamok** (Vyborg Castle), sitting on an island between the two halves of the town, dates largely from the

The northern lights over the Kola peninsula.

THE SAMI OF RUSSIA

The indigenous people of the Kola Peninsula in the far north of the region are called the Sami, a hardy, semi-nomadic group whose traditional lifestyle has come under threat time and time again over the centuries. Despite collectivisation in the 1920s and repression of their language and culture throughout the Soviet period, there has been something of a resurgence in Sami culture since the fall of communism, helped along by more frequent contact with their Scandinavian cousins across the border in Norway, Sweden and Finland. Sami crafts such as bone carving, leather working and beadwork are being taken up by an increasing number of people and the language has witnessed a rebirth. However, alcoholism and land grabs by big mineral companies remain serious problematic issues.

16th century, and there are defensive towers from the 14th, but buildings from all periods survive, and the early 20th-century Art-Nouveau structures are especially striking. If you like follies, then the early 19th-century castle burial vault will be of interest. The **Ermitazh Vyborg** (Vyborg Hermitage; 10am–6pm) has special exhibitions borrowed from the St Petersburg Hermitage that change every 6 months or so.

Some 30 km (18 miles) east of St Petersburg towards Lake Ladoga, **Shlisselburg** ⓲ (Schlusselberg) was known between 1944 and 1992 as Petrokrepost. World War II buffs will know that the town played a pivotal role in lifting the siege of Leningrad in 1944. The main sight here is the **krepost** (fortress), which was used as a prison in pre-Revolutionary times. Peter the Great's sister was imprisoned here, some of the Decembrists were kept here before being exiled to Eastern Siberia, and in 1887 Lenin's brother, Alexander Ulyanov, was executed in the yard for his role in an attempt on Alexander III's life. A

Veliky Novgorod's Kremlin.

pleasantly bucolic day-trip from St Petersburg, **Staraya Ladoga** ⓳, 100 km (60 miles) along the south side of the lake, is noted for the 12th-century **Tserkov Giorgiya Pobedonostsa** (Church of St George) filled with marvellous frescoes, and other 17th-century buildings. You'd never guess it today, but this sleepy village claims to have been Russia's first capital. Sixty kilometres (37 miles) to the southeast is **Tikhvin** ⓴, worth a visit for its 16th- and 17th-century monuments and the **Dom Muzei Rimskovo-Korsakova** (Rimsky-Korsakov House Museum). The composer was born and grew up here in the mid-19th century.

Going west along the south bank of the Gulf you pass Petrodvorets and the imperial summer palaces, before reaching the border with Estonia at **Narva** ㉑. Jump out on the Russian side, which is called **Ivangorod** ㉒, and take a look around the fortress there. Despite over four decades of co-existence in the USSR, the difference in lifestyle between the Russian and Estonian sides of the border is marked.

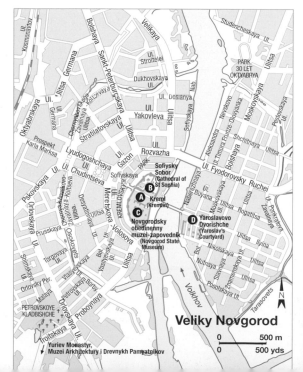

South of St Petersburg

Novgorod and Pskov ruled the north when the Tatars took over the rest of ancient Rus, building up trading links with the Hanseatic League and protecting themselves against attacks by the Poles and Livonians with heavy fortifications. Both principalities were renowned for their democratic institutions as well as magnificent arts and architecture.

When Russia was united under the rule of the Moscow princes at the end of the 15th century, Ivan III invited Pskov and Italian architects and craftsmen to help in the building of the churches in the Moscow Kremlin. The local monasteries were centres of learning, and Novgorod's historical chronicles and texts, scratched on pieces of dried birch bark, are known to historians all over the world.

The area suffered appallingly from the Nazi occupation. Whole villages were burned, their inhabitants shot en masse. Buildings of interest that have survived or have been restored are concentrated in the two main towns.

Veliky Novgorod ㉓ has a rich past and is arguably the most historically interesting northern Russian city. At its height, the principality ruled from here to the White Sea and west to present-day Poland. In 1570 Ivan the Terrible butchered some 60,000 of Novgorod's citizens and brought the city under Moscow's rule. Despite all the wars and destruction, the city has numerous monuments. The **Kremlin Ⓐ** built on the bank of the River Volkhov is at the heart of the old city. It is dominated by the magnificent 11th-century **Sofiysky Sobor Ⓑ** (Cathedral of St Sophia), Russia's oldest place of worship. Inside are 12th-century frescoes, including a portrait of Constantine and Helen, and the remains of 11th-century mosaics. One of the most surprising things to be found here is the east portal, with 12th-century bronze doors made at Magdeburg, taken – according to legend – from the fortress of Sigtunain in 1187. They are a superb example of Western European Romanesque metalwork tucked away in the heart of Russia.

Novgorod United Museum has a wealth of icons.

The **Novgorodsky obedinenny muzei-zapovednik**  (Novgorod United Museum; Wed–Mon 10am–6pm) is also housed here. It has a wealth of icons and church utensils as well as birch-bark manuscripts and woodcarvings. The huge monument outside the building, erected to commemorate the millennium of Russia in 1862, is by the sculptor Mikhail Mikeshin and portrays many important figures from Russian history.

On the opposite bank of the river is **Yaroslavovo Dvorishche**  (Yaroslav's Courtyard), a pretty ensemble of 12th- to 16th-century churches. It was thought to have been the residence of the princes of Yaroslav until the end of the 14th century. There are plenty of other churches in town, some in the most unexpected places. If you count fewer than 30 as you wander round you have missed a fair number. Outside the town, only a short bus trip away, are two more sights. The **Yuriev Monastyr** (St Yuri Monastery; Wed–Mon 10am–6pm), and the excellent **Muzei Derevyannovo Narodnovo Zodchestvo Vitoslavits** (Vitoslavlitsy Museum of Wooden Architecture) just across the road.

South of Novgorod, on the other side of Ilmen Ozero (Lake Ilmen) at the confluence of two rivers, is **Staraya Russa** ㉔. More intimate than Novgorod, the town is also rich in churches, for this was the centre of salt production. Fyodor Dostoyevsky and his family spent their summers in Staraya Russa from 1872, and much of *The Brothers Karamazov* was written and set here. His house is now a museum: the **Dom-Muzei Dostoevskovo** (Dostoyevsky House Museum; Tue–Sun 10am–5.30pm), an unmissable stop for fans of Russian literature, as is the Nauchno-kulturny tsentr Dostoevskovo, which hosts temporary exhibitions on Dostoyevsky themes.

For many people outside Russia, all they know about **Pskov** ㉕ is that it was here, in the royal train, that Nicholas II signed his abdication. Lake Chudovo, where the hero of Eisenstein's film *Alexander Nevsky* defeated the Teutonic Knights in the famous battle on the ice in 1242, is not far from the city.

Staraya Russa, setting of The Brothers Karamazov.

Like Novgorod the town is dominated by its fortress and churches. They played a bigger defensive role than those in Novgorod, because of the ever-present danger from across the nearby border. Pskov's **Kremlin** is more fairytale in appearance than that of Novgorod. Instead of square red-brick towers, here we see heavy, round, squat towers with wooden roofs.

The **Troitsky Sobor** (Trinity Cathedral), built in 1669 on the site of a much older church, still dominates any view of the town. This white structure was not only a church, but also the place where the state council sat in session and where important state documents were kept. The **Kutekrom Bashnya** (tower) in the corner of the Kremlin walls was where the poet Pushkin liked to look down over the river. The **Pskovsky Gosudarstvenny obedinenny istoriko-arkhitekturny i khudozhestvenny muzei-zapovednik** (Pskov State United Museum of History and Architecture; Tue–Sun 11am–6pm) is another highlight with an eclectic exhibition on Pskov's history.

Outside the old town are yet more religious buildings. The magnificent **Spaso-Preobrazhensky Sobor** (Cathedral of the Transfiguration) within the Mirozhsky Monastyr, decorated in the 12th century by Greek masters and their Russian apprentices, is a world in itself. The frescoes dating from that time definitely merit a visit.

About 30 km (18 miles) along the main road to the west of Pskov, you find **Izborsk** ㉖. The village is built around the remains of a medieval fortress. Another 20 km (12 miles) further on, nestling in a deep ravine, is the 16th-century **Pskovo-Pecherskaya Lavra** (Pskov Monastery of the Caves) at **Pechory** ㉗, its picturesque beauty matched only by the strangeness of its caves, used as burial vaults for monks. Of particular note is the **Uspensky Sobor** (Dormition Cathedral), erected on the site of an ancient cave church.

The monastery is once again a religious institution, and it is possible to come here for a retreat.

Pushkin's estate

Even Russians indifferent to the medieval history of the Pskov area are not unaffected by its connection with the poet Alexander Pushkin (1799–1837). The **Mikhailovskoye** estate at **Pushkinskiye Gory** ㉘ (Pushkin Hills), 130 km (80 miles) south of Pskov, belongs to an ensemble of three estates and the nearby **Svyatogorsky Monastyr**, all restored after the war. Amble slowly round the grounds and drop into Pushkin's study, where he worked during his exile from St Petersburg on the tsar's order, then take a peek into the small cottage where his old nanny lived (Tue–Sun 9am–5pm).

The other estates here, **Petrovskoye** and **Trigorskoye**, are all reflected in Pushkin's poetry and prose. Mikhailovskoye and Trigorskoye form the background to *Evgene Onegin*, and the monastery features in *Boris Godunov*.

Dostoyevsky's desk and manuscripts at the Dom-Muzei Dostoevskovo.

Pskov's Kremlin.

The Mother Russia memorial of Mamaev Kurgan in Volgograd was built to commemorate the Battle of Stalingrad, 1942.

SOUTHWEST OF MOSCOW

The cathedrals, fortresses and war memorials
of the southwestern steppe bear witness
to the region's many rulers. It was here
that Ivan Turgenev found inspiration.

Smolensk's Dormition Cathedral.

Southwestern Russia is a fundamentally Russian place, a land of Tolstoy and Turgenev, Pushkin and Dostoyevsky, of Kremlins and cathedrals, sleepy 19th-century towns and the slow-moving rivers of the Eurasian plain. It was here that the Russian Empire was forged.

Kievan Rus, which covered western Russia and parts of present-day Ukraine and Belarus, emerged after the 860s when the Varangians (Vikings) arrived to lord over and protect the Slavic tribes. It was as Rus that the area gained its Slavic identity and from this word we get *russkiy*, meaning Russian.

From 1054, Kievan Rus was divided into principalities. These lasted into the 12th century from which point the history of **Smolensk** ㉙ offers a typical catalogue of the tumultuous battles and power struggles which have marked Russian history, causing Rus to expand into imperial Rossiya in an attempt to survive.

From the 12th century to the 20th, Smolensk and its region have passed from Kievan to Tatar, Lithuanian, Muscovite, Polish, Russian, French, German, Soviet and now finally back to Russian rule. Situated on the upper River Dnieper (Dnepr), "the gate of Russia" was first mentioned in 863. It soon became an important centre along the trade route between Moscow, 390 km (242 miles) to the northeast, and the West. Indeed, the town gets its name from the Russian word for tar, *smola*, because it was here that the river traders tarred their boats.

At the centre of the old town is Cathedral Hill on which the vivid green and white **Uspensky Sobor** (Dormition Cathedral) stands, on ground hallowed since 1101. This 18th-century church has a gilded interior and a wooden iconostasis carved by the Ukrainian Sila Trusitsky. The town's three 12th-century churches – Sts Peter and Paul, St John the Divine and the Archangel Michael – are also worth a visit.

The main attraction of Smolensk is the **city wall**. Built by 300,000 people

between 1596 and 1602, the 15-km (9-mile) -long, 15-metre (49-ft) -high wall was known as "the precious necklace of Russia". Napoleon ordered it destroyed as he went through the city in 1812, but he only blew up eight of the 38 towers. Today 17 remain.

For art lovers, the **Khudozhestvennaya galereya** (Art Gallery; ulitsa kommunisticheskaya 4; Tue–Sun 10am–5pm), has a valuable collection including pieces by Repin, 18th-century icons and some European masters. The **Muzei Smolensky lyon** (Smolensk Flax Museum; ulitsa Marshala Zhukova 6; Tue–Sun 10am–6pm) may not sound that interesting but it turns out to be quite a fascinating place, with exhibits and demonstrations illustrating just how important the flax industry was to Smolensk.

City in the forest

Founded in 985 on the River Desna by Prince Vladimir, **Bryansk** ⑳, 325 km (200 miles) southwest of Moscow, lies in the heart of a 12,000-sq km (4,630-sq mile) forest and has a rich and brutal history. The forest has ensured the survival of the inhabitants of Bryansk on many occasions, most notably during World War II when 60,000 people fled from the invading Germans and lived in huts in the woods, forming a formidable partisan movement. The Bryansk fighters are remembered at **Partizanskaya Polyana** (Partisan Field) on the Orel road, just outside Bryansk where there is a museum (daily 10am–5pm), preserved huts, and a wall on which are recorded the names of the 8,000 partisans who died. You may also spot some of the wild boar, brown bears and elk which roam the forest.

South of the city, the working **Svensky Monastyr** (Sven Monastery) is a reminder of the days when Bryansk was also a significant trading town. Furs and jewellery were sold here at the Sven Fair, which reached its zenith in the 17th century. The huge **Uspensky Sobor** (Dormition Cathedral), commissioned by Ivan the Terrible, has not withstood the test of time, but the two gate churches have been restored. The view from here is splendid.

The region has been home to many artistic heroes. In **Ovstug** ㉛, 48 km (30

Inside Smolensk's Flax Museum.

miles) northwest of Bryansk, the picturesque estate of nature poet Fyodor Tyutchev makes an interesting day trip (Tue–Sun 10am–5pm).

Heart of the region

The heart of Russia's southwest is the triangle formed by three wonderfully characterful places, Yasnaya Polyana, Oryol and Yelets. These are places that recapture the past and are a world away from the brash arrogance of Moscow and the Kremlin.

Leo Tolstoy fans will be familiar with the name **Yasnaya Polyana** ❸ (Tue–Sun 9am–5pm), the estate 190 km (120 miles) south of Moscow where he was born, lived and died. He wrote *Anna Karenina* and *War & Peace* in what is now known as the Tolstoy House where the rooms have been left exactly how they were on his death in 1910. There's a Tolstoy exhibition in the nearby Kuzminsky House and the writer's unmarked grave lies deep in the forest.

Drowsy **Yelets** ❸ 350 km (217 miles) south of Moscow provides a delightful journey back in time, with wooden houses and dilapidated churches

lending it some authentic historical character. The highlight here is the incredibly decorative **Voznesensky Sobor** (Ascension Cathedral; ul pushkinskaya) designed by Konstantin Ton, the architect behind the Cathedral of Christ the Saviour in Moscow. At 74 metres (243 ft) tall, the cathedral tower is one of the highest in Russia. Yelets is famous for its lace and some fine examples can be seen at the quaint **Dom Eletskogo kruzheva** (House of Yelets Lace; ulitsa Oktyabrskaya 108).

Some 165 km (103 miles) west of Yelets, **Oryol** ❸ has bags of pre-1917 charm and is a city of literary museums and aristocratic architecture. A single 100-rouble ticket covers house museums dedicated to 12 men of letters who lived and/or worked in Oryol in the 19th and early 20th centuries. The two best known names are Nobel Prize winner Ivan Bunin, who died here, and Ivan Turgenev, who lived 70 km (43 miles) north of here at the family estate in **Spasskoye Lutovinovo** ❸ (daily 10am–5pm). It was there that he penned *Fathers and Sons* and *A Nest of Gentlefolk* in the 1850s.

THE KALININGRAD ENCLAVE

Completely detached from Mother Russia, the Kaliningrad enclave is an usual part of Russia often overlooked by visitors. Surrounded today by EU members Lithuania and Poland, until 1945 this was old Prussian Königsberg, capital of East Prussia, with a mixed German, Jewish and Polish population. During World War II the RAF flattened the city, which was then annexed by the Soviet Union. The Germans were expelled to Germany and Russians from across the USSR arrived to take their place.

Kaliningrad (named after Bolshevik revolutionary and Stalinist henchman Mikhail Kalinin) was never rebuilt, the Soviets preferring instead to completely redesign the city as a utopia of thundering boulevards and high-rise blocks. The city is as bland as Soviet cities come, with just a tiny reserve intended for use by tourists. This includes the Sobor-Kaliningrad **(cathedral)**, a Unesco world heritage site containing the tomb of Immanuel Kant, the city's most famous son. To see what old Königsberg looked like before the bombs fell visit the **Friedland Gate** (10am–7pm), where a 40-minute multimedia show presents early 20th-century footage of the city. Occupying the Dohna Tower, the **Amber**

Museum (Tue–Sun 10am–6pm) has 6,000 pieces of prehistoric resin, found in large amounts along the Baltic coast.

Vastly more engaging than the city of Kaliningrad is the Baltic coast. Here, resorts such as **Zelenogradsk**, **Svetlogorsk** and **Yantarny** are hemmed by long white beaches and sand dunes. Yantarny is where 90 percent of the world's amber is sourced (the name means 'Amber' in Russian). The **Curonian Spit** (Kurshskaya Kosa) is the region's top attraction, a 98-km (61-mile) -long sandbar (only 50km/31 miles in Russia) which is now a national park. There are lots of opportunities for hiking, cycling, camping and mushroom picking along its forested length. It's accessible by bus from Kaliningrad.

Apart from a single flight to Berlin and a few cross-border buses from Poland and Lithuania, Kaliningrad is pretty much cut off from the rest of Europe. Visitors still need a full visa to enter even for the day, and locals complain of their isolation from their neighbours and expensive flights to Moscow. Kaliningraders tend to be less hostile towards the West than those in Russia proper and Kremlin propaganda has less of an impact here, hence the huge military presence.

ALONG THE VOLGA

The mighty Volga, Europe's longest river, has played a major role in the development of Russia, as the ancient towns and villages along its banks testify.

For many centuries the Volga has been like a mother feeding the Russian nation. It has witnessed numerous battles and wars, and has always stirred strong feelings in Russian hearts. It begins just north of Moscow in Valdayskaya Vozvyshennost (the Valdai Hills), not far from the picturesque Lake Seliger, and flows 3,530 km (2,195 miles) south to the Caspian Sea.

From time immemorial, people have gravitated to the river. One of the best preserved of the early settlements is **Veliky Bulgar** (Great Bulgar), the former capital city of the Volga Bulgars, near **Posileniye Bulgar** (Bulgar Village) in Tatarstan. Other great sites include the remnants of Itil and Sarai, former capital cities of the Golden Horde, not far from Nizhny Volgograd and Astrakhan.

Kazan

The **Povolzhye** (Volga Region) comprises the middle and lower parts of the river from Kazan to Astrakhan. **Kazan** ❶ is the capital city of Muslim Tatarstan, a sovereign republic within the Russian Federation. It was founded in the second half of the 13th century, and in the mid-15th century became the capital of the Kazan khanate. In the second half of the 15th and in the early 16th centuries Moscow princes besieged the city repeatedly. In 1552 it became part of the Russian state and in the 18th century

developed into a major administrative, trade, industrial and cultural centre. Today it is a booming place awash with Kremlin cash and oil industry money.

The **Kazan Kremlin** is a marvellous ensemble of 16th-century architecture and today houses government departments, churches, museums, the magnificent Kul-Sharif Mosque and lots of parkland. Particularly handsome are the towers. They include the **Spasskaya Bashnya**, a 45-metre (147-ft) high clock-bearing tower begun in 1555, and the seven-tier 55-metre (180-ft) -high

Riverside frolics, Volgograd.

Along the Volga

Suyumbiki with its stone dome and gate leading to the Sovereign's yard. Of the museums, pick of the bunch is the **Ermitazh Kazan** (Kazan Hermitage; Tue–Thu and Sat–Sun 10am–5.30pm, Fri noon–8.30pm) which has rotating exhibitions supplied by the Hermitage in St Petersburg.

The city has many universities, theatres and museums, including the **National Museum of Tatarstan** (2 Kremlyovskaya ulitsa; Tue–Sun 10am–6pm) in the former merchants' chambers opposite the entrance to the Kremlin, which has a fine collection of historical and ethnographic exhibitions.

Around 74 km (46 miles) downstream, travelling southwest from Kazan, the Volga joins the Kama, its largest tributary. Just south of here is the town of **Ulyanovsk ❷** (formerly Simbirsk), occupying both banks. It was founded in 1648, and parts still evoke an old merchant city. Best known as the birthplace of Vladimir Lenin, whose real surname was Ulyanov, the city has many memorial sites dedicated to the leader. Perhaps more interesting is the fact that writer Ivan Goncharov, author of Oblomov, hailed from what was then Simbirsk and the Muzei Goncharova (Goncharov Museum; ulitsa Lenina 134; Tue–Sun 10am–6pm) is arguably the city's most interesting sight.

Another 125 km (78 miles) downstream from Ulyanovsk the **Zhiguli Hills** begin, the most beautiful part of the Volga. On the left bank of the river, opposite the village of **Usolye**, stands **Tolyatti ❸** at the bottom of the Zhiguli Hills. A modern city, it is well known for its **Volzhsky Avtozavod** (Volga Car Factory).

Samara

Further downstream, approximately half-way down the Volga's entire length, stands the town of **Samara ❹**, extending for dozens of kilometres along the bank. A broad staircase leads from the bank to the city centre, and a cast-iron grille adorns a riverside park. Named after the Samara River which flows into the Volga at this point, the town was built in 1586 as a fortress on the Volga's left bank. Once an important trading and industrial centre, it has many fine pre-Revolutionary structures, including the Drama Theatre, done in fantastic Russian Revival style. During World War II as the Germans advanced on Moscow, the government and diplomatic missions were moved here. **Stalin's Bunker** (ulitsa Frunze 167; pre-booked groups only), a huge underground kremlin, was prepared for the leader. Stalin never used it, but visitors can marvel at it today. The **Khudozhestvenny muzei** (Art Museum; ulitsa Kuybysheva 92; Wed–Sun 10am–6pm) provides more cultural enjoyment with its exhibits of Russian art.

After Samara the Volga turns sharply to the west. The landscape here is stunningly beautiful. The right bank with its steep and high cliffs is mountainous while the left bank is a lowland of emerald-green meadows.

Saratov

After Samara comes **Saratov** ❺, a modern industrial town, founded on the left bank of the Volga in 1590 and once home to a large population of ethnic Germans. In 1674 the town was moved to the right bank, to a sloping hollow surrounded by the **Lysaya**, **Altynnaya** and **Uvekskaya mountains**. In the first 100 years of its existence it was little more than a small fortress designed to protect river trade routes from raids by nomads. During the reign of Peter the Great, the city's central square was called Gostinaya, on account of the **Gostiny Dvor** (rows of shops) built for merchants. The **Sobor Svyatoi Troitsi** (Trinity Cathedral) was built in Gostinaya Square in 1695. Yuri Gagarin lived in Saratov and studied at the local university, now named in his honour. Possibly the city's most engaging sight is the **Muzei Gagarina** (Gagarin Museum; ulitsa Sakko i Vanzetti 15; Mon–Fri 9am–4pm, Sat 8am–3pm), which provides a biography of the first man in space. Interestingly his Vostok 1 capsule crash landed just 40km (25 miles) from the city, a huge coincidence if ever there was one.

In 1798 Saratov was made the centre of a *guberniya* (a pre-Revolution term

Statue of a Mongol soldier at the National Museum of Tatarstan.

Musicians in traditional costume, Kazan.

Statue of Felix Dzerzhinsky, Lenin's faithful ally and director of the infamous Cheka police, outside Saratov railway station.

This former saw-mill was left untouched as a monument to the Battle of Stalingrad.

equivalent to "province", which has now been reintroduced) and awarded a coat of arms. Like many other Russian towns, Saratov was a wooden town and as a result, it often suffered from fires. There was a particularly devastating fire in 1810, which prompted new city planning. In 1865 a new theatre was built of stone; this has survived as the **Teatr Operi i Balleta** (Opera and Ballet Theatre) on Teatralnaya ploshchad 1 (Theatre Square).

Also here is the **Radishchevsky Muzei** (Radischev Museum; ulitsa Pervomaiskaya 75; Tue–Sun 10am–6pm), which opened in 1885. It contains rich collections of paintings, sculptures, porcelain and furniture. The city's main street, Moskovskaya ulitsa, leads to Muzeinaya ploshchad (Museum Square), a remnant of old Saratov. Its major feature is the **Stary Sobor** (Old Cathedral), the former theological seminary, with arcades and columns.

Volgograd

Some 394 km (244 miles) downstream from Saratov stands the major city of **Volgograd** ❻. During the 13th century the area was occupied by the Golden Horde. When the Kazan and Astrakhan khanates eventually collapsed in the second half of the 16th century, a new town called Tsaritsyn was built on the island where the Tsaritsyn River flows into the Volga. It was designed to protect the country's southeastern borders.

The town suffered numerous raids by nomads, and the Don Cossacks, who rose in rebellion against the ruling regime, entered the town more than once. Peter the Great attached great importance to the town and built a barrage more than 60 km (38 miles) long and a rampart about 12 metres (40 ft) high. In 1765, Catherine the Great issued a decree allowing foreigners to settle in Russia. Among Tsaritysyn's newcomers from Western Europe was a sizeable colony of Germans, whose neighbourhood became known as Sarepta.

By the 19th century the town had lost its function as a fortress and become a trading and industrial centre. With the introduction of railways, industry developed rapidly, and soon saw-mills and cast-iron foundries were operating.

In the winter of 1942–3 the town (by then called Stalingrad) was the focus of the key battle which marked the turning point in World War II. Fierce fighting lasted for 200 days and nights; some 300,000 of Hitler's crack troops lost their lives and the whole city lay in ruins.

After the war, the town was rebuilt from scratch. It extended along the Volga for nearly 100 km (60 miles). New factories, houses and parks were built. The memorial on **Mamaev Kurgan** (Mamaev Mound) by the sculptor Vuchetich and architect Belopolsky was built to commemorate the battle. It depicts a group of grieving citizens carrying wreaths to put on the heroes' graves. Behind the sculpture is a ramp paved with granite slabs and on both sides of the ramp are granite blocks resembling anti-tank teeth; they are engraved with the dates of all the major battles that took place near the town. The ramp ends with an 11-metre (36-ft) -high sculpture of a warrior with a sub-machine gun and a grenade in his hand. Behind him, near a terrace bright with red flowers, rises a wide staircase with high walls on both sides showing the town's ruins. The staircase leads to a gigantic, 72-metre (23-ft) high sculpture of a female figure symbolising the Mother Russia, a sword held high in her hand.

There are many museums in the city dedicated to World War II, including the **Panorama of the Stalingrad Battle** (ulitsa Marshala Chuykova 47; Tue–Sun 10am–6pm). For a break from the war, visit the **Muzei-zapovednik Staraya Sarepta** (Old Sarepta Museum Reserve; ulitsa Vinogradnaya 6; Tue–Sun 9am–5.30pm), an hour's bus ride from the city centre. Once the home to ethnic Germans this small museum tells their story in several preserved buildings.

Astrakhan

Downstream from Volgograd, the river turns to the southeast, flowing along the sandy-clay steppe of the lower Volga area. The right bank of the river near **Astrakhan** ❼ (the last town on the Volga) is 12 metres (40 ft) high. Astrakhan lies in the Volga's delta, straddling 11 islands separated by channels and rivulets and has a population of just over half a million.

Socialist Realist statuary adorns Volgograd's railway station.

NIZHNY NOVGOROD

Perhaps the most successful city after Moscow in terms of economic development in post-Communist Russia, is **Nizhny Novgorod** ❽ (known as Gorky in the Soviet era, after the writer Maxim Gorky who was born here). Situated 250 km (155 miles) upstream from Kazan at the confluence of the Volga and Oka rivers, Nizhny, as it is known, was once most famous for its annual fair, which drew traders and shoppers from all over the Volga region. Two giants of Soviet engineering have their roots here: MiG, the soviet aircraft manufacturer, and GAZ, the Gorky Avto Zavod (Gorky Car Plant), producer of the old Volga saloon car. In the mid-1990s, GAZ alone had 350,000 employees. The city became infamous for being the place of exile for the dissident, physicist and Nobel prize winner, Andrei Sakharov in the 1980s. His flat is now a museum, **Muzei A.D. Sakharova** (Prospekt Gagarina 214; Sat–Thu, 9am–5pm). Nizhny Novgorod was founded in the early 13th century. Its dramatic hilltop **Kremlin** houses the **Arkhangelskoye Sobor** (Cathedral of the Archangel Michael), built in 1631, the 19th-century governor's house and a plethora of worthwhile museums, including the State Art Museum, the National Centre for Contemporary Art and the Western European Art Collection.

In the 18th century Astrakhan was on the Caspian Sea; today the sea falls short by some 200 metres/yards).

In the 8th century, 10–12 km (6–7 miles) upstream on the Volga's right bank stood **Itil**, the capital city of the Khazar (Turkic-speaking nomadic tribes). The name "Astrakhan" was first used in the 13th century. In 1556 Ivan IV's troops captured Astrakhan without a fight and annexed it to Moscovy. Another turning point in the town's history was 1558, when New Astrakhan was founded on the opposite, left bank. The first wooden fortifications were built here. Between 1582 and 1589 they were replaced by a stone fortress: the **Astrakhan Kreml Ⓐ** (Kremlin; daily 7am–7pm). This has seven towers, three of them with gates. **Krasnie** (Red) and **Nikolskie** (St Nicholas) gates, located in the Kremlin's northwestern part, led to the Volga. The third **Prechistenskaya Bashnya** (Prichisten Tower), with a bell tower incorporated in the eastern wall, led to the suburb **Bely Gorod** (White Town). Close to the Prechistensky Gate is the **Uspensky Sobor Ⓑ** (Dormition Cathedral). The cathedral

is a marvellous monument built by the serf-architect, Dorofei Myakishev, in 1698. From all sides, it is surrounded by a two-tier gallery decorated with filigree carved stone, creating an impression of light and air. The upper church with five graceful domes rises from this unusual, seemingly weightless pedestal. The Dormition Cathedral together with Lobnoye mesto, where executions took place and announcements were made, and a high bell tower, built in the 19th century, make up a majestic architectural ensemble. The pseudo-Russian details overload the facades of the structure, but its tiers, evenly diminishing as they rise, make the bell tower look austere.

The **Troitsky Sobor Ⓒ** (Trinity Cathedral), built between the late 16th and 18th century on the opposite side of the Kremlin territory, looks modest compared with the Cathedral of the Assumption. But in terms of craftsmanship, it is a large and intricate complex.

Many of the Kremlin's architectural structures date from the 19th century. Of particular interest are the Guard House (1807) and the **Kirillovskaya**

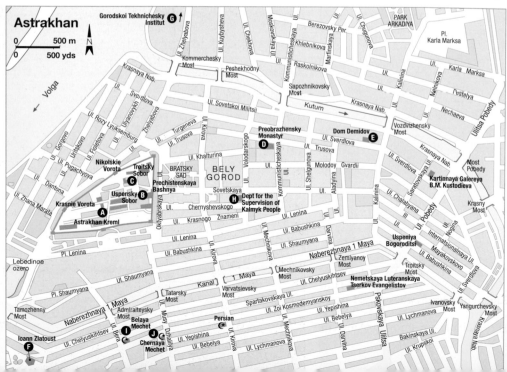

Astrakhan

Chasovnya (St Kiril Chapel). In the early 19th century, the chapel's original 17th-century structure was enclosed in a classical shell. The main portal (17th-century) is hidden behind the short massive Doric columns. Another architectural structure that has survived on the territory of the former Bely Gorod is the Tower of the **Preobrazhensky Monastyr D** (Transfiguration Monastery). Its snow-white octahedron, adorned with multi-coloured belts and insets and crowned with a dome, is magnificent.

Not far from the Preobrazhensky Monastery there is the **Demidov Homestead E** (ulitsa Sverdlova 55), another architectural legacy of the 17th and 18th centuries. It was the largest and the most important home in the town. The Demidovs were an ancient merchant family in Russia. The size of the building was immense and even today it occupies half the block.

Among the churches that have survived outside the Kremlin's boundaries is the **Ioann Zlatoust F** (St John Chrysostom; ulitsa Volzhskaya 14). It was built in 1763, and its octahedron-on-tetrahedron composition was common in Central Russia. The church was reconstructed more than once, the final version in the form of a cross, incorporating the decor associated with classicism. The entrance to the church is adorned with a figure of Christ. The bent figures of angels on the western facade of the belfry express grief.

Buildings in classical style became a regular feature in towns after 1769. The early 19th century gave rise to such imposing and outstanding buildings as the **City Technical School G** and the **Department for the Supervision of the Kalmyk People H** at ulitsa Volodarskoga 22. Stone structures were built not only in the centre of Astrakhan but in the outskirts, too. A striking example is the surviving building of the hospital on Parobichev Hill. Eastern merchants, who enjoyed extensive privileges, settled in Astrakhan. They built their trade rows and lived in tight-knit communities in the centre of Bely Gorod. The surviving structures of the Tatar and Persian homesteads were built in the 19th century.

Foreign merchants also built their own religious institutes, hence the **Belaya Mechet I** (White Mosque; ulitsa Zoi Kosmodemyanskoi 41), and the **Chernaya Mechet J** (Black Mosque; ulitsa Musy Dzhaliya 26), erected by Strakhan Tatars in the mid-19th century. In the eastern part of town, at the confluence of the Kutum River and the canal stands a Roman Catholic church, **Katolicheskaya Tserkov**, dating from the 18th century. Such architectural imports form a magnificent contrast to Astrakhan's other buildings.

Equally impressive are the commercial buildings that served the merchants. The merchants' estates on the Kutum's northern bank also illustrate the luxury of the times. One of the most interesting features of Astrakhan's architecture of the 19th century is the elaborate metalwork. A strong Oriental influence is evident in the fancy grilles, balconies, arches and gates.

Boat tour on the Volga delta.

The modern face of Yekaterinburg along the city pond.

THE URALS

Marking the border between Europe and Asia, the Ural Mountain region is the industrial heartland of Russia, where modern cities rise out of a landscape of forests and lakes.

The Urals lie in the centre of the vast Russian Federation, an area rich in natural resources, from minerals to timber. Once one of the centres of Soviet industry, the region has never attracted many visitors, partly because Soviet leaders declared most of the Urals off-limits to foreigners – restrictions that were lifted only during the perestroika years.

There are still some areas of outstanding natural beauty where lakes and hiking paths dot the landscape, and new tourist facilities make them accessible for everyone with a bit of effort. The 2,000-km (1,250-mile) -long Ural Mountain range – stretching between the Kara Sea in the north and Kazakhstan in the south – is not the insuperable geographical barrier one imagines: in fact, it is less than 2,000 metres (6,500 ft) at its highest point and has never been a serious obstacle to invasion from either direction. But in the absence of any other geographical feature it has long been taken to mark the divide between European Russia and Siberia, and by extension, between Europe and Asia.

The Ural Mountains date back 250 million years. Until the 15th century they were sparsely inhabited by a variety of local tribes. In the 17th and 18th centuries, many Old Believers settled here, bringing with them traditions of hard work and stern morality. By

contrast, today's Urals accommodate more than 20 million inhabitants, covering five regions: Sverdlovsk, Perm, Chelyabinsk, Orenburg, Kurgan, and two republics, Udmurtiya and Bashkortostan. The Urals' rich reserves of iron ore, coal, precious minerals and ferrous and non-ferrous metals eventually attracted large-scale European migration in the 18th century. Between 1752 and 1762 alone, 55 factories were built in the region, and industrial centres sprouted up in Yekaterinburg, Perm and Orenburg.

Main Attractions

Yekaterinburg
Perm
Kungur ice caves
Ufa
Orenburg

Neo-Gothic Sevastyanov's House.

Industry moves in

Russia's devastation during World War II brought a boom to the Urals. After the German army roared across much of the European part of the USSR Stalin moved 1,300 factories and hundreds of thousands of people to beyond the Urals for protection – not only from ground troops, but also from the *Luftwaffe*. The new Ural industrial base tripled capacity and was able to supply 40 percent of the Soviet Union's military needs for the war. The German armies never came close to the Urals, and historians cite Stalin's relocation of Soviet industry as a decisive factor in the outcome of World War II.

Following the war, Soviet authorities continued to expand heavy industry and the manufacturing of weapons. Traditional rural life in the region changed permanently as people flocked to the cities to work. Between 1940 and 1979, the Urals' urban population more than doubled. Even though the Urals still has one of the lowest population densities in Russia, it claims one of the highest outputs in heavy industry and defence sectors.

Skateboarding in front of the Monument to the Founders of Yekaterinburg.

By the final years of Soviet power, the Urals accounted for a third of the country's steel production and a quarter of its cast iron. "The economic region of the Urals plays an important role in building the material and technical base of Communism", the country's main encyclopaedia enthused. The intense industrialisation has also made the Urals a relatively polluted region though things have improved since the Soviet period.

Capital of the Urals

Yekaterinburg ❶, which was omitted from many tourist maps until 1990, is the Urals' most important urban centre and is Russia's fourth city. Known as Sverdlovsk during the Soviet decades (the region in which it lies is still called Sverdlovskaya oblast and you might still see the old name on railway timetables), it is the first major Russian city in Asia; 40 km (25 miles) to the west along the highway, a 4-metre (13-ft) high memorial marks the Asian-European border. Yekaterinburg spreads out around the Iset River and is surrounded by taiga (forests).

The winter here lasts for about five months, from November to the beginning of April, and the temperature may fall to -40°C (-40°F). The summer, which normally lasts no more than two months, maintains an average temperature of 20°C (68°F).

Like most major cities in the Urals, Yekaterinburg's history has been closely associated with industry. The city was founded in 1723, and within five years the area had set up an ironworks, the first of many industrial enterprises attracted by the abundant raw materials of the region. It remained modestly populated for many decades with just 10,000 people at the start of the 19th century, but the population exploded under socialism, climbing from 100,000 in 1917 to four times that number at the end of World War II. The war triggered an industrial boom in the city, and the area became one of the Soviet Union's most important manufacturing centres for years afterwards. Up until 2015, the Putin era had seen Yekaterinburg thrive, with industry injecting money into a booming economy. Russia's economic downturn and Western sanctions will no doubt hit the city hard.

Yeltsin's home town

Modern Yekaterinburg is best known for its political sons, the first president of the Russian Federation, Boris Yeltsin, and Nikolai Ryzhkov, prime minister during Gorbachev's presidency. Yeltsin was born into a poor family some 150 km (93 miles) from Yekaterinburg, in **Butka**. He spent most of his life in Yekaterinburg, first studying at the Urals Polytechnic (now the Urals State Technical University), then building a career in the construction industry while rising through the ranks of the Communist Party.

Many remember Boris Yeltsin as a tough but popular leader, and some local people still recall the day that party officials came to visit in 1985. Yeltsin was later summoned to the capital to become chief of the Moscow party, effectively taking up the post of mayor of the city. With Gorbachev's blessing he used this post as a power-base for reform at the heart of the Soviet Empire. He did not know

Memorial plaque on the site of the execution of the royal family; the Church on the Blood was built on the spot where the infamous Ipatyev House once stood.

DEATH OF A TSAR

Yekaterinburg is most famous in the history books not for its industry, but for its role in the execution of Tsar Nicholas II following the Bolshevik Revolution. After seizing power in 1917, the Communists imprisoned Nicholas and his family, moving them to several locations before bringing them to Yekaterinburg in April, 1918. The family was confined to a brick home formerly belonging to a local businessman, Ipatyev. Accounts of the royal family's end were wrapped in secrecy throughout the Soviet period, but historians believe that guards treated the family cruelly during their final days. In July the Bolsheviks decided to dispose of the tsar once and for all, to avoid him being recaptured by the anti-Bolshevik forces that were then threatening the town. The tsar was moved into the basement of the house and informed that he was about to die. The historian William Henry Chamberlain wrote: "The tsar did not understand, and began to say 'What?' whereupon Yurovsky shot him down with his revolver. This was the signal for the general massacre. The other executioners emptied their revolvers into the bodies of the victims." The bodies were taken into the surrounding woods and left in a shallow grave. In 1998 their remains were removed to St Petersburg for reburial.

Statue of Vladimir Vysotsky, one of Russia's most famous singers.

at the time that he would be staying on in Moscow as president of a new Russian state.

Exploring Yekaterinburg

Town planners have thankfully kept most of the industry outside the town centre, creating instead pleasant wide avenues lined with trees and modern apartment blocks and offices.

Start your sightseeing by walking south, away from prospekt Lenina (Lenin Avenue), the city's main street, along ulitsa Karl Liebknecht. The first sight – a few minutes' walk, to the right – is the **Dom Poklevskikh-Kozell** Ⓐ (Poklevsky-Kozell House; ulitsa Malisheva 46; Wed–Sun 11am–6pm). Here you'll find an interesting historical collection, special exhibitions on local and folk themes and a permanent collection giving a rundown of Yekaterinburg's history. A five-minute walk north up ulitsa Karl Liebknecht is the **Khram na Krovi** (Church on the Blood), the golden-domed church which was consecrated in July 2003 on the 85th anniversary of the execution of Russia's last tsar and his family. The

church is built on the site where the tsar, Nicholas II, his wife Alexandra and his five children were shot dead.

The executions took place in the basement of a house belonging to an engineer named Ipatyev and this house came to represent a link with earlier times in the decades following the revolution. However, in 1977, the Kremlin, increasingly worried that the **Dom Ipatyeva** Ⓑ (Ipatyev's House) could become a place of worship, ordered the local party boss, Boris Yeltsin, to remove it. A few days later the bulldozers were driven up to the house in the middle of the night. By the next morning, nothing was left of the building. There is an exhibition on the lower level about the last days of the Romanov family.

City museums

There are several museums a few blocks west of Prospekt Lenina. In an area that is the site of the city's original settlement is the **Yekaterinburgsky muzei izobrazitelnykh isskustv** Ⓒ (Yekaterinburg Fine Art Museum; ulitsa Voyevodina 5; Tue –Sun 11am–7pm, Wed–Thu until 8pm), home to mostly

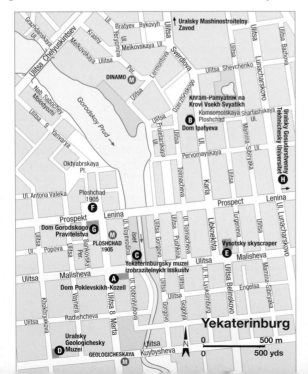

Yekaterinburg

Russian paintings. The large building's centrepiece is a 4.5-metre (15-ft) -high iron pavilion crafted in an intricate Oriental style for display at the Paris Expo in 1900. Other highlights include local metal sculptures, a popular and traditional art form of the area.

The **Uralsky Geologichesky Muzei**  (Urals Geological Museum; ulitsa Khokhryakova 85; Tue–Sat 11am–5.30pm) houses an interesting collection of almost 600 minerals found in the Urals, including malachite, topaz, a 748-kg (1,650-lb) crystal and meteorites. The **Uralsky Mineralogichesky Muzei** (ulitsa Krasnoarmeyskaya 1; Mon–Fri 11am–7pm, Sat–Sun 11am–5pm) was the first private museum in the city and contains a quirky collection of stones and minerals from the locality and around the world. Not far from here rises the **Vysotsky skyscraper** **E** (ulitsa Malysheva 51; viewing platform: daily 1–11pm, Vysotsky Museum: Wed–Sat 10am–7pm, Sun 11am–6pm). At the top is a viewing tower with panoramic views of Yekaterinburg and beyond. The name of the skyscraper is a play on words – it sounds like the Russian word for "high"

but is in fact the name of one of Russia's most famous singers, Vladimir Vysotsky. There's a small museum dedicated to his memory here, too.

If you return to prospekt Lenina and walk one block to the east, you'll come to **ploshchad 1905** (1905 Square) **F**, Yekaterinburg's main square and the home to the **Dom Gorodskogo Pravitelstva** **G** (City Hall; prospekt Lenina 24), which was built between 1947 to 1954 by German prisoners captured during World War II. Here you will also find a large statue of Lenin erected in 1957.

On the east side of town, where Prospekt Lenina starts, is the **Uralsky Gosudarstvenny Tekhnichesky Universitet** **H** (Urals State Technical University), the largest university in the Asian part of Russia, which once had 20,000 students, 7,000 teachers and employees and occupied several blocks of town with its own hospital, hostels and hotels. Known for its strong science and engineering departments in particular, the school has produced a series of prominent Soviet and Russian officials, including Boris

The Afghanistan War Memorial.

The bustling city centre.

Yeltsin and his wife, Naina, who met as students here.

Rural surroundings

Despite the industrial development, the area around Yekaterinburg is delightful, full of beautiful rivers, lakes and forests. There are a great number of sights near the city, such as the **Border of Asia and Europe** (marked by an obelisk 4-metre (13-ft) high), a wooden architectural museum in **Nizhnaya Sinyachikha**, and several sites where gold, emeralds and semi-precious stones are mined. For outdoor adventurers, there are fishing, hiking, spelunking, skiing, and even dog-sledding tours.

In and around Perm

On the European side of the Urals and a stop on the Trans-Siberian Railway, **Perm ❷** is a large industrial centre. It was founded in 1723 as a village around a factory. Today it is a rapidly growing city with an interesting hotchpotch of architecture that sprawls along the Kama River. One of Perm's highlights is the **Gosudarstvennaya**

The Iceberg Modern shopping centre in Perm.

Khudozhestvennaya Galereya (State Art Gallery; Komsomolsky prospekt 4; Tue–Sun 11am–6pm), with its fine display of 16th- to 19th-century icons, local wood sculptures and Russian and foreign paintings. More art, this time of a contemporary nature, can be viewed at the **Muzei sovremennogo iskusstva PERMM** (PERMM Museum of Contemporary Art; ulitsa Monastyrskaya 2; Tue–Sun noon–9pm) which has changing exhibitions of a high quality. Russia has many open-air museums of architecture but one of the best is the the **Arkhitektekturno-Etnografichsky Muzei Khokhlovka** (Khokhlovka Ethnographic Architecture Museum; daily 10am–6pm) at **Khokhlovka**, 45 km (28 miles) north of Perm, which preserves some interesting examples of pre-20th-century rural buildings. It is best reached by bus.

Some 75 km (50 miles) southeast of Perm lies the town of **Kungur**, a small town with a big attraction – the **Kungur Ice Cave** (daily 10am–4pm). It's around 5 km (3 miles) long, but only about 1.5 km (1 mile) is open to the public. Guided tours of this frozen

world of ice formations and underground lakes leave every two hours.

Bashkortostan

Ufa ❸ is the capital of Bashkortostan, an autonomous republic within the Russian Federation. Vastly outnumbered by Russians, the indigenous population are the Bashkirs, Turkic Muslims who can be found living throughout the Ural Mountains and beyond. Oil-rich Ufa is the place to experience their culture and a good place to start is the **Natsionalny muzei Bashkortostana** (Bashkortostan National Museum; ulitsa Sovietskaya 14; Tue–Fri and Sun 11am–6pm, Sat 1–9pm) which has exhibits on the republic's natural history and the Bashkirs themselves.

Eastern Bashkortostan is a superb place for lovers of the great outdoors. Rafting, skiing and horse riding are popular pursuits – contact local tour agencies in Ufa. **Lake Turgoyak** and the **Zyuratkul National Park** are other places to seek out if you fancy a bit of fresh air and exercise, though they are both tricky to reach without assistance.

Orenburg

Orenburg ❹, an industrial centre founded in 1735, is famous for its destruction during the Pugachyov rebellion in 1773–4, and for being visited by writer Alexander Pushkin when he was gathering material for his *History of the Pugachyov Rebellion* and novella *The Captain's Daughter*. It is also known for its lacy shawls, made from goat wool (similar to the fine wool produced by the Pashmina and Kashmiri goats). Much pre-Revolutionary architecture has survived in the city, and it has a number of interesting museums, such as the **Orenburg Museum of Regional Studies** (ulitsa Sovetskaya 28; Wed–Sun 10.30am–6pm) and the **Orenburg Museum of Fine Arts** (ulitsa Kashirina 29; Wed–Sun 10.30am–6pm), which have good collections of local historical and cultural artefacts, respectively.

The area around Orenburg offers lots of interest to outdoor enthusiasts, with good fishing, hunting and other sports. There are also plenty of caves, mines and quarries that can be visited; and in some places you can pan for gold or dig for mineral treasures.

White river rafting in eastern Bashkortostan.

Lenin mural, Sochi.

Sochi's public beach.

THE EUROPEAN SOUTH

This is Russia with a southern flavour. Here, you can soak up the sun in the Black Sea resort of Sochi or sample the curative mineral waters of the Caucasian Mountains.

Main Attractions

Sochi
Krasnaya Polyana
Stalin's Dacha
Mineralnyye Vody

The European south, or northern Caucasus as it is also called, stretches across the south of the Russian Federation, bounded by the Black Sea and Sea of Azov to the west and the Caspian Sea to the east. The scenery is diverse: from the fertile black-earth steppe of the Don to the north, to the snow-capped Caucasian mountains to the south; from the subtropical Black Sea coast to the semi-desert areas by the Caspian. The vegetation is equally varied: coniferous forests at the foot of the mountains, subtropical vegetation along the shores, high meadows carpeted with mountain flowers and rush-filled river valleys.

Both the subtropical climate and the mineral-rich soil in the northern Caucasus make it an extremely fertile area and a wide variety of fruits and vegetables grow in abundance. Just north of Sochi at **Dagomys** ❶ are the most northerly tea plantations in the world, producing Krasnodarsky tea, a large percentage of which goes for export. Tobacco, including rare oily kinds, is another important resource. Despite the harsh legislation during Mikhail Gorbachev's anti-alcohol campaign when nearly one-sixth of the Soviet Union's vineyards were destroyed, the northern part of the Caucasus is still renowned for its vineyards. In the small town of **Abrau-Dyurso**, west of

the Black Sea port of Novorossiysk, vintners have been producing one of Russia's best champagnes for more than 150 years.

The Caucasus has been home to dozens of different peoples over time, resulting in the ethnic diversity which characterises the region to the day. It covers more than six autonomous republics and is home to Ukrainians, Russians, Circassians, Adygeis, Kabardians, Balkars, Ossets, Ingushi, Chechens, Greeks, Abkhazians, Georgians, Armenians and Estonians. The

Railway station in Adler, a resort near Sochi.

Woman with a sign offering a room to rent, Adler railway station.

Kuban Cossacks (named after the river which runs through Krasnodar) and their descendants live on the plains to the north of the Caucasus. Their capital is **Krasnodar ❷**. Before the Revolution, Krasnodar was called Yekaterinodar – from *Yekaterina* (Catherine) and *dar* (gift). Catherine the Great gave this city to the Kuban Cossacks in return for conquering southern lands for the Russian crown. Today it is the capital of the **Krasnodarsky Kray** region, an area rich in minerals, especially oil, and famous for its wheat.

The Black Sea coast

The Black Sea is an internal and virtually isolated body of water which laps the shores of six countries. Although marine life is sustainable only in the top 200 metres/yards, the Black Sea supports a variety of different fish, three species of dolphin and more than 13 types of jellyfish. It is fed by a large number of rivers, which dilute the salt content and keep the sea clean. **Novorossiysk ❸** is southern Russia's principal port. It

is Russia's only Black Sea naval base actually in Russia proper (not counting Sevastopol in occupied Crimea), making it an important military location and probably not one visitors should head for, especially with the war in East Ukraine simmering to the north and a military build-up in nearby Crimea. Another vital Black Sea port is **Tuapse ❹**, south of Novorossiysk, where most of the Russian oil tankers berth.

Sochi

Russia's most popular beaches stretch along the east coast of the Black Sea from Tuapse to Georgia. The best known resort is **Sochi ❺** which hosted the 2014 Winter Olympics. Like the rest of the coast, Sochi is protected from cold northerly winds by the Caucasus and enjoys a subtropical climate. The area around Sochi has evidence of habitation dating back to prehistoric man. The first official Russian settlement on the River Sochi was the coastal fortress of Aleksandria, founded in 1838 to prevent Ottoman expansion in the area.

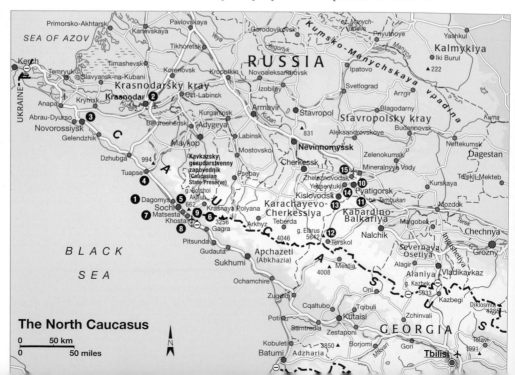

The North Caucasus

Sochi began developing as a tourist destination in the late 19th century. In the Soviet period it became a popular holiday destination among Russians and their leaders. You can still see the *dachas* (country houses) of some the politicians – Stalin, Khrushchev, Brezhnev – who spent holidays here.

Sochi's popularity is further boosted by its numerous *sanatorii* (therapeutic hotels) and *doma otdykha* (rest-houses), which offer cures and treatments for various illnesses using local spa therapies. Sochi and its environs have all the makings of a great resort with a distance of only about 56 km (35 miles) between snowy alpine mountains and a subtropical, palm-lined coast, part of the reason the Olympics were awarded to the city. Tourists can swim in oceans or pools, enjoy typical resort nightlife, go river rafting, take spa cures, visit tea plantations, take safari trips to mountain waterfalls, or stroll through picturesque parks – not to mention enjoying fabulous skiing. An estimated

$50 billion was spent on basically rebuilding Sochi in preparation for the winter games, improving the visitor experience immensely.

Like all the Russian Black Sea beaches, those in Sochi are pebble rather than sand. They drop away steeply into the sea making them excellent for swimming. You can walk most of the coast along the romantic seafront promenades and through the parks lush with magnolia palm and cypress. Most popular of Sochi's parks is the botanical garden, **Park Dendrariy Ⓐ**, with more than 1,600 different types of trees. Next to Dendrariy Park you will find the **Derevo Druzhby** (Tree of Friendship). Although it looks similar to an orchard, it is in fact one tree to which, in honour of visiting foreign representatives, 40 different citrus fruits have been grafted – Japanese tangerines, Italian lemons, American oranges and Indian grapefruits, to name a few.

Kurortny prospekt Ⓑ is the main street in Sochi, where most of the major hotels are situated. The

TIP

The best time to visit Sochi is in autumn when there are long hours of sunshine and the humidity is low. Spring comes early to the coast and flowers bloom in late March.

Waiting for the fish to bite, Sochi.

A TASTE OF THE CAUCASUS

The cuisine of the northern Caucasus and the Black Sea coast is influenced both by the bordering country of Georgia and by the local inhabitants. Here you will find Ukrainian *borshch* (beetroot soup) alongside Georgian *kharcho* (a spicy meat and tomato broth). You can try Russian *pelmeni* (a type of ravioli served with sour cream or vinegar) and Georgian *khinkali* (a larger spicier version of *pelmeni*). As well as traditional Russian breads there are Armenian *lavash* (a soft pancake-thin unleavened bread) and Georgian *khachapuri* (a delicious hot cheese-filled bread). On the beach vendors often come by selling hot corn on the cob, roasted hazelnuts and *semochki* (sunflower seeds). Another unusual seaside snack is *churchikhela*, a Georgian sweet made of hazelnuts or walnuts strung on a piece of string and coated with hot grape juice, which solidifies as it cools. An integral part of summer picnics is *shashlik*, a type of marinated kebab cooked on long skewers over charcoal embers. The Armenian version is wrapped in *lavash* and cheese. In the seafront cafés try locally caught trout in delicious Georgian *bazha* (walnut and coriander sauce), and finish your meal with an excellent Turkish or Greek-style coffee and a *paklava* (pastry) made with fresh mountain honey.

prospekt begins in the north at Platanovaya alleya (Platan Alley, named for the plane trees which line it) at **Park Rivyera** 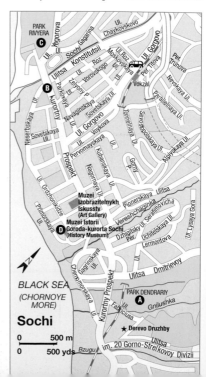 and traverses the length of Sochi crossing several small rivers. In the evening, life shifts from the seafront cafés to restaurants and cafés along Kurortny.

The **Muzei istorii goroda-kurorta Sochi** (Sochi History Museum; ulitsa Vorovskogo 54; daily 9am–7.30pm), contains exhibits from the earliest evidence of prehistoric habitation through to the modern day, as well as the 1970 Soyuz 9 capsule which was piloted by two locals.

The foothills of the Caucasus

Most compelling of all is the countryside around Sochi. This area is very popular with the Russian political elite and President Putin has often skied here. If you don't have a car, there are plenty of tour operators located on Kurortny who arrange moderately priced bus trips into the mountains surrounding Sochi. One of the most spectacular routes is the journey to

the mountain village of **Krasnaya Polyana** (Beautiful Glade), 50 km (30 miles) from Sochi and 600 metres (1,970 ft) above sea level. It was here that the skiing events at the 2014 Winter Olympics took place, the village receiving a complete facelift and a couple of world-class ski resorts. You can now reach Krasnaya Polana by high-speed train from Sochi, another legacy of the games.

The road up to Krasnaya Polyana snakes along ledges cut into steep mountain gorges providing breathtaking views. A fork in the road takes you to a place called **Medvezhy Ugol** (Bears' Corner), an allusion to the brown bears that roam these parts, along with wild boar and deer. There is also a Narzan mineral water spring. Archaeological finds suggest that the area was first inhabited in the Stone Age. At the turn of the 20th century it was a hunting preserve for the tsar and his family. Today, as the **Caucasian State Preserve**, it is famous for its herd of bison.

Krasnaya Polyana is surrounded by snowy mountain peaks, at the foot of

LITERARY HERO

Mikhail Yurevich Lermontov (1814–41) is one of Russia's leading romantic writers whose life and works are integral to the Caucasus. He is best known for his novel *Hero of our Time*, a large part of which is based in Pyatigorsk. As a child, Lermontov visited the region on several occasions and his earliest poems refer to the local landscape and culture. Lermontov was exiled to the Caucasus in 1837 for writing a poem alleging that the tsarist regime was to blame for Pushkin's death. A year later he returned to St Petersburg, where his reputation as a writer grew. His work was characterised by his cynical views on contemporary society and his criticism of the tsarist regime. In 1840 he was exiled to the Caucasus again, this time to a military post. The following year, in a scene strangely reminiscent of the plot of *Hero of Our Time*, Lermontov quarrelled with another officer and was killed in a duel just outside Pyatigorsk. You can still visit the Academic Gallery, Bulvar Gagarina, where the character "Pechorin" first sees "Princess Mary", and the Spa Research Institute, prospekt Kirova, site of the fashionable balls in the novel. The author's cottage can be seen at the Lermontov Museum (ulitsa Lermontova; Wed–Sun 10am–5pm).

which are dense forests. Footpaths lead to an arboretum and the remains of the tsar's hunting lodge, and to river valleys, waterfalls and alpine meadows. There are several places to stay that make a good base for hiking trips in the summer months and skiing in the winter. **Matsesta** ❼, 12 km (7 miles) southeast of Sochi, is the region's main spa town. In local Circassian, *matsesta* means "fire water". The sulphur waters turn bathers' skins bright red; they also help to treat systemic disorders, ulcers, and skin diseases. The marble *banya* (baths) date from tsarist times.

If you are curious about life in Sochi during the Soviet era, you might visit **Stalin's dacha** (Kurortny prospekt 120; daily 9am–6pm), part of the Zelyonaya Roshcha (Green Grove) sanatorium complex. His personal *dacha*, a peculiarly Soviet combination of stately and Spartan, has been preserved for curious tourists; wealthy visitors can opt to stay at one of the private bungalows once reserved for the political elite.

About 25 km (15 miles) from Sochi is **Khosta** ❽, another spa with hot mineral springs. It can be reached by train, bus, or boat. The pleasant beaches here are less populous than those in the centre of Sochi. Three kilometres (2 miles) inland is a forest preserve containing trees as old as 800 years. Here, too, is all that remains of an 11th-century fortress believed to have been built by Genoans. Nearby is a collection of cork oaks brought from Portugal, France, Spain and Algeria.

Mt Bolshoi Akhun ❾ with a 662-metre (2,171-ft) observation tower, is 20 km (12 miles) inland from Sochi. From the top of the tower there is an excellent view of the snow-topped peaks of the high Caucasus, the coastline beyond Sochi, and even the Abkhazian resort of Pitsunda. A little way from the tower are the **Agurskiye vodopady** (Agur waterfalls). There are good restaurants at the foot of the tower and by the waterfalls serving Caucasian food and wine.

Spa towns of the northern Caucasus

Mineralnyye Vody (Mineral Waters) is a resort region made up of four

View of the mountains and the Black Sea from the Sochi cable car.

main towns: Kislovodsk, Pyatigorsk, Zheleznovodsk, and Yessentuki, all of which are connected by trolleybuses. The area is located on the northern spur of the central Caucasus. Summers are warm, 20° to 25°C (68°–77°F) and long, winters are mild and the sun shines nearly 300 days a year. The marvellous climate, curative waters, lush vegetation and mountain scenery have lured the health-conscious for nearly two centuries. The region is also known for its abundance of fruits and vegetables, dry and sweet wines, cognacs and, of course, drinking waters. Today there are numerous old-fashioned *sanatorii*, and more modern hotels are appearing.

Pyatigorsk ❿ (Five Peaks), the region's oldest spa, was founded 200 years ago on the southern slopes of **Mt Mashuk** (993 metres/3,257 ft). It has 43 mineral springs and its own research institute for the development of new cures. You cannot visit Pyatigorsk without coming across reference to the Russian poet and author Mikhail Lermontov (1814–41) who died here fighting a duel. The **Lermontovskaya Galereya** (Lermontov Gallery) is situated in the town's central park among the mineral springs and grottoes. **Ozero Tambukan** ⓫ (Lake Tambukanskoye), 11 km (6 miles) from Pyatigorsk, is renowned for its mud, which is said to improve muscle tone and blood vessels.

Gora Elbrus ⓬ (Mt Elbrus), Europe's highest peak, is a 168-km (104-mile) drive south. The region is noted for its horse farms. Races are held at the local hippodrome from May to September.

Kislovodsk ⓭ (Sour Waters), 40 km (25 miles) southwest of Pyatigorsk, claims to have the best climate in the region. Founded in 1803, Kislovodsk is renowned for its Narzan mineral water. In the local language, *narzan* means "drink of the gods"; it is used in medicinal baths. The town is surrounded by beautiful landscapes, including a 12-hectare (30-acre) artificial lake. Nearby is a strange rock formation known as the **Zamok Kovarstva i Lyubvi** "Castle of Perfidy and Love" from which, the story goes, a young shepherd boy and wealthy local girl who were in love but forbidden to marry made a pact to throw themselves to their deaths. The shepherd jumped, but the girl did not.

Halfway between Pyatigorsk and Kislovodsk is **Yessentuki** ⓮, named after a local mineral water that is prescribed for stomach, intestinal, and urological disorders. Built in the early 19th century, the spa is known for its Gothic and Greek-style architecture and for its mud baths. **Zheleznovodsk** ⓯ (Iron Waters), the smallest of the four spa towns, is 630 metres (2,066 ft) above sea level. It was built at the recommendation of the General Aleksei Yermolov who fought in the Caucasian war. Local sites include the Mauritanian-style **Ostrovsky Baths** (1893), the **Emir of Bukhara's palace**, and the **permafrost caves**.

Treatment in progress at the Pyatigorsk spa.

Raketa hydrofoil on Lake Baikal.

The scenic Altai Mountains,
a hiker's paradise.

SIBERIA

Siberia may seem overwhelming in size, but the delights of Irkutsk's old timber architecture, the rugged mountains of Altai and the wonders of Lake Baikal are just a plane or train journey away.

In 1982, Russian geologists exploring a remote region of the Siberian taiga near Gornaya Khasiya, found a family of *raskolniki* (Russian Orthodox Old Believers) generations of whom had been living in hiding since tsarist times and knew nothing of the fall of the tsar and the rise of Soviet rule. Such is the vastness of the great Siberian plain.

Exploring Siberia's vast sweep of geography is really a lifetime's ambition, not a holiday, though connections between cities have improved in recent years. But for a determined and hardy traveller, much of the flavour of this remote part of the world can still be savoured in the Russian and Soviet-era outpost towns that dot the vast Siberian taiga from the Urals to Lake Baikal, the Arctic Ocean to Mongolia. Most travellers tackle Siberia by train, stopping off at the various cities which it links together. From these jumping off points, trips are possible off the trains to places the rails have yet to reach and probably never will. Long gone are the Soviet travel restrictions, though care should be taken around the border areas where, in theory at least, permits are required.

Travel around Siberia is fairly straightforward these days, though train journeys can eat into your visa time. Even off-the-beaten track places have a daily bus to the nearest big

city and there are even some flights between Siberia's cities. Irkutsk has become a major tourist hub with many new hotels and even backpacker hostels opening up.

The region's geography

Siberia's vast area means it is more a geo-political invention rather than a physical, geographical identity. The name Siberia probably comes from the Mongolian *sib ir* which means "sleeping land". It encompasses a wide range of terrain, related by little more than

Main Attractions

Omsk
Novosibirsk
Altai
Krasnoyarsk
Khakassia
Republic of Tuva
Lake Baikal
Irkutsk
Ivolginsk
Ulan-Ude

Typical wooden house in Listvyanka.

the remoteness of European Russia to the west and China and Mongolia to the south. The Buryats in Ulan-Ude consider themselves residents of Siberia just as much as the students and businessmen of Novosibirsk.

A journey from west to east Siberia starts at the rolling Urals and passes immediately on to the great primeval forests of the taiga. The taiga is almost equal in size to the whole of Western Europe. It stands pretty much as it has for millions of years, since logging is economically impractical in the remote forests.

Further east is the River Ob, running north from the Altai Mountains through Gorno-Altaisk to Barnaul, Novosibirsk, just missing Tomsk and then meandering north towards the Arctic Circle where it enters the Obskaya Guba. This is Russia's longest river, 5,410 km (3,362 miles), and the first of a network of rivers flowing north to the Arctic Ocean. The others include, from west to east, the Yenisey, Angara and Lena. To the south of the taiga is the world's biggest bog, the Urmany. The region has some of the richest oil and gas reserves in the world and has until now provided an easy source of revenue for the Kremlin. Oil money has brought some prosperity to a few communities in Siberia but most of the cash earned stays put in Moscow, a fact that disgruntles many Siberians. Further east is Ozero Baikal (Lake Baikal), "the Pearl of Siberia", and the boundary between Siberia and the Russian Far East. Baikal is for many the highlight of a trip across Russia and the most popular stop on the Trans-Siberian Railway between Moscow and points further east.

A little history

Though sporadic fur trading was underway by the 11th century, the process of "opening" Siberia to Russia did not really begin until 1552 – the year Ivan the Terrible liberated Kazan from the Tatars and created a gateway for expansion.

Siberia has endured two great waves of exploration and settlement. The first occurred during the expansion of tsarist Russia, when Russian Cossacks reached the coast of California. Expansion was characterised by brutal suppression of native peoples followed by waves of exiles and serfs seeking freedom. The explorer credited with doing most to open up Siberia is the Cossack Yermak, an outlaw who travelled with a band of mercenaries in the hope of winning the tsar's favour and pardon. Yermak was killed in 1564, but not before founding the fortress of Tomolosk on the River Ob. The building of the Trans-Siberian Railway opened up Siberia even more in the early 20th century and settlers continued to arrive right up to the time of the Bolshevik Revolution in 1917.

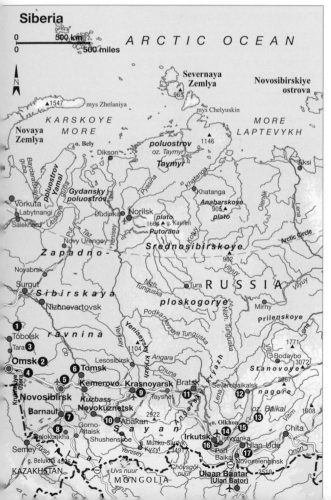

The greatest wave of Siberian settlement came with Stalin's first Five-Year Plan in 1929, which called for the rapid transformation of Russia from an agrarian to an industrial society. This daring, ultimately brutal, programme led to the founding of thousands of small and medium-sized industrial towns across Siberia. Another group of people who found themselves in Siberia, though not through choice, were the many hundreds of thousands of political prisoners sent to the gulag camps of Siberia. On release some chose not to return to European Russia.

Industrial expansion led to ecological disasters for many regions, as improper care was taken to guard the delicate environment. Though many of the excesses of the Soviet Union have been cleaned up and factories such as the paper pulp factory on the shores of Lake Baikal have closed, Siberia is still vulnerable to environmental catastrophe despite its vastness.

During the Soviet period of settlement, enthusiastic komsomoltsy (young Communists) were encouraged to go to Siberia to work on one of the hundreds of large industrial projects designed to transform Russia into a modern, industrial power. It was a heroic undertaking, embarked upon in the most idealistic years of Soviet rule. One of the biggest projects was the construction of the Baikalo-Amurskaya magistral, the BAM Railway that stretches from Tayshet to the Pacific, a distance of over 3,000 km (1,864 miles). The final cost of this incredible piece of hardly-required infrastructure was around $25 billion, an expenditure which contributed to the collapse of the USSR.

The Trans-Siberian Railway

The world's longest continuous train journey, the Trans-Siberian Railway, crosses seven times zones along its 9,299-km (5,778-miles) route from Moscow to Vladivostok, passing for a stretch across the north Gobi Desert and even over a 4,000-metre (13,125-ft) high mountain pass in the remote Amur Mountains. It actually comprises three routes: the Trans-Siberian, the Trans-Mongolian and the Trans-Manchurian

FACT

Two of Siberia's most attractive Buddhist temples are situated in Aginskoe and Tsugol, accessible from the city of Chita on the Trans-Siberian Railway.

Young Buryat man travelling on the Ulan Ude–Irkutsk train.

railways, the last two making the connection to Beijing. The railway was built to counter Western Europe's commercial shipping fleets and to break their monopoly on trade with the Orient. Tsar Alexander III dreamed of creating a faster route to the Orient. Due to political upheavals this aim was never achieved, but the Trans-Siberian Railway did support Russia's expansion into Central Asia and allowed it to keep a grip on its Far East holdings as far south as Vladivostok.

The ability of Russia to transport troops and weapons quickly to these remote areas allowed the country to become the world's largest empire. Construction began in 1890. At the time, it was the world's most ambitious engineering project. The entire stretch from St Petersburg to Vladivostok was finished in 1905 (see page 128).

Western Siberia

A side trip from the Trans-Siberian Railway, the former Siberian capital of **Tobolsk ❶** has a sleepy atmosphere, lorded over by a magnificent **kremlin** built in the 17th century. The city's museums tell the story of the city, from top dog as the 18th- and 19th-century capital to decline following the decision to run the *trakt* (post road) and then the railway to the south.

Siberia's second-largest city, **Omsk ❷**, approximately equidistant at 800 km (497 miles) from Yekaterinburg in the northwest and Novosibirsk in the southeast, is also one of its oldest, though you'd hardly know it today. It was founded in 1716 as a fort city and later became a place of exile. Among those banished here was Dostoyevsky, who spent four years in Omsk until 1854. Before the 18th century, Omsk traders supplied Asian markets with slaves, who were kept on **Katonsky Ostrov** (Katon Island) until they could be sold. Two forts can still be visited: **Staraya Krepost** (Old Fort), built in 1716, and **Novaya Krepost** (New Fort), built by the Russians at the end of the 18th century. Today, Omsk is the administrative centre of western Siberia and has grown rich thanks to the oil and gas industry. The city has one of the best museums of fine art in Siberia, the **Muzei izobrazitelnykh iskusstv** (Fine Arts Museum; ulitsa Lenina 23; Tue–Sun 10am–6pm), featuring a collection of 7,000 artworks, as well as exhibits on peasant life of different peoples.

From Omsk there are day tours to **Tara ❸**, a Siberian fort town 300 km (186 miles) north, founded in 1594. It is also possible to visit **Krutinskiye Ozera ❹** (Steep Lakes), comprising three beautiful natural lakes (Ik, Saltaima and Tenisa), 200 km (125 miles) to the northeast of Omsk. During the warm summer months, these lakes and the surrounding area are popular among local families as a weekend getaway for hiking and swimming.

Some 700 km (435 miles) east of Omsk, **Novosibirsk ❺**, Siberia's largest city, is the quintessential, dull Soviet city smothered in pre-fab housing blocks. It was built predominantly as an industrial centre. Indeed, the city is a virtual monument to Stalin's

Tobolsk's 17th-century Kremlin and cathedral covered in snow.

single-minded drive to industrialise Russia. Its airport is Siberia's hub and even handles some direct flights from Western and Eastern Europe. Despite its big city business image, the city does have some worthwhile sights. The **Muzei Rerikha** (Rerikh Museum; Kommunisticheskaya 38; daily 10am–6pm) has reproductions of, Nikolai Rerickh's (also known as Nicholas Roerich) works as well as other items relating to his activities as a writer and explorer. The original Rerikhs can be found at the **Khudizhestvenny Muzei** (Art Museum; Krasny prospekt 5; Tue–Fri 11am–7pm, Sat–Sun 1–7pm) which has around 60 of his paintings.

The old Siberian town of **Tomsk ❻**, founded 400 km (248 miles) northeast of Novosibirsk in the early 17th century, is perhaps best known for its academic prowess: it has the oldest university in Siberia and more professors (and students) per head than any Russian city. There are plenty of churches, museums and theatres here, especially in and around Lenin Square. Pick of the museums must be the **Memoralny muzei "Sledstvennaya tyurma NKVD"** (NKVD Prison Museum; prospekt Lenina 44; daily 10am–6pm), in the former KGB headquarters, which takes a long hard look at the gulag system and some of the figures that passed through it.

The Altai

The territory of Altaisky Kray, in the south of Western Siberia, bordering Kazakhstan and the Respublika Altay (Republic of Altai), is an ideal place for the adventure tourist to experience the Russian outback. With its natural beauty – one-third of the territory is covered by woods – mountains, low rainfall and pleasant summer temperatures of around 20°C (68°F), it makes an ideal centre for hiking, rafting and climbing. It also has Siberia's highest peak, Mt Belukha (4,506 metres/14,783 ft) and no less than 7,000 lakes.

The starting point for exploring the region is **Barnaul ❼**, the administrative centre of the territory, founded in 1730. It lies 230 km (143 miles) southeast of Novosibirsk on the River Ob and is accessible by train and bus

FACT

Arshan is a spa town in a dramatic setting at the foot of the Eastern Sayany Mountains. Take the waters before heading out onto the hiking trails that head up to some breathtaking spots. Buses head here from Irkutsk and Slyudyanka.

Gate to an Old Believers' enclave.

Lake Baikal souvenirs.

from Novosibirsk. The only worthwhile museum to see in town is the **Muzei istorii literatury, iskusstva i kultury** (Literature, Art and Culture Museum; Tolstogo 2; Tue–Sat 10am–6pm) which displays items relating to the local Altai culture as well as some works by Rerikh and several icons.

In the resort of **Belokurikha** ⑧, 200 km (124 miles) to the south, the combination of the local spring waters and pure mountain air creates an ideal atmosphere for the Russian sanitorium and indeed it is home to several specialised *doma otdykha* (rest homes, similar to Western health farms). Here, you can ski, trek, make use of the medical facilities or simply enjoy the scenery. **Lake Teletskoe**, Altai's largest, lies in the west of the Altai and is a mini-Baikal of sorts. It can be reached by bus from Gorno-Altaisk. The road heading south to the border with Mongolia is called the **Chuysky Trakt** and is one of the most dramatic road routes in all Russia, passing through superbly remote mountain ranges and following rushing alpine rivers for much of the way.

Krasnoyarsk has witnessed a recent boom in tourism.

Eastern Siberia

An increasingly popular stop on the Trans-Siberian Railway, **Krasnoyarsk** ⑨, 1,000 km (620 miles) from Novosibirsk is a youthful, energetic city which has also benefitted greatly from Russia's oil and gas industry. Founded in 1628 along the River Yenisey, Krasnoyarsk became a place of political exile and subsequently an industrial centre during the years of Soviet rule. Tourism has budded here with a new ski resort and several new hotels opening up, though it receives a fraction of the visitors Irkutsk does. Top billing is shared here between the **Stolby Nature Reserve**, an area of bizarre rock formations to the south of the city through which you can hike; and the superb **Kraevedchesky muzei** (Regional Museum; Dubrinskogo 84; Tue, Wed and Fri–Sun 10am–6pm, Thu 1–9pm) housed in an Art Nouveau mock Egyptian temple. It's one of the best museums east of the Urals examining every aspect of the region's past, from Cossack explorers to life in the USSR.

Khakassia

Heading south from Krasnoyarsk you soon enter the Republic of Khakassia, a small region by Russia's standards with its early 20th-century capital **Abakan ⑩**, the only town of any real size. A leafy, quite pleasant transport hub, the town does have a very engaging museum, the **Khakassky natsionalny kraevedchesky muzei** (Khakassia National Museum; Pushkina 96; daily 10am–6pm) where you can learn about local standing stones in a strikingly modern environment.

A short bus ride away, **Minusinsk** is a much older settlement with some impressive, if derelict, old architecture harking back to its days as a centre of European culture. It, too, has a very good museum, the **Muzei Martyanova** (Martyanov Museum; Martyanova 6; daily 10am–6.30pm) which packs countless rooms with shamanic knicknacks, standing stones and exhibits on the Europeans to have settled in these parts.

Another short bus ride from Abakan brings you to **Shushenskoe**, a town famous for having hosted Lenin during his years of Siberian exile in the late 19th century. The only sight here is the **Istoriko-etnografichesky muzei-zapovednik Shushenskoe** (Shushenskoe Historical and Ethnographic Museum; daily 10am–6pm) which once focused on Lenin's rather productive time here but is now more of an open-air museum of Siberian architecture with a bit of Lenin thrown in at the end for old time's sake.

Tuva

Cut off from the rest of the Russian Federation by the Yergaki Mountains, the Republic of Tuva is a fascinating corner of Asia few ever get to see. Only accessible by bus from Abakan, this small republic is a land of yurts and nomads, grassland and mountains, active shamanism and throat singing, the main draw for tourists. The capital **Kyzyl** is one of the few cities in Russia to still be dominated by the original inhabitants – the Tuvans, a proud Mongolian people who speak a language belonging to the Turkic group. Despite its remoteness, Kyzyl has no less than three blockbuster sights; the first is the **Natsionalny muzei** (National Museum; Titova 30; Wed–Sun 10am–6pm) where the definite highlight is the gleaming collection of Scythian gold, unearthed at the Arzhaan I burial site to the northwest of Kyzyl. The second is the **Centre of Asia Monument** – a English explorer calculated Kyzyl to be at the geographic centre of Asia and new monument marks the spot by the river. The third place you should not miss is the **Tsentr traditsionnoi tuvinskoi kultury** (Centre for Tuvan Culture; ulitsa Lenina) an arts centre which brings together all of Tuva's traditional culture, focusing specifically on the republic's folk music and throat singing (see page 125).

Along the BAM Railway to Lake Baikal

The BAM Railway, the "other" Trans-Siberia Railway built by the Soviet

Irkutsk–Listvyanka hydrofoil on Lake Baikal.

Union in the 1970s and 80s to link Siberia with the Pacific (but avoiding the sensitive Chinese border area), begins at **Tayshet**, a former gulag town and transit point for hundreds of thousands of prisoners. There are some pleasant, off-the-map trips here to places like **Biryusinsk**, an old timber-processing town on the old Trakt, the post road that once linked Europe with Asia. Railway buffs will enjoy the town's railway connections. Founded in the late 1600s by Cossacks, **Bratsk ⓫**, 600 km (373 miles) east of Krasnoyarsk, has been overtaken by progress – literally. The old city is now under the reservoir of the **Bratsk Hydroelectric Station**, once the largest in the world and an impressive sight – you might be able to arrange a tour through one of the local travel companies. New Bratsk, founded in 1955 as the logging and wood processing centre of central Siberia, is a dreary, confusing Soviet creation.

Around a day on the train from Bratsk the BAM has a brief encounter with Lake Baikal. The lakeside town of **Severobaikalsk ⓬** was established

in the mid-1970s as a camp for those building the railway but has developed into the largest settlement on Lake Baikal's shores. This is a superb base for striking out into the wilderness and for accessing parts of the Great Baikal Trail, an ambitious project that aims to construct a hiking trail around the whole of Lake Baikal. Otherwise the town's main attraction is the **Muzei BAMa** (BAM Museum; Mira 2; Tue–Sat 10am–1pm and 2–6pm), where nostalgia-inducing exhibits tell the story of the BAM builders.

Lake Baikal

No trip to Siberia is complete without seeing the "Pearl of Siberia," **Ozero Baikal** (Lake Baikal) ⓭, a 636-km (395-mile) long stretch of water which lies 66 km (41 miles) east of Irkutsk. One of the world's great lakes, Baikal is more than simply Siberia's top tourist attraction, it is a force of nature. For once, Russian statistics are not gratuitous. The lake holds 20 percent of the world's fresh water and its maximum depth plunges to 1,637 metres (5,370 ft) (see page 276). Lake Baikal offers so many endemic species (1,500) and so much geological diversity that the study of the lake has created a new scientific discipline: Baikology.

Whatever the season, weather on Baikal is unpredictable. The lake is ruled by a microclimate in which storms may rise and fall without passing over the shoreline. Weather often bears little relation to that in Ulan-Ude or Irkutsk. Even on the lake, it may change drastically in minutes. The first snow appears in early October, and the lake is frozen from January to May. This is the time when ice roads are created, vastly reducing the time it takes to drive from communities on one side of the lake to those on the other.

The lake's most famous indigenous species is the *nerpa*, the world's only freshwater seal. Sturgeon and *omul* (similar to salmon and trout) feature among the marine life. The lakeside

Classic Soviet car parked by the harbour, Listvyanka.

village of **Listvyanka** ⑭ makes an interesting day trip from Irkutsk; here the extraordinary ecology of the area is best explained in the small **Baikalsky Muzei** (Baikal Museum; 9am–7pm). On the other side of the Angara River is **Port Baikal**, a drowsy village linked to Listvyanka by a lazy ferry four times a day. Before the section of the Trans-Siberian Railway that skirts the southern shores of Lake Baikal was built, entire trains were loaded onto ice breakers here and carried over the lake to where the tracks started again.

In the summer months, Lake Baikal becomes a popular destination for Russians looking to cool off in its ever-chilly waters. The best beaches can be found on the southeast coast and on **Ostrov Olkhon** ⑮ (Olkhon Island) on the lake's west shore, about five hours northeast by road from Irkutsk. A place steeped in spiritual meaning and legend for the local shamanist Buryats, the island is a beautifully tranquil almost uninhabited place, except for the mini-capital Khuzhir which has become an unlikely tourist hotspot.

Irkutsk

Located on the Angara River around 66km from the lake, **Irkutsk** ⑯ is arguably the most appealing Siberian city and the one best developed to accommodate tourists. Most visitors arrive on the rails, and if there's one stop on the Trans-Siberian that no one misses, it's Irkutsk, with its easy access to Lake Baikal. The city centre is generally a pleasant place with many decent places to stay and some excellent eateries. Irkutsk has missed out on Siberia's oil wealth, which has pushed tourism up the local agenda, and it's one of the few cities east of the Urals to have a proper tourist office, street map boards and lots of English-speaking assistance available.

It was founded in 1662 by Russian Cossacks, as a fort from which they collected a fur tax from the local Buryats. It later grew rich on trade and was the launch pad for many expeditions into Asia by wealthy Russian explorers. So civilised were the citizens of Irkutsk when it was the capital of all Russia's territory east of the Urals (including California and Alaska), that it earned

Street sign in Russian and Buryat, Irkutsk.

Traditional wooden house, Irkutsk.

Buddha at the Khangalov Museum of Buryat History.

Buddhist temple (Datsan), Ulan-Ude.

itself the nickname "Paris of Siberia". This image was partly created by the city's most famous residents, a few Decembrists, who ended up here after being exiled further east following an unsuccessful coup against the tsar in December 1825. Two of the city's highlights are museums dedicated to the Decembrists – the **Dom-muzei Volkonskogo** (Volkonsky House Museum; Pereulok Volkonskogo 10; Tue–Sun 10am–6pm) and the **Dom-muzei Trubetskoi** (Trubetskoi House Museum; Dzerzhinskogo 64; Wed–Mon 10am–6pm) which both tell the emotional story of their Siberian exile.

Many of Irkutsk's wooden houses may have witnessed the Decembrists tale, though some are in a sorry state. To address the problem with these wooden structures and to mark the city's 350th birthday in 2012, the authorities created the **130 Kvartal** (130th Block; Sedova and Iyulya), an entire block of wooden buildings, some moved here from other parts of the city, others built from scratch. These are now packed with shops, restaurants, bars and hotels creating a kind of Irkutsk Disneyworld for the tourists.

In addition to the Decembrist houses, Irkutsk certainly has no shortage of other museums. The **Krayevedchesky Muzei** (Local History Museum; Karla Marksa 2), housed in the former Siberian Geographical Society building, contains interesting exhibits on various aspects of Siberian life. The newer **Muzei istorii goroda Irkutska** (Irkutsk History Museum; ulitsa Frank-Kamenetskogo 16a; Thu–Tue 10am–6pm) tells the story of the city with limited space. Some 47 km (29 miles) southeast of Irkutsk on the road to Listvyanka is the region's best outdoor museum, the **Arkhitekturno-etnograficheský muzei Taltsy** (Taltsy Museum of Architecture and Ethnography; daily 10am–5pm), a collection of old Siberian dwellings, churches, shops and watermills saved from various sites along the Angara River that have been submerged by reservoirs.

Republic of Buryatia

This large, Buddhist Republic on the east side of Lake Baikal is a fascinating

RUSSIA'S SEAT OF BUDDHISM

One of Buryatia's greatest attractions is the Ivolginsk Datsan, the seat of Buddhism in Russia, some 30 km (19 miles) west of the town. The temple was opened in the 1960s ostensibly to show the world that religious tolerance existed in the Soviet Union. In reality, it was all a charade. The KGB had secretly sent a dozen agents to Ulan Bator, Mongolia, to become sufficiently familiar with the rituals of Buddhism to open the datsan. The KGB agents enjoyed large *dachas* in the mountains and were driven to the temple each day in *Zil* limousines. In the late 1980s the pretence became reality as more and more curious Buryats attended the temple. The temple, which has grown rapidly in recent years, is in a splendid setting with snow-capped peaks towering over the plain and a small mountain stream running nearby. Its colourful interiors contain numerous images of the Buddha, Buryat paintings and a museum. When visiting follow the path along the datsan's inside walls: the prayer wheel (spin it gently as you pass) is said to write a prayer 1,000 times for each spin. You may visit a service at the main temple – generally held in the morning. To get there, take a minibus from Ulan-Ude bus station to Ivolga, then change onto special minibuses that run to the temple.

country within the Russian Federation which shares much more with Mongolia than it does with the rest of Russia. Its people are Buryat Mongolians and their capital is **Ulan-Ude** ⑰, an exotic, very un-Russian place with enough attractions to keep visitors away from the railway for a week at least. First stop for most is Ploshchad Sovietov (Soviets Square) where the largest **Lenin Head** in the world was erected in 1970 on the occasion of what would have been Lenin's 100th birthday. Nearby the **Muzei istorii Buryatii im. M.N. Khangalov** (Khangalov Museum of Buryat History; Profsoyuznaya 29; Tue–Sun 10am–6pm) may be housed in an ageing building but the Buddhist art inside is unmissable. New *datsany* (Buddhist temples) have sprung up all over Buryatia in the past two decades – the most recent addition in Ulan-Ude is the **Rinpoche Bagsha Datsan**, high on a hilltop above the city. Around 6 km (4 miles) from the city centre the **Etnografichesky muzei** (Ethnographic Museum; Verkhnyaya Berezovka; Wed–Fri and Sun 9am–5pm, Sat 10am–6pm) is an open-air affair with seven different areas, each one dedicated to the architecture and traditional culture of a different Buryat tribe or group. Back in town, take a look at the **Buryatsky teatr opery i baleta** (Buryat Opera and Ballet Theatre; Lenina 51), a striking building restored to its original Stalinist state a decade ago – this included a couple of depictions of Stalin himself, a rare sight in Russia.

Heading south from Ulan-Ude towards the border with Mongolia, the first settlement of note is Novoselenginsk where there's an interestingly remote **Muzei Dekabristov** (Decembrist Museum; Lenina 53; Wed–Sun 10am–6pm) if little else. Russia turns into Mongolia at the dusty frontier town of Kyakhta. By the mid-19th century this small town had grown fat on the tea trade with China, building several monumental cathedrals and filling a **Kyakhta Museum** (Lenina 49; Tue–Sun 10am 6pm) with treasures from far and wide. The tea millionaires have long since gone, ruined by the Trans-Sib and the Suez Canal, but the museum and the hulks of their churches remain.

FACT

Buryatia's Barguzin Valley is an enchanting, mountain-hemmed area of grassland, lost villages, grazing horses and strange rock formations. Tours run from Ulan-Ude and Ust-Barguzin.

Buryat Opera and Ballet Theatre, Ulan-Ude.

SIBERIA'S ADVENTURE PLAYGROUND

With its vastness of forests, endless lakes and rivers, remote mountains, varied wildlife and an off-the-map feel, Siberia is a paradise for outdoor adventurers.

When it comes to the great outdoors, there is no greater adventure playground on earth than Siberia and the Russian Far East. With some good research, a little local assistance and judicious preparation Siberia can provide the adventure of a lifetime.

Some of the best places to trek are the ranges of the Altai and Sayany mountains. The Altai's Katunski Range is the highest in Siberia, a land of peaceful high valleys and snowcapped peaks, with Mt Belukha towering at 4,506 metres (14,783 ft). For serious mountaineers, the glacier-shrouded high Altai offers challenging climbs. The Great Baikal Trail project aims to ring Lake Baikal with hiking paths. Olkhon Island and the Stolby Nature Reserve on the outskirts of Krasnoyarsk, with its spectacular rock formations, are great hiking areas.

Prefer your adventures on water? Then Siberia's wild rivers will get your adrenalin pumping. Flowing with snow and glacial meltwater from the mountains in the south, rivers like the Katun, Argut, Bashkaus, Chulyshman, Chuya and Chulcha are white-water rafting heaven. Lake Baikal is also a great location for kayaking, diving and sailing.

Kamchatka

Just the word makes the hearts of outdoor adventurers everywhere beat a little faster. This spearhead-shaped peninsula in the Russian Far East is dotted with active volcanoes, spouting geysers, giant plants and fields of boiling mud. June to September are the best times for adventure tourism. Any later than September and things get too cold and snow-bound.

That's not to say there is no outdoor adventure here in winter. There's a growing number of downhill resorts most notably in Krasnoyarsk and Baikalsk. Between November and April, cross-country skiing can be enjoyed just about everywhere.

For guided adventures websites, see page 307.

The remote lands of the Sayan and Altai mountains, which border Mongolia in Siberia's south, are carpetted with wildflowers in summer.

Kamchatka is known for its active volcanoes, such as the Chodutka. Trek up or choose a helicopter ride for some stunning vistas. However going it alone here can be dangerous so enlist the help of an experienced guide.

Brown bear fishing in Kamchatka.

SIBERIA'S WILDLIFE

With such a vastness of virgin land, wildlife is another of Siberia's outdoor attractions. The dreamy taiga forests and the open northern steppe shelter bears, deer, wolves, lynx, elk, beaver and caribou. Kamchatka on the other hand is abundant with bears and there are Stellar's Sea eagles, foxes, killer whales and deer to spot also. Wildlife watching is a growing aspect of adventure tourism in Russia, and to see a rare Siberian tiger in the Amur forests is a nature lover's holy grail. Plenty of wildlife means hunting and fishing are also on the agenda. Tour operators can arrange guiding and permits for exciting trophy hunting all year round. For anglers, Siberia's lakes and rivers are a paradise in summer. The Angara, which drains Lake Baikal, offers one of the best locations.

Top-notch hiking is for the taking in Kamchatka, with plentiful wildlife as a bonus. Also popular are the area around Lake Baikal and the Sayany mountain ranges.

Rafting down the Urik river, Sayany.

Fly-fishing is also popular.

LAKE BAIKAL

The most beautiful jewel in Siberia's crown is Ozero Baikal, the world's deepest lake, which attracts scientists and tourists alike to its shores.

The word Baikal is derived from the Turkish word Bai-Kul, meaning 'a rich lake'. The Unesco-listed lake certainly lives up to its name. Its crystal clear waters cut a north–south swathe through the mountains and taiga of Siberia, creating a rich habitat for a flora and fauna unique to this region.

Baikal is roughly the size of Belgium. It covers 32,000 sq km (12,352 sq miles), holds one-fifth of the world's fresh water and is more than a mile deep (1,637 metres/5,370 ft) at some points.

Endemic Species

The lake's most renowned resident, the *nerpa* (Baikal seal), is believed to have been trapped here when the last Ice Age retreated. The seal then slowly adapted to the freshwater environment of its new home. Today, the grey-coloured *nerpa* is a protected species – the best places to spot them are areas away from tourists such as Olkhon Island, the Svyatoy Nos Peninsula and the remote northern shores.

More than 50 species of fish can be found in the waters. Among the more interesting fish is the *golomyanka*, which lives up to 1.5 km (1 mile) below the surface and gives birth to living young. The highly prized Baikal sturgeon can produce up to 9 kg (20 lb) of caviar on reaching maturity, and the omul, a member of the salmon family, often appears on the menu as a local speciality.

For five months of the year the lake is frozen to a depth of 10 metres (30 ft).

Omul, also known as Baikal omul, is endemic to Lake Baikal. A local delicacy, it is the object of one of the largest commercial fisheries on Lake Baikal, but over-fishing has led to it become an endangered species.

The ambitious Great Baikal Trail project aims to build a hiking trail around the entire shoreline of the lake.

Lake Baikal is fed by more than 300 rivers, but drained by just one, the Angara. The River Selenga forms a large delta on the eastern shoreline, an important habitat for birds.

EXPLORING THE LAKE

Helicopter trips, horse-riding, hiking and fishing are just some of the summer excursions on offer around Baikal, while in winter, dog sled rides, skiing and skating top the list. Irkutsk is the best launching point for trips. Hydrofoils and ferries make regular journeys to lakeside settlements in summer. In winter the lake is frozen solid to a depth of 1.5 m (5 ft) – ice roads criss-cross its expanse at this time. The southwestern side of the lake is the most accessible. One of the best places to view the world's oldest lake is from the tourist village of Listvyanka, 66 km (41 miles) east of Irkutsk. For the more adventurous, a trip to the Khamar-Daban Mountains south of Baikal offers the chance to explore taiga, alpine tundra and glacial lakes. To the northwest is Olkhon Island, the largest island in Lake Baikal, which has huge significance for local shamanist Buryats. At the northern end of the lake is Severobaikalsk, a railway town surrounded by hot springs.

Wooden homes are typical of the lakeside villages. The Museum of Wooden Architecture near Irkutsk contains fine examples of Siberian buildings.

The construction of the Irkutsk hydroelectric station in the 1950s led to a rise of 1 metre (3 ft) in the depth of water and caused serious ecological problems.

Getting ready to dive in the icy lake, Olkhon Island.

Deepest winter in the bay of Vladivostok.

Brown bears fishing in the Kamchatka Peninsula.

The new Zolotoy Bridge (Golden Bridge) in Vladivostok.

RUSSIAN FAR EAST

Six to eight times zones east of Moscow, this huge sweep of the planet is a land of ice and fire, of political exile and nomadic tranquillity.

Often mistaken for Eastern Siberia, roughly east of Lake Baikal begins Russia's Far East, a vast stretch of the country that ends at the Pacific. Colder, wilder and more sparsely populated than Siberia, this can seem a forbidding place, but the two railway lines, the Trans-Siberian and BAM Railway chug along through this wilderness, stopping off at interesting towns and cities along the way.

It's estimated that Russia's easternmost region has a population of just 6.3 million – one person per square kilometre – making it the least densely inhabited part of the planet. The population is also on the decline with many deciding to up sticks and move to Moscow. With temperatures regularly dipping below -40ºC/ºF, that possibly comes as no surprise. Inhabitants of these chilly parts who won't be moving on are the Far East's indigenous groups – the Sakha of the Sakha Republic (often mistakenly called Yakutia), the Even, Itclmcni and Koryak of Kamchatka and the Nanai along the River Amur.

Most take a linear route through the Far East, continuing their city-hopping along the Trans-Siberian and BAM railways. However, the tracks certainly don't reach everywhere here and to places like Kamchatka

and Yakutsk you'll have to fly. The Far East also has a few more internal flight connections given the distances and the condition of the roads. The road network here was only hooked up to the rest of the Russian Federation in 2010 and the vast majority of highways are unpaved.

Along the Trans Siberian

The first worthwhile stop on the Trans-Sib after leaving the Republic of Buryatia is **Birobidzhan** ⑱, capital of the Jewish Autonomous

Main Attractions

Birobidzhan
Khabarovsk
Vladivostok
Komsomolsk-na-Amure
Yakutsk
Sakhalin Island
Kamchatka

Visitors being dropped off to see the geysers in the Kamchatka Peninsula.

Region, an entity that exists in name only. Stalin came up with the idea of a 'home for the Jews' in the early 1930s and Birobidzhan did attract around 30,000 Jews from other parts of the Soviet Union and other countries, but the experiment didn't last long. In the late 1930s the Soviets began to close synagogues and ban the use of Yiddish, rendering a Jewish autonomous region virtually obsolete. Around 20,000 stayed until the collapse of the USSR; most have now left for Israel. Some Jewish heritage remains – ask around at the **Jewish Cultural Centre** (Lenina 19; Mon–Fri 9am–5pm) for someone to show you round.

The most engaging stop between Lake Baikal and Vladivostok is the city of **Khabarovsk** ⓳, at the confluence of the Ussuri and Amur Rivers, which both help to form the border with China. The 600,000 or so souls who call this frontier city home enjoy a surprisingly pleasant city with many historical, pre-1917 buildings and a lively waterfront. Apart from strolling the wide boulevards and

along the Amur in the City Park, a diverting few hours can be spent at the **Khabarovsky kraevoi muzei** (Khabarovsk Regional Museum; Shevchenko 11; Tue–Sun 10am–6pm) which contains an eclectic exhibition on all aspects of Russian history and local indigenous peoples. Amur cruise boats leave every two hours from the riverfront. Passenger boats also leave twice a day for Fuyuan in China but you'll need a Chinese visa even for an overnight trip.

After seven days of clanking rails, the locomotive's brakes on the trans-Russia Rossiya train service are applied for the last time at **Vladivostok**. Sometimes called the "San Francisco of Russia", due to its Pacific location and steep streets, it was first taken from the Chinese in 1860 and has since become the country's main port in the Far East. The climate here is pleasant with summer temperatures reaching 20°C (68°F) and winter lows rarely dipping below -15°C (5°F) and this, plus the city's vibrant atmosphere and Tsarist-era architecture make Vladivostok a fitting

It's a long way up to the Assumption Cathedral in Khabarovsk.

climax to a journey across the vastness of the Russian Federation. Local history can be explored at the **Obedinenny muzei im. V.K. Arseneva** (Arsenev United Museum; Svetlanskaya 20; Tue–Sun 10am–7pm) which was first opened in 1890 and does a good job of telling the city's story from Chinese outpost to post-Soviet boomtown. Vladivostok also has the best dining east of Lake Baikal as well as the most energetic nightlife, which can come as a refreshing surprise after weeks of travel. Moving on, there are ferries to both South Korea and Japan from here, trains to China and many flights back to Moscow.

BAM – Lake Baikal to the Pacific

The lonely tracks of the BAM Railway quickly leave the shores of Lake Baikal behind and push on through extremely remote backcountry for 27 hours until it reaches **Tynda**. This purely Soviet town's short history only began in 1974 when it became the BAM builders' central headquarters. Born of the BAM, there's little to see here except the **Muzei istorii BAMa** (BAM History Museum; Sportivnaya 22; Tue–Fri 10am–6pm, Sat 10am–7pm), the definitive BAM museum about how the line was built. The vast majority of towns and village on the BAM line were built to house railway construction workers and then railway workers themselves, meaning lots of Soviet concrete and drab prefab blocks. The one exception is the attractive city of **Komsomolsk-na-Amure**, which was established in the 1930s and hence sports many Stalinist neo-classical facades. The city was built by the Komsomols (Communist Youth Movement), which also gave this settlement of 280,000 its name. Packed full with Soviet-era mosaics, monuments, red stars, hammers and sickles and square-jawed proletariat emerging from blocks of stone, this is as near to the model Stalinist city as you will find anywhere in Russia.

Unlike its better-known cousin the Trans-Siberian Railway, which ends in style at Vladivostok, the BAM peters out with a whimper at the lonely and wholly uninteresting port of Vanino/Sovietkaya Gavan.

Diamond-studded Yakutia

In theory you can reach Yakutsk from the BAM Railway by boat. The mighty Lena River meanders north from from Ust-Kut around the Udokan Mountains towards the Verkhoyansky Mountains where it widens and continues north to the Arctic Ocean. In summer you might just find a passenger ship making the journey, but it's very hit and miss. Where the Lena widens, the capital city of the Sakha Republic, **Yakutsk** ⓴, which dates

from the first wave of Russian exploration in 1632, can be found. It is best reached by air on regular flights from Moscow, Irkutsk and Vladivostok, though there are plans to extend the railway this far north.

Like most outposts of its kind, Yakutsk was founded by Cossacks, working to please the tsar, who permitted them freedom in an empire of serfs. Later it became one of the cruellest places of exile, notorious for its brutal cold.

The city might have remained a simple outpost had it not been for the discovery of enormous mineral riches in the region, including diamonds, gold, oil and gas. This has brought wealth to some who are erecting new buildings in what had become a pretty drab Soviet city. One interesting feature of Yakutsk is that many buildings stand on stilts due to the fact that the entire place was constructed on permafrost – the stilts are to stop the buildings subsiding into the summer mud.

Yakutsk offers an excellent base for exploring the native Yakut and

Cross-country skiing on Moroznaya Mountain, Kamchatka.

Tolbachik Volcano is very much active on Kamchatka.

Evenki villages on the tundra with local tour companies. In town there's the excellent **Khudozhestvenny muzei** (Art Museum; Kirova 9; Wed–Sun 10am–6pm) where you'll find handcrafts and decorative items used and made by the Sakha people. The **Muzei mamonta** (Mammoth Museum; Kulakovskogo 48; Mon–Fri 10am–5pm) displays mammoth skeletons that have been preserved in the permafrost, while the adjacent **Muzei arkheologii i etnografii** (Museum of Archaeology and Ethnography; Kulakovskogo 48; Tue–Fri 10am–5pm, Sat 11am–4pm) has an excellent collection relating to the traditional culture of the Far East's indigenous peoples.

Another popular activity is the hydrofoil trip to the **Lenskiye Stolby** (Lena Pillars), giant rock formations about an hour upstream from Yakutsk.

Russia's Alaska

The island of **Ostrov Sakhalin** ㉑ has long held an exotic allure for Russians as a remote land of possibilities. Rich in natural resources

KAMCHATKA

Dubbed the "land of ice and fire" the Kamchatka Peninsula is a place of snow and volcanoes, cloud-wreathed mountains, nomadic natives and foraging bears – lots of them. It was claimed for Russia by Cossacks in 1696, but for most of its history has remained off-limits to ordinary Russians. Since 1991 the area has opened up to tourists, though generally only rich ones who can afford the cost of helicopter rides out into the wilderness. But prices are coming down and arranging a tour out of the dreary capital Petropavlovsk-Kamchatsky to see the peninsula's geysers, Lake Kurilskoe and Mt Mutnovskaya is now possible on a modest budget. The only way to reach the city is by air – Kamchatka has virtually no roads and is not linked to the rest of Russia by any terrestrial transport infrastructure.

such as oil, gas and non-ferrous metals, it is Russia's Alaska. Passed between Japan and Russia during the 19th and 20th centuries, Russia finally occupied Sakhalin in the last days of World War II. The capital of **Yuzhno-Sakhalinsk 22** was founded in 1881 at the base of Mt Bolshevik. Surrounding the city are virgin forests blanketing mountainous terrain, which provide a spectacular backdrop. The only sane way to reach Sakhalin is by air as ferry services are few and far between.

Volcanic isles

The **Kurilskiye Ostrova** (Kurile Islands) **23**, a chain of volcanic islands extending from Kamchatka to the northern Japanese island of Hokkaido, would probably be unheard of outside Sakhalin if they were not the subject of a territorial dispute between Russia and Japan over the South Kuriles, which Japan claims, but which Russia took in World War II.

The islands are stunningly beautiful all year round, with towering volcanoes sloping into violent seas.

The Russians have done very little to develop them, except for creating a number of small fishing villages and a naval base situated on Shikotan. The journey by sea takes one and a half days from the closest port, **Korsakov**, on Sakhalin.

With a population of 6,000, **Yuzhno-Kurilsk 24**, a fishing village on the island of **Ostrov Kunashir**, is the capital of the Kurile chain, and the most accessible destination in the group. At its southern tip, the island is within 12 km (7 miles) of Japan, whose hills are clearly visible from most points on the island. The village itself is little more than a maze of rickety huts and a fishing plant.

The island has a small **Muzei Yestestvoznaniya** (Museum of Natural History) in the town square. At the entrance a Japanese face is carved into a stone, a compelling reminder of the island's former landlords. From Yuzhno-Kurilsk it is possible to arrange boat trips to nearby **Ostrov Shikotan 25**, the most beautiful island in the chain, with a sunny microclimate.

Shikotan Island.

TRAVEL TIPS
RUSSIA

TRANSPORT

GETTING THERE AND GETTING AROUND

GETTING THERE

By Air

Almost every European international airline and several others around the world connect Moscow's Domodedovo, Sheremetyevo and Vnukova airports with destinations outside of Russia. Domodedovo is a modern airport in the south of the city which has taken a lot of business away from Sheremetyevo. Domodedovo is linked by special express train to Paveletsky Vokzal (railway station) next to Paveletskaya Metro Station, and by minibus to Domodedovskaya Metro station.

Flights take about 9 to 10 hours from New York, 4 hours from London, Paris and Rome; from Frankfurt it takes 3 hours, 2 from Stockholm, 6 from Delhi and 8 hours from Beijing.

In addition to Moscow, some international carriers also fly to Pulkovo Airport in St Petersburg and some have even found their way to regional airports such as Kazan, Nizhny Novgorod, Yekaterinburg and Novosibirsk. Note that there are no flights from Europe or America to Eastern Siberia or the Russian Far East. These destinations always require a change of planes in Moscow.

The national airline is still Aeroflot but it now shares the skies with other Russian carriers, most notably S7 Siberian Airlines.

By Sea

Unless you are on a cruise ship that calls at St Petersburg you are unlikely to arrive in Russia by ship. There are some ferry services between St Petersburg and Helsinki, Tallinn, Stockholm and Lubeck as well as

between South Korea/Japan and Vladivostok.

By Rail

Railways are the most important means of passenger transport within Russia and connect the largest cities (Moscow, St Petersburg) with some Eastern and Western European capitals. Nowadays these services are normally through carriages rather than dedicated trains.

Passengers in transit through Belarus to Russia need a Belarus visa which must be obtained before departure. A double-transit visa is needed if the return journey is on the same route. Most nationals of European and North American countries do not need a visa to cross Ukraine, but check with the nearest Ukrainian Embassy if you are unsure.

It takes two to three days to reach Moscow from Western Europe by train, with a change of gauge on reaching Russia.

The most popular rail routes for international traffic are Helsinki to St Petersburg, Helsinki to Moscow, Riga/Tallinn to Moscow and Kiev to Moscow. The website of Deutsche Bahn (www.bahn.de) is a good place to look up timetables etc.

By Road

During the past few years marked changes have taken place in the quality of services along Russian roads. There are numerous service and repair stations for all types of car across the country. However, you should still be cautious of travelling into Russia by car. It can be dangerous and road borders can take a long time to cross due to customs

Boarding a plane to Ulan-Ude at Domodedovo Moscow Airport.

checks. Outside towns petrol stations are now very frequent and petrol is very cheap by Western standards.

GETTING AROUND

By Train

With over 140,000 km (90,000 miles) of tracks, the railway system of Russia, operated by Russian Railways (RZD) is the longest in the world. It is a means of transport used for around 4 billion individual trips per year. The busiest lines in European Russia connect Moscow with St Petersburg.There are many trains between the two cities, which take between four and nine hours to reach their destination. Some are sleeper trains with berths, others are high-speed Sapsan bullet trains that cut the journey time in half. See http://pass.rzd.ru/ for train timetables, prices and online tickets.

In overnight sleeping cars, tea and some limited food is always available and trains travelling long distances have a restaurant car attached though this can be a disappointing affair. Commercial trains across Russia offer a more comfortable service, sometimes with showers and food. Cheaper trains certainly do not include any extra services. There are three types of carriage: Platskart is an open carriage with around 50 berths; kupe is a four-berth compartment and SV is a luxury two-berth compartment. Most opt for the four-berth kupe as it gives the best price to comfort ratio.

Reservations On busy routes you might want make your reservation several days ahead as berths can be in short supply, especially in 2nd class kupe carriages, which are cheap but fairly comfortable. You can reserve your seat through a travel agent, at railway stations, at your hotel or online. Booking tickets for Russian trains in your own country is the most expensive way to go and is quite unnecessary.

There are booking offices in the railway stations of every major city. To buy a ticket you will need your passport, which you must show when boarding. You'll also need to know your destination, class of carriage and train number (or time you'd like to leave). Check your ticket carefully on purchase. Remember that the entire Russian rail system works on Moscow time so make sure you factor in the correct time difference and turn up at the station at the right time.

Trans-Siberian Railway

This rail link from Europe to Russia's east and beyond is the longest in the world. Over a period of around seven days the train crosses seven time zones from Moscow to Vladivostok, passing through much of the diversity of Siberian Russia and the Far East. It makes many scheduled stops along the way, but never lingers longer than 30 minutes. If you want to explore further than a few hundred yards from the tracks, you must disembark and rejoin a later train. Stop-offs should be scheduled ahead of time – there are no hop-on hop-off tickets..

Once in your compartment there are a few points of railway etiquette you should follow. Most people change into comfortable clothes (track suits, even pyjamas) and slippers once on board and store the attire in which they boarded on hangers next to their bunk. You should do the same. Compartments are mixed sex so men should leave for five minutes or so when women want to get changed. Getting to know the people you'll be cooped up with for the next 12 hours is the done thing, as is sharing food. However, it's not a great idea to get involved in card games, vodka drinking or political discussions. Your sheets and pillow case are brought to you by the carriage attendant who will also make tea on request.

Popular stops along the Trans-Siberian between Moscow and Vladivostok include Nizhny

The Russian railways website (www.rzd.ru) has a lot of information in English.

By Car

Car Hire

Western car companies can be found in the major cities and you will find branches at international airports. Cars can also sometimes be hired with a driver. Check up-to-date details before you leave or at hotels, which advertise such companies. Note that unless you have considerable experience in driving conditions in Second/Third World countries, taking a car onto the Russian roads is probably not advisable.

All the big Western hire companies such as Avis, Budget, Eurocar, Hertz and Thrifty operate on the Russian

Novgorod, Kazan, Ekaterinburg, Novosibirsk, Krasnoyarsk, Irkutsk, Ulan-Ude and Khabarovsk. The most popular halt by far is Irkutsk which is a fascinating city in its own right but is also the closest jumping off point for Lake Baikal, the undisputed highlight of any trip across Russia.

Few know that the Trans-Siberian has a country cousin – the BAM Railway - which leaves the main line at Tayshet and travels 3,100 km (1,920 miles) through some unbelievably remote wilderness to the Pacific. There are only a couple of passenger trains a day on the line but some of the views are stupendous.

Many imagine the Trans-Siberian Railway to be one express train but this is not the case. Many trains run along the line linking various points along it – Novosibirsk to Khabarovsk, or Ekaterinburg to Irkutsk for instance. Only one semi-luxury service does the entire run – the Rossiya. It's Russia's premier train service and tickets are more expensive than on other services.

If you don't fancy the Moscow–Vladivostok run there are other options. From Ulan-Ude you can take the Trans-Mongolian route down to the Mongolian capital Ulaanbaatar and then onto Beijing. From Chita another branch heads down to Beijing. You can also cross from BAM to Trans-Sib or vice versa on the "Little BAM" between Tynda and Skovorodino.

market. Car hire is rare in Siberia and the Far East.

Rules of the Road

Russia is a signatory to the International Traffic Convention. Rules of the road and road signs correspond to international standards. The basic rules, however, are worth mentioning. Vehicles are driven on the right side of the road.

It is prohibited to drive a car after consuming any alcohol, even the smallest amount. If you test positive for alcohol, the consequences may be very serious. It is also prohibited to drive a car under the effect of drugs or any powerful medicine.

You must have an international driving licence and documents verifying your right to drive the car.

Vehicles must carry the national registration code and a national licence plate.

Using the horn is prohibited within city limits except in emergencies.
Seat belts for the driver and front seat passenger are compulsory.
The speed limit in populated areas (marked by blue coloured signs indicating "town") is 60 kph (37 mph); on most arterial roads 90 kph (55.5 mph). On highways the limit can differ, so look out for road signs specifying other speeds.

On Foot

Don't assume Russian drivers will stop when you cross the road – they'll expect you to jump out of their way and are likely to hit you if you don't understand this convention.

While walking, be aware of a traditional Russian hazard still very much in evidence: the manhole without a cover. And don't expect heavy doors, such as in the metro, to have dampers fitted – they're likely to swing towards you with enough force to knock you off your feet.

Hiking is now a popular pastime across Russia and a great way to see the country where it is possible. One very ambitious project is the Great Baikal Trail, which aims to ring Lake Baikal with hiking paths.

By Boat

Relying on passenger ships and other boats to get around Russia is folly indeed. Usually only available in summer, these services are erratic at best, non-existent at worst. The most reliable services are between Moscow and St Petersburg, with many companies running cruises between the two cities. Passengers ships also ply the Volga and the Yenisei and hydrofoils buzz up and down Lake Baikal from June to September.

By Plane

Plane is the naturally the quickest way to get around this vast country. Gone are the days when Aeroflot had a monopoly on the market – others have taken over, though, it has to be said, with very mixed results. Many domestic flights are operated by a plethora of single-plane companies that have traditionally had very short lifespans. Stick to the following big companies to be certain.
Aeroflot (www.aeroflot.ru) is still a big domestic player, linking Moscow with all major Russian cities.
S7 Siberian Airlines (www.S7.ru) connects many cities across the Russian Federation. The service is up

The busy Moscow Metro.

to Western standards and fares are competitive.
UTair (www.utair.ru) is a Khanty-Mansiysk-based airline that flies to many out-of-the-way places across Russia.
Rossiya (www.rossiya-airlines.com), based at St Petersburg's Pulkovo Airport, links the city with the rest of Russia and beyond.

By Bus

Since the demise of the USSR, buses have become a much more popular way of getting around, especially for journeys of less than 500 km (310 miles) when an overnight train journey is not worth the fuss. Bus fares are far cheaper than the train, but journeys on substandard roads can be long and uncomfortable. Vehicles can range from luxury coaches to rattling mini-vans. Drivers usually stop at mealtimes. Bus stations are not the chaotic mess they once were and are fairly regimented, even in deepest Siberia. Tickets can be bought from station ticket offices and usually a couple of travel agents in each city, and must be booked in advance where possible. Overnight minivans (*marshrutki*) often leave from in front of railway stations.

City Transport

Moscow

Buses and Trolleybuses
Buses and trolleybuses are slow, because of traffic conditions, but cheap. Buy tickets from the driver or conductor. The metro is usually much more convenient.

Taxis
There are many reliable taxi companies in Moscow and the major cities. Hotels can provide recommendations. Never take

unlicensed cabs at night and don't even think of getting into a tout's taxi at any airport. In Moscow and St Petersburg you could pre-book a transfer with your tour operator. In other cities contact local travel companies. Taxi fares are reasonable across Russia though meters are rare.
The Metro
The Moscow Metro system is famous for its architecture. It is also fast, reliable and cheap and the best way to travel around Moscow. Buy tickets for 1, 2, 5, 10, 20 rides from the ticket windows in the entry halls or, if you can, buy a monthly pass. Each station, including those which are at the same location but on different lines, has its own name.

St Petersburg

Buses, Trams and Trolleybuses
These run from 6–1am the following morning. To make full use of the system, it is essential to have a special map called Marshruty Gorodskovo Transporta – Trolleibus, Avtobus i Tramvai (Town Transport Routes for Trolleybuses, Buses and Trams). Ask your hotel receptionist where to buy a copy.

Stops marked by an "A" sign serve buses, while stops marked "T" serve trolleybuses. The latter are less crowded than buses during rush-hour. Tram signs hang from wires above the middle of the road.
Taxis
Taxis in St Petersburg are cheap and reliable. Determine the price of a journey before setting out. It's advisable to pre-book a taxi from the airport through a tour operator.
The Metro
Like St Petersburg's buses and trams, the Metro runs from 6–1am. Famous for its architecture and murals, the Metro is the fastest way to get around town, and it is worth trying to get to grips with routes and Cyrillic signs.

EATING OUT

RECOMMENDED RESTAURANTS, CAFES & BARS

WHAT TO EAT

Restaurants in Russia today cater for a variety of tastes, from local cooking done the traditional way and national dishes with a modern twist, to food from all over the globe. Travelling in the Russian Federation also gives you the opportunity to sample Georgian, Armenian, Uzbek and other cuisines from the Caucasus and Central Asia, which provide a spicy and unusual counterpoint to the more mainstream fare.

Russian

The most famous dishes are beef Stroganov and Beluga caviar. Russian cuisine includes dishes like *bliny* (pancakes with butter and sour cream, caviar, meat, jam etc), *shchi* (sour cabbage soup with meat), *pelmeny* (boiled dumplings with meat) and *kasha* (a type of porridge made with different grains).

Georgian

Georgian food has always been popular in Russia, and you will find Georgian cafés and restaurants almost everywhere, as well as Caucasian favourites served in most Russian restaurants. Georgian cuisine is famous for its *shashlik, tsyplyata tabaka* (chicken fried under pressure), *basturma* (spicy salted and smoked meat), *suluguni* (salted cheese), green and red *lobio* (beans), aubergines in a myriad of variations, and *satsyvi* (chicken). It can be served with *lavash* (a flat bread), or with *khachapuri* (a roll stuffed with cheese) flavoured with various spices, such as *tkemali*, or with a delicious *bazha* sauce.

Ukrainian

Ukrainians love their food, and their traditional cuisine is also pretty tasty. Signature dishes include *borshch* (beetroot soup with cabbage, meat, mushrooms and other ingredients), *varenyky* (filled dumpling served with sour cream) and *holubtsi* (cabbage leaves filled with mince meat and rice).

In Ukrainian restaurants you will inevitably come across *salo* (raw lard spiced with garlic) served with black bread. This is eaten raw and used as an ingredient in many dishes.

Ethnic

Siberia is particularly varied when it comes to eating out. In Buryatia everyone at some point tries *buuzy* (sometimes known as *pozy* – golf ball-sized dumplings filled with combinations of meat and fat). Horse meat specialities are common in Yakutsk and Tuva; expect lots of fish dishes around Lake Baikal.

WHERE TO EAT

These days cafés and restaurants abound and it really isn't difficult to get a meal to suit any budget just about anywhere. Hotel and tourist restaurants can be good, but also very expensive; some of the best food is often to be found in small cafés, where, if you look in the kitchen, it's grandma running the show from the stove. The quality of the food and of the service varies, as does the accuracy of the translated menus, if they are translated at all. In the big cities, expensive restaurants usually take credit cards but cafés generally do not, while cash is the only way to go in most smaller cities. Reservations

are advised for elite eateries. Self-service canteens are now very popular places to fill a hungry stomach. These are cheap and good for non-Russian speakers as you simply have to point at what you want.

WHAT TO DRINK

Everyone knows what they drink in Russia: vodka, and tea from the samovar. This is only half the truth: there are many other drinks to accompany different cuisines. Russians are drinking more and more beer, owing to the country's booming beer industry. And in summer, Russians prefer to drink kvas, a refreshing beverage prepared from bread fermented with water and yeast. As far as wine goes, it's best to stick to foreign imports. Some Moldovan wine is very drinkable and, due to recent events in the region, there may now be more Crimean wine available in restaurants. Russians have caught the coffee bug in the last decade or so and you can get a pretty good latte virtually anywhere.

Plov, a rice dish popular in Siberia.

MOSCOW

Russian & Ukrainian

Café Buloshnaya
Lyalin pereulok 7/2, korpus 1
Tel: (495) 917 3295/916 2693
Pastries and light fare in a soothing antique setting. **$–$$**

Café Pushkin
Tverskoy bulvar 26A
Tel: (495) 739 0033
Considered Moscow's best restaurant, with creatively updated Russian cuisine in a lovely faux-19th-century setting. Reservations essential. **$$$**

Chemodan
Gogolevsky bulvar 25
Tel: (495) 695 3819
Almost every species of animal found in Russia inhabits the menu at this restaurant specialising in anything you can hunt. **$$$**

Dacha na Pokrovke
Pokrovsky bulvar 18/15
Tel: (499) 764 9995
Enjoy simple and affordable Russian food amidst knicknacks of yesteryear. **$**

Godunov
Teatralnaya ploshchad 5/1
Tel: (495) 698 4480
Touristy medieval Muscovy decor, but good food and a fun atmosphere. **$$$**

Korchma Taras Bulba
ulitsa Pyatnitskaya 14
Tel: (495) 951 3760
Ukrainian chain restaurant. **$$**

Odessa-Mama
Pereulok Krivokolenny 10
An incredible fusion of Slavic, Jewish and southern European fare is dished up at this essentially Ukrainian and vaguely nostalgic restaurant. **$$**

Stolovaya 57
GUM, Krasnaya ploshchad (Red Square)
Within the GUM shopping mall, this place is incredibly cheap for the super-central location. **$**

Yolki-Palki
Neglinnaya ulitsa 8/10

A chain that provides tasty Russian food in a rustic setting. Good salad bar. **$–$$**

Caucasian & Central Asian

Café Khinkalnaya
Neglinaya ulitsa 15
Tel: (495) 276 1500
Very atmospheric, very authentic Georgian restaurant frequented by the local Georgian community. **$$**

Darbazi
ulitsa Nikoloyamskaya 16
Very authentic, family-run Georgian restaurant serving some of the best and most reasonably-priced Caucasian fare in the Russian capital. **$$**

Kish Mish
ulitsa Novy Arbat 28
Tel: (495) 690 0703
Uzbek restaurant with waiters in traditional dress and heaps of *plov* (pilau rice) and manti (meat-filled dumplings). **$$**

Madame Galife
prospekt Mira 26
Antique-dotted Georgian restaurant a cut above its peers. **$$**

Noev Kovcheg (Noah's Ark)
Maly Ivanovsky pereulok 9
Tel: (495) 917 0717
Authentic Armenian cuisine in a lovely decor. **$$$**

U Pirosmani
Novodevichy Proyezd 4
Tel: (499) 255 7926
Named after a famous Georgian painter, this is probably the finest (and most expensive) Caucasian restaurant in town. It has a beautiful interior and a good view. Quiet live music. **$$$**

European

Björn
Pyatnitskaya ulitsa 3
Tel: (495) 953 9059
Sleek Scandinavian restaurant with a venison-, herring- and salmon-rich menu and faultless Nordic service. **$$$**

Jean-Jacques
Nikitsky bulvar 12
Tel: (495) 290 3886
Snug French café with excellent, simple food. **$$**

Mario
Klimashkina ulitsa 17
Tel: (495) 253 6505
Expensive and excellent Italian cuisine. **$$$**

The Most
Kuznetsky Most 6/3
Tel: (495) 660 0706.
Upmarket restaurant with sumptuous decor and both "classical" and "creative" French brasserie-style menus. Reservations advised. **$$$**

Other

Avocado
Chistoprudny bulvar 12/2
Tel: (495) 621 7719
Vegetarian food, whole plantations of tea and occasional live music. **$$**

Beloe Solntse v Pustyne (White Sun in the Desert)
Neglinnaya ulitsa 29/14
Tel: (495) 625 2596
Kitsch decor, high prices, but authentic Uzbek, Azeri, Arabic and Chinese specialities. **$$$**

Expeditsia
Pevshevsky pereulok 6
Tel: (495) 775 6075
Upmarket restaurant serving Arctic cuisine. Striking interior design and surprisingly good food. **$$$**

Khajuraho
Shmitovsky proezd 14
Tel: (499) 256 8136
If you are looking for authentic Indian food to add a bit of spice to your time in Moscow, this is the place to go. **$$**

Jagannath
ulitsa Kuznetsky Most 11
Tel: (495) 928 3580
One of Moscow's very few vegetarian restaurants. Includes a take-away section and food shop. **$$**

Starlite Diner
Strastnoy bulvar 8A
Tel: (495) 989 4461
Superb American diner with red-leather booths and monster burgers. **$$**

Tibet-Himalaya
ulitsa Nikolskaya 10
Tel: (495) 287 2021
Tranquil setting and Indian/Asian food. Every Tuesday night the famous 'Curry Club' takes place here. **$$**

Yugos
Rozhdestvensky bulvar 10/7
Discover the hot cuisine of Serbia and the wines of the Balkans. **$$**

Alfresco lunch in Moscow.

ST PETERSBURG

Russian

1913
Voznesensky prospekt 13/2
Tel: (812) 315 5148
Perhaps the finest Russian cuisine for the price. **$$$**

Abrikosov Café
Nevsky prospekt 40
Tel: (812) 312 2457
Good bistro food and confectionery in a 1906 café. **$$**

Café Idiot
Naberezhnaya Moika 82
Tel: (812) 315 1675
The pseudo-bohemian decor and atmosphere are popular with tourists and ex-pats. Vegetarian fare. **$**

Caviar Bar
Mikhaylovskaya ulitsa 1/7
Tel: (812) 329 6622
Silver Age bar in the Grand Hotel Europe with countless kinds of ice cold vodka and three types of fresh caviar. **$$$**

Da Vinci
Malaya Morskaya 15
Tel: (812) 315 9334
Russian cuisine in flashy, neon club with tawdry, fun nightclub acts. **$$$**

Dvoryanskoe Gnezdo
Dekabristov ulitsa 21
Tel: (812) 312 0911
Set in a pavilion of the Yusupov Palace and serving French-influenced aristocratic cuisine. **$$$**

Feodor Dostoevsky
Vladimirsky prospekt 9
Tel: (812) 334 2244
Elegant setting in which to enjoy traditional Russian dishes. **$$$**

Lya Rus
Konnogvardeysky bulvar 15
Tel: (812) 571 2946
Simple, rustic café with good home cooking. **$**

Mechta Molokhovets
Radishcheva ulitsa 10
Tel: (812) 929 2247
Considered one of the city's best restaurants and serving updated recipes from Russia's first cookbook. Reservations essential. **$$$**

NEP Café
Nab. reki Moiki 37
Tel: (812) 571 7591
The NEP (New Economic Policy) recreates the café atmosphere of the 1920s, with fine Russian cuisine and a fun cabaret show. **$$–$$$**

Old Customs House
Tamozhenny pereulok 1
Tel: (812) 327 8980
Fine Russian and European cuisine in a historic interior. **$$$**

Palkin
Nevsky prospekt 47
Tel: (812) 703 5371
The Palkin restaurants were considered the city's finest before the Revolution. This restaurant recreates one of the original sites, and has hyped but excellent aristocratic and international cuisine. **$$$**

Podval Brodyachey Sobaki (The Stray Dog Cellar)
ploshchad Iskusstv 5/4
Tel: (812) 312 8047
Once a famous pre-Revolutionary art and poetry venue and now reopened with some of the original 1912 recipes. Bistro setting. **$$–$$$**

Restoran
Tamozhenny pereulok 2
Tel: (812) 327 8979
Chic decor and fine Russian cuisine. **$$$**

Sadko Restaurant and Wine Bar
ulitsa Glinki 2
Tel: (812) 903 2373
Creative and fresh updated Russian cuisine under some amazing chandeliers. **$$**

Tsar
ulitsa Sadovaya 12
Tel: (812) 640 1900
Feel like royalty among thrones and grand chandeliers as you feast on an imperial era banquet. **$$$**

Troika
Zagorodny prospekt 27/21
Tel: (812) 407 5343
Russian cuisine and folk show, catering to tourists. **$$$**

European

Bistro Garçon
Nevsky prospekt 95
Tel: (812) 277 2467
Fine French cuisine in cosy Parisian-style setting. **$$$**

Café Berlin
Italyanskaya ulitsa 2
Tel: (812) 943 2332
Cosy café with a focus on reasonable pricing, design and a friendly welcome. **$$**

Il Lago dei Cigni
Severnaya doroga 21
Tel: (812) 602 0707
Swan Lake is a gourmet Italian restaurant on Krestovsky Island. **$$$**

Il Palazzo
Nab. Reki Fontanki 34
Tel: (812) 595 6338
Milanese cuisine in a smartly restored part of the Sheremetev Palace. **$$$**

Receptoria
Admiralteysky prospekt 10
Tel: (812) 312 7967
Airy white restaurant serving exquisite and creative French- and Italian-inspired cuisine. **$$$**

Teatro
Glinki ulitsa 2
Tel: (812) 900 4488
Airy and comfortable decor and a superb spot for a pre-theatre dinner. **$$**

Other

Aragvi
Nab. reki Fontanki 9
Tel: (812) 570 5643
Clean, minimalist decor and excellent Georgian food. **$$–$$$**

Baku
Sadovaya ulitsa 12/23
Tel: (812) 941 3756
Azeri cuisine in a sultan's palace hall. **$$$**

Kavkaz
Karavannaya ulitsa 18
Tel: (812) 312 1665
A local Georgian favourite. **$$**

Khutor Vodograi
Karavannaya ulitsa 2
Tel: (812) 570 5737
Ukrainian theme restaurant with costumed musicians and authentic cuisine. **$$**

Le'Chaim
Lermontovsky prospekt 2
Tel: (812) 572 5616
St Petersburg's only kosher restaurant – elegant cuisine and setting. **$$–$$$**

Russkaya Rybalka
Yuzhnaya Doroga
Tel: (812) 323 9813
One of the city's most enjoyable piscine venues. You catch the fish in the pond, and they cook it for you. **$$$**

Tandoori Nights
Voznesensky prospekt 4
Tel: (812) 312 8772
Indian food, including a good, varied vegetarian selection. **$$**

Tinkov
Kazanskaya ulitsa 7
Tel: (812) 458 7788
Centrally located restaurant; one of the coolest and largest in town. Serves sushi, pizza, and US-style salads, and has its own micro-brewery. **$–$$**

PRICE CATEGORIES

Price categories are based on a meal for one.
$ = Less than US$20
$$ = US$20–50
$$$ = more than US$50

THE GOLDEN RING

Kostroma

Roga i Kopyta
ulitsa Sovetskaya 2
The theme here is a well-known 1920s
Russian literary figure called Ostap
Bender. Great interior in which to enjoy
the simple, tasty fare on offer. **$**

Slavyansky
Molochnaya Gora 1
Tel: (4942) 317 769
Rustic decor, home-brewed beer and
hearty food. **$**

Rostov-Veliky

Ruskoye Podvorye
ulitsa Marshala Alezeyeva 9
Russian food as it once was before
the arrival of the potato, tomato or
corn. **$$**

Suzdal

Chaynaya
ulitsa Kremlovskaya 10G

In the town's crafts market, this café
has some unusual combinations on
the menu but everything is filling and
tasty. **$**

Losos i Kofe
ulitsa Lenina 63A
In the town's trading arches, 'Salmon
and Coffee' may not sound the best
combination, but the food here is
good and the atmosphere relaxing.
$$

Vladimir

Oblomov
Bolshaya Moskovskaya, 19
Tel: (4922) 326 818
Superb cuisine, excellent service and
stylish interior combine to make this
Vladimir's top place to dine. **$$**

**Restaurant U Zolotykh Vorot (By
the Golden Gates)**
Letne-Perevozinskaya, 1A
Tel: (4922) 324 162

Mostly European cuisine served
up within charming surroundings,
with an open fireplace to boot.
$

Yaroslavl

Pivoteka Pinta
ulitsa Sovietskaya 8
Popular beer restaurant in the city
centre. **$**

Podbelka
ulitsa Bolshaya Oktyabrskaya 28
Erstwhile dumpling café that has
been transformed into a trendy
place, but one that still specialises
in *pelmeni* (Russian ravioli) and its
cousins from across Eurasia.
$$

Traktir Na Naberezhnoy
Volzhskaya Nab. 17/1
Tel: (4852) 308 996
Hearty, imaginative Russian cuisine
overlooking the Volga. **$$**

THE EUROPEAN NORTH

Murmansk

Terrasa
prospekt Lenina 69
Restaurant with a cosmopolitan
menu by day, cocktail spot by night.
$$

Traktir Zhily-Bily
ulitsa Samoylovoy 5
This enjoyable place has a rustic
Russian folk theme and the food is
as traditional as it comes.
$

Veliky Novgorod

Detinets (Fortress)
Novgorod fortress
Tel: (8162) 774 624
The best place in town to eat is in
the fortress itself, which provides
warming sustenance in winter and
has an open veranda for hot summer
days. **$$**

Kolobok
ulitsa Bolshaya Moskovskaya 28
Cheap cafeteria popular with
students and low-income locals,
where the Soviet past lives on.
$$

Skazka
ulitsa Bolshaya Vlasyevskaya, 1
Tel: (8162) 961 902
The name of this restaurant means
'fairy tale' – the Uzbek food may
not be worthy of a bedtime story but
it certainly fills you up and doesn't
empty your wallet.
$$

Petrozavodsk

Café Kivach
prospekt Lenina 28
Student café open 24 hours a day,
and serving respectable pizzas and
pastas for a fistful of roubles. **$**

Karelskaya Gornitsa
Engelsa ulitsa 13
Tel: (8142) 785 300
Traditional Karelian fare (including
reindeer, bear and elk). A Karelian
cottage, medieval hall and even
prehistoric caves have all been
reconstructed on the premises. **$$**

Pskov

Dvor Podznoeva
ulitsa Nekrasova 1
Complex of eateries with everything
from a simple bakery to sit-down
restaurant. **$–$$**

Old Krom Grill & Pub
ulitsa Gorkogo 4V

Russian fast-food chain Russky Dvor in Smolensk.

Tel: (811) 229 8136
Steak and beer restaurant with
Chesterfield-style seating and brisk
service. **$$**

Vologda

Gud'OK
ulitsa Chekhova 51
Tel: (8172) 762 436
The obvious choice in Vologda, with
its sophisticated cosmo interior and
very good food. **$$**

Puzaty Patsyuk
Sovietsky prospekt 80
Ukrainian restaurant with imaginative
dishes. **$$**

Vyborg

Kruglaya Bashnya
Rynochnaya ploshchad 1
Founded in 1923 on the top
floor of a battlement tower.
$$

SOUTHWEST OF MOSCOW

Oryol

3 Etazh
ulitsa Pushkina 6
Sandwiches, pizzas, waffles, pastas and salads served in a friendly Western atmosphere. **$$**
Traktir Pelmenov
ulitsa Saltykova-Shchedrina 34
A timber-rich interior, well-drilled serving staff and traditional menus make this a sound choice. **$$**

Smolensk

Samovar
ulitsa Lenina 14
Self-service canteen serving up sweet pies and soft drinks.
$
Russky Dvor
Glinka Gardens
Cheap, friendly café in the city's main park.
$

Tirol
ulitsa Marshala Zhukova 9
Intimate little place done up like a Russian grandmother's abode. **$$**

Yelets

Stary Gorod
ulitsa Mira 100
With a menu of Russian favourites this is the place to head for a full-blown dinner. **$$**

THE URALS

Yekaterinburg

Kuznya
ulitsa Melkovskaya 3
Rustically themed restaurant serving an eclectic menu of Russian and Urals food. Popular with locals – always a good sign.
$$
Troekurov
ulitsa Malysheva 137

Refined, updated Russian aristocratic cuisine and modern inventions in beautifully recreated 19th-century splendour. **$$$**
Uralskie Pelmeni
Lenina prospekt 69/1
Tel: (343) 350 7150
Popular venue divided into separate halls for Russian, Georgian and Uzbek food. **$–$$**

Perm

Karin
ulitsa Mira 45B, Hilton Garden Inn Hotel
An international menu is served at this excellent Western-standard hotel restaurant. **$$**
Khutorok
ulitsa Krisanova 24
Friendly Ukrainian restaurant with hearty food. **$$**

THE EUROPEAN SOUTH

Sochi

Beliye Nochi
ulitsa Ordzhonikadze 9
The 'White Nights' serves a mix of European fare and food from the Caucasus. **$$**
Dom 1934
Pereulok Morskoy 2

Laid-back place with lots of sofas and great pasta dishes that won't break the bank. **$$**
Promenad
ulitsa Vorovskogo 3
Tel: (862) 264 3867
Much-lauded restaurant with a sunny terrace and well-crafted food. **$$**

Stary Bazar
ulitsa Neserbskaya 4
Overlooking the harbour, this popular place has a wide-ranging menu of Caucasian and International favourites.
$$

SIBERIA

Irkutsk

Bierhaus
ulitsa Gryaznova 1
Bavarian-style tavern boasting an international beer menu and hearty Russian/European fare to go with it. **$$**
Figaro
ulitsa Karla Marksa 22
Siberia's best Italian restaurant is an incredibly authentic affair, despite Russian sanctions on the import of Western ingredients. A real Italian chef keeps the pastas and pizzas coming and there are very unusual dishes on the menu such as wild boar and duck.
$$
Kochevnik
ulitsa Gorkogo 19
Tel: (3952) 200 459

One of Irkutsk's best places to eat, with filling Mongolian dishes, impeccable service and foreign wines. **$$**
Liverpool
ulitsa Sverdlova 28
British-themed pub and club with decent food, lots of beer and live music. **$$**
Mamochka
ulitsa Karla Marksa 41
Self-service canteen but with a difference – the food is a cut above the normal canteen and the Soviet theme is low key. **$**
Rassolnik
130 Kvartal (ulitsa 3 Iyulya 3)
Soviet-themed nostalgia restaurant in the 130 Kvartal development. Some great Soviet-era antiques and a menu to fit the design. Great fun. **$$**

Krasnoyarsk

Gastropub Tolsty Kray
ulitsa Lenina 116
Faux medieval cellar where the International and Russian food is served by serving staff fluent in English.
$$
Kalinka-Malinka Stolovaya No 2
prospekt Mira 100
Soviet-themed self-service canteen serving dishes from every former Soviet republic. **$**

PRICE CATEGORIES

Price categories are based on a meal for one.
$ = Less than US$20
$$ = US$20-50
$$$ = more than US$50

TRANSPORT

EATING OUT

ACTIVITIES

A – Z

LANGUAGE

Omul for sale in Listvyanka.

Mama Roma
prospekt Mira 50A
Tel: (391) 266 1072
Best Italian eatery in Krasnoyarsk.
$$

Novosibirsk

Tiflis
Sovetskaya ulitsa 65
Tel: (3832) 228 181
Good Georgian cuisine in a lively
atmosphere. One of the best spots to
dine in Novosibirsk. **$$**

Tinkoff
Lenina ulitsa 20
Tel: (383) 2222 703
One of a chain of pub-breweries, this
restaurant has an American Wild
West theme, but the food is very
Russian. Excellent meals – and good
beer to go with them. **$$**

U Nikolaya
ulitsa Uritskogo 25
Tel: (383) 2180 355
This little café is situated in a
beautiful old building near the centre
of town. Good Middle Eastern food
and value for money. **$$**

Ulan-Ude

Baatarai Urgöö
Barguzinsky Trakt, Verkhnyaya Berezovka
Yurt restaurant a little out of town
serving authentic Buryat fare
amid Mongol suits of armour and
traditionally dressed serving staff. **$$**

Chay Khana
ulitsa Baltakhinova (Europa Business Centre)
Superb Uzbek restaurant on the top
floor of a high-rise business centre.
Great views to accompany the well-
crafted food. **$$**

Churchill
ulitsa Lenina 55
British-themed pub restaurant
opposite the Lenin Head. **$$**

Kyzyl

Fusion
ulitsa Tuvinskykh Dobrovoltsev 13
International food in a European
setting in the heart of Asian Kyzyl. **$$**
Subedey
ulitsa Druzhby 149
Yurt restaurant serving traditional
Tuvan food as well as more familiar
European standards. **$$**

Tobolsk

Ladeiny
ulitsa Revolyutsionnaya 2
Tel: (3456) 222 111
Tobolsk's top eatery, housed in a
vernacular Siberian timber building
and serving the region's traditional
fare. **$$**

Omsk

Kochegarka
ulitsa Lermontova 77
Tel: (3812) 532 909
Great beer restaurant with good
service and stylish decor. **$$**

Abakan

Kafe Abakan
prospekt Lenina 80
Khakassia-themed self-service
canteen bang in the centre of town,
serving cheap meals in a pleasant
setting. **$**
Tokana
ulitsa Chertygasheva 112
Surprisingly stylish café serving
Khakassia's best coffee. **$**

FAR EAST

Vladivostok

Kapitan Kuk
Devyataya ulitsa 14
Tel: (4232) 215 579
For curiosity's sake, you can't walk
past Kapitan Kuk. It serves Australian
steak, crocodile, shark and ram's ribs
as well as Australian wine and beer –
even when the temperature is -30°C
and the city's in a whiteout. **$$$**
Nostalgiya
ulitsa Pervaya Morskaya 25
Tel: (4232) 410 513
Russian imperial-themed restaurant
with café and souvenir shop.**$$**
Pyongyang
ulitsa Verkhneportovaya 68B
It's not every day you can sample the
cuisine of the world's most secretive
dictatorship, but this North Korean

restaurant south of the city centre
provides a convenient opportunity. **$$**

Khabarovsk

Gatsby
ulitsa Istomina 49
Tel: (4212) 604 333
Stylish bar-restaurant-lounge serving
tasty bar food. **$$$**
Russky Restoran
Ussuriysky bulvar 9
Tel: (4212) 306 587
Russian theme restaurant split bet-
ween the rustic and imperial past. **$$**

Komsomolsk-na-Amure

Shinok Pervach
ulitsa Dzerzhinskogo 34
There are few better places to eat
in Komsomolsk-na-Amure than this

Ukrainian restaurant. **$$$**

Yakutsk

Chochur Muran
Vilyusky Trakt
Excellent place to sample authentic
Sakha cuisine. **$$**
Tygyn Darkhan
ulitsa Ammosova 9
Tel: (4112) 343 406
Sakha specialities such as frozen raw
fish and horse meat. **$$**

PRICE CATEGORIES

Price categories are based on a
meal for one.
$ = Less than US$20
$$ = US$20-50
$$$ = more than US$50

ACTIVITIES

NIGHTLIFE, SHOPPING AND SPORTS

NIGHTLIFE

Moscow

Nightclubs

Bilingua
Krivokoleny pereulok 10
Metro: Chistiye Prudy
Tel: (495) 923 9660
Art café; nice atmosphere.

Night Flight
Tverskaya ulitsa 17
Tel: (495) 629 4165
Legendary Moscow club with surprisingly good food.

Opera
Trekhgorny val 6
Tel: (495) 205 9822
Hip, very pricey and highly exclusive.

Icon Club
Bolotnaya naberezhnaya 9

Clubbing in Moscow.

Metro: Kropotkinskaya
Tel: (495) 364 0909
Experience Moscow's inimitable glitz and extravagance.

Propaganda
Bolshaya Zlatoustinsky pereulok 7
Metro: Kitai Gorod
Tel: (495) 624 5732
Flies in DJs from Britain and the US.

Gogol Club
Stoleshnikov pereulok 11
Tel: (495) 514 0944
Multi-tasking club with something for everyone.

Club Garage
Brodnikov pereulok 8
Tel: (495) 238 7075
One of Moscow's longest established clubs attracting a local crowd.

Music

Moscow's best venues for live jazz, reggae and rock concerts:

DOM
Bolshoi Ovchinnikovsky pereulok 24
Tel: (495) 953 7236
Featuring an unusual line up of concerts, such as festivals of Tuvan throat singing. At times completely empty, at times crowded. Call in advance. English spoken.

Nest of Wood Grouse (Gnezdo Glukharya)
Tsvetnoy Bulvar 30
Good venue to hear bards/singer-songwriters.

BB King
Sadovaya-Samotechnaya ulitsa 4
Tel: (495) 699 8206
Cool jazz venue.

Rythm and Blues Café
Starovagonkovsky perculok 19
Tel: (495) 697 6008
American-themed country and blues spot.

Vermel
Raushskaya Naberezhnaya 4/5
Tel: (495) 959 3303
Popular among students and expats. Occasional film screenings.

St Petersburg

Nightclubs

ArcticA
ulitsa Beringa 38
Good spot for rock and folk concerts.

City Bar
Furshtatskaya ulitsa 20
Tel: (812) 448 5837
Classic expat-favoured club.

Fish Fabrique
Ligovsky prospekt 53
Tel: (812) 764 4857
Legendary St Petersburg club/ music venue that is very popular with students and local artists alike.

GEZ-21
Ligovsky prospekt 53

Tel: (812) 764 5258
Experimental music, jazz, rock and
arty performances.
Griboedov
Voronezhskaya ulitsa 191
Tel: (812) 164 4355
In an old underground bomb shelter.
Jambala
Bolshoy prospekt 80
Tel: (812) 332 1077
St Petersburg's only Reggae club.
Liverpool
ulitsa Mayakovskogo 16
Tel: (812) 579 2054
Friendly club with a kitsch Beatles
theme.
Purga 1 and 2
Nab. reki Fontanky 11
Tel: (812) 570 5123
Fun bar-clubs where it's New Year's
Eve every night at midnight.
Sinners (Greshniki)
Griboyedov Canal 28
Tel: (812) 570 4291
Funky gay club.
Metro
Ligovsky prospekt 174
Tel: (812) 766 0204
Youthful multi-level club with
mainstream music.

Jazz and Blues clubs

Since Soviet times, St Petersburg
has had Russia's most vibrant jazz
scene.
Jazz Philharmonic Hall
Zagorodny prospekt 27
Tel: (812) 764 8565
JFC Jazz Club
Shpalernaya ulitsa 33
Tel: (812) 272 9850
Jimi Hendrix Blues Club
Liteiny prospekt 33
Tel: (812) 279 8813
Neo Jazz Club

Solyanoy pereulok 14
Tel: (812) 273 3830

SHOPPING

What to Buy

Goods are as plentiful throughout
the Russian Federation as they are
in the West, especially in the big
cities. Huge out-of-town malls are
becoming more common, though
the vast majority of Russians
still regularly shop at traditional
markets. Despite what you might
have heard bargaining does not
take place anywhere.

In the large cities, shopping hours
are more in line with those of the
West, especially in the large malls.
Standard opening hours elsewhere
are Mon–Sat 10am–8pm. Some
smaller shops take a lunch break
from 2–3pm. Small 24-hour shops
are common.

Souvenirs

Inexpensive souvenirs, toys and
other knick-knacks abound on
Russian streets and at markets.

The "must see" street in Moscow
is the Arbat, where Moscow
painters and woodcarvers sell
their works. Prices are quite high,
so don't be in a hurry to buy a
set of Russian *matryoshkas* (the
wooden dolls which fit inside one
another) – the same set may be
found much cheaper somewhere
else. The Izmailovo market in the
city's northeastern suburb (metro
Izmailovsky Park) is worth a trip.

There are places similar to Arbat in
St Petersburg (Ostrovskoro ploshchad)

Shopping centre in Moscow.

and in other big cities. More upmarket
souvenirs can be bought in specialist
shops, art-salons and curio shops.
Beware of the possible problems
waiting at customs: according to
Russian regulations, antiquities,
precious metals and artworks may not
be exported without prior approval. The
risk of confiscation is real. Customs
officials are particularly strict about
antique icons and military medals.
Many art galleries will provide the
necessary documentation. For further
information on Customs, see page 303.

Outside Moscow and St
Petersburg, look out for lace, jewellery
(in Veliky Ustiug), painted wooden
objects (in Archangelsk) and carved
ivory (especially in the village of
Lomonsovo, near Archangelsk).
Birch bark items are just one of
the souvenirs travellers bring back
from Lake Baikal, along with various
minerals crafted into jewellery.

These days communist-era
badges, flags, hats and watches are
likely to be Chinese-made fakes,
though the real deal can still be
found. Flea markets are surprisingly
rare and second-hand shops almost
unheard of.

Where to Shop

Moscow

Department stores
GUM (State Department Store)
Krasnaya ploshchad 3 (Red Square)
This famous arcade has been
commandeered by branches of
foreign stores, and you won't
find many Russian goods here

Festivals

Since the fall of communism many
church and pagan holidays and
festivals have been revived. Almost
everywhere, a week-long celebration
called Maslenitsa (Butter Week)
precedes the long Lent before
Easter. This farewell to winter
involves piles of bliny, buckets of
alcoholic beverages, and usually
games and competitions.

Throughout the year cities hold
various arts and other festivals.
In Russia, the best known festival
is the White Nights celebration in
St Petersburg with its non-stop
programme of cultural events
and performing arts. Sailing
competitions and festivals are
hosted by the Bay of Finland.

Moscow holds classical, jazz
and ethnic music festivals in the
summer, many in the concert
halls of palaces and museums.
The prestigious International
Tchaikovsky Competition (www.
tchaikovsky-competition.ru) is held
every fourth year in Moscow. In
the autumn the concert season
kicks off, with festivals of early
and avant-garde music in St
Petersburg, as well as other special
cultural events in Moscow and
the other cities. A second peak
occurs around New Year, with many
museums and palaces holding
concert series on their premises,
and special programmes taking
over the concert halls.

apart from a few handicrafts and souvenirs. Foreign-made goods will probably be more expensive than at home. However, it is worth visiting, if only for the fabulous decor.

Petrovsky Passage
Petrovka ulitsa 10
Another magnificent arcade, as expensive as GUM.

Speciality shops
It is no longer hard to find souvenir, craft and gift shops in Russia; they are easily located in city centres and just about anywhere tourists congregate. More interesting and artistic crafts and gifts can be found in kiosks or stands in the lobbies of major museums. Traditional gifts, such as crystal, Gzhel (similar to Delftware), ceramics, and china can be found without the tourist mark-up in department stores and arcades. There are plenty of jewellery stores selling silver and traditional rose gold ornaments; ask about native Russian diamonds faceted in Smolensk – they are renowned for their brilliance and clarity. There are also fur shops galore, selling a variety of domestic and imported outerwear. Check the seams to be sure they are tight and be sure that the hairs are firmly attached (if they seem to fall out, the pelt may be old and dry).

St Petersburg
One of the best places to buy souvenirs is at the three bridges, next

Cooling down after the sauna.

to the cathedral of Our Saviour on the Blood, right on Kanal Griboyedova.

Department stores
Gostinny Dvor
Nevsky prospekt 35
Most famous of St Petersburg's department stores.
Passage
Nevksy prospekt 48
Another big department store.

China
Imperial Porcelain Factory
Obukhorskoy Oborony prospekt 151.

SPORTS

Football

Football (soccer) is one of Russia's national sports and the country is due to host the 2018 FIFA World Cup (controversially some might add). Most matches pass off without incident but Russia has a hooligan problem similar to the UK of the 1970s and 80s and racism is rife.

In St Petersburg the main team is Zenith, in Moscow there are Dinamo, CSKA, Spartak and Lokomotiv. Other big teams include Rubin from Kazan and FC Anzhi Makhachkala from the Republic of Dagestan. Tickets are usually cheap and can be purchased at the stadium box offices and online. Big games sell out quickly, and touts are still common.

Ice Hockey

Ice hockey is Russia's winter sport. The country exports a lot of players to the US NHL and the national team is one of the world's most successful. In Moscow the teams to watch are Dinamo, CSKA and Spartak. Matches are played in the Sports Palace or at the Luzhniki Small Sports Arena. Spectators are better humoured than soccer crowds and the atmosphere much friendlier.

Traditional Sports

Siberia's ethnic groups engage in some more traditional sporting pastimes. In Buryatia Surkharban is a big annual event that demonstrates the locals' incredible horsemanship. In the Republic of Tuva wrestling is the main sport.

Spas and Bathhouses

The healing properties of the mineral waters in the Mineralnyye Vody Region (Caucasian Spa District) have been known for centuries. This area, and the customs of resort people, were described by the writer Mikhail Lermontov, author of *A Hero of Our Time*, who was killed in a duel in the spa town of Pyatigorsk.

Pyatigorsk mineral waters are still popular and are used to treat bowel complaints, the neural system, dyspepsia, pathological metabolism, and vascular, gynaecological and skin problems. Other spas in this region – Essentuki, Kislovodsk and Zheleznovodsk – are just as famous as Pyatigorsk. Sochi and Matsesta are in the vicinity of the Kavkazskiye Mineralniye Vody Region, on the Black Sea coast close to the spa of Tskhaltubo.

Another option is the day spas of the major cities which offer a variety of relaxing and reviving treatments.

Whether a simple log-house in rural surroundings or in palatial city premises, the *banya* (bathhouse) is a tradition close to Russians' hearts. In Moscow, the most famous *banya* is Sandunovskie Bani, or Sanduny (14 Neglinnaya ulitsa; tel: (495) 928 4631; www.sanduny.ru). Here the men's section is decked in marble and gold. In most *banyas*, a 2-hour session costs around 600 roubles (more in big cities) including use of towel and slippers. Other services are extra. Most guesthouses around Lake Baikal have traditional *banyas*.

A – Z

A HANDY SUMMARY
OF PRACTICAL INFORMATION

A

Accommodation

The last 10 years have seen a sharp improvement in the number, services and class of hotels. All the same, gaps persist. In Moscow there is a dearth of medium-class hotels in the city centre. Budget travellers either have to opt for hotels in the outskirts (near to metro stations) or consider renting a serviced flat. In other cities visitors may have to make do with modernised Soviet-era hotels. However, luxury establishments and privately owned boutique hotels are cropping up in smaller touristy towns. Mini-hotels are small hotels offering basic services: clean rooms and simple breakfasts. Most hotels provide some form of Internet access, a range of concierge services, and breakfast.

In Russia hotels are required by law to list prices in roubles.

B

Business Hours

Most stores in Russia open 10am to 8pm, though in the centre of major cities it is not difficult to find 24-hour convenience food stores and chemists. Lunch breaks are more or less a thing of the past, though don't be surprised if you encounter a locked door between 1pm and 3pm, especially outside of big cities. Banks are normally open 9am to 6pm weekdays and in some cases Saturdays, too. Restaurants are generally open between 11am–11pm.

C

Climate

Russia spans a huge range of climatic zones, from the arctic tundra of northern Siberia to the steppes of Central Asia. Almost everywhere is extremely cold in winter, the exception being a small area along the Black Sea coast, where January temperatures remain above freezing. By contrast, most places average around −20°C (−4°F), with the cold intensifying to the northeast. In northeast Siberia, winter temperatures are usually somewhere near −50°C (−57°F), and have been known to plummet as low as −68°C (−90°F). The Pacific coast and European Russia are milder; Moscow has January daytime temperatures of around −9°C (16°F), St Petersburg −7°C (1either have to opt for 9°F).

Most of the country experiences warm summers, the exceptions being the arctic north and the Pacific coasts, where cold ocean currents keep temperatures down. Across much of Siberia summer daytime values are around 20°C (68°F), but can sometimes rise to 38°C (100°F). In Moscow, July daytime temperatures average 23°C (73°F), but vary widely from year to year. Southern Russia has hotter and more humid summers. Most of Russia has a summer maximum of rainfall, with thunderstorms common in early summer. Eastern regions are drier.

Children

Taking children to Russia is not the trial people might imagine. Russians are very welcoming to little ones and if there's a way to jump queues, melt the cold heart of bureaucracy and avoid harassment by the police it's to have a tot in tow. For babies all Western brands of milk and nappies are available. Changing facilities are rare. A trip across Russia is a fascinating experience for older children – wildlife is pretty accessible in rural areas and museums across the land are thinking more about young visitors.

Crime and Safety

Crime against tourists in Russia is no worse than in any Western country. The most common form of crime in the city centres are pickpockets who take advantage of crowds. Violent crime is rare and tourists are hardly ever targeted. However, those with dark skin should take extra care as racism is on the increase across Russia.

A few simple rules to observe to avoid becoming the victim of a crime: Don't carry all your cash in one place, and avoid displaying large sums of money. You should change

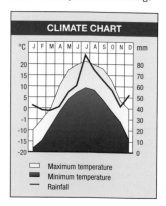

CLIMATE CHART

Maximum temperature
Minimum temperature
Rainfall

money only at exchange booths and make sure you take all the cash out of the drawer (sometimes a note sticks to the drawer thanks to a bit of glue). ATMs are generally safe to use, but you should use normal precautions when using street machines. Watch out for scams, like someone "dropping" a wad of bills (if you pick it up, the owner will return for it and claim there was more than what you have in hand). Tuck your bag and camera firmly under your arm while shopping. Be sure to lock your door in your hotel and if travelling on an overnight sleeper train. Never get into card games with "new friends" at railway stations.

When travelling by train, you will need to book your seat in advance. Never buy tickets from the casual person apparently returning an unwanted ticket at the railway station, and ensure that your ticket reflects your passport details as you will be required to show it to the conductor.

Russian police (politsia) officers have a mixed reputation. Most try to be helpful to foreign tourists (there are even dedicated "Tourist Police" in Moscow though you'd be lucky to see one), but some may try to "fine" tourists for supposed registration or other offences. If a police officer asks for your documents, hand them over (but not your purse or wallet). If you are asked to pay a fine, ask to be taken to a police station to do so – there are no on-the-spot fines in Russia and the officers will in this case probably just give up and let you go. Never ever offer a policeman a bribe – this cannot be emphasised enough.

Until recently taking photographs of just about anything was OK, but with the current heightened tensions over Ukraine and return of Soviet-era paranoia about the West, it's probably best to refrain from photographing railway stations, bridges, anything

Gender Etiquette

Russian etiquette on male-female relations is in flux, and you are likely to come across a wide variety of behaviour. In general, society veers towards the more traditional roles. Men are expected to open doors for women, help them with their coats, carry heavy parcels and suitcases, and offer a hand to a woman getting on or off a bus. Men will invariably pay for meals or drinks and may be

vaguely military, pro-government demonstrations or power stations etc, especially away from big cities. Also, border zone restrictions have recently been tightened – these means everyone (even locals) needs a permit to go within a certain distance of Russia's border. Permits take a month to get and you have to have a good reason to want one, especially when it comes to sensitive frontiers such as Ukraine and China.

Customs Regulations

When you arrive in the country, you must fill out a customs declaration for any cash over US$10,000. In this case, be sure to use the Red Channel at the airport and have the customs officer stamp your declaration.

The only time some foreigners get caught out by Russia's customs laws is when they try to take anything out of the country which looks old. A tourist with a Repin tucked under their coat might get through, a Russian living in London trying to take retro 1970s light fittings for their home might get stopped and the items confiscated. If you are unsure about something you have bought, the Ministry of Culture (ulitsa Akademika Korolyova 21, tel: 499 391 4212) are supposed to be able to assess whether an item can be exported.

Emergency Numbers

All Russian cities have unified emergency telephone numbers which can be dialled free from public telephones:
Fire 01
Police 02
Ambulance 03
Gas Emergency 04
General Emergency 112
Officials responding to these calls will speak little English, so a knowledge of Russian is needed to make yourself understood.

D

Disabled Travellers

Russia is not a barrier-free environment and travelling to the country with mobility problems should arguably not be attempted. The most expensive hotels in the main cities may provide one wheelchair-accessible room, and the major museums now have ramps and lifts. But getting around cities and towns or visiting cultural sites is likely to be almost impossible, especially when it

offended if a woman reaches for her purse. Women expect this kind of attention, including from foreigners, in social settings and in some business ones.

Sexual harassment is rare, but if you are bothered by a man, the best person to help is an older woman – matrons and babushki usually put males in their place with a few harsh words.

comes to public transport. People who use a wheelchair should consider a light-weight manual chair for their trip so that assistance can be provided. Hiring a local guide who knows the terrain is also a good idea.

E

Electricity

Electrical supply is 220v. Sockets require a continental-type two-pin plug. Take adaptors with you as they are not available in Russia.

Embassies and Consulates

Moscow
Australia
Podkolokolny pereulok 10A/2
Tel: (495) 956 6070
Canada
Starokonyushny pereulok 23
Tel: (495) 105 6000
Ireland
Grokholsky pereulok 5
Tel: (0495) 937 5911
New Zealand
Povarskaya ulitsa 44
Tel: (495) 956 3579
South Africa
Granatny pereulok 1, bldg 9
Tel: (495) 540 1177
UK
Smolenskaya Naberezhnaya 10
Tel: (495) 956 7200
US
Bolshaya Devyatinsky pereulok 8
Tel: (495) 728 5000

St Petersburg
Australia
Italyanskaya ulitsa 1
Tel: (812) 325 7333
UK
ploshchad Proletarskoy Diktatury 5
Tel: (812) 320 3200
US
Furshtatskaya ulitsa 15
Tel: (812) 331 2600

Entry Requirements

Today the best way to get a visa is to go through a specialist visa agency in your own country. The process otherwise takes a long time and involves a lot of paperwork. In the UK Real Russia (www.realrussia.co.uk) are a very professional outfit. Note that applicants in the UK must visit the Russian embassy visa application centre to provide fingerprints. In the US Visa HQ (www.visahq.com) are the people to turn to.

There are essentially three types of visa: tourist visas valid for a maximum of 30 days, business visas valid for up to a year and transit visas valid for 72 hours. The only time you won't need a visa to enter Russia is if you are a passenger arriving on a cruise ship in St Petersburg.

When you arrive in the country, you will have to fill out a migration card, usually provided on board the plane. You must keep the stamped migration card with your passport and surrender it upon leaving the country.

You are obliged to have your passport and visa registered within seven working days of arrival and every time you move to another town. Taking weekends into account, this in theory gives you 11 days in which to register. Hotels will do this for you. If you are staying with a friend he or she can, in theory, register you at the post office. It is sensible to carry your passport and visa at all times, while you are in Russia since the police have the right to check your identity at will. However the police do not have the right to fine you if you are unregistered. They must hand you over to the immigration authorities, who should open an official case against you. This is rarely done.

Etiquette

The Soviet years had an unfortunate effect on Russian manners, and some sales assistants and service personnel may be brusque or unfriendly. In Russia eye contact does not have to be established between customer and shop assistant/ticket seller for the transaction to begin – this can be disconcerting for Westerners. The Russians also have a saying – "A smile without reason is a sign of stupidity" (it rhymes in Russian) so what you consider a friendly smile can be interpreted in quite a different way by strangers in public situations.

It is considered bad manners for men to wear their hats indoors or for anyone to keep their coat on or with them in a restaurant, museum or theatre. (They need to be checked in the garderobe – cloakroom.) Before entering churches, men should take off their hats and women should cover their heads; you should not turn your back to the altar or speak loudly. In some churches and most monasteries women will not be admitted in trousers. In theatres when taking your seat in the middle of a row, it is bad form to walk with your back to those already seated. On public transport, the rule is to give up your seat to older people, women with children, or the infirm, although this is no longer an absolute standard.

Remember to take off your shoes when entering a house and put on the slippers provided. Failure to eat and drink what your host offers will be taken as offence – stating "medical reasons" will get you off the hook. Russians don't like small talk and don't be surprised if you are asked questions that most Westerners would find too personal and intrusive (How much do you earn? You are 25! Why don't you have any children?). Many Russians these days want to talk geopolitics. Getting into discussions of this sort is the quickest way to lose new friends so diplomatically try to change the subject.

G

Gay Travellers

Russia was always a conservative society and the hostility towards "alternative lifestyles" that Putin's regime has created has made things even worse. Open hostility is rare, but public displays of affection between members of the same sex might at best evoke ridicule, at worst lead to arrest. There is a gay scene in every city but it's kept very low key for obvious reasons.

H

Health Care

Pharmacies

Apteki (pharmacies) in the major cities are well-stocked with domestic and imported medicines. Most pharmacists will understand the Latin name of a drug, not brand names. If you need special medication it is best to bring it with you. Doctors and hospitals may expect immediate cash payment for health services. Medical insurance is essential, preferably with supplementary medical insurance with specific overseas coverage, which includes repatriation.

Moscow

In Moscow and the major Russian cities there are many Western-style pharmacies, such as the chain 36.6 which have a full array of Western and local OTC drugs and healthcare products. The chain Arbat Prestizh carries familiar Western brands of toiletries and beauty products. In all cities there are round-the-clock pharmacies, usually marked with a clearly visible "24". Your hotel can provide assistance to find the closest one.

Take precautions

It is recommended that you wash fruit and vegetables before eating them. Never drink tap water especially in Russia's cities. Water comes through very old pipes almost everywhere, but it is particularly important not to drink St Petersburg's tap water, even in small quantities. Bottled mineral water is available everywhere.

Be careful when buying alcohol from kiosks. It's been known for brand-name bottles to be emptied of their original contents and refilled with homebrew of dubious quality.

Doctors

Your hotel service bureau will find a doctor to come to your hotel room or will refer you to the nearest clinic. Medical standards in Moscow and St Petersburg are reasonable; they're not so great in rural areas. Emergency treatment should, in theory, be free.

Several medical centres provide Western-style medical care with English-speaking staff:

Moscow
MEDSI International Clinic
Grokholsky pereulok 1
Tel: (495) 290 9386
International SOS Clinic
Grokholsky pereulok 31, 10th floor
Tel: (495) 937 5760
European Medical Centre
Spiridonsky pereulok 5
Tel: (495) 933 6655

St Petersburg
American Medical Clinic
Nab. reki Moiki 78
Tel: (812) 740 2090

MEDEM International Clinic and Hospital
Marata ulitsa 6
Tel: (812) 327 0301

Health Regulations

No vaccinations are required for visits to Russia, but immunisation against tetanus and diphtheria are recommended. It is also advisable to be inoculated against Hepatitis A. If you are travelling to certain areas of Siberia protection against tick-borne encephalitis and possibly rabies is also advised.

Visitors from regions suspected to be infected by yellow fever, especially some African and South American territories, require an international certificate of vaccination against yellow fever.

I

Identity Papers

According to Russian law, everyone should carry their passport (Russians have an internal one) at all times. Foreigners also need to carry their registration receipts and possibly used plane and railway tickets, too. Some visitors choose to carry photocopies, fearing their documents may be stolen, and indeed it is extremely difficult to replace a lost or stolen visa. The best idea is to make copies of all your documents and leave them in the hotel. If you are stopped by the police and they find a problem with your papers, ask to be taken to the nearest police station. Never pay a fine on the spot as this is just the policemen looking for a bit of cash from a foreigner.

Internet

Almost all hotels in the major cities provide some form of internet these days, usually free or paid Wi-Fi, or sometimes the use of the a computer. Hotspots are also to be found advertised on café doors in the big cities. As across Europe, internet cafés are virtually a thing of the past. When using a smartphone, get a local SIM card as roaming charges in Russia are astronomical.

M

Money

The currency in Russia is the rouble, which consists of 100 kopeks. There

Maps

Particularly recommended for Moscow and St Petersburg are the German Falk plan maps, available from large bookshops.

are bills in denominations of 50, 100, 500, 1,000, and 5,000, and coins of one, five, ten, and 50 kopeks, as well as one, two, five and ten roubles.

Travellers' cheques are not worth the bother for the security they offer. In Russia they are difficult and expensive to exchange for cash and no restaurant, shop or hotel will accept them.

ATMs (called *bankomat*) can be found throughout major cities and are secure. In big cities they issue both dollars and roubles; in smaller cities they usually only issue roubles. The ATM exchange rate is as good as (and sometimes better than) exchange counters. Cash should only be exchanged in banks and at exchange offices; these days, rates are usually better in banks.

Major credit cards are accepted at hotels and many stores, and an increasing number of restaurants. However, Russia is still largely a cash economy, and you should be prepared to pay in roubles for tours, food, and most services, especially outside the big cities.

N

Newspapers

Foreign-language press

Most large hotels provide cable or satellite television with a full array of English-language news and entertainment stations, and in the major cities there are also sports bars and other venues that broadcast English-language programming. Newsstands in major hotels as well as foreign-owned supermarkets in the big cities have current English-language magazines and newspapers.

In Moscow, *The Moscow Times* (www.moscowtimes.ru) takes a rare critical view of the Kremlin and is a good read. Its sister newspaper in St Petersburg is *The St Petersburg Times*. Both have entertainment listings. The glossy monthly *Pulse* (www.pulse.ru) provides feature stories and cultural listings, as does *Where*, which can be found in hotels and many restaurants. Less interesting is the monthly Neva News (www.

nevanews.com). Several other official and unofficial (i.e. commercial) guides can be found free of charge around the city. They are published quarterly, with cultural listings and feature articles.

Russian-language press

The Russian media has changed since Putin came to office in 2000 – the major television stations (the main source of news for Russians) are strongly managed by the state and do not provide a diversity of information and opinion. However, the print media, internet, and to some extent radio have a certain degree of independence, although they reach a far smaller portion of the population. Tabloids and glossies are very popular; the Russian edition of *Cosmopolitan* is the magazine's second biggest seller. For an entertaining taste of the absurd propaganda Russians are exposed to on a daily basis, but in English, log onto www.english.pravda.ru.

O

Overseas Missions

Russian Missions Abroad

Canada
285 Charlotte Street, Ottawa
Tel: (613) 235 4341
Visa Department
Tel: (613) 236 7220
UK
6/7 Kensington Palace Gardens, London W8 4QP
Tel: (020) 7229 6412
Consulate, 58 Melville Street
Edinburgh EH3 7HF
Tel: (0131) 225 7098
US
Embassy, 2650 Wisconsin Avenue, N.W. Washington DC 20007
Tel: (202) 298 5700
Consulate, 9E 91st Street, New York, NY 10128
Tel: (212) 348 1717

Public Holidays

1–5 January (New Year Holidays)
7 January (Orthodox Christmas Day)
23 February (Defence of the Motherland)
8 March (Women's Day)
1 May (Labour Day)
9 May (Victory Day)
12 June (Independence Day)
4 November (Unity Day)

TRANSPORT

EATING OUT

ACTIVITIES

A – Z

LANGUAGE

P

Photography

Generally speaking, taking photographs in galleries, museums and exhibitions is permitted; but visitors should take care not to take photographs of military installations or anything else that might be seen as a threat to security. This could, in theory, include railway stations, bridges, factories and tunnels. Innocent photographers are still sometimes detained for taking photos on and around train stations, especially away from large cities.

Postal Services

Post offices open Mon–Sat 9am–6pm; they often close at midday for an hour, and are closed on Sundays. Some post offices, however, open only from 9am–3pm or 2–8pm. The mail service in Russia provides an increasing variety and standard of services, including fax, courier, mail and sometimes internet. Not all post offices accept international mail bigger than a standard letter. International postal delivery can be slow – it may take two or three weeks for a letter from Moscow to reach Western Europe and sometimes even a month or more to reach the US. Theft of postal items is now rare.

R

Religious Services

The main religion in Russia is the Orthodox Church, although the constitution provides for religious freedom and most of the world's major religious denominations have

Time Zones

Russia has eight time zones. Moscow and St Petersburg are three hours ahead of Greenwich Mean Time. Moscow time is adopted nearly everywhere west of the Urals.

When it is noon in Moscow, it is 2pm in Yekaterinburg, 3pm in Novosibirsk, 4pm in Krasnoyarsk, 5pm in Irkutsk, 6pm in Chita, and 7pm in Vladivostok. All Russian trains, including those on the Trans–Siberian Railway use Moscow time.

Dialling Codes

Country codes
US and Canada – 1
UK – 44
Australia – 61
New Zealand – 64
Russia – 7
City prefixes
Moscow – 495 or 499
St Petersburg – 812
When making a call within Russia, dial 8 before the city code, and wait for the dial tone.

houses of worship. Most Orthodox churches hold services daily at about 9am and 5pm. The Church of St Catherine the Great Martyr at Bolshaya Ordynka 60/2 sometimes holds services in English; for information call (495) 959 1296.

In both St Petersburg and Moscow there are a number of Catholic, Protestant, and Jewish congregations that worship in English. For up-to-date listings in Moscow see www.moscowtimes.com; for St Petersburg, see the Friday edition of the *St Petersburg Times*.

Outside the main cities you are unlikely to find non-Orthodox congregations.

T

Telephones

The mobile phone signal in Russia covers most inhabited areas. Local SIM cards are cheap, but you'll have to get a local to buy one for you as you must have a resident's permit to do so. Calls are relatively cheap, but using a SIM card bought in Moscow for calls in Siberia can become expensive (this is essentially roaming even though you are in the same country).

The main type of public phone box uses plastic cards, available in units of 5, 10, 20 or 50 at metro stations and kiosks. Insert the card and dial the number. When your call is answered press the # button to complete the connection.

International phone fees as charged by hotels are exorbitant. Most travellers to Russia now rely on Skype calls.

Tipping

The tipping etiquette in Russia is confusing. Some guidebooks recommend adding 10 percent to

the bill but most serving staff would be bewildered by such an amount. Rounding up the bill is now common, but the general rule is only tip if you are actually satisfied with the service.

Tourist Offices

UK
202 Kensington Church Street, London, W8 4DP, UK
Tel: (020) 7987 1234
US
224 W. 30th St., Ste. 701, New York, NY 10001
Tel: (877) 221 7120

Tour Operators

Using a tour operator gives peace of mind that all your arrangements have been made by a professional, insured company but adds a hefty amount to the cost of the trip. Booking direct with local fixers and guides makes things a lot cheaper but doesn't provide the guarantees Western tour operators can. Nowadays Intourist, the former state travel agency, is now just one of many tour operators active in the market.

UK

Intourist
7 Princedale Road, London W11 4NW
Tel: (0844) 875 4026
www.into-russia.co.uk/
Voyages Jules Verne
21 Dorset Square, London NW1 6QE
Tel: (0845) 166 7003
www.vjv.com
Offers cruises and more expensive, specialist tours.
Noble Caledonia
2 Chester Close, Belgravia, London SW1X 7BE
Tel: (020) 7752 0000
www.noble-caledonia.co.uk
Offers cruises.
Cox & Kings Travel
30 Millbank, London SW1P 4EE
Tel: (020) 7873 5000
www.coxandkings.co.uk
Tailor-made journeys throughout Russia.
Regent Holidays
Tel: (020) 7666 1244
www.regent-holidays.co.uk
Provides flights, bespoke tours, trips on the Trans-Siberian Railway and can book hotels all over Russia.
Trans-Siberian Experience
Tel: (0845) 521 2910
www.trans-siberian.co.uk
Organises informal trips for individuals featuring family stays, trans-Siberian trips and trekking.

Real Russia Limited
3 The Ivories, Northampton Street, Islington, London N1 2HY
Tel: (020) 7100 7370
www.realrussia.co.uk
Visas, railway tickets, hotels and expert assistance.

Scott's Real Life Tours Ltd
141 Whitfield Street, London W1T 5EW
Tel: (020) 7383 5353
www.scottstours.co.uk

The Russia House Limited
Chapel Court, Borough High Street, London SE1 1HH
Tel: (020) 7403 9922
www.therussiahouse.co.uk

US

Incredible Adventures
6604 Midnight Pass Road, Sarasota, FL 34242
Tel: (800) 644 7382
www.incredible-adventures.com
Specialises in flights on MIGs as well as tours.

GO TO RUSSIA Travel
309 Peters Street, Unit A, Atlanta, GA 30313
Tel: (888) 263 0023 or (404) 827 0099
www.gotorussia.net
The biggest Russia specialists in the US

Russian-American Consulting Corp
45 West 34th Street, Suite 703, New York, NY 10001
Tel: (212) 268 9336 or (877) 268 2677
www.russianconsulting.com
Tours across the Russian Federation.

Kosmos Travel
8539 West Sunset Boulevard, Suite 22, Los Angeles, CA 90069
Tel: (818) 713 1717
www.kosmostravel.com

W

Websites

There are thousands of sites with information about Russia in English. Here is our selection:

Moscow
www.mbtg.ru/index.php?language=en
The Moscow Business Telephone Guide; addresses and phone numbers.
www.moscow-city.ru
Less than convincing official tourist information for the city of Moscow.
www.moscowtimes.ru
Moscow Times
www.moscowcity.com
Information about Moscow.
www.moscow.info
Moscow city information portal.

Local Travel and Tours

Local travel can be arranged by most hotels, local travel agencies, local guides and through the growing number of tourist offices across the Russian Federation. Forums such as www.expat.ru and www.redtape.ru are other good ways to find a guide.

Moscow
Patriarshy Dom
Tel: (495) 795 0927;
www.toursinrussia.com
Capital Tours

St Petersburg
www.nevsky-prospekt.com
Guide to St Petersburg's most famous street.
http://eng.ispb.info/
St Petersburg tourist information.
www.petersburgcity.com
General information for St Petersburg.
www.saint-petersburg.com
Comprehensive city information.

Russia
www.russia-travel.com
Russian tourist office official site.
www.russianembassy.org
Information on visas.
www.museum.ru
Museums in Russia.
www.russiatourism.ru/eng
General reference site with useful links.
www.gotorussia.com and www.redtape.ru and www.expat.ru
Helpful information and forums.
www.menu.ru
Contact information on restaurants and clubs.
www.restoran.ru/spb
Fairly complete and updated restaurant listings, plus a reservation service; English version available.
www.waytorussia.net
Comprehensive information on travel and life in Russia.
www.destinationrussia.com
Hotels, apartments and travel information.
www.raftsiberia.com
White-water rafting in Siberia.
www.travelkamchatka.com and www.travelkamchatka.com/
Adventure tourism in the Kamchatka peninsula.
http://siberiansafari.com/en
Wildlife-watching; hunting, fishing.
www.seat61.com
Trans-Siberian journey planning.
www.sibtourguide.com
Hiking trips and Siberian journeys from Krasnoyarsk.
www.visittuva.ru
National tourist office of Tuva.
www.privet-baikal.ru

Tel: (495) 232 2442; www.capital tours.ru

St Petersburg
Eclectica-Guide.
(tel: (812) 610 0540; www.eclectica-guide.ru

Lake Baikal
Baikaler
Tel: (3952) 336240; www.baikaler.com
Denis Sobnakov
Tel: 902 455 2222; www.uuhostel.com

Portal for the north of Lake Baikal.
www.greatbaikaltrail.org
Website of the Great Baikal Trail project.
www.irkutsk.org
Irkutsk information portal.
www.irkvisit.info
Official Irkutsk information portal.
http://eng.rzd.ru/
Look up timetables and ticket prices for all Russian Railways services.

What to Wear

You can pretty much dress as you would these days in Russia's big cities. The old advice was to dress down to avoid attracting attention, but these days some Russians, especially women, dress to the nines just to go to the supermarket for a pint of milk. However, out in the countryside your clothes may mark you out as a foreigner, especially if you dress in hiking gear.

Coming to Russia in the cold months (November to March), be prepared to encounter temperatures of 25° to 30°C below zero (−13°F to −22°F) and to dress accordingly, not forgetting a warm hat and gloves. It's best to dress in layers of clothing to cope with the variations in temperature between the frozen outdoors and the overheated indoors. Waterproof shoes are a necessity in winter, since the legendary Russian frost is often interrupted by periods of thawing. Russia may be cold in winter, but it's equally sweltering in summer so shorts and T-shirts are definitely in order.

Smart casual is now acceptable for theatre visits. Some VIP restaurants in Moscow and St Petersburg will only allow admittance to men in jackets. At nightclubs across Russia rigorous 'face control' is employed to keep out anyone who might not be suitable clientele.

When travelling on overnight sleeper trains, be sure to have slippers and something comfortable to change into for the journey – a tracksuit or jogging trousers and a sweatshirt are ideal.

TRANSPORT
EATING OUT
ACTIVITIES
A – Z
LANGUAGE

LANGUAGE

UNDERSTANDING THE LANGUAGE

LINGUISTIC HISTORY

Russian belongs to the Slavonic branch of the Indo-European family of languages. English, German, French, Spanish and Hindi are its relatives.

It is important when speaking Russian that you reproduce the accent (marked here before each stressed vowel with the sign') correctly to be understood well.

Historically Russian can be called a comparatively young language. The evolution of the language to its present form on the basis of the spoken language of Eastern Slavs and the Church-Slavonic written language is thought to have occurred between the 11th and 14th centuries.

Modern Russian has absorbed a considerable number of foreign words. Very few tourists will be puzzled by Russian words such as *telefon, televizor, teatr, otel, restoran, kafe, taxi, metro, aeroport.*

What intimidates people making their first acquaintance with Russian is the Cyrillic alphabet. In fact the alphabet can be remembered easily after a few repetitions and the difference with the Latin alphabet is only minimal. An understanding of the Russian alphabet permits one to make out the names of the streets and the shop signs.

The Russian (or Cyrillic) alphabet was created by two brothers, philosophers and public figures Constantine (St Cyril) and Methodius, both born in Solun (now Thessaloniki in Greece). Their purpose was to facilitate the spread of Greek liturgical books to Slavonic speaking countries. Today the Cyrillic alphabet with different modifications is used in the Ukrainian, Belarusian,

Bulgarian and Serbian languages, among others.

TRANSLITERATION

There are four systems of transliteration of Russian words into English (*see The Transliteration of Modern Russian for English Language Publications* by J.T. Shaw, the University of Wisconsin Press, 1967). If necessary, the systems can be combined so that one letter or a group of letters is transliterated according to one system and the other according to another. To transliterate some Russian letters, English letter combinations are used: ж = zh, х = kh, ц = ts, ч = ch, ш =sh, щ = shch, ю = yu, я = ya, ё = yo. The Russian letter combination кс is transliterated both as *ks* and as *x*. Russian letters are transliterated (with a few exceptions) in a similar way: й, ы – y, е, ё – e.

To transliterate the Russian soft sign between the consonants and before no-vowel, the apostrophe is used, or the soft sign is ignored, as before vowels. The transliteration of nominal inflections has a number of peculiarities: ый, ий = y, ие, ье = ie, ия = ia.

If the traditional English spelling in names differs from their letter-by-letter transliteration they are mostly translated in their English form: Moscow (city), but river Moskva.

The Genitive inflections in the names of streets and other objects are translated according to their pronunciation, and not their spelling: площадь Горького, (ploshchad' Gór'kogo) = pl. Gorkovo in this book. The transliteration in this section shows the way to pronounce Russian

words and therefore does not correspond exactly with their spelling.

The city maps and their captions use Russian words and abbreviations: ul. (*úlitsa*) means street; per. (*pereúlok*) – lane; prosp. (*prospékt*) – avenue; pl. (*plóshchadь*) – square; *alléya* – alley; *bulvár* – boulevard; *magistrál* – main line; *proézd* – passage; *shossé* – highway; *spusk* – slope.

The Russian system of writing out house numbers is as follows *prosp. Kalinina 28* (*28 Kalinin Avenue*).

Language Centres

A relatively inexpensive way to visit Russia is through institutes that run Russian language courses. Among these are the Lomonosov and Lumumba universities and the Pushkin Institute of Russian Language in Moscow, the University of St Petersburg, the Shevchenko University in Kiev and other universities and linguistic co-operatives. They are all able to arrange visas and inexpensive accommodation during the study period.

To communicate directly with the universities you should contact the cultural attaché of the Russian embassy or consulate.

When selecting courses, care should be taken to ensure that the teaching is on a professional level. It is also worth contacting the Russian departments of universities at home. Many are now running short (one- or two-week) overseas study tours (which includes flights, accommodation and transport within Russia and tuition fees) for the general public.

The Alphabet

The first two columns show the printed letter in Russian upper and lower case. The third column demonstrates how the Russian letters sound; the final letters in bold are the name of the letter in Russian.

А а **a**, archaeology **a**
Б б **b**, buddy **be**
В в **v**, vow **v**
Г г **g**, glad **ge**
Д д **d**, dot (the tip of the tongue close to the teeth, not the alveoli) **de**
Е е **e**, get **ye**
Ё ё **yo**, yoke **yo**
Ж ж **zh**, composure **zhe**
З з **z**, zest **ze**
И и **i**, ink **i**
Й й **j**, yes **jot**
К к **k**, kind **ka**
Л л **l**, life (but a bit harder) **el'**
М м **m**, memory **em**
Н н **n**, nut **en**

О о **o**, optimum **o**
П п **p**, party **pe**
Р р **r** (rumbling – as in Italian, the tip of the tongue is vibrating) **er**
С с **s**, sound **es**
Т т **t**, title (the tip of the tongue close to the teeth) **te**
У у **u**, nook **u**
Ф ф **f**, flower **ef**
Х х **kh**, hawk **ha**
Ц ц **ts**, (pronounced conjointly) **tse**
Ч ч **ch**, charter **che**
Ш ш **sh**, shy **sha**
Щ щ **shch**, (pronounced conjointly) **shcha**
ъ (the hard sign)
Ы ы **y** (pronounced with the same position of a tongue as when pronouncing G, K) **y**
ь (the soft sign)
Э э **e**, ensign **e**
Ю ю **yu**, you **yu**
Я я **ya**, yard **ya**

USEFUL WORDS AND PHRASES

Numbers
1 *adín* один
2 *dva* два
3 *tri* три
4 *chityri* четыре
5 *pyat'* пять
6 *shes't'* шесть
7 *sem* семь
8 *vósim* восемь
9 *d'évit* девять
10 *d'ésit* десять
11 *adínatsat'* одиннадцать
12 *dvinátsat'* двенадцать
13 *trinátsat'* тринадцать
14 *chityrnatsat'* четырнадцать
15 *pitnátsat'* пятнадцать
16 *shysnátsat'* шестнадцать
17 *simnátsat'* семнадцать
18 *vasimnátsat'* восемнадцать
19 *divitnátsat'* девятнадцать
20 *dvátsat'* двадцать
21 *dvátsat' adín* двадцать один
30 *trítsat'* тридцать
40 *sórak* сорок
50 *pidisyat* пятьдесят
60 *shyz'disyat* шестьдесят
70 *s'émdisyat* семьдесят
80 *vósimdisyat* восемьдесят
90 *divinósta* девяносто
100 *sto* сто
200 *dv'és'ti* двести
300 *trísta* триста
400 *chityrista* четыреста
500 *pitsót* пятьсот
600 *shyssót* шестьсот
700 *simsót* семьсот
800 *vasimsót* восемьсот
900 *divitsót* девятьсот
1,000 *tysicha* тысяча
2,000 *dve tysichi* две тысячи и
10,000 *d'ésit' tysich* десятьтысяч
100,000 *sto tysich* сто тысяч
1,000,000 *milión* миллион
1,000,000,000 *miliárd* миллиард

Pronouns

I/we *ya/my* я/мы
You *ty* (singular, informal)/*vy* (plural, or formal singular) ты/вы
He/she/they *on/aná/aní* он/она/они
My/mine *moj* (object masculine)/*mayá* (object feminine)/*mayó* (neutral or without marking the gender)/*maí* (plural) мой/моя/моё/мои
Our/ours *nash/násha/náshe/náshy* (resp.) наш/наша/наше/наши
Your/yours *tvoj* etc. (see My)/*vash* etc. (see Our) твой/ваш
His/her, hers/their, theirs *jivó/jiyó/ikh* его/её/их
Who? *khto?* Кто?
What? *shto?* Что?

GREETINGS AND ACQUAINTANCE

Hello!
zdrástvuti (neutral, and often accompanied by shaking hands, but this is not necessary) Здравствуйте!
zdrástvuj (to one person, informal) Здравствуй!
alo! (by telephone only) Алло!
priv'ét! (informal) Привет!

Good afternoon/Good evening *dóbry den'/dobry véchir* Добрый день/Добрый вечер
Good morning/Good night *dobrae útra/dobraj nóchi* (= Sleep well) Доброе утро/Доброй ночи
Goodbye
dasvidán'ye (neutral) До свиданья
ciao! (informal) Чао!
paká! (informal, literally "until") Пока!
Good luck to you! *shchislíva!* Счастливо!
What is your name? *kak vas (tibya) zavút?/kak váshe ímya ótchistva?* (the second is formal) Как вас (тебя) зовут?/Как ваше имя и отчество?
My name is.../I am... *minya zavut.../ya...* Меня зовут.../Я...
It's a pleasure *óchin' priyatna* Очень приятно
Good/excellent *kharashó/atlichno* хорошо/отлично
Do you speak English? *vy gavaríti pa anglíski?* Вы говорите по-английски?
I don't understand/I didn't understand *ya ni panimáyu/ya ni pónyal* Я не понимаю/Я не понял
Repeat, please *pavtaríti pazhálsta* Повторите, пожалуйста
What do you call this? *kak éta nazyvaitsa?* Как это называется?
How do you say...? *kak skazat...?* Как вы сказаиь...?
Please/Thank you (very much) *pazhálsta/(bal'shóe) spasíba* Пожалуйста/(бальшоэ) спасибо
Excuse me *izviníti* Извините

GETTING AROUND

Where is the...? *gd'e (nakhóditsa)...?* Где находится...?
beach *plyazh* ...пляж
bathroom *tualet* ...туацет
bus station *aftóbusnaya stántsyja/aftavakzál* ...автобусная станция/автовокзал
bus stop *astanófka aftóbusa* ... остановка автобуса
airport *airapórt* ...аэропорт
railway station *vakzál/stántsyja* (in small towns) ...вокзал/станция
post office *póchta* ...почта
police station ...*milítsyja* ... милиция
ticket office *bil'étnaya kássa* ... билетная касса
market place *rynak/bazár* ...рынок/базар
embassy/consulate *pasól'stva/kónsul'stva* ...посольство/консульство
Where is there a...? *gd'e z'd'es'...?* Где здесь...?

Terms of Address

Modern Russian has no established and universally used forms of salutation. The old revolutionary form *tavárishch* (comrade), still used among some party members, lacks popularity among the rest of the population. Alternatives include: *Izviníti, skazhíte pozhálsta…"* (Excuse me, tell me, please…) or *Izviníti, mózhna sprasít…)* or *I ozhálst* (Excuse me, can I ask you…).

If you want to sound original and show your understanding of the history of courteous forms of greeting, you can address a man as *gospodin* (sir), and a woman as *gospozha* (madam). These are very formal honorifics, used with a person's last name.

If you know the name of the father of the person you are talking to, the best and the most neutral way of addressing them is to use their first name and patronymic, formed by adding *-ich* to their father's name if it is a man, and *-orna* if it is a woman.

You will hear the common parlance forms *Maladói chelavék!* (Young man!) and *Dévushka!* (Girl!) directed toward a person of any age, and also *Zhénshchina!* (Woman!) to women in the bus, in the shop or at the market. These forms should be avoided in conversation.

currency exchange *abm'én val'úty* … обмен валюты
pharmacy *apt'éka* …аптека
(good) hotel *(kharóshyj) atél'/* *(kharoshaya) gastinitsa* … (хороший)отель/(хорошая) гостиница
restaurant *ristarán* …ресторан
bar *bar* …бар
taxi stand *stayanka taxi* …стоянка такси
subway station *mitró* …метро
service station *aftazaprávachnaya stantsyja/aftasárvis* … автозаправочная станция
news stand *gaz'étnyj kiosk* … газетный киоск
public telephone *tilifón* …телефон
supermarket *univirsám* … универсам
department store *univirmák* … универмаг
hairdresser *parikmákhirskaya* … парикмахерская
jeweller *yuvilírnyj magazine* … ювелирный магазин

hospital *bal'nítsa* …больница
Do you have…? *u vas jes't'…?* У вас есть…?
I (don't) want… *ya (ni) khachyu…* Я (не) хочу…
I want to buy… *ya khachyu kupít'…* Я хочу купить…
Where can I buy… *gd'e ya magú kupít'…* Где я могу купить…
cigarettes *sigaréty* …сигареты
wine *vinó* …вино
film *fotoplyonku* …фотоплёнку
a ticket for… *bilét na…* …билет на…
this *éta* …это
postcards/envelopes *atkrytki/ kanv'érty* …открытки/конверты
a pen/a pencil *rúchku/karandásh* … ручку/карандаш
soap/shampoo *myla/shampún'* … мыло/шампунь
aspirin *aspirn* …аспирин
I need… *mn'e núzhna…* Мне нужно…
I need a doctor/a mechanic *mn'e núzhyn dóktar/aftamikhánik* Мне нужен доктор/автомеханик
I need help *mn'e nuzhná pómashch'* Мне нужна помощ
Car/plane/trains/ship *mashyna/ samal'yot/póist/karábl'* машина/самолёт/поезд/корабль
A ticket to… *bil'ét do…* билет до…
How can I get to… *kak ya magu dabrátsa do…* Как я могу добраться до…
Please, take me to… *pazhalsta atvizíti minya…* Пожалуйста, отвезите меня…
What is this place called? *kak nazyváitsa eta m'ésta?* Как называется это место?
Where are we? *gd'e my?* Где мы?
Stop here *astanavíti z'd'es'* Остановите здесь
Please wait *padazhdíti pazhalsta* Подождите, пожалуйста
When does the train [plane] leave? *kagdá atpravl'yaitsa poist [samalyot]?* Когда отправляется поезд (самолёт)?
I want to check my luggage *ya khachyu sdat bagázh* Я хочу сгатб багаж
Where does this bus go? *kudá id'yot état aftóbus?* Куда идёт этот автобус?

SHOPPING

How much does it cost? *skól'ka eta stóit?* Сколько это стоит?
That's very expensive *eta óchin' dóraga* Это очень дорого
A lot, many/A little, few *mnóga/ mála* много/мало
It (doesn't) fits me *eta mn'e (ni) padkhódit* Это мне (не) подходит

AT THE HOTEL

I have a reservation *u minya zakázana m'esta* У меня заказановнецто
I want to make a reservation *ya khachyu zakazát' m'esta* Я хочу заказать место
A single (double) room *adnam'éstnuyu (dvukhmestnuyu) kómnatu* одноместную (двухместную) комнату
I want to see the room *ya khachyu pasmatrét' nómer* Я хочу посмотреть номер
Key/suitcase/bag *klyuch/ chimadán/súmka* ключ/чемодан/сумка

EATING OUT

Waiter/menu *afitsyánt/minyu* официант/меню
I'd like a table for… people *bud'tye dobri stolik na…* Будьте добры, столик на…
Do you have…? *yest' li u vas* Есть ли у вас…?
a set menu/a children's menu *komplyeksniye obyedi/dyetskoye myenyu* комплексные обеды/детское меню
What do you recommend? *chto vi posovyetuyetye* Уто вы посоветуете?
What's this? *chto eto takoye* Уто это такое?
I want to order… *ya khachyu zakazat'…* Я хочу заказать
Breakfast/lunch/supper *záftrak/ ab'ét/úzhyn* Завтрак/обед/ужин
the house speciality *fírminnaya blyuda* фирменное блюдо
Mineral water/juice *minirál'naya vadá/sok* минерал'ьная вода/сок
Coffee/tea/beer *kófe/chai/píva* кофе/чай/пиво
What do you have to drink (alcoholic)? *shto u vas jes't' vypit'?* Что у вас есть выпить?
Ice/fruit/dessert *marózhynaya/ frúkty/disért* мороженое/фрукты/дессерт
Salt/pepper/sugar *sol'/périts/ sákhar* соль/перец/сахар
Beef/pork/chicken/fish/shrimp *gavyadina/svinína/kúritsa/ryba/ kriv'étki* говядина/свинина/курица/рыба/креветки
Vegetables/rice/potatoes *óvashchi/ris/kartófil'* овоши/рис/картофель
Bread/butter/eggs *khleb/másla/ yajtsa* хлеб/масло/яйца
Soup/salad/sandwich/pizza *sup/ salát/butyrbrót/pitsa* суп/салат/бутерброд/пицца

Fork/knife/spoon *vilku/nozh/lozhku*
вилку/нож/ложку
A plate/a glass/a cup/a napkin
tar'élka/stakán/cháshka/salf'étka
тарелка/стакан/чашка/салфетка
The food is cold *yeda kholodnaya*
Еда холодная
May I change this? *dayte mnye
pozhaluysta chto nibud' drugoye*
Дайте мне, пожа-луйста, что-нибудь
другое?
The bill, please *shchyot pazhalsta*
Счёт, пожалуйста
Is service included? *chayeviye
vklyuchyeni* Чаевые включены?
We'd like to pay separately *mi
budyem platit' porozn'* Мы будем
платить порознь
What's this amount for? *a eto za
chto* А зто за что?
Do you accept traveller's cheques?
hyeryotye li vi dorozhniye chyeki
Берёте ли вы дорожные чеки?
Delicious/Not so good *fkúsna/ták
sibe* вкусно/так себе
I want my change, please *zdáchu
pazhalsta* Сдачу, пожалуйста

MONEY

**I want to exchange currency
(money)** *ya khachyu abmin'át'
val'yutu (d'én'gi)* Я хочу обменять
валюту (деньги)
Do you accept credit cards? *vy
prinimáiti kridítnyi kártachki?* Вы
принимаете кредитные карточки?
Can you cash a traveller's cheque?
*vy mózhytl razminyat' darózhnyj
chek?* Вы можете разменять
дорожный чек?

What is the exchange rate? *kakój
kurs?* Какой курс?

TIME

What time is it? *katóryj chas?*
Который час?
Just a moment, please *adnú
minútachku* Одну минуточку
How long does it take? *skól'ka
vrémini eta zanimáit?* Сколько
времени это занимает?
Hour/day/week/month *chas/den'/
nid'élya/m'ésits* час/день/неделя/
месяц
At what time? *f kakóe vrémya?* В
какое время?
This (last, next) week *eta (próshlaya,
sl'édujshchiya) nid'elya* эта (прошлая,
следующая) неделя
Yesterday/today/tomorrow *fchirá/
sivód'nya/záftra* вчера/сегодня/завтра
Sunday *vaskris'én'je* воскресенье
Monday *panid'él'nik* понедельник
Tuesday *ftórnik* вторник
Wednesday *sridá* среда
Thursday *chitv'érk* четверг
Friday *pyatnitsa* пятница
Saturday *subóta* суббота
The weekend *vykhadnyi dni*
выходные дни

SIGNS AND INSCRIPTIONS

вход/выход/входа нет *fkhot/vykhat/
fkhóda n'et* **Entrance/exit/no
entrance**
туалет/уборная *tual'ét/ubórnaya*
Lavatory

Ж (З)/М (М) *dlya zhén'shchin/dlya
mushchín* **Ladies/gentlemen**
зал ожидания *zal azhidán'ya* **Waiting
hall**
занято/свободно *zánita/svabódna*
Occupied/free
касса *kassa* **booking office/cash
desk**
медпункт *medpúnkt* **Medical
services**
справочное бюро *správachnae bzuro*
Information
вода для питья *vadá dlya pit'ya*
Drinking water
вокзал *vakzál* **Terminal/railway
station**
открыто/закрыто *atkryta/zakryta*
Open/closed
запрещается/опасно *zaprishchyaitsa/
apásna* **Prohibited/danger**
продукты/гастроном *pradúkty/
gastranóm* **Grocery**
булочная/кондитерская
búlachnaya/kan'dítirskaya **Bakery/
confectionery**
закусочная/столовая *zakúsachnaya/
stalóvaya* **Refreshment room/
canteen**
самообслуживание
samaapslúzhivan'je **Self-service**
баня/прачечная/химчистка
bánya/práchichnaya/khimchístka
Bathhouse/laundry/dry cleaning
книги/камыттовары *knígi/
kantstaváry* **Books/stationery**
мясо/птица *m'ása/ptítsa* **Meat/
poultry**
овоши/фрукты *óvashchi/frúkty*
Green-grocery/fruits
универмаг/универсам *univirmák/
univirsám* **Department store/
supermarket**

FURTHER READING

HISTORY

The Blackwell Encyclopaedia of the Russian Revolution, edited by H. Shukman.
Catherine the Great, by J.T. Alexander.
Comrades 1917 – Russia in Revolution, by Brian Moynahan.
History of Soviet Russia, by E.H. Carr.
A History of the Soviet Union, by G.A. Hosking.
A History of Twentieth Century Russia, by Robert Service.
The Icon and the Axe, by James Billington.
The Last Tsar, by Edvard Radzinsky.
The Making of Modern Russia, by L. Kochan and R. Abraham.
A People's Tragedy, by Orlando Figes.
Nicholas II: Emperor of all the Russians, by Dominic Lieven.
Peter the Great: His Life and Work, by Robert K. Massie.
Soviet Colossus: History of the USSR, by Michael Kort.
Stalin, Man of Contradiction, by K.N. Cameron.
Stalinism and After: Road to Gorbachev, by Alec Nove.

LITERATURE

And Quiet Flows the Don and *The Don Flows Home to the Sea*, by Mikhail Sholokhov.
Blue Lard, by Vladimir Sorokin.
Children of the Arbat, by Anatoli Rybakov.
Crime and Punishment, *The Brothers Karamazov*, *The Devils*, by Fyodor Dostoyevsky.
Dead Souls Diary of a Madman and Other Stories, by Nikolai Gogol.
Doctor Zhivago, by Boris Pasternak.
Eugene Onegin, by Alexander Pushkin.
Fathers and Sons, *On The Eve*, *A Hero of Our Time*, by Mikhail Lermontov.
Lady with Lapdog and Other Stories, by Anton Chekhov.
The Life of Insects, by Victor Pelevin.
The Master and Margarita, by Mikhail Bulgakov.
Red Cavalry and Other Stories, by Isaac Babel.
Soviet Russian Literature: Writers and Problems and The Epic of

Russian Literature, by Mare Slonim.
Sportsman's Sketches, by Ivan Turgenev.
We, by Evgeny Zamyatin.
War and Peace, *Anna Karenina* and *The Death of Ivan Ilyich and Other Stories*, by Leo Tolstoy.

BIOGRAPHY/MEMOIRS

Black Earth, by Charlotte Hobson.
An English Lady at the Court of Catherine the Great, edited by A.G. Gross.
The Gulag Archipelago, by Alexander Solzhenitsyn.
The House by the Dvina, by Eugenie Fraser.
In the Beginning, by Irina Ratushinskaya.
Into the Whirlwind; Within the Whirlwind, by Eugenia Ginzburg.
The Making of Andrei Sakharov, by G. Bailey.
On the Estate: Memoirs of Russia Before the Revolution, edited by Olga Davydoff Bax.
Russia: Despatches from the Guardian Correspondent in Moscow, by Martin Walker.
Ten Days that Shook the World, by John Reed.

ART

History of Russian Painting, by A. Bird.
The Irony Tower, by Andrew Solomon.
The Kremlin and its Treasures, by Rodimzeva, Rachmanov and Raimann.
New Worlds: Russian Art and Society 1900–3, by D. Elliott.
Russian Art of the Avant Garde, by J.E. Bowlt.
Russian Art from Neoclassicism to the Avant Garde, by D.V. Sarabianov.
Street Art of the Revolution, Tolstoy, V.I. Bibikova and C. Cooke.
Travel and Natural History Among the Russians, by Colin Thubron.
The Big Red Train Ride, by Eric Newby.
Caucasian Journey, by Negley Farson.
Epics of Everyday Life, by Susan Richards.
First Russia, Then Tibet, by Robert Byron.

The Food and Cooking of Russia, by Lesley Chamberlain.
Imperial Splendour, by George Galitzine.
Journey into Russia, by Laurens van der Post.
The Natural History of the USSR, by Algirdas Kynstautas.
The Nature of the Russia, by John Massey Stewart.
The New Russians, by Hedrick Smith.
Portrait of the Soviet Union, by Fitzroy Maclean.
Sailing to Leningrad, by Roger Foxall.
The Taming of the Eagles: Exploring the New Russia, by Imogen Edwards-Jones.
The Trans–Siberian Rail Guide, by Robert Strauss.

OTHER INSIGHT GUIDES

Other Insight Guides to this region include: **Poland** and **Estonia, Latvia & Lithuania**.

Send Us Your Thoughts

We do our best to ensure the information in our books is as accurate and up-to-date as possible. The books are updated on a regular basis using local contacts, who painstakingly add, amend and correct as required. However, some details (such as telephone numbers and opening times) are liable to change, and we are ultimately reliant on our readers to put us in the picture.

We welcome your feedback, especially your experience of using the book "on the road". Maybe we recommended a hotel that you liked (or another that you didn't), or you came across a great bar or new attraction we missed.

We will acknowledge all contributions, and we'll offer an Insight Guide to the best letters received.

Please write to us at:
 Insight Guides
 PO Box 7910
 London SE1 1WE
Or email us at:
 hello@insightguides.com

CREDITS

Insight Guide Credits

Distribution

UK
Dorling Kindersley Ltd
A Penguin Group company
80 Strand, London, WC2R 0RL
sales@uk.dk.com

United States
Ingram Publisher Services
1 Ingram Boulevard, PO Box 3006,
La Vergne, TN 37086-1986
ips@ingramcontent.com

Australia and New Zealand
Woodslane
10 Apollo St, Warriewood,
NSW 2102, Australia
info@woodslane.com.au

Worldwide
Apa Publications (Singapore) Pte
7030 Ang Mo Kio Avenue 5
08-65 Northstar @ AMK
Singapore 569880
apasin@singnet.com.sg

Printing
CTPS-China

All Rights Reserved
© 2016 Apa Digital (CH) AG and
Apa Publications (UK) Ltd

First Edition 1990
Fourth Edition 2016

Every effort has been made to provide accurate information in this publication, but changes are inevitable. The publisher cannot be responsible for any resulting loss, inconvenience or injury. We would appreciate it if readers would call our attention to any errors or outdated information. We also welcome your suggestions; please contact us at: hello@insightguides.com

www.insightguides.com

Editor: Carine Tracanelli
Author: Marc Di Duca
Head of Production: Rebeka Davies
Update Production: AM Services
Picture Editor: Tom Smyth
Cartography: original cartography Geodata, updated by Carte

Contributors

Marc Di Duca has been criss-crossing the former communist world for the past 25 years. He is the author of several guides to Moscow, St Petersburg, Lake Baikal and Eastern Siberia, a confident Russian speaker and a regular visitor to Russia.

About Insight Guides

Insight Guides have more than 40 years' experience of publishing high-quality, visual travel guides. We produce 400 full-colour titles, in both print and digital form, covering more than 200 destinations across the globe, in a variety of formats to meet your different needs.

Insight Guides are written by local authors who use their on-the-ground experience to provide the very latest information; their local expertise is evident in the extensive historical and cultural background features. All the reviews in **Insight Guides** are independent; we strive to maintain an impartial view. Our reviews are carefully selected to guide you to the best places to eat, go out and shop, so you can be confident that when we say a place is special, we really mean it.

Legend

City maps

	Freeway/Highway/Motorway
	Divided Highway
	Main Roads
	Minor Roads
	Pedestrian Roads
	Steps
	Footpath
	Railway
	Funicular Railway
	Cable Car
	Tunnel
	City Wall
	Important Building
	Built Up Area
	Other Land
	Transport Hub
	Park
	Pedestrian Area
	Bus Station
	Tourist Information
	Main Post Office
	Cathedral/Church
	Mosque
	Synagogue
	Statue/Monument
	Beach
	Airport

Regional maps

	Freeway/Highway/Motorway (with junction)
	Freeway/Highway/Motorway (under construction)
	Divided Highway
	Main Road
	Secondary Road
	Minor Road
	Track
	Footpath
	International Boundary
	State/Province Boundary
	National Park/Reserve
	Marine Park
	Ferry Route
	Marshland/Swamp
	Glacier Salt Lake
	Airport/Airfield
	Ancient Site
	Border Control
	Cable Car
	Castle/Castle Ruins
	Cave
	Chateau/Stately Home
	Church/Church Ruins
	Crater
	Lighthouse
	Mountain Peak
	Place of Interest
	Viewpoint

INDEX

Main references are in bold type